PERSONALITY ASSESSMENT
IN
POLICE PSYCHOLOGY

ABOUT THE EDITOR

Peter A. Weiss is currently Assistant Professor of Psychology at the University of Hartford, where he teaches courses in psychological assessment, forensic psychology, and psychotherapy in their APA-accredited doctoral program in clinical psychology. He earned his B.S. in Psychology from the College of William and Mary and his Ph.D. in Clinical Psychology (2001) from Long Island University. Prior to coming to the University of Hartford, Dr. Weiss worked at Interfaith Medical Center in New York City, where he supervised psychology interns in their APA-accredited internship program, and was the unit chief for two inpatient psychiatric units there. Dr. Weiss has been very active as a practitioner and researcher in police psychology and forensic psychology, especially with regards to applications of personality assessment instruments to these fields. He is the current (2009) President of the Society for Police and Criminal Psychology and has been an editorial board member of the *Journal of Police and Criminal Psychology* since 2002. He maintains an active research program, mainly focusing on the MMPI-2, Personality Assessment Inventory, and Rorschach Comprehensive System. He is the senior author of one other book, *Self-Esteem: A Study of Methods of Measurement* (Weiss, Mcguire, Ritzler, Kose, & Watson, 2008) published by VDM. He has also published numerous articles and book chapters, mainly on personality assessment, but also on psychotherapy and counseling as well. He has been a regular presenter and symposium chair at professional meetings, particularly the Society for Police and Criminal Psychology and the Society for Personality Assessment. He lives in Hartford, Connecticut.

PERSONALITY ASSESSMENT IN POLICE PSYCHOLOGY

A 21st Century Perspective

Edited by

PETER A. WEISS, PH.D.

CHARLES C THOMAS • PUBLISHER, LTD.
Springfield • Illinois • U.S.A.

Published and Distributed Throughout the World by

CHARLES C THOMAS • PUBLISHER, LTD.
2600 South First Street
Springfield, Illinois 62704

©2010 by CHARLES C THOMAS • PUBLISHER, LTD.

ISBN 978-0-398-07914-7 (hard)
ISBN 978-0-398-07915-4 (paper)

Library of Congress Catalog Card Number: 2009037926

With THOMAS BOOKS *careful attention is given to all details of manufacturing and design. It is the Publisher's desire to present books that are satisfactory as to their physical qualities and artistic possibilities and appropriate for their particular use.* THOMAS BOOKS *will be true to those laws
of quality that assure a good name and good will.*

Printed in the United States of America
CR-R-3

Library of Congress Cataloging-in-Publication Data

Personality assessment in police psychology : a 21st century
perspective / edited by Peter A. Weiss.
    p. cm.
 Includes bibliographical references and index.
 ISBN 978-0-398-07914-7 (hard) -- ISBN 978-0-398-07915-4 (paper)
 1. Police psychology. 2. Law enforcement--Psychological aspects.
3. Personality and occupation. 4. Personality tests. I. Weiss, Peter A.
II. Title.

HV7936.P75P47 2010
363.201'9--dc22
                                                      2009037926

CONTRIBUTORS

Michael G. Aamodt, Ph.D., was a professor at Radford University for 26 years, then he took advantage of an early retirement option in 2009 and is now a Principal Consultant with DCI Consulting Group. Mike is the author of several books including *Research in Law Enforcement Selection, Industrial-Organizational Psychology: An Applied Approach* (6th edition), *Human Relations in Business,* and *Understanding Statistics in I/O Psychology.* He has published extensively in such areas of police psychology as employee selection methods, police suicide rates, and police divorce rates. He received his bachelor's degree from Pepperdine University and his Ph.D. from the University of Arkansas.

JoAnne Brewster received her Ph.D. in experimental psychology from McMaster University in 1978, and subsequently completed clinical training at the University of Virginia. She was in private practice until 1992, when she joined the faculty at James Madison University. She is currently a professor in the Department of Graduate Psychology, and teaches Abnormal Psychology, Forensic Psychology, and Police Psychology. She has been a consultant to police departments since 1981. She is a past president and current secretary of the Society for Police and Criminal Psychology, and a member of the Police Psychological Services Section of the International Association of Chiefs of Police and Division 18 of the American Psychological Association.

Michael R. Cunningham, Ph.D., completed his B.A. at Carleton College, his Ph.D. in Psychology at the University of Minnesota, and he taught at Macalester College, Elmhurst College, and the University of Louisville. Dr. Cunningham has worked as a Psychometrician with Vangent, Inc. and its predecessors, since 1984. Dr. Cunningham also served as a consultant for the Jefferson County, Kentucky Police Department for ten years. Dr. Cunningham has presented research at the Society of Industrial/Organizational Psychology, Association of Test Publishers, and the American Psychological Association, and has published in the *Journal of Applied Psychology, Journal of Business and Psychology*, and many other journals.

Kelly D. Dages, Ph.D., is a Senior Organizational Psychologist and Program Evaluator with Vangent, Inc.'s Human Capital Division. She has been with Vangent for eight years. She received her Ph.D. in I/O Psychology from Northern Illinois University. Dr. Dages oversees program evaluation activities measuring the business impact of client's assessment programs. She develops customized assessment solutions for customers in private and government organizations to assist clients in organizational development, selection, and performance management. She consults with clients to develop competency models and preemployment assessment content.

Robert D. Davis, Ph.D., M.P., is a licensed Medical Psychologist, Clinical Psychologist, and Clinical Neuropsychologist in Baton Rouge, Louisiana. He is a partner in Matrix, Inc., the Police Psychological Services Corporation. Dr. Davis is known nationally for the development of inferential statistical models for the actuarial prediction of discrete liabilities in law enforcement. Dr. Davis is the senior author for the M-PULSE Inventory, a stand-alone screening test used for officer selection in the pre-offer phase which can be used for rank ordering potential candidates. He is also senior author of the M-PULSE: Psychological Methodology, a comprehensive post-offer battery for police psychologists utilizing impressionistic decision-making models to predict each of 18 liabilities in law enforcement. He is also a co-author of *A Handbook for Psychological Fitness-For-Duty Evaluations in Law Enforcement* (Rostow & Davis, 2004), and more than two dozen peer reviewed publications.

Dr. James S. Herndon has been a police psychologist for more than twenty years. He served as the Staff Psychologist for the Orange County (FL) Sheriff's Office from 1992–2002. Prior to that, he was the Executive Director of Police Psychological Services of Hampton Roads, Inc. in Virginia. He is a past president of the Council of Police Psychological Services (COPPS), as well as a past president of the Society for Police and Criminal Psychology (SPCP). He holds a Diplomate in police psychology from SPCP, and is the current Chair of the Diplomate Committee. He also serves on the editorial board of the *Journal of Police and Criminal Psychology*. He consults with law enforcement agencies on organizational and operational issues and serves as an adjunct professor at four colleges and universities in Florida. His Ph.D. is in industrial/organizational psychology from Old Dominion University and his Ed.D. is in counseling psychology from the University of Sarasota.

Dr. John H. Hitchcock is an assistant professor in the Department of Educational Studies housed within the College of Education at Ohio University. His professional interests lie in promoting evidenced-based practice and developing psychological interventions for special needs populations. He is also interested in special education research, experimental design, and mixed method (i.e., quantitative and qualitative) designs. He is currently serving as a principal investigator/consultant on several federal research initiatives in education, and he has produced several scholarly works presented in peer-reviewed journal articles and at national conferences.

Robin Inwald received her Ph.D. in psychology from Columbia University in 1976. She founded Hilson Research, Inc. in 1980 and has served as a psychological consultant to hundreds of law enforcement agencies and companies worldwide. The author of over 40 published psychological tests and several books, she is a Fellow of the American Psychological Association and holds diplomates in forensic psychology, assessment psychology and police psychology. In March, 2007, Dr. Inwald sold Hilson Research, which is now part of the Public Safety and Security Division of the Institute for Personality and Ability Testing, Inc. (IPAT). Dr. Inwald can be reached at Inwald Research, Inc. (CA-CI.com), PO Box 73, Cleverdale, NY 12820 or 917-757-9063.

John W. Jones, Ph.D., ABPP is Vice President and Chief Scientist of Vangent, Inc.'s Human Capital Division. Dr. Jones serves as the principal thought leader in the research, development, and delivery of Vangent's Assessment and Hiring Solutions portfolio. In more than 25 years of experience in the human capital management business, Dr. Jones has held a number of executive positions, including the role of President and Senior I-O Psychologist for IPAT, Inc. He has served as past Chair of both the Association of Test Publisher's Industrial Division and the Standards Committee where he oversaw the development of the Model Guidelines for Preemployment Integrity Testing. His numerous publications include *Personnel Testing: A Manager's Guide; Applying Psychology in Business: A Handbook for Managers and Organizations*, Virtual HR, and Advances in e-Business and Psychology. He is also the founder of the *Journal of Business and Psychology*. Dr. Jones received his Ph.D. in applied psychology from DePaul University and his MBA from the Keller Graduate School of Management. He was awarded diplomat status in I-O psychology from the American Board of Professional Psychology, and is a licensed clinical psychologist in both Illinois and Virginia. Dr. Jones is a member of the American Psychological Association, the American Psychological Society, the Society for Industrial-Organizational Psychology, the Society for Police and Criminal Psychology, and the Psychological Services Section of the International Association of Chiefs of Police, among others.

Ali Khadivi earned his Ph.D. at the New School in New York City. He is Associate Clinical Professor of Psychiatry and Behavioral Sciences at The

Albert Einstein College of Medicine, Division of Law and Psychiatry. He is a Chief of Psychology at the Bronx Lebanon Hospital Center and director of Clinical and Forensic Psychological Assessment Services. He has conducted conditional second opinion psychological evaluations for major law enforcement agencies. He has an active practice in forensic assessment and psychotherapy in New York City.

Rosemarie O'Conner, Ph.D., is an educational measurement and research scientist at ICF International. Dr. O'Conner has over 10 years experience as a program evaluator, research methodologist, survey designer, and applied statistician. Her research and evaluation interests are concentrated in the area of survey construction and validation, classroom assessment, adolescent literacy, intensive academic instruction for at-risk youth, and teacher professional development. She has published her research in peer-reviewed journals and is co-editor and author of the book *A Pig Don't Get Fatter the More You Weigh It* (Teachers College Press, 2007).

Eric Ostrov, Ph.D., J.D., ABPP, is a licensed attorney and licensed clinical psychologist who is board certified in Forensic Psychology (American Board of Professional Psychology). His expertise is in the fields of police psychology, violence risk assessment, child custody, sex offenders, tort cases, criminal cases, and psychological disability. He is the co-author of five books and 35 articles. He has provided consultation services as a police psychologist since 1982, conducting evaluations and implementing screening programs for agencies such as the Chicago Police Department, the Drug Enforcement Agency and the FBI. He has worked extensively as a forensic psychologist, providing assessment and expert testimony with respect to civil, criminal and administrative litigation-related issues.

Cary Dennis Rostow, Ph.D., M.P., grew up in Brooklyn, NY where his father was a NYC police commander. Dr. Rostow attended the University of Illinois in Chicago and received his Ph.D. in Clinical Psychology at Northern Illinois University in DeKalb, IL. He has held a number of academic appointments during his long career. He is licensed as a Clinical Psychologist, Clinical Neuropsychologist and Medical Psychologist (Prescribing Psychologist) in the State of Louisiana. He is a member of the American Psychological Association, the Association of State and Provincial Psychology Boards, the National Academy of Neuropsychologists, the Society for Police and Criminal Psychology and the Psychology Section of the International Association of Chiefs of Police. He holds a Post-Doctoral Masters Degree in Psychopharmacology. He holds the Diplomate in Police Psychology from the Society for Police and Criminal Psychology. He is the President of

Matrix, Inc., a professional police psychology corporation. Dr. Rostow is the senior author of *Psychological Fitness-for-Duty Evaluations for Law Enforcement Executives* (with Robert Davis, 2004). He is also an author of the *Matrix-Psychological Uniform Law Enforcement Selection Evaluation (M-PULSE)*, a methodology and inventory for the determination of the probability of civil rights violations and other misconduct in law enforcement officers and law enforcement officer candidates, now in publication with MHS. He may be reached at 225-216-9422 or at 740 Colonial Drive, Baton Rouge, LA 70806 or at drrostow@idsmail.com.

Gerald F. Serafino, Ph.D., is a licensed psychologist who completed his Ph.D. at the University of Pittsburgh (1974) while he was Director of a local substance abuse center and a consultant (doing ride-alongs and training sessions) with the McKeesport, PA, Police Department. In 1978, he was appointed Director of the Forensic Evaluation Team for Southeastern New Mexico and continued his career as a police psychologist by working for more than 30 local, state, and federal law enforcement agencies. He was awarded the Diplomate in Police Psychology by the Society for Police and Criminal Psychology (1989), served on the New Mexico State Board of Psychologist Examiners (1997-2000), and has continued active memberships in the SPCP, APA, IACP, and his local FOP.

Michael L. Stoloff earned his doctoral degree from Johns Hopkins University in 1980. He is currently Professor and Head of the Department of Psychology at James Madison University. He has been a member of the Society for Police and Criminal Psychology since 1995. He currently serves as Webmaster and member of the Board of Directors of that organization. Since 1998, Dr. Stoloff has contributed to collaborative research regarding psychological assessment of police officer candidates.

William U. Weiss has worked for 40 years as a clinical psychologist, police psychologist, and researcher. He obtained his B.A. from The Johns Hopkins University and his Ph.D. in 1969 from the University of Maryland at College Park. From 1976 to 2008, Dr. Weiss was a member of the Psychology Department of the University of Evansville in Evansville, Indiana with the title of Professor of Psychology. He is now Professor Emeritus of Psychology at the University of Evansville. He currently teaches at Portland State University in Portland, Oregon, where he is Adjunct Professor of Psychology. He is a former editor of the *Journal of Police and Criminal Psychology* and he has authored numerous peer-reviewed journal articles on personality assessment and police psychology. Dr. Weiss also maintains a private practice in Vancouver, Washington.

Phillip W. Wickline is a doctoral graduate student at the University of Virginia. He has been an active participant at both the Society for Police and Criminal Psychology and Society for Personality Assessment Conferences over the past several years. One of his main interests is in the application of the Rorschach Comprehensive System to police psychological assessment.

INTRODUCTION

The story of how this book came to be written is a long and interesting one. My involvement in police psychology goes back to 1999, when I attended my first Society for Police and Criminal Psychology (SPCP) conference, held that year in Port Jefferson, New York. I was a graduate student at the time and (had been for some time since entering graduate school) very keenly interested in personality assessment. One of the things I noticed at the conference right away was that many of the psychologists presenting at the conference (including several whose chapters are included in this book) were using personality assessment instruments in police psychology and conducting research on them. As a result, I began an interest in applications of personality assessment to police psychology that has continued, and over the years continued to discuss this application with other psychologists, particularly in SPCP.

One of the things that I noticed fairly quickly (many of my colleagues noticed it, too) was that there were a wide range of assessment instruments used in police psychology, and what was used depended on the preferences of the psychologist. Moreover, people had a lot of information on using personality assessment for purposes of pre-employment screening of law enforcement officers, but not on much else. In addition, the presentations that I attended, and journal articles I read, usually dealt with only a few instruments–the MMPI-2 and the Inwald Personality Inventory (IPI) were about it in those days. Exploring the use of additional methods seemed to be of less interest.

Now, ten years later, all of these situations are changing. New instruments have been developed or investigated for use in police psychology, and there are more peer-reviewed research studies on using personality assessment in police psychology than ever before. Since that time, the Personality Assessment Inventory (PAI) and Rorschach Comprehensive System were investigated for use in police work, the M-PULSE was developed, and the Hilson Test Battery (of which the IPI is a part) has been expanded. With so much information available and an almost bewildering array of tests, the police psychologist needs a handy information resource on personality assessment.

Moreover, psychologists are more involved in law enforcement work than ever before, and in a wider variety of roles. The purpose of this book is to provide a "how to" primer which will help psychologists understand the essentials of conducting various police evaluations, and also understand the pros and cons of various tests in order to help with test selection. When we began work on this book, my co-contributors and I realized that no such resource existed, but that such a book would be invaluable to the police psychologist. Important information on conducting evaluations can be found in the sections of this book dealing with different tests and specific evaluations. Of course, background information and evaluation basics are covered in the introductory section.

However, this book is not oriented exclusively towards practitioners. With the movement in psychology towards evidence-based practice, police psychologists must justify their practice-based decisions in terms of research findings. The question will always be asked, "Does this assessment method work for this purpose?" For this reason, a three-chapter section has been included on research methods in police psychology. The purpose of this section is to help psychologists better understand current research, particularly using the ever-popular personality inventories, but also to better understand research findings, and, in the chapter on future research, we hope to stimulate further research in the field of personality assessment in police psychology. Reflecting this empirical orientation, all of the practice-oriented chapters cite relevant research studies as well in the spirit of continuing to promote evidence-based practice.

The event that actually precipitated this book is more immediate, however. As a result of my interest in personality assessment, I also became involved in the Society for Personality Assessment (SPA), and it was suggested to me for the 2008 conference in New Orleans that I host a symposium on using personality assessment in police psychology. So I assembled a group of presenters whom I knew from both SPA and SPCP, and we had a very interesting set of lectures and discussions on a variety of issues in police psychology. We felt that the symposium was quite successful, and it promoted our thinking more about how personality assessment is actually used in police applications. After discussions with several of the contributors in this book, especially James Herndon, whose presentation at SPA on the politics of assessment in police agencies was a big hit, we felt that a resource on using personality assessment for police work was needed, for the reasons that I have briefly described above. We hope that this book will become a valuable resource for the current generation of police psychologists. We have tried to be as comprehensive as possible and to include up-to-date information. We have also attempted to cover as many types of applications, and as many tests, as were reasonable within this space. While in such rapidly changing fields as applied psychology, it is nearly impossible to have everything within one cover, we sincerely hope that this volume will be viewed as an important reference by police psychologists everywhere. Never before has so much information on personality assessment in police psychology been found in one place.

I would like to acknowledge the efforts of a number of individuals without whom this book would not have been written. First and foremost, I would like to thank all of the contributors to this book–after all it would not exist without their efforts. Among that group, several people deserve special mention. Robin Inwald was an enthusiastic supporter of this project from the very beginning, and she provided invaluable assistance in helping me trace the history of personality assessment in police psychology. She was perhaps the ideal person to do this, as she was one of the pioneer police psychologists doing personality assessment in the early days. James Herndon, Phil Wickline, JoAnne Brewster, Michael Stoloff, John Hitchcock, and Rose O'Conner all contributed in one way or another to the SPA 2008 symposium that evolved into this book, and their contributions were very important. James Herndon also deserves special thanks for helping to convince me that a volume such as this was sorely needed, as do JoAnne and Phil for agreeing with me that exploring the use of the Rorschach in police psychology was something worth doing. I would like also to thank Gerry and Anne Serafino, and Ali Khadivi, for the many hours that they spent with me talking police and assessment psychology and, essentially, cheering this project on to its completion.

Finally, thanks goes out to both of my parents. My father, William U. Weiss, has been a longtime police psychologist and former editor of *Journal of Police and Criminal Psychology*, and has proven to be a better collaborator on all things related to assessment and police psychology than I ever could have hoped for myself. My mother, Judith Weiss, used her editing skills to assist with assembling the book manuscript and her assistance is greatly acknowledged.

My co-contributors and I all sincerely hope that this volume will be invaluable to you in whatever area of police or assessment psychology you may be involved in.

Peter A. Weiss
West Hartford, CT and Vancouver, WA

CONTENTS

Page

Introduction xi

Chapter

PART I: Introduction and Basic Principles

1. A BRIEF HISTORY OF PERSONALITY ASSESSMENT IN
   POLICE PSYCHOLOGY–*Peter A. Weiss & Robin Inwald* 5

2. FUNDAMENTAL ISSUES IN POLICE PSYCHOLOGICAL
   ASSESSMENT–*Gerald F. Serafino* 29

**PART II: Major Assessment Instruments Used
in Police Psychology**

3. USING THE THE MMPI-2 IN POLICE PSYCHOLOGICAL
   ASSESSMENT–*Peter A. Weiss & William U. Weiss* 59

4. USE OF THE PERSONALITY ASSESSMENT INVENTORY
   IN POLICE AND SECURITY PERSONNEL SELECTION–
   William U. Weiss & Peter A. Weiss 72

5. USE OF THE INWALD PERSONALITY INVENTORY,
   HILSON TESTS, AND INWALD SURVEYS FOR SELECTION,
   "FITNESS-FOR-DUTY" ASSESSMENT, AND
   RELATIONSHIP COUNSELING–*Robin Inwald* 91

6. THE USE OF THE M-PULSE INVENTORY IN LAW
   ENFORCEMENT SELECTION–*Robert D. Davis &*
   Cary D. Rostow 132

7. PRE-OFFER POLICE INTEGRITY TESTING: SCIENTIFIC
   FOUNDATION AND PROFESSIONAL ISSUES–*John W. Jones,*
   Michael R. Cunningham, & Kelly D. Dages 159

8. USING THE RORSCHACH COMPREHENSIVE SYSTEM
   IN POLICE PSYCHOLOGY–*JoAnne Brewster, Phillip W. Wickline,*
   & Michael L. Stoloff 188

**PART III: Research Methods in Police
Psychology Personality Assessment**

9. PREDICTING LAW ENFORCEMENT OFFICER
   PERFORMANCE WITH PERSONALITY INVENTORIES–
   Michael G. Aamodt 229

10. EFFECT SIZES IN POLICE PSYCHOLOGY PERSONALITY
    ASSESSMENT RESEARCH: A PRIMER–*John H. Hitchcock,*
    Rosemarie O'Conner, & Peter A. Weiss 250

11. THE FUTURE OF PERSONALITY ASSESSMENT RESEARCH
    IN POLICE PSYCHOLOGY: WHAT'S NEXT AND WHAT DO
    WE NEED?–*John H. Hitchcock, Peter A. Weiss, William U. Weiss,*
    Robert D. Davis, & Cary D. Rostow 279

**PART IV: Applications of Personality Assessment
in Police Psychology**

12. PROCEDURAL CONSIDERATIONS IN SECURITY
    PERSONNEL SELECTION–*William U. Weiss* 299

13. ISSUES IN THE LAW ENFORCEMENT FITNESS-FOR-
    DUTY EVALUATION–*Cary D. Rostow & Robert D. Davis* 317

Contents

14. CONDITIONAL SECOND OPINION PSYCHOLOGICAL
    EVALUATION OF LAW ENFORCEMENT CANDIDATES–
    Ali Khadivi 333

15. USING MULTIPLE SOURCES OF INFORMATION WHEN
    CONDUCTING MANDATORY OR REQUIRED POLICE
    PSYCHOLOGICAL EVALUATIONS–*Eric Ostrov* 347

16. THE POLITICS OF PERSONALITY ASSESSMENT IN
    POLICE AGENCIES–*James Herndon* 362

Index 373

PERSONALITY ASSESSMENT
IN
POLICE PSYCHOLOGY

Part I

INTRODUCTION AND
BASIC PRINCIPLES

Chapter 1

A BRIEF HISTORY OF PERSONALITY ASSESSMENT IN POLICE PSYCHOLOGY[1]

PETER A. WEISS AND ROBIN INWALD

Since the 1960s, the application of psychological services and research to law enforcement settings (henceforth referred to as "police psychology") has gone from being practically nonexistent to being almost universal in a relatively short period of time (Scrivner, 2006). In the early twenty-first century, psychologists are involved in providing a variety of services to law enforcement agencies, including performing evaluations for pre-employment selection, "fitness-for-duty" evaluations (FFDE), and providing counseling and treatment to psychologically troubled officers.

The extensive use of personality assessment instruments in police psychology is not surprising given the fact that psychologists have traditionally concerned themselves with issues of psychological measurement and test construction. In the contemporary practice of police psychology, assessment using personality measures is essential, being utilized in all of the previously mentioned evaluations, in addition to other occasional applications (Weiss, Weiss, & Gacono, 2008).

Before the 1960s

Even though most of the current trends in police psychology date back only to the 1960s, the use of psychological assessment in law enforcement is

---

[1]This writing is based on records obtained by the authors at the time of this writing. An ongoing project to fully develop and verify the history of "police assessment psychology" is underway. It will be appreciated if readers contact the authors with any corrections and/or additions (such as the names of additional early conference participants).

not a recent phenomenon. Lewis Terman, who is probably best known for developing the Stanford-Binet (the first intelligence test widely used by psychologists), attempted to use psychological assessment techniques to predict the performance of law enforcement officers over 90 years ago (Terman, 1917). Terman conducted a study in which he gave the original Stanford-Binet intelligence test to applicants for employment in the San Jose, California, police department in 1916. Terman discovered that the Stanford-Binet scores were related to several external correlates that could have an impact on an applicant's performance as a law enforcement officer. While Terman's techniques deviated from contemporary practice in police psychology, his original study is important in that it foreshadows contemporary test usage.

While Terman's (1917) study was the first to suggest that testing might be useful for pre-employment evaluations, he noted that his results were tentative because he lacked information about the true criterion-related validity of the Stanford-Binet for this application (selection of police officers). However, he did feel that testing would be potentially valuable as a selection tool for certain types of occupations, and stressed the importance of establishing correlations between the test scores and future performance, and also in establishing norms of performance for different occupational groups. While Terman's study was speculative and did not involve the kinds of personality tests utilized in law enforcement selection today, he established the basis for these evaluations and for obtaining the necessary research data to make these evaluations viable.

While Terman (1917) made an important first step, psychological testing of any kind was not widely used in law enforcement until seven decades later.

Prior to the 1960s, a few experimental investigations of psychological testing on police attitude and performance were conducted. For example, L. L. Thurstone (1922) gave the Army Alpha Intelligence test to a group of officers serving in the Detroit Police Department. He found that, in general, patrolmen were more intelligent than the lieutenants who commanded them. Thurstone concluded that this may have been due to the fact that the most intelligent law enforcement officers often moved to other, higher paying occupations rather than wait for promotion. Kates (1950) administered the Rorschach Inkblot Method (Klopfer system) to a group of New York City police officers and found that some Rorschach variables could be used to predict job satisfaction and motivation for promotion. In 1954, the Los Angeles Police Department began screening all of its officers using the Minnesota Multiphasic Personality Inventory ("MMPI"), a group Rorschach, a tree drawing and a brief psychiatric interview (Blau, 1994; Fabricatore, 2009). A few other attempts to develop and validate instruments for police selection exist in the literature, but, by and large, psychological tests were not widely used in law enforcement settings in the years leading up to and immediately following World War II.

The nature of police departments changed dramatically after the 1950s, and this included increased involvement by collateral professions in police work, such as psychology (Scrivner, 2006). According to Janik (1994), part of this had to do with psychology expanding beyond its academic origins during World War II. During the War, psychologists were employed by the military to assist Selective Service Boards in identifying individuals who were psychologically unfit for military service. In addition, they became involved in conducting evaluations for purposes of selecting spies, saboteurs, and intelligence operatives (Janik, 1994). Most notable in this area was the work of Henry Murray and colleagues, who used personality assessment instruments to perform personnel selection evaluations for the Office of Strategic Services (OSS), the forerunner of the CIA (Weiner & Greene, 2008). Given that they had some degree of success in these enterprises, it was not surprising that psychologists would continue with their expanded applied roles in postwar civilian life. Becoming involved in selecting law enforcement personnel was a natural extension of the activities that they had engaged in during WWII.

Changes in the 1960s

Legal and cultural changes/events in the 1960s, including the 1963 "Onion Fields" kidnap-murder of officer(s) and the 1965 Watts riots, led to the expansion of psychologists' roles and applications in the law enforcement field. In 1963, James Shaw of Washington was appointed by the King County Sheriff's Department as the first "in-house" police psychologist working half-time, conducting research, providing consultations, and pre-employment evaluations for sheriff's deputies.

In 1967, the release of two federal government reports on law enforcement resulted in the eventual universal psychological screening of law enforcement candidates (Ostrov, 1986; Janik, 1994). The Presidential Commission on Law Enforcement and the Administration of Justice (1967) emphasized the importance of assessing emotional stability in officer candidates. The National Advisory Commission on Annual Justice Standards and Goals (1967) recommended that, by 1975, every law enforcement agency employ a trained professional who could administer psychological tests for purposes of evaluating applicants for characteristics that would be detrimental to police work.

As a result of these and other developments in the late 1960s, the concept of pre-employment selection evaluations for police candidates became more acceptable to police administrators than it had in the past. Still, during the late 1960s and 1970s, most chiefs continued to believe that the pre-employment interviews they conducted themselves, along with their medical and physical examination requirements, were sufficient for selecting the best candidates for the job.

In 1968, the Law Enforcement Assistance Administration (LEAA), as part of the Department of Justice, funded new programs including studies of psychological testing. That same year, Martin Reiser of California was hired as the first full-time staff psychologist for the Los Angeles Police Department. He became the first major city "in-house" police psychologist who provided counseling, but not assessment, services.

Some psychologists at that time consulted and conducted research as external consultants to law enforcement agencies (Baehr, Furcon, & Froemel, 1968) and agencies began to have more direct contact with psychologists and the services they could provide through grant projects. For example, in 1969, Joseph Fabricatore of California began working as a graduate student Research Associate for the LA Sheriff's Department on an LEAA study focused on predicting patrol officer behavior from psychological variables.

Changes in the 1970s

In October, 1971, Michael Roberts of California was hired by the San Jose Police Department as the first full-time police psychologist whose responsibilities, among others, included assessment services.

The idea for a national police psychologist's group grew as the result of initial efforts by Nelson Watson. Watson, who retired from the FBI to an executive position with the International Association for Chiefs of Police (IACP), had an ongoing interest in developing psychological services within law enforcement and promoted the idea at national leadership conferences (Shaw, 2009). On September 25, 1973, the IACP hosted a meeting at its annual conference in San Antonio, TX that was organized by Terry Eisenberg of MD, IACP's "Research Scientist" in its Professional Standards Division. The conference was funded by the Police Foundation, with 56 participants from 44 organizations attending, including police psychologists James Shaw, Martin Reiser, and Michael Roberts. Representing 14 universities and 19 police agencies, among others, psychologists and professionals working in law enforcement met in order to "improve communications between social/behavioral scientists." While this meeting ended without direction, the idea of a national police psychologist's group continued (Shaw, 2009).

In September, 1975, Joseph Fabricatore was hired by the Department of Personnel of the City of Los Angeles as the first full-time police psychologist devoted solely to providing assessment services, including pre-employment screening and fitness-for-duty evaluations.

In 1975 and 1976, Charles J. Galbo, a psychologist from California, chaired the first two meetings of the Society for Police and Criminal Psychology in Tucson, Arizona and Gulf Park, Mississippi. Joseph Fabricatore was the only practicing assessment psychologist to attend those first meetings. This society, with its continued annual conferences, provided a forum for academics, psychologists and criminologists to discuss new roles, techniques and methods related to the law enforcement field.

In the mid-1970s, some states had one-sentence guidelines, intended primarily for physicians conducting pre-employment medical examinations, that required officers to be "free of significant psychopathology" or "free of any psychopathology" without mention of how that psychopathology related to actual police work or police officer performance. In order to further define police officer performance, Frank Landy and his colleagues published a study in 1976 using behaviorally anchored scales for rating the performance of police officers (Landy et al., 1976).

When the Equal Employment Opportunity Commission's (EEOC's) *Uniform Guidelines on Employee Selection* was published in 1978, this document defined "adverse impact" and included requirements for the validation of all selection tests, including psychological testing for public safety officer candidates. U.S. police agencies soon became aware of their need to follow test validation procedures in order to defend against class action lawsuits and any formal charges of "adverse impact" in their departments. These guidelines made it clear that validation of all selection tools, including any tests or psychological interviews used as a component of police officer selection, was necessary in order to properly defend hiring decisions (Inwald, 1984). The Uniform Guidelines had a major impact on discussions about testing in the police field and provided verification that more comprehensive validation studies were needed in order to justify police psychologist's evaluation techniques used in employee selection.

From October 26–29, 1976, the first "National Working Conference on the Selection of Law Enforcement Officers," sponsored by the FBI and LEAA of the Department of Justice, was held at the FBI Academy in Quantico, VA. Along with a number of university-based research psychologists were police psychologists James Shaw, Terry Eisenberg, Joe Fabricatore, and Michael Roberts.

From May 29 to June 1, 1979, the second national conference focusing on police selection was held at the FBI Academy in Quantico, VA. University-based researchers, such as Charles Spielberger (FL), John Furcon (IL), and Allen Shealy (AL) presented data on the relationship between personality test variables and police work. With approximately 55 participants, this three-day conference included practicing psychologists James Shaw, Joseph Fabricatore, Michael Roberts, Robin Inwald of New York and Mark Zelig of

Utah, who were conducting pre-employment assessments of officer candidates for law enforcement agencies at that time.

During the late 1970s, the personality tests most commonly used with public safety office candidates included the MMPI, California Psychological Inventory ("CPI"), 16 Personality Factor ("16 PF"), Edwards Personal Preference Schedule "(EPPS"), and various projective tests (Fabricatore et al., 1978; Fabricatore, 1979; Inwald, 1982; Ostrov, 1986).

Since the MMPI was the most widely used nonprojective personality assessment instrument available to clinical psychologists at the time, it was a natural choice to be used by psychologists who began working in the police and public safety officer selection field (Murphy, 1972). First used in police research in an attempt to predict police academy grades (King, Norrell, & Erlandson, 1959), articles suggesting the usefulness of the MMPI in police settings, particularly for pre-employment screening, began to appear in the 1970s (Azen, Snibbe, & Montgomery, 1973; Azen, 1974; Saccuzo, Higgins, & Lewandowski, 1974; Saxe & Reiser, 1976).

However, the MMPI originally had been developed and normed for use with inpatients in psychiatric hospitals and not with more highly functioning, and symptom-denying, job applicants for law enforcement officer positions. It was noticed by practitioners that the norms for the MMPI often showed "normal" ranges for individual candidates, while the job histories and antisocial behavior patterns discovered in background investigations and psychological interviews for these same individuals suggested potential difficulties for high risk positions (Inwald, 1982). There was growing concern about the inadequacy of available instruments, and, in one study, it was reported that there was "no evidence (found) to support the MMPI as a predictor of police performance" (Mills & Stratton, 1982).

In November, 1979, after conducting over 1,000 pre-employment assessments, Robin Inwald completed the Inwald Personality Inventory (IPI), the first comprehensive personality inventory that was designed and validated specifically for public safety officer selection and that used public safety officer norms (Inwald, 1980). This also was the first personality assessment instrument that included biographical/behavioral data items, such as arrest history, driving record, work history, and alcohol/drug use, as well as scales identifying the presence of psychopathology and antisocial attitudes. Several weeks later, she founded Hilson Research, Inc., the first police and public safety-focused psychological test publishing company.

Changes in the '80s

The 1980s represented a decade of change, with much growing interest and development in police/public safety personality testing. A larger number of research articles and instrument publications began to appear in the 1980s as more psychologists became involved in conducting pre-employment evaluations for police departments and the need to firmly establish the validity of the instruments used for this application was recognized.

In 1980, a psychologically-oriented "Law Enforcement Personal History Questionnaire" was written by Robin Inwald. The first of its kind to be widely distributed to police psychologists, this "PHQ" often was used as a psychologist's interview aid along with computer-scored personality inventories such as the MMPI, CPI and/or IPI (Inwald, 1980; Inwald & Knatz, 1980; Inwald, Knatz & Levitt, 1980; Inwald, 1984; Inwald, 1985).

In 1981, the Law Enforcement Assessment and Development Report ("LEADR,") was published, a derivative of Raymond Cattell's 16-PF (1949) published by IPAT, with a public-safety-related narrative report (Dee-Burnett, Johns, & Krug, 1981).

In 1981, police psychologists became aware of an important lawsuit in New York City. On December 20, 1976, NYC Police Officer I.A. Bonsignore used his "off-duty" revolver to shoot his wife and then to commit suicide. His wife suffered brain damage and serious motor dysfunction as a result. In the lawsuit that followed, the jury awarded his wife $425,000 damages on her claim for negligently causing her injuries (*Bonsignore v The City of N.Y.*, 521 F.Supp. 394 (S.D.N.Y. 1981), aff'd 683 F.2d 635 (2d Cir. 1982). This was a very important case in the development of police psychological screening programs in that its outcome persuaded many reluctant chiefs that they could have serious difficulties defending hiring decisions if they failed to provide adequate psychological screening at the outset.

While the LEAA was abolished in 1982 due to lack of government funding, this did not stop the growing interest in improving police selection techniques. At the ninetieth annual convention of the American Psychological Association in Washington, D.C. (August, 1982), Harvey Goldstein (of MD) chaired a symposium entitled, "A Futurist View of Psychology's Emerging Role in Police Agencies." At that same conference, he organized the first meeting of police/public safety psychologists at APA with eleven other psychologists in attendance, including Martin Reiser, Joseph Fabricatore, Robin Inwald, Ellen Scrivner of Maryland, and Al Somodevilla of Texas. This was the first national organization consisting solely of Ph.D.-level psychologists who were working in-house or as consultants providing direct psychological services to police and/or public safety agencies. After the first officer elections were held in 1983, Robin Inwald chaired the meetings for this newly-named "Police and Public Safety" Section of APA's Division 18 (Psychologists in Public Service) from 1984 through 1986. Annual section discussions during these years focused primarily on issues related to pre-employment screening and personality assessment techniques.

In September, 1984 (17th–21st), James T. Reese (from the FBI) and Harvey Goldstein organized and conducted the five-day National Symposium on Police Psychological Services at the FBI Academy in Quantico, VA. It was at this conference where approximately 147 police psychologists and other professionals working in the field from around the country began to develop a strong national network. During and after the presentations at this conference, there were many active discussions about various testing programs and selection techniques.

Draft guidelines written by Robin Inwald for "mental health professionals conducting pre-employment psychological screening programs in law enforcement agencies" were presented at this conference (Inwald, 1984; Blau, 1994). Inwald then conducted an opinion survey of these guidelines and published results for the 54 FBI conference participants who responded (Inwald, 1985; Scogin & Beutler, 1986). Using this information, she continued to collect additional surveys, edited the guidelines accordingly, and chaired discussions at APA and other organizations in order to reach a consensus in the field related to pre-employment assessment (Inwald, 1984).

After an informal meeting at the 1984 FBI conference, Susan Saxe-Clifford of California and James Shaw worked to arrange the first organizational Ad Hoc committee meeting for Police Psychology at the International Association of Chiefs of Police in Salt Lake City, UT. On October 23, 1984, Saxe-Clifford, Shaw, and six other psychologists, including Robin Inwald and James Chandler of Illinois, attended that committee meeting. The focus of discussion was on the organization's mission and the immediate need for professional guidelines for pre-employment psychological assessment. In October, 1986, members were appointed to the new IACP Police Psychological Services Section, with James Shaw as the first elected Chairman, Susan Saxe-Clifford as Vice-Chair, and Robin Inwald as Liaison Officer. At that meeting, Inwald's amended guidelines for pre-employment assessment were further edited and then adapted as the formal guidelines of the IACP Police Psychological Services Section. The American Psychological Association eventually rejected the police psychology section's request to formalize such guidelines under APA due to concerns regarding legal ramifications and enforcement.

After another informal meeting at the 1984 FBI conference, Gabriel Rodriguez of Lousiana and Douglas Gentz of Oklahoma named and organized the Consortium of Police Psychologists (COPPS). Approximately ten psychologists attended the first COPPS meeting that took place in New Orleans during Mardi Gras in March, 1985. These included Rodriguez, Gentz, Scott Allen (FL), Tom Hickey (TN), and Leo Shea (NH), among others, who were conducting police assessments at that time. This group continues to focus on assessment techniques and other practical issues for police psychologists at its annual conferences each year.

Many research articles were published in the 1980s establishing the validity of Hathaway and McKinley's (1940) 566-item MMPI for screening police/public safety officers, including those by Bernstein (1980), Beutler, Storm, Kirkish, Scogin, & Gaines (1985), Costello, Schoenfeld, & Kobos (1982), Hartman (1987), Hiatt & Hargrave (1988), and Inwald (1988).

Research articles by James, Campbell, & Lovegrove (1984), Hargrave (1985); and Hargrave, Hiatt, & Gaffney (1986) also showed the increased use of Harrison Gough's CPI (1956), a 434-item test that shared 194 items with the original MMPI yet focused on common personality factors rather than on psychopathology.

Meanwhile, the shorter, 310-item IPI soon gained considerable popularity with police psychologists, especially as its validity for pre-employment screening became established during the 1980s. Several research publications and independent studies were completed, including the first longitudinal cross-validation studies and the first publications that directly compared law enforcement candidate test results by gender and ethnicity (Inwald & Shusman, 1984; Ostrov, 1985; Scogin & Beutler, 1986; Los Angeles Police Department, 1986; Mesnick et al., 1988; Malin et al., 1987; Inwald, 1988). Also at this time, there was some early recognition of the emerging area of police/public safety assessment by professional psychology organizations. For example, in 1982, the NY State Psychological Association's "Meritorious Research Award" was presented to Inwald for "Contribution to test construction in an important new area."

After the IPI computerized report was published in 1982, specifying how test results could be interpreted using public safety officer applicant norms, National Computer Systems (NCS) introduced an MMPI computer-generated narrative report, the "Minnesota Report: Personnel Selection System," in 1984. The original MMPI clinical norms still were used in the MMPI profile graphs and no cut-off scores were suggested for law enforcement officer candidates or for other job applicants.

In 1985, police psychologists began to expand their practices to include "fitness-for-duty" testing. When some psychologists, who were using the IPI for pre-employment screening, began to readminister this test as an aid for determining fitness for duty of already hired officers (Rice, 1985), it was clear that there was a need for more specialized assessment instruments. In 1986, the first comprehensive personality inventory developed for "fitness-for-duty" evaluations of public safety officers, the Hilson Career Satisfaction Index (HCSI), was developed and validated by Robin Inwald (Inwald & Kaufman, 1989).

In the late 1980s, Inwald also wrote the first "Proposed Fitness-for-Duty Evaluation Guidelines." These were revised and later published for wider review in August, 1990 (Inwald, 1990; Blau, 1994).

Several important national and international conferences followed the 1984 meeting at the FBI. In 1985 (May 7–15), John Yuille of Canada organized the NATO Conference on Police Selection and Training, where approximately 80 police psychologists from Canada, Europe and the United States were invited to meet in Skiathos, Greece for 9 days of meetings on selection techniques and training. Later that same year (December 15–19), James T. Reese organized the FBI World Conference on Police Psychology in Quantico, VA. In 1986, Reese also organized the 2nd National Symposium on Police Psychological Services, also held at the FBI Academy in Quantico.

At these conferences and in other forums throughout the country, specific procedures for using actuarial tests, along with personal history questionnaires and psychological interviews, were presented and actively discussed (Inwald, 1985, 1986; Pendergrass, 1987).

Now aware of recent court cases and the growing potential for publicity and lawsuits in this area, practicing police psychologists worried about either "negligent hiring" cases (when officers were hired who initially had "passed" the psychological evaluations and then did something "wrong") or charges of "discrimination" (when candidates were not hired and believed the psychological assessments were "unfair"). Robin Inwald searched for a credential, beyond the Ph.D. and state license to practice psychology that would add credibility in the courtroom for those who conducted police evaluations. In 1985 and '86, respectively, after a rigorous tape-recorded examination by skeptical forensic psychologists, she became the first full-time practicing police psychologist to be granted Diplomate status by the American Board of Forensic Psychology (ABFP) and the American Psychological Association's American Board of Professional Psychology (ABPP). Unfortunately, this was not the perfect home for "police assessment psychologists," since most of the forensic psychology work focused on other areas, quite different from police work. Nevertheless, 11 additional active police psychologists have been granted their ABFP and ABPP Diplomates since that time.

In 1988, at the IACP annual convention, Inwald introduced the Hilson Personnel Profile/Success Quotient ("HPP/SQ"), the first comprehensive personality inventory measuring "emotional intelligence" (Inwald & Brockwell, 1988; Inwald & Brobst, 1988; Inwald, 2008). Validated for police personnel hiring and promotion, and based on Inwald's "Success Quotient Theory," this measure focused on a combination of characteristics such as initiative, "winner's image," work ethic, popularity/"charisma" and social sensitivity. Norms were collected for police chiefs at the 1988 IACP convention and, after validation data were analyzed for law enforcement officer applicants throughout the country, the HPP/SQ became a standard addition to many police psychologist's pre-employment and promotional test batteries.

In 1988, Inwald also added discriminant-function-derived prediction equations for termination, absence, lateness and disciplinary actions to the IPI's computerized report. These equations were based on the first five-year longitudinal prediction study, including cross-validation, for public safety officers that was published in the *Journal of Applied Psychology* (Inwald, 1988).

In 1989, a major revision of the MMPI was published (Butcher et al., 2001), resulting in the MMPI-2, which in turn caused police psychologists to attempt further validation studies with the new test. While welcoming obsolete item revisions, police psychologists, who were accustomed to interpreting MMPI profiles using the original clinical norms, expressed concern that the new updated norms showed far fewer elevations for the more "normal" and defensive police/public safety officer candidates. This led many psychologists involved in pre-employment assessment to add additional tests to their standard batteries in order to either augment or to replace the MMPI-2.

Also in 1989, Michael Roberts and Michael Johnson, of Johnson, Roberts & Associates, published their automated Johnson, Roberts Personal History Questionnaire ("PHQ"), a 300-item questionnaire for evaluating public safety officer applicants (Roberts, 2009).

When the Polygraph Act of 1988 banned the use of the pre-employment polygraph for non-federal police agencies, newly-unemployed polygraph examiners became interested in promoting the use of "paper-and-pencil honesty tests" that could take the place of the polygraph. In his 1994 book, Theodore Blau wrote, "More than 40 integrity tests are available in the field today; however, few studies of these tests have been published in peer-reviewed journals."

Because of complaints about "honesty/integrity" tests received by members of Congress, its Office of Technology Assessment launched an investigation into the validity of these tests now flooding the market (though mostly in the retail area). With similar concerns, the American Psychological Association also organized a special Task Force to review available research. At this time, practicing police psychologists expressed growing concerns about claims of validity for tests not previously used to screen law enforcement applicants. Since these tests, with little or no published research connected with police performance, were being marketed directly to police chiefs and others for use without the input of a psychologist, several articles and research reviews were published on the subject (Sackett & Harris, 1984; Inwald, 1987, 1988; Sackett et al., 1989; Inwald, 1989, 1990). When the final reports from OTA (1990) and APA (1991) were published, they showed con-flicting results. The OTA report concluded that "existing research is insuffi-cient as a basis for supporting the assertion that (honesty tests) can reliably predict dishonest behavior in the workplace," while the APA Task Force con-cluded that the available research was not unlike that for many other tests used in the field of psychology. That report also relied on, and cited, a preprint version of Deniz Ones' (IA) meta-analysis that included "a substan-tial amount of data from IPI research indicating its validity for police selec-tion" (Ones et al., 1993; Ones, 2009). In any case, the Polygraph Act and sub-sequent "honesty test debate" of the late 1980s certainly encouraged in-creased scholarship and validation research in the area of public safety/police assessment.

Changes in the 1990s

While personality assessment in law enforcement settings came of age in the 1970s and 1980s, reflecting changes in both society and in the profes-sional role of psychology, the 1990s were a decade of continued expansion. In 1990, a survey of 72 major law enforcement agencies was conducted in order to determine the tests used for applicant selection. Results of this sur-vey revealed that 51 percent did not use any psychological tests, while the three most widely used tests were the MMPI, CPI and IPI (Strawbridge & Strawbridge, 1990; Blau, 1994).

In 1990, the Americans with Disabilities Act was passed by Congress. This law prohibited "pre-conditional offer psychological/medical" testing and became effective in 1992. Passed with the American Psychological Asso-ciation's written support, and before APA executives had notified Division 18 police psychologists of ADA's ramifications for their assessment work, this new law had a major, mostly negative, impact on police assessment. Police psychologists, prior to 1992, were saving departments large sums of money and resources by inquiring about alcohol/drug use during the early stages of applicant investigations and screening. Robin Inwald and Michael Roberts, who, between them, then had the largest collection of pre-employment test data in the country, pooled these data from various testing instruments and databases. They collaborated on an article about the job-relatedness of such questions (Inwald, Kaufman & Roberts, 1991) in an attempt to influence the writers of the government's upcoming ADA Guidance report (guidelines for the new law). Despite the admittedly clear evidence that patterns of alcohol and/or past drug use on written personality/psychological instruments did, in fact, predict poor police officer performance across many test scales and performance variables, Inwald and Roberts' campaign for an ADA exclusion of public safety organizations on behalf of practicing police psychologists failed. The published ADA guidelines required that police agencies adhere to the requirement that such questions only be asked after a bonafide "conditional offer of employment" had been made near the end of the screening process. While some psychologists continued to conduct "psychological/medical" screenings using the MMPI or IPI prior to conditional job offers in their departments, most police psychologists changed their pre-employment assessment practices after the passage of the ADA in order to avoid lawsuits.

A second law passed in the 1990s, the Civil Rights Act of 1991, also had a strong impact on assessment practices and instrument development in the police/public safety field. With concerns that police assessment validity would be decreased should it become illegal to use separate gender norms, APA's Diane Brown organized a meeting with EEOC's representatives and two researchers in the field. Paul Sackett and Robin Inwald presented research data supporting the value of using separate group norms to best predict police and other employee's performance. Despite their efforts to preserve the best predictions possible for employee selection, the Civil Rights Act of 1991 resulted in responsible selection test publishers having to change available separate norms by gender and ethnicity and merge groups into one overall norm. It became illegal to consider ethnicity or gender during employee selection, thus making the most accurate prediction equations also illegal.

In 1991 (October), the IACP's Psychological Services Section formally adapted Inwald's revised "Fitness-for-Duty Evaluation Guidelines" at its Annual Section Meeting. In a conference program entitled "Fitness for Duty: Standards and Practices for the '90s," that included presentations by Catherine Flanagan (NY), Stephen Curran (MD), and James Janik (IL), Robin Inwald formally presented these guidelines to the IACP membership during the 98th Annual IACP Conference in Minneapolis, MN.

Rather than alter items and scales of the IPI so that it could continue to be used as a "pre-conditional offer" test under the new ADA guidelines, Inwald wrote a series of new personality assessment instruments that were normed and validated on public safety officer applicants and did not contain items that would reveal psychopathology or past substance abuse (included in the ADA definition of "medical" diagnoses). In 1992, the Inwald Survey 5 (IS5), that included scales measuring areas of "integrity" and anger management, among others, was published by Hilson Research (Inwald & Gebbia, 1992). Inwald developed the IS5 in an effort to give police psychologists critical behavioral information at the "pre-conditional offer" phase of screening, since the administration of the IPI or MMPI now was illegal under ADA. Police agencies began to use this test as part of their "pre-conditional-offer" screening programs and many police psychologists also added it to their "post-conditional-offer" and "fitness-for-duty" batteries.

In 1993 (July 27–30), the FBI sponsored a conference on "Law Enforcement Families: Issues & Answers" at the FBI Academy in Quantico, VA. Robin Inwald conducted a research study for this conference and developed the Hilson Spouse/Mate Inventory, the first assessment instrument for evaluating relationship issues specific to police personnel and their spouse/partners (Inwald, 1993).

In 1993, Deniz Ones "published a monograph in the *Journal of Applied Psychology* that included the IPI validity data mentioned in the APA Task Force report. "This study established the generalizability and test validities of 'integrity' tests and stopped the movement to ban these instruments" (Ones, 1993; Ones, 2009).

In 1995 (January 23–27), the FBI sponsored a conference on "Organizational Issues in Law Enforcement" at the FBI Academy in Quantico. At this conference, Robin Inwald presented summary research on those police/public safety officers who had been tested during the 1970s or 1980s and later became involved in inappropriate violent behavior as officers (Inwald, 1995). As a direct result of discussions at this FBI conference, the Inwald Survey 2 ("IS2") was published by Hilson Research the following year (Inwald et al, 1996). This 110-item inventory, along with its shorter version, the "Inwald Survey 8" ("IS8"), was the first personality inventory developed for public safety officers and applicants that focused specifically on the identification of characteristics associated with violent behavior.

In 1995, Inwald's Hilson Safety/Security Risk Inventory (HSRI) was published for use in pre-conditional offer police screening (Inwald, 1995). The HSRI, with its scales focusing on attitudes and behaviors related to safety issues, as well as self-control in other areas, was developed for use in the police/public safety field after police administrators continued to complain about the recurring problem of vehicular accidents in their departments. Inwald's instruments saw increased use by police psychologists in the 1990s as evaluators sought to use personality instruments that tapped job-related behavioral characteristics in pre-employment, FFDE, and treatment-based evaluations.

Also in 1995, Consulting Psychologist's Press published Michael Roberts' "CPI Police & Public Safety Selection Report" for evaluating public safety applicants using Harrison Gough's CPI. With its addition of public safety applicant norms, this report gained immediate popularity with CPI users in the field (Roberts, 2009).

In 1996, Hilson Research published Robin Inwald's "Hilson Management Survey – HMS," a test that was developed for promotional screening. This instrument was used, initially, for public safety officer promotions and public safety administrator screening, including some assessments being conduced by police psychologists for police chief and assistant chief positions (Inwald et al., 1996).

Since many police psychologists and public safety administrators who conducted or organized pre-employment screening programs often complained about the length of the personality inventories being administered, Inwald then developed the "Hilson Life Adjustment Profile ("HLAP)," a 110-item inventory for identifying psychopathology as well as assessing a police candidate or officer's actual functioning in personal, social and family life. Also published in 1996, this inventory was offered as a possible replacement for the much lengthier MMPI and correlations between these two instruments were included in the HLAP Technical Manual (Inwald et al., 1996).

In 1997, Psychological Assessment Resources, Inc. published the "PAI Law Enforcement, Corrections, and Public Safety Selection Report" to be used with Les Morey's 1991 Personality Assessment Inventory ("PAI"-Roberts et al., 2004). Like the IPI and the other Hilson Research test reports, this report relied upon law enforcement norms for evaluating public safety applicants.

The first comprehensive "psychological" job analysis, focusing on personality variables found in published psychological tests and documenting their relative importance to "subject matter experts," such as police chiefs and administrators, was conducted by Michael Cuttler and Robin Inwald in the mid-1990s. In this study, over 1,500 police administrators, representing every public safety agency in the state of North Carolina, identified those personality variables they believed to be most important for police officer performance on the Hilson Job Analysis Questionnaire ("HJAQ"). Using this and other studies, the HJAQ was published in 1998 and was the first computerized job analysis assessment tool used by administrators to evaluate the relative importance of different personality variables in their agencies (Inwald, 1998).

In the fall of 1998 (September 14–18), as the result of increasing concerns about domestic violence in police families, the FBI sponsored a "Domestic Violence by Police Officers" conference at Quantico. After the week-long presentations and discussions on this topic concluded, Robin Inwald developed a scale for identifying those individuals most likely to become involved in domestic violence. This scale was added to the updated and renormed Inwald Survey 5-Revised ("IS5R") in 1999.

Additional IPI studies from independent researchers also were published in the 1990s (Mufson & Mufson, 1998), including one linking the IPI and MMPI with the "Big Five" Personality Factors (Cortina et al., 1992). During this time, several researchers continued to examine the validity of the revised MMPI-2. Examples from this period include articles by Brewster & Stoloff (1999); Hargrave, Hiatt, Ogard, & Carr (1994); and Kornfeld (1995).

However, research efforts in the field soon were hampered by the fact that police departments, unlike in earlier years, began to take their psychologist's ratings very seriously. During the '80s, police administrators continued to hire many officers despite their questionable suitability based on psychological tests. This allowed for validation studies to be conducted where there were a larger number of "failures." This situation changed during the '90s, when police psychologists had gained respect in their departments and when the testing came at the end of the screening process (due to the ADA). Now agencies rarely hire officers with "questionable" psychological results. While good for society, the rejection of nearly all poorly-rated candidates restricted the range of officers who could be followed in predictive research studies, limiting researcher's ability to directly compare the validities of different tests.

In 1999, Deniz Ones began a project for the California Police Officer Selection and Training (POST) organization in their efforts to update psychological screening guidelines. At this time, she "collected over 19,000 validity coefficients from all personality-based tests available at the time. These results were presented at numerous professional conferences, firmly establishing the validity of personality tests, such as the MMPI, CPI, and IPI, among others" (Ones, 2009).

Changes in the 2000s

In 2004, Gary Aumiller of New York obtained the trademark "Diplomate in Police Psychology" on behalf of the Society for Police and Criminal Psychology. Over 40 police psychologists nationwide have received this diplomate status as of 2009.

New instruments for public safety assessment purposes also have been developed during the first decade of the twenty-first century.

In 2000, Law Enforcement Services, Inc. (LESI) published Michael Cuttler's "onlinePHQ," for evaluating public safety officer applicants. This new instrument grew from research conducted on the validity of individual life history items that was published in the *Journal of Applied Psychology* in 1998 (Sarchione et al., 1998).

In 2002, Hilson Research published Robin Inwald's Hilson Trauma Recovery Inventory ("HTRI"), also developed as a result of discussions at the 1998 FBI Conference on Domestic Violence by Police Officers and the recent influx of officers returning from overseas military duty in the Middle East (Inwald, 2002; Inwald, 2006).

Additional independent IPI validation research was completed during these years (Detrick et al., 2001; Detrick & Chibnall, 2002; Chibnall &

Detrick, 2003), including comparisons of IPI scores with those of newly-developed research scales for the MMPI-2 (Ben-Porath, 2007).

In 2005, IntegriQuest, LLC published Andrew Ryan's "RPIQ," an automated biodata collection instrument for public safety officer candidates.

In 2007, Inwald Research, Inc. published the Inwald Couples Compatibility Questionnaire ("ICCQ,") Inwald Partners Personality Inventory ("IPPI,") Inwald Personality Survey ("IPS,") and the Inwald Attitude Survey ("IPS,") for use with police couples (Inwald, 2006; Inwald, 2008).

In 2008, Multi Health Systems, Inc. (MHS) published Robert Davis & Cary Rostow's "M-PULSE," a personality test developed for public safety officer screening (Davis & Rostow, 2008).

[handwritten margin note: l-ck A M-PULSE]

In 2008, Peter Weiss, William Weiss and Carl Gacono reviewed the use of the Rorschach Inkblot Method (Exner, 2003) for police psychological assessments (Zacker, 1997; Weiss, 2002; Weiss, Weiss, & Gacono, 2008). This review was completed for several reasons: One was the wealth of personality-related information that can be gleaned from the Rorschach Comprehensive System and another was the impression management limitations of self-report measures.

In 2008, Pearson Assessments, Inc. published the MMPI-2 Restructured Form ("MMPI-2RF"), a revised form of the MMPI-2 that includes a set of law enforcement norms in its technical manual (Tellegen & Ben-Porath, 2008).

SUMMARY

In 2008, Dave Corey (of OR, petitioner for the American Psychological Association), Gary Aumiller (of NY, petitioner for the Society for Police & Criminal Psychology), Herb Gupton (HI), Phil Trompetter (CA), and Michael Cuttler (NC, committee members) led an initiative resulting in the APA Council of Representatives approving recognition of "Police Psychology" as a proficiency in professional psychology.

Given the history of police psychology, it is not surprising that of the four domains recognized as part of police psychology proficiencies by Aumiller and Corey (2007), the assessment domain contains the largest number of proficiencies (20 out of the total of 57). While police psychologists are engaged in a very wide range of activities, psychological assessment remains a very important part of their professional activity at the beginning of the twenty-first century. Many of these activities involve the use of personality assessment instruments. While "personality assessments" per se are not mentioned in the description of the proficiencies, a number of them, particularly "pre-employment," "post-offer psychological evaluations of job candidates," "pre-offer suitability screening of job applicants," "test development," "assessment-related education and training," and "assessment-related research" contain language relating to personality assessment instruments. In addition, personality assessment methods are often used in a number of other police psychological assessments, particularly fitness-for-duty evaluations. A perusal of the article (Aumiller & Corey, 2007) identifying the activities of police psychologists reveals an extraordinary range of activities, and it is likely that the application of personality assessment instruments to different kinds of police and public safety evaluations will continue to increase in the future.

REFERENCES

look for citations

Aumiller, G.S., & Corey, D. (2007). Defining the field of police psychology: Core domains & proficiencies. *Journal of Police and Criminal Psychology, 22,* 65–76.

Azen, S.P. (1974). Predictors of resignation and performance of law enforcement officers. *American Journal of Community Psychology, 2,* 79–86.

Azen, S.P., Snibbe, H.M., & Montgomery, H.R. (1973). A longitudinal predictive study of success and performance of law enforcement officers. *Journal of Applied Psychology, 57,* 190–192.

Baehr, M.E., Furcon, J. El, & Froemel, E.C. (1968). Psychological Assessment of Patrolmen: Qualifications in relation to field performance. Chicago Industrial Relations Council (unpublished).

Ben-Porath, Y. (2007). Restructured scales of the MMPI-2. Presentation at the 2007 annual meeting of the IACP Police Psychological Services section, San Diego, CA. October.

Bernstein, I.H. (1980). Security guards' MMPI profiles: Some normative data. *Journal of Personality Assessment, 44,* 377–380.

Beutler, L.E., Storm, A., Kirkish, P., Scogin, F., & Gaines, J.M. (1985). Parameters in the prediction of police officer performance. *Professional Psychology: Research and Practice, 16,* 324–335.

Blau, T. (1994). *Psychological services for law enforcement.* New York: John Wiley & Sons.

Brewster, J., & Stoloff, M.L., (1999). Using the good cop/bad cop profile with the MMPI-2. *Journal of Police and Criminal Psychology, 14*(2), 29–34.

Butcher, J.N., Graham, J.R., Ben-Porath, Y.S., Tellegen, A., Dahlstom, W.G., & Kaemmer, B. (2001). *MMPI-2: Manual for administration, scoring, and interpretation, revised edition.* Minneapolis: University of Minnesota Press.

Chibnall, J.T. & Detrick P. (2003). The NEOPR-R, Inwald Personality Inventory, and MMPI-2 in the prediction of police academy performace: a case for incremental validity. *American Journal of Criminal Justice, 27,* 233–248.

Cortina, J.M., Doherty, M.L., Schmitt, N., Kaufman, G., & Smith, R.G. (1992). The "Big Five" personality factors in the IPI and MMPI: Predictors of police performance. *Personnel Psychology, Inc., 45,* 119-140.

Costello, R.M., Schoenfeld, L.S., & Kobos, J. (1982). Police applicant screening: An analogue study. *Journal of Clinical Psychology, 38*, 216–221.

Davis, R.D., & Rostow, C.D. (2008). *M-PULSE technical manual.* Toronto: Multi Health Systems, Inc.

Detrick, P., Chibnall, J.T. & Rosso, M. (2001). MMPI-2 in police officer selection: normative data and relation to the Inwald Personality Inventory. *Professional Psychology: Research & Practice, 32*, (5), 484–490.

Detrick, P. & Chibnall, J.T. (2002). Prediction of police officer performance with the Inwald Personality Inventory. *Journal of Police & Criminal Psychology, 17* (2), 9–17.

Exner, J.E., Jr. (2003). *The Rorschach: A Comprehensive System: Basic foundations and principles of interpretation* (Vol. 1). New York: Wiley.

Fabricatore, J.M., Azen, S., Schoentgen, S. & Snibbe, H. (1978). Predicting performance of police officers using the 16 personality factor questionnaire. *American Journal of Community Psychology, (6)* 1, 63–70.

Fabricatore, J.M. (1979). Pre-entry assessment and training: Performance evaluation of police officers, In *Police selection and evaluation* (Ed) Spielberger, C.D. New York: Hemisphere Publishing Corporation.

Fabricatore, J.M. (2009). Personal communication with the second author.

Gough, H.G. (1987). *California psychological inventory administrator's guide.* Palo Alto, CA: Consulting Psychologists Press, Inc.

Hargrave, G.E. (1985). Using the MMPI and CPI to screen law enforcement applicants: A study of reliability and validity of clinicians' decisions. *Journal of Police Science and Administration, 13*, 221–224.

Hargrave, G.E., Hiatt, D., & Gaffney, T.W. (1986). A comparison of MMPI and CPI test profiles for traffic officers and deputy sheriffs. *Journal of Police Science and Administration, 14*, 250–258.

Hargrave, G.E., Hiatt, D., Ogard, E.M., & Karr, C. (1994). Comparison of the MMPI and MMPI-2 for a sample of peace officers. *Psychological Assessment, 6*, 27–32.

Hartman, B.J. (1987). Psychological screening of law enforcement candidates. *American Journal of Forensic Psychology, 1*, 5–10.

Hathaway, S.R., & McKinley, J.C. (1940). A multiphasic personality schedule (Minnesota): I. Construction of the schedule. *Journal of Psychology, 10*, 249–254.

Hiatt, D., & Hargrave, G.E. (1988). MMPI profiles of problem peace officers. *Journal of Personality Assessment, 52*, 722–731.

Inwald, R. (1980). "Personality characteristics of law enforcement applicants and development of assessment instruments." Paper presented at the meeting of the American Psychological Association, Montreal, Canada, September.

Inwald, R. (1980). "Psychological screening of correction officers." Paper presented at the meeting of the International Personnel Management Association Assessment Council, Boston, MA, July.

Inwald, R.; Knatz, H. (1980). "Techniques for conducting psychological interviews with law enforcement candidates." Paper presented at the meeting of the American Psychological Association, Montreal, Canada, September.

Inwald, R.; Knatz, H.; Levitt, D. (1980). "Pre-employment psychological evaluation as a predictor of correction officer job performance." Paper presented at the meeting of the American Psychological Association, Montreal, Canada, September.

Inwald, R. (1982). Psychological screening test helps police, corrections save money, avoid legal battles. *Criminal Justice Journal, 1* (8), 1–1, 3–6.

Inwald, R.E. (1982). *Inwald Personality Inventory (IPI) Technical Manual.* New York: Hilson Research, Inc. Reprinted (2008), Chicago, IL: IPAT, Inc., a subsidiary of OPP Ltd.

Inwald, R. (1984). Law enforcement officer screening: A description of one pre-employment psychological testing program. Submitted to the National Symposium on Police Psychological Services FBI Academy, Quantico, VA. September 17–21.

Inwald, R. (1984). "Issues & guidelines for mental health professionals conducting pre-employment psychological screening programs in law enforcement agencies." Paper prepared and presented at the National Symposium on Police Psychological Services, FBI Academy, Quantico, VA, September 17–21.

Inwald, R. & Shusman, E., (1984). The IPI and MMPI as predictors of academy performance for police recruits. *Journal of Police Science and Administration, 12* (1), 1–11.

Inwald, R. & Shusman, E., (1984). Personality and performance sex differences of law enforcement officer recruits. *Journal of Police Science and Administration, 1 2* (3), 339–347.

Inwald, R. (1984). "Ethical Guidelines for screening for high risk occupations." Paper presented at the meeting of the American Psychological Association, Toronto, Canada, August.

Inwald, R. (1984). Pre-employment psychological testing for law enforcement: ethical and procedural issues : What should administrators do? *Training Aids Digest, 9* (6), 1–7.

Inwald, R. (1984). Proposed guidelines for providers of pre-employment psychological testing services to law enforcement agencies, version III. Submitted to APA Task Force of Division 18, Section of Police and Public Safety Psychology.

Inwald, R. (1984). Psychological screening: Legal, ethical and administrative questions. *The Police Chief, 51* (1), 26.

Inwald, R. (1985). Administrative, legal, and ethical practices in the psychological testing of law enforcement officers. *Journal of Criminal Justice, 13*, 367–372.

Inwald, R. (1985). Professional opinions on a set of proposed guidelines for mental health practitioners conducting pre-employment psychological screening programs in law enforcement agencies. *Corrections Digest, 16* (7).

Inwald, R. (1985). Proposed guidelines for conducting pre-employment psychological screening programs. *Crime Control Digest, 19*(11), 1–6.

Inwald, R. (1985). Use of psychologists for selection and training police. In H.W.M. & P. Unsinger (Eds.), *Police Managerial Uses of Psychology & Psychologists.* Springfield, IL: Charles C Thomas.

Inwald, R. (1985). "A personality inventory developed specifically for screening law enforcement officer candidates." Presentation at NATO Conference on Police Selection & Training. Skiathos, Greece, May.

Inwald, R. (1985). "Establishing standards for psychological screening." Presentation at the FBI-sponsored World Conference on Police Psychology, Quantico, VA, December.

Inwald, R. (1986). Why include individual interviews for all law enforcement candidates? *Criminal Justice Digest, 5*(3), 1–3.

Inwald, R. (1986). The development of guidelines for psychological screening in law enforcement agencies. In J.T. Reese & J.M. Horn (Ed.) *Police psychology: Operational assistance* (pp. 233–240). U.S. Department of Justice, FBI, Washington, D.C. Reprinted in *Crime Control Digest, 20* (36), 6–9.

Inwald, R. (1986). "Law enforcement officer screening: a description of one pre-employment psychological testing program." Paper prepared and presented at the National Symposium on Police Psychological Services, FBI Academy, Quantico, VA, December.

Inwald, R. (1987). Paper and pencil psychological tests for security personnel. *Security Systems, 16* (2), p. 24. Reprinted as Psychological/honesty test buyers beware: how to evaluate pre-employment paper and pencil tests. *Criminal Justice Digest, 6*(11), 1–6. Reprinted in *Corporate Security Digest, 1* (12), 1–4. Reprinted in *Personnel Journal,* (1988), *67* (5), 40–46. Reprinted in *Security Management,* (1988), *32*(2), 75–80.

Inwald, R.E. (1988). Five year follow-up study of departmental terminations as predicted by 16 pre-employment psychological indicators. *Journal of Applied Psychology, 4,* 703–710.

Inwald, R. & Brockwell, A. (1988). *Success quotient profiles of law enforcement administrators.* New York: Hilson Research, Inc.

Inwald, R. & Brobst, K.E. (1988). *Hilson Personnel Profile/Success Quotient (HPP/SQ) Technical Manual.* New York: Hilson Research, Inc. Reprinted (2008), Chicago, IL: IPAT, Inc., a subsidiary of OPP Ltd.

Inwald, R., Hurwitz, H. & Kaufman, J. (1989). Uncertainty reduction in retail and public safety/private security screening. *Forensic Reports. 4*(2), 171–212.

Inwald, R. (1989). How to detect those "little white lies" or "seven deadly sins" of honesty test vendors. *Corporate Security Digest, 3* (36), 1, 3, 4–7. Reprinted in *Security Management,* (1990), *34* (4), 73–76. Reprinted in *Personnel,* (1990), *67* (6), 52–58.

Inwald, R. & Kaufman, J.C. (1989). *Hilson Career Satisfaction Index (HCSI) Technical Manual.* New York: Hilson Research, Inc. Reprinted (2008), Chicago, IL: IPAT, Inc., a subsidiary of OPP Ltd.

Inwald, R. & Knatz, H. (1983). A process for screening out law enforcement candidates who might break under stress. *Criminal Justice Journal, 2* (4), 1–5.

Inwald, R. (1990). Proposed fitness-for-duty evaluation guidelines. *Criminal Justice Digest, 9* (8)

Inwald, R., Kaufman, J. & Roberts, M. (1991). Alcohol use, drug use, and past psychiatric history. *Criminal Justice Digest, 10* (7), 1-8.

Inwald, R., & Gebbia, M.I. (1992). *Inwald Survey 5 (IS5) Technical Manual.* New York: Hilson Research, Inc. Reprinted (2008), Chicago, IL: IPAT, Inc., a subsidiary of OPP Ltd.

Inwald, R. (1993). "Police spouse-mate relationships: Hilson Spouse/Mate Inventory." Presentation at the Law Enforcement Families: Issues & Answers Conference, Federal Bureau of Investigation Academy, Quantico, VA, July 27–30.

Inwald, R. (1995) "Workplace violence: A study of line officer characteristics." Presentation at the Organizational Issues in Law Enforcement Conference at the FBI Academy, Quantico, VA, January 23-27.

Inwald, R. (1995). *Hilson Safety/Security Risk Inventory (HSRI) Technical Manual*. New York: Hilson Research, Inc. Reprinted (2008), Chicago, IL: IPAT, Inc., a subsidiary of OPP Ltd.

Inwald, R., Resko, J. A. & Favuzza, V. (1996). *Hilson Life Adjustment Profile (HLAP) Technical Manual*. New York: Hilson Research, Inc. Reprinted (2008), Chicago, IL: IPAT, Inc., a subsidiary of OPP Ltd.

Inwald, R., Resko, J. A., & Favuzza, V. (1996). *Inwald Survey 2 (IS2) & Inwald Survey 8 (IS8) Technical Manual*. New York: Hilson Research, Inc. Reprinted (2008), Chicago, IL: IPAT, Inc., a subsidiary of OPP Ltd.

Inwald, R.E., Traynor, B., & Favuzza, V.A. (1998). *Hilson Management Survey (HMS) Technical Manual*, New York: Hilson Research, Inc., Reprinted (2007), Chicago, IL: IPAT, Inc., a subsidiary of OPP Ltd.

Inwald, R. (1998). *Hilson Job Adjustment Questionnaire (HJAQ) Technical Manual*. New York: Hilson Research, Inc. Reprinted (2008), Chicago, IL: IPAT, Inc., a subsidiary of OPP Ltd.

Inwald, R. (1998). "Psychological Profiles of Police and Public Safety Officers Involved with Domestic Violence." Paper prepared and presented at the Domestic Violence by Police Officers Conference, FBI Academy, Quantico, VA, September 17–18.

Inwald, R. (2002). "Case Studies of Violent Adult and Juvenile Offenders/Hilson Trauma Recovery Inventory (HTRI)." Consortium of Police Psychological Services, 2002 Annual Conference, Marathon, FL, May 10.

Inwald, R. (2006). "Inwald Couples Evaluation Program (ICEP): An Evaluation of the Profiles and Problems of Police Couples." 2006 Annual Conference of the Society for Police and Criminal Psychology, Washington DC, October 26.

Inwald, R. (2006). "Use of a Customized Hilson Research Test Battery to Identify Stress Susceptibility in Returning Military Veterans." 2006 Annual Conference of the International Association of Chiefs of Police, Boston, MA, October 15.

Inwald, R.E. (2008). The Inwald Personality Inventory (IPI) and Hilson Research Inventories: Development and Rationale. *Journal of Aggression and Violent Behavior, 13*, 298–327.

James, S.P., Campbell, I.M., & Lovegrove, S.A. (1984). Personality differentiation in a police selection interview. *Journal of Applied Psychology, 69*, 129–134.

Janik, J. (1994). Why psychological screening of police candidates is necessary: The history and rationale. *Journal of Police and Criminal Psychology, 10*(2), 18–23.

Kates, S.L. (1950). Rorschach responses, Strong blank scales, and job satisfaction among policemen. *Journal of Applied Psychology, 34*, 249–254.

King, P., Norrell, G., & Erlandson, F.L. (1959). The prediction of academic success in a police administration curriculum. *Educational and Psychological Measurement, 19*, 649–651.

Kornfeld, A.D. (1995). Police officer candidate MMPI-2 performance: Gender, ethnic, and normative factors. *Journal of Clinical Psychology, 51*, 536–540.

Landy, F.J., Farr, J.L., Saal, F.D., & Freytag, W.R. (1976). Behaviorally anchored scales for rating the performance of police officers. *Journal of Applied Psychology, 61,* 750–758.

Los Angeles Police Department, Behavioral Sciences Section (1986). Personality characteristics of police officers who continue or terminate employment within eighteen months of hiring. Unpublished research abstract.

Malin, S.Z., Luria, J., & Morgenbesser, L.I. (1987). "New York state pre-employment screening program: Longitudinal validation study. Paper presented at the annual meeting of the American Psychological Association, New York, NY.

Mesnick, P., Ostrov, E. & Cavanaugh, J. (1988). "A comparison of the IPI scores of police recruit applicants with and without a history of psychiatric disturbance." Paper presented at the annual meeting of the American Academy of Forensic Sciences, Philadelphia, PA.

Mills, M.C. & Stratton, J.G. (1982). MMPI (Minnesota Multiphasic Personality Inventory) and the prediction of law enforcement performance. *FBI Law Enforcement Bulletin, 51,* 10–15.

Morey, L.C. (2007). *Personality Assessment Inventory professional manual* (2nd ed.). Lutz, FL: Psychological Assessment Resources.

Mufson, D.W. & Mufson, M.A. (1998). Predicting police officer performance using the Inwald Personality Inventory: An illustration from Appalachia. *Professional Psychology: Research and Practice, 29* (1), 59–62.

Murphy, J.J. (1972). Current practices in the use of psychological testing by police agencies. *Journal of Criminal Law, Criminology, & Police Science, 63,* 570.

Ostrov, E. (1985). "Validation of police officer recruit candidates' self-reported drug use on the Inwald personality inventory drug scale." Presented at the American Psychology Law Society Mid-Year Meeting.

Ostrov, E. (1986). Police/law enforcement and psychology. *Behavioral Sciences and the Law 4* (4), 353–370.

Ones, D.S., Viswesvaran, C., & Schmidt, F.L., (1993). Comprehensive meta-analysis of integrity tests validities: Findings and implications for personnel selection and theories of job performance. *Journal of Applied Psychology, 78,* 679–703.

Ones, D. (2009). Personal communication with the second author.

Pendergrass, V.E. (1987). Psychological assessment of police for entry-level selection. *Chief of Police, 2* (1) Winter, 31.

Rice, D. (1985). Employee assistance (emotional): A law enforcement necessity. *Crime Control Digest, 7* (22)

Roberts, M.D., Thompson, J.A., & Johnson, M. (2004). *PAI law enforcement, corrections, and public safety selection report: Manual.* Lutz, FL: Psychological Assessment Resources.

Roberts, M. (2009). Personal communication with the second author.

Saccuzzo, D.P., Higgins, G., & Lewandowski, D. (1974). Program for psychological assessment of law enforcement officers: Initial evaluation. *Psychological Reports, 35,* 651–654.

Sackett, P.R., & Harris, M.M. (1984). Honesty testing for personnel selection: A review and critique. *Personnel Psychology, (17),* 221–245.

Sackett, P.R., Burris, L.R., & Callahan, C. (1989). Integrity testing for personnel selection: an update. *Personnel Psychology, (42)*, 491–529.

Sarchione, C.D., Cuttler, M.J., Muchinsky, P.M., & Nelson-Grey, R.O. (1998). Prediction of dysfunctional job behaviors among law enforcement officers. *Journal of Applied Psychology, 83*(6), 904–912.

Saxe, S.J., & Reiser, M. (1976). A comparison of three police applicant groups using the MMPI. *Journal of Police Science and Administration, 4,* 419–425.

Scogin, F. & Beutler, L. (1986). Psychological screening of law enforcement candidates. In P. Keller & L.G. Ritt (Eds). *Innovations in clinical practice, a source book (5),* 317–330. Florida: Professional Resource Exchange.

Scrivner, E. (2006). Psychology and law enforcement. In I.B. Weiner & A.K. Hess (Eds.), *The handbook of forensic psychology* (3rd ed.) (pp. 534–551). New York: Wiley.

Shaw, J. (2009). Personal communication with the second author.

Strawbridge, P. & Strawbridge, D. (1990). A networking guide to recruitment selection and probationary training of police officers in major departments of the united states. Unpublished report. New York: John Jay College of Criminal Justice.

Super, J.T. (2006). A survey of pre-employment psychological evaluation tests and procedures. *Journal of Police and Criminal Psychology, 21*(2), 83–90.

Tellegen, A. & Ben-Porath, Y.S. (2008). *MMPI-2-RF (Minnesota Multiphasic Personality Inventory-2): Technical manual.* Minneapolis: University of Minnesota Press.

Terman, L.M. (1917). A trial of mental and pedagogical tests in a civil service examination for policemen and firemen. *Journal of Applied Psychology, 1,* 17–29.

Thurstone, L.L. (1922). The intelligence of policemen. *Journal of Personnel Research, 1,* 64–74.

Weiner, I.B., & Greene, R.L. (2008). *Handbook of personality assessment.* New York: Wiley.

Weiss, P.A. (2002). Potential uses of the Rorschach in the selection of police officers. *Journal of Police and Criminal Psychology, 17*(2), 63–70.

Weiss, P.A., Weiss, W.U., & Gacono, C.B. (2008). The use of the Rorschach in police psychology: Some preliminary thoughts. In C.B. Gacono & F.B. Evans (Eds.), *Handbook of Forensic Rorschach Assessment* (pp. 527–542). New York: Routledge.

Zacker, J. (1997). Rorschach responses of police applicants. *Psychological Reports, 80,* 523–528.

Chapter 2

FUNDAMENTAL ISSUES IN POLICE PSYCHOLOGICAL ASSESSMENT

GERALD F. SERAFINO

INTRODUCTION

The purpose of this chapter is to describe the pros and cons of certain fundamental psychological issues in working with law enforcement agencies. It is primarily for the practicing police psychologist but it will have useful information for police executives, students, and psychologists who are thinking about adding police psychology to their practice. General fundamental principles of police psychology, problems of police culture, psychological assessment, special evaluation procedures, legal/ethical issues, and the use of multiple practice guidelines are examined from the point of view of the author.

General Fundamental Principles of Police Psychology

While there are some novel suggestions in this chapter, most of the information is neither new nor sufficient. Where I have devoted a paragraph or a section to a particular idea, others have written books, taught courses, and offered weeklong seminars. During a 30-year career (1971 to 2001) as a counselor, teacher, trainer, and forensic and police psychologist, the present author has encountered many problems which most practicing police psychologists will recognize. While there may be a variety of ways these problems can be solved, psychologists will do their best work if they stay consistent with fundamental principles even if there are differences in how those principles are implemented. Readers are invited to learn more, explore alternatives, and reconsider ongoing practices to find their own way among the many fundamentals of police psychological assessment.

This chapter first explores general fundamental principles of psychology which have special relevance in police settings such as respecting the police culture, use of informed consent, and being as honest as possible with all parties at all times. Second, particular fundamentals for a variety of police psychological assessments are examined. The suggestions herein may be applicable to pre-employment assessments, mandatory Fitness-for-Duty Examinations (FFDE), exams for potential civil or criminal court, evaluations for stress reactions and disabilities, and other types of psychological evaluations. Third, specific recommendations for practicing psychologists and the police who hire and oversee them are offered.

There are some case examples that have been suitably disguised to protect confidentiality; even so, the essence remains intact. The chapter explores some of the strategies used by successful police psychologists whether they are doing psychological assessments, training, and counseling, consulting, or providing referral services for troubled employees. Throughout this chapter, the author assumes that the reader is interested in doing things correctly. Whether one is a police executive or a psychologist, it is important to be sure that the police psychological assessment services used are consistent with the best possible practice for the jurisdiction in which one is working.

There are so many fundamentals of police psychological assessment that it is difficult to limit oneself to the available space. Complicating the problem is the fact that not all police psychologists agree on what constitutes fundamental principles nor do they agree on how to implement them. This is common in psychology. Nevertheless, the range of fundamentals must be known by the practicing police psychologist and the police executives who hire them. To ignore these issues or be unaware of them is to put the psychologist, the police, or even the public in danger.

There are some general principles of psychology that take on special relevance in police agencies. Most police psychologists agree that knowing the history, laws, ethics, and guidelines related to police psychology is fundamental; that using an informed consent procedure for assessments is fundamental; and using appropriate risk management strategies such as proper documentation of one's work is also fundamental. These fundamentals take on special relevance because a police agency is not a psychological setting such as a mental health center or psychiatric hospital. A police department is like few other employment settings. It has its own culture, its own way of doing things, and its own very important mission: To protect and to serve the public. The police deal with life and death daily, people in crisis, and issues affecting the health, welfare, and safety of everyone 24 hours a day, 365 days a year.

Because the police psychologist works in an alien environment where many of the psychological fundamentals are unknown to the users of the psychological services, the psychologist may be asked to engage in dual or multiple relationships, to practice outside of one's area of expertise, or to do other unethical things. When asked to do any of the above it is incumbent on the psychologist to clarify the roles, educate the consumer, and professionally demonstrate a commitment to the applicable laws, relevant court precedents, ethical principles, and practice guidelines.

Jeff Younggren, Ph.D., of the American Psychological Association Insurance Trust (APAIT), teaches that complaints and lawsuits are best avoided or defended when psychologists use informed consent with all parties, proper documentation, and consultation with other professionals (Young- gren, 2008). These fundamentals take on even more importance in police agencies because virtually anything a police psychologist does in his or her official capacity may end up being dealt with in court. Because of the police culture and the paramilitary command structure of most law enforcement agencies, it is even more important for psychologists to know their ethics, limitations, governing rules, and be willing to actively inform others of them.

Police psychologists must be able to recognize potential conflicts and have a plan to avoid them, or if unavoidable, have a plan to resolve the conflicts with the least potential for harm to the client, the examinee, or the person whom the psychologist encounters. To do this, police psychologists must know, understand, and respect the police culture.

Respect the Police Culture

It is fundamental to know the police to be able to serve them in meaningful ways. One of the salient features of police agencies is the adherence to the lines of communication described in the chain of command. Psychologists are not necessarily familiar with the police practice of following the chain of command in all communications with the department. To fail to consistently follow the chain of command may cause a psychologist to be criticized, reprimanded, or even fired. To avoid miscommunication and misunderstanding, the psychologist must find out who, what, when, why, and how communications are to be made. The chief or the chief's designee should be able to answer these questions for the psychologist. Once known, it is vital for the psychologist to follow these lines of communication consistently.

It is fundamental for the psychologist to recognize the mission of the police (protect and serve) and the many tasks that entails for even the most novice officer. In order to understand the many different facets of policing, it is important to read books and articles published on police psychology, test interpretation, and ethical dilemmas. It is equally important to become involved in the everyday activities of the police. This kind of involvement takes time, effort, permission and arrangements from the command staff, and acceptance by officers at all levels.

With proper introduction and orientation, psychologists can learn first-hand about police culture by directly observing police work. This includes engaging in ridealongs with officers during different shifts, attending meetings and briefings, observing officers testifying in court, observing interviews with victims, witnesses and offenders, and attending school resource officer job functions. It could also include attending department sponsored picnics and other formal and informal functions, when invited to do so by the psychologist's supervisor or liaison. To avoid multiple relationships, the psychologist should not attend any private parties.

According to a fundamental chapter written many years ago by Nancy Bohl, Ph.D:

> . . . the mental health professional should engage in what we call the joining process. That would include riding with police officers in their patrol cars and visiting homicide scenes with detectives. . . . In addition to developing empathy and understanding for the feelings of law enforcement personnel, the mental health professional will reap another reward: a bonding process occurs. Officers become familiar with the mental health professional, getting to know him or her on a first-name basis. Also they are impressed when they see that the mental health professional is sufficiently concerned about them to volunteer time in order to learn more about them and their job. (Bohl, nd, p. 129)

Michael Aamodt, Ph.D., also points out the utility of ridealongs when studying the job descriptions, job analyses, and essential job functions of police officers in preparation for pre-employment exams, FFDE referrals, and specialty assignment evaluations:

> Observations are useful job-analysis methods, especially when used in conjunction with other methods such as interviews. During a job-analysis observation, the job analyst observes incumbents performing their jobs in the work setting. The advantage to this method is that it lets the job analysts actually see the worker do his or her job. (Aamodt, 1996, p. 87)

During these observations, active participation from the psychologist is neither desired nor necessary. In most situations, the psychologist will learn the most by simply preparing beforehand (by reading the relevant job analysis or job description) and observing the many tasks that police officers engage in as they implement their essential job functions. In addition to the rapport which should develop, the psychologist can see how often the officers must multi-task, how many different kinds of people they must deal with, and how many pieces of equipment they use as a daily part of their work. Psychologists usually end their first ridealong with a sense of amazement about the complexity of the job.

While knowing, understanding, and respecting the police culture is fundamental, it is also important for the psychologist not to be overtaken by it. Respecting the police culture will not be possible if that respect requires condoning any forms of discrimination, inequity, or other acts that might be illegal or unethical. For example, at various times in the past, psychologists administering pre-employment assessments have been asked to eliminate women, gay men, older persons, or others for reasons unrelated to the applicants' abilities. Psychologists have been asked to betray confidences, falsify data, or ignore certain things while doing assessments. Still others have been asked if they would be willing to go drinking with an off-duty officer to diagnose whether or not the officer was an alcoholic.

At these times, the psychologist must educate the police about the illegality or unethical nature of the request and emphasize the psychologist's commitment to the American Psychological Association (APA) Ethics Code without exception. If the police executive actually tells the psychologist to bend the rule the psychologist should reiterate the objection adding something like: "I'd never risk my psychologist's license just to do something I don't agree with. Remember, friends don't ask friends to break the law." If this answer with the accompanying humor does not resolve the issue, the psychologist may want to seek alternate employment.

There are other occasions when psychologists are asked to do certain things that are not as blatantly wrong as the earlier examples. Psychologists who work as evaluators are sometimes asked to become counselors to the same people they might be evaluating in the future. The psychologist might be asked to send a copy of a three-year-old pre-employment evaluation report to an attorney who is representing an officer in a child custody dispute, or may be asked to perform a secret evaluation of an officer (without any informed consent). Other requests may include practicing outside of one's area of expertise doing marital counseling, profiling, psychological autopsies, or hypnosis of a witness. In no case should a psychologist be lured into doing something illegal or unethical because of a desire to be everything to everyone, or a misplaced need to become part of the police culture. This is not always easy to do in a police environment where camaraderie, cohesion, and loyalty to the group are valued.

The law enforcement agency needs a real psychologist willing to share expertise and relevant police psychological literature, and to perform all the other services a good police psychologist can provide. The police do not need a "cop groupie" who becomes so immersed in the police culture that he or she loses their effectiveness as a psychologist.

Often the police psychologist is asked to do something unethical simply because the police do not know about the many laws, rules, regulations, ethics, practice guidelines, and other maxims which guide the profession. Other times it is because of an executive's desire to maintain order and discipline on the force and his or her perceived understanding of what that required in the past. Sometimes it is due to outright prejudice on the part of the police.

To avoid or manage these inappropriate requests, the psychologist can use the APA Ethics Code, the International Association of Chiefs of Police (IACP) Guidelines, and other references to respectfully but assertively educate the police about the proper role of psychologists working with the police. Dietz and Reese (1986) wrote an article describing strategies to "reduce professional conflicts without compromising operational effectiveness" (Dietz & Reese, 1986, p.385). The article cautions the psychologist to be honest with everyone, respect the chain of command, recognize one's limitations, avoid overidentification, and respect confidentiality. Understanding the basic tenets of this article is fundamental to being a successful police psychologist.

After some time as an interested observer and an active listener, the psychologist will find himself or herself better able to perform pre-employment, fitness-for-duty, and specialty assignment evaluations. The psychologist will gain the trust and respect of the officers, as long as he or she has acted appropriately during the observations. The psychologist will develop an emotional and behavioral understanding of the stresses of police work, not just a theoretical or actuarial understanding. Further, the psychologist will be able to respect the police culture because he or she will have experienced it first-hand.

Some words of caution here: While observing, if asked, psychologists should always identify themselves honestly with something like, "I'm a psychologist here to learn about police procedure." Psychologists should not expect to be compensated for their learning, at least not at the usual hourly rate, if at all. Psychologists are not there to carry a gun, although the department may require them to wear a bulletproof vest. Psychologists are not there to teach or ask questions at the scene, although they should get all their questions answered afterwards. Psychologists are not there to interview victims, witnesses, or suspects; they are there to observe and listen.

While some police psychologists consider these kinds of activities to be fundamental, others do not. Those who have chosen to not engage the police with observations and ridealongs cite lack of time, discomfort, lack of billable hours, and other reasons for not participating. They may still be effective and competent police psychologists but they miss the richness, humanness, complexity, sophistication, emotionality, and action-oriented nature of police work.

Know the History but Be Open to New Ideas

It is important for police psychologists to know the history of research concerning psychological test instruments, but it is fundamental for them to know the present state of research. The 2002 APA Ethical Principles of Psychologists and Code of Conduct make it clear that all psychologists "undertake ongoing efforts to develop and maintain competence" (Bersoff, p. 18). Furthermore, in a section entitled "Failure to attend to changes in the knowledge base," Leonard J. Haas states:

> . . . deficient knowledge is a major threat to competence. . . . This is a strong argument for continuing education and continuing self-examination... A considerable number of ethics and malpractice complaints could be avoided if the psychologist were to become acquainted with (and use) current, well-validated assessment instruments. (Haas, 2008, p. 463)

In the 1970s and 80s most of the California Peace Officer Standards and Training (POST) research examined the effectiveness of only two personality instruments: The Minnesota Multiphasic Personality Inventory (MMPI) and the California Personality Inventory (CPI). (1984, p. 22–23). In 1982, Dr. Robin Inwald published the Inwald Personality Inventory (IPI) (Inwald, 1982), which uses behaviorally anchored scales rather than empirically derived scales. Dr. Inwald also tracked the applicants for the first two years of their careers and was able to derive predictions of performance based on disciplinary, attendance, and retention criteria. While the POST study actually recommended the MMPI and the CPI, there are now many other instruments that could be used. The MMPI has also been revised and there is an updated, shortened version (MMPI 2RF) as of 2008. This particular version of the MMPI also has police norms. Many of these instruments are discussed in individual chapters later in this book.

Having a readily available battery of alternative personality tests is important when re-evaluating an applicant who has become test-wise. Some applicants who fail a psychological pre-employment exam might have received feedback which may have been a little too specific, enabling the applicant to become test-wise. Other candidates may have gotten on the web and learned how to "beat the test" through some of the available programs. Any of the alternative tests can be used as long as the psychologist has been trained to use them and feels confident in defending the reliability, validity, relevance to essential job functions, lack of adverse impact, and consistency with local, state, and federal rules, regulations, and laws.

For example, most of the above referenced tests should be given after a Conditional Offer of Employment (COE), but some are permissible even before the COE. Others may not be permitted in states where "Integrity Questions" are prohibited. Integrity questions frequently involve asking the applicant about a history of antisocial acts and/or antisocial attitudes. Their use is controversial but some research suggests that they do have utility, especially for retail applications (Aamodt, 1996). In any case it is fundamental for the police psychologist to stay abreast of the new research, laws, and court cases, which might impinge on the tests chosen for a particular location and application.

It is fundamental for psychologists to develop current, local norms for the populations being tested and the efficacy of the tests chosen. Follow-up studies are important as well as recognizing that some of the historical research may not be relevant. This is even more important when some minorities may have been inadvertently excluded from the original groups upon whom the historical norms were developed. For example, the early literature sometimes referred to "Hispanics" or "Latinos" as general terms. But, recently emigrated Mexicans who grew up in small, rural towns and villages along the southern borders of Texas, New Mexico, and Arizona may test very differently than Cuban-Americans from Miami or Puerto-Ricans from New York City. Yet, they may have all been described by a singular generic term that may be meaningless or, even worse, misleading. It is incumbent on the psychologist to know the limitations of history and to stay abreast of the newer research and the development of local norms. This exercise is not just fundamental; it is also quite interesting.

Governance and Guidance of Police Psychology

There are a variety of federal laws, state laws, court precedents, and regulations embodied in the administrative codes and Law Enforcement Academy (or Board) rules and regulations that govern the practice of police psychology. There are also ethical principles and codes of conduct which recommend certain behaviors (such as maintaining competence) that may or may not be incorporated into the laws in some of the states. There are too many to attempt to list all the laws and regulations, which may affect one's practice in the different states and territories of the United States. Suffice it to say it is simply fundamental that the police psychologist be aware of the laws and regulations that affect the practice of police psychology in his or her area. An ethical police psychologist, whose practice conforms to the ethical code, will be able to address many federal concerns by simply not discriminating against anyone:

> 3.01 Unfair discrimination. In their work-related activities, psychologists do not engage in unfair discrimination based on age, gender, gender identity, race,

ethnicity, culture, national origin, religion, sexual orientation, disability, socio-economic status, or any other proscribed by law. (APA Ethical Principles and Code of Conduct, Bersoff, 2008, p. 18)

Other aspects of federal law and the regulations and court decisions related to those laws are not so easily addressed. For example, any test which purports to examine an applicant's mental or emotional condition is viewed the same as a medical test by the Americans with Disabilities Act. As such, it cannot be administered to any applicant until that applicant has been given a COE. Further, the psychologist should have virtually no contact with the applicant until the COE has been given.

However, because of the variety of activities, the risk of forensic involvement for virtually any service, and the need for appropriate risk management procedures, there are many other sources of governance or guidance for the police psychologist. Again, some of the following may be implicitly or explicitly related to the state administrative codes for the practice of psychology in your area. Be that as it may, many useful guidelines can aid the police psychologist:

- APA Ethical Principles of Psychologists and Code of Conduct (APA, 2002)
- APA Statement on Disclosure of Test Data (APA, 1996)
- APA Guidelines for Providers of Psychological Services to Ethnic, Linguistic, and Culturally Diverse Populations (APA, 1993)
- APA Specialty Guidelines for Forensic Psychologists (American Psychology and Law Society, 1991)
- APA Record Keeping Guidelines (APA, 2007)
- IACP Guidelines for Consulting Police Psychologists (IACP, 2007)
- IACP Guidelines for Pre-employment Psychological Evaluation Services (IACP, 2004)
- IACP Guidelines for Fitness-For-Duty Evaluations (FFDE) (IACP, 2004)
- IACP Guidelines for Officer Involved Shooting (IACP, 2004)
- IACP Guidelines for Peer Support (IACP, 2007)
- Assessment of Test User Qualifications (Moreland, Eyde, Robertson, Primoff, and Most, 1995)
- Health Insurance Portability and Accountability Act (HIPAA), for those who will be transferring records electronically (American Psychological Association Practice Organization, 2002)
- Standards for Educational and Psychological Testing (American Educational Research Association, 1999)

There are other idiosyncrasies that vary by state. For example, some states permit applicants to provide their own psychological statement from any psychologist in the state, whether or not the psychologist has any expertise or training in police psychology. Other states will only take reports from psychologists who have been hired by the department. Some states allow the psychologists to specify levels of acceptance whereas others mandate the psychologists to simply state yes or no. In any case it is fundamental for psychologists to know the rules and laws that apply in their jurisdictions, to practice them consistently, to document properly, to consult with others when necessary, and to not practice outside their areas of expertise or beyond the level of their competence.

Most of the best police psychologists are members of one or more of the police psychology organizations in the country. Some are members of all three. The International Association of Chiefs of Police (IACP), Police Psychology Section has published the guidelines noted in this chapter. They periodically revise the guidelines to stay current with new research, legislation, or court decisions that might affect the practice. Their annual conference offers APA approved Continuing Education Units (CEU) and special seminars on ethical issues. The conference, the website, and the membership all aid the police psychologist with opportunities for networking and consulting with other psychologists who practice police psychology.

The Society for Police and Criminal Psychology (SPCP) publishes the *Journal of Police and Criminal Psychology*, holds an annual conference with APA approved CEU's, and offers a Diplomate in Police Psychology, which requires a number of steps similar to the APA's American Board of Professional Psychology (ABPP) certification. The SPCP also offers excellent opportunities for networking and even more opportunities for doing joint research with academicians and practicing police psychologists collaborating.

The Police Psychology Section (PPS) of the APA in the Division of Psychologists in Public Service (Division 18) also provides good networking opportunities for those who are members of APA. PPS has also sponsored workshops and seminars of interest to police psychologists. Membership in one or more of these groups is fundamental and active participation would be even better. The APA has recently (2008) recognized Police Psychology as a "distinct proficiency" within psychology. There are active committees in each of these groups which are working on solutions to some of the most contentious and vexing problems facing police psychologists. The organization benefits from the psychologist's participation, and the psychologist benefits from the organization's efforts.

While the many guidelines (noted above) do not necessarily carry the weight of law they can be very persuasive when dealing with administrators who may want to save money by asking the psychologist to take some shortcuts, responding to others who may want the psychologist to do something unethical, or confronting a civil or criminal court action. The psychologist who has been practicing within the guidelines will feel more confident as he or she enters the courtroom.

Be Honest and Expect Honesty from Others

While it may seem to be a truism, police psychologists need to make especially assertive efforts to demonstrate their honesty. The APA Ethics are replete with admonitions regarding the need for "honesty . . . clarity . . . truthfulness . . . trust . . . accuracy. . ." (APA Ethical Principles and Code of Conduct, 2002). If there is any potential for misunderstanding the psychologist must attempt to inform the people and clarify the issues to prevent the misunderstanding. The APA Ethics suggest the psychologist actively and assertively educate clients, organizations, and the public in order to avoid confusion, misinformation, or deception. Consistent adherence to the principle of honesty in all police psychological contacts will make the work of a police psychologist possible and acceptable to the police.

Importantly, honesty does not mean violating confidentiality. If a police administrator requests that a police counseling psychologist reveal confidential, privileged, or protected information, the police psychologist can honestly state that it would be impossible because it would be unethical.

Honesty in performing psychological assessments must first start with the psychologist being honest with himself or herself. Is the psychologist, in fact, competent to provide this service? Can he or she actually fail an applicant and defend the opinion in court, if necessary? Might they have biases that could preclude their ability to do the job? Can aspiring police psychologists accept the responsibility to fail an applicant or an employee, knowing that the psychologist may have his or her work examined by an ethics committee, a personnel board, a police union representative, a committee of police psychologists, or even a federal or state court with direct and cross examinations? These questions must first be honestly answered to oneself.

Second, honesty with employing agencies must be addressed. Again, it is necessary to be assertive in clarifying roles, job descriptors, contractual obligations, and ethical imperatives affecting the nature and relationship of the police psychologist and the department. To facilitate this honesty, it is recommended that the police psychologist provide the employing law enforcement agency with the following:

- An information sheet describing the services to be provided, the (relevant) qualifications of the psychologist(s), the cost for the services, and how to make a referral.

- An explanation of the tests, assessment procedures, and scoring criteria.
- A copy of the Informed Consent form(s) to be used in the evaluations.
- A sample report (suitably disguised).
- Any other information to help clarify any issues that might be misinterpreted. (This may be included in a cover letter or on a separate sheet.)

When meeting with law enforcement executives, the psychologist may want to verbally emphasize his or her commitment to the applicable ethics, codes, guidelines, and regulations governing these kinds of evaluations in the local jurisdiction. If the psychologist has published relevant articles, book chapters, or other references, they can be provided in order to give the employing agency an even fuller understanding of the psychologist's orientation, techniques, and opinions or research findings. Dietz and Reese (1986) actually recommend providing the law enforcement agency with a copy of the "Principles of Ethics of one's discipline before accepting employment or a consulting agreement" (Dietz & Reese, 1986, p. 387).

The psychologist should also ask the police personnel if they have any questions, issues, or disagreements with anything in the information packet. Even though the packet of information may not be read entirely by the police, it will surely be examined if there is some conflict requiring outside intervention (such as mediation, arbitration, or court action). In any case, the psychologist has assertively demonstrated honesty with the agency and a willingness to actively seek the agency's feedback concerning the information provided by the psychologist.

The third area of honesty concerns the variety of people a police psychologist may encounter, especially if they go on ridealongs: employees, victims, alleged victims, offenders, alleged offenders, traffic violators, the general public, persons with mental retardation, inebriated persons, others with or without psychiatric diagnoses who are in crisis, children, adults, the elderly, and anyone else who may have a reason to interact with the police.

No matter whom the police psychologist encounters, it would be inappropriate to misrepresent oneself to anyone. For example, if the police psychologist goes on ridealongs with police to better understand how the police implement their essential job functions (an integral part of any job analysis) he or she will surely encounter traffic violators, victims, offenders, and the general public. Victims or offenders may utter something overheard by the psychologist, who then may become a fact witness in court (not an expert witness, which requires special parameters of professional practice). Further, people may start talking to the psychologist, assuming that what they say will be kept confidential because of the stated occupation. The ridealong psychologist must politely but immediately clarify that there is no confidentiality or privilege in this situation.

It benefits and behooves psychologists to be honest with all examinees with a complete informed consent procedure, not just with a form to be signed. When administering an informed consent procedure to a group of applicants, I recommend reading the entire form aloud to the group, asking if anyone has any questions, and letting the group know that they will have another opportunity to ask questions at the beginning of their individual interviews. In addition, at this point, the group may be told that one of the most frequent reasons applicants fail the psychological is because they do not pass the lie scales and the validity scales.

The use of a well-thought-out informed consent form and procedure cannot be overemphasized. The person being evaluated, post-Conditional Offer of Employment (COE), has the right to know:

• The limits of confidentiality.
• The potential uses of the exam.
• The recipients of the written report.
• Whether or how feedback will be offered to the applicant.
• Their rights and responsibilities (consistent with state, local, and institutional dictates).
• The purpose and scope of the exam.

In order to address the issue of "consent" I recommend using the title: "Statement of Understanding" instead of "Informed Consent Form." The applicants are not requesting to be tested and all they really need to do is be informed and understand the parameters of the exam. According to London and Bray (2008) "Ethical treatment of employees during and after evaluation is another obligation of psychologists. How employees or applicants are treated when they are evaluated can influence the results of the evaluation and their acceptance of the ensuing decision" (London & Bray, 2008, p. 284). The authors emphasize the necessity of equal treatment, enabling examinees to do their best, and providing "direct and honest answers to examinees' questions" (Bersoff, 2008, p. 284). Some might say that this kind of attention is not necessary or it may interfere with the examinees' level of cooperation. The present author (Serafino, 1990) has found just the opposite:

> We have found virtually no reluctance whatsoever on the part of either applicants or employees to participate in an evaluation once they have been informed and their questions concerning the evaluation have been answered. Police officers in particular appear to appreciate the direct and straightforward manner that these potential conflictual issues are being dealt with by the psychological examiners.

Understanding Essential Job Functions

It is important to remember that the psychologist's battery must be based on job-related criteria. One of the best ways to do this is to examine the job description and the job analysis, and go on a series of ridealongs with the police on different shifts. It is very valuable for the psychologist to learn about how the essential job functions are implemented in the real world. An unanticipated consequence of the ridealong has to do with the psychologist's credibility with the command staff and officers. When the police see that their psychologist is actually interested in their work, the increase in the psychologist's reputation is incalculable. But even before the ridealong, a good police psychologist has examined the job description and the job analysis. A good understanding of job analysis includes the following:

> Job analysis is the basic analytical process of a personnel management system, including selection, training, etc. Without job analysis information it is not possible to determine accurately what kind of training is needed, what kind of employee should be hired, and what might constitute acceptable performance. (New Mexico Law Enforcement Academy, 1991, p. 9)

This excerpt came from a document that described 583 separate essential job functions, equipment lists which the employee must be able to use (after training), and hundreds of learning objectives that the employee must be able to successfully master and then implement. Furthermore, the officer will have to implement the learning alone (after their field training) during a crisis or at least in stressful situations.

Of the 583 detailed descriptors in the NM job/task analysis project report, approximately 120 are psychological tasks which include reading, writing, communication, comparing, analyzing, interrogating, reviewing records, instructing, advising, collecting facts, providing information to individual in need of social services, among other tasks (New Mexico Law Enforcement Academy, 1991).

A more recent POST study, authored by Shelley Spilberg, Ph.D., describes 123 personality-based requirements for entry-level patrol officers (Spilberg, 2002). The IACP committee studying evaluation methods for police specialty assignments identified 113 "personality-related position requirements" for public safety employees in applying for those positions. It is fundamental for the practicing police psychologist to be aware of this body of literature and to strive to have consistency with the personality test results and the essential job functions.

One of the earliest studies, The Commission on Peace Officer Standards and Training (1977) research in California, identified a number of areas where psychologists can offer relevant information, including:

- Communication skills.
- Problem-solving skills.
- Learning.
- Judgment under pressure.
- Observation.
- Willingness to confront problems.
- Interest in people.
- Interpersonal sensitivity.

Strict and consistent adherence to the spirit and letter of the criteria, whether it is embodied in the law, rules, or regulations for your area is necessary. In California the criteria is essentially a "screen out" one: "Peace officer applicants shall be free from job-relevant psychopathology, including personality disorders, as diagnosed by a qualified professional" (Commission on Peace Officer Standards and Training, 1984).

It is fundamental for the police psychologist to know the verbatim criteria applicable in his or her area. The practicing police psychologist should commit the criteria to memory. Hence, when asked (during a consult or while being deposed for court or during cross-examination in court) the psychologist should be able to answer the criteria question with a verbatim quote that matches the legal requirement. This simple act will substantially increase the psychologist's credibility and standing within the police culture.

During the informed consent procedure, applicants should be told that they are expected to be honest and that attempts to fake good on the tests and during the interview may result in their being "not recommended" for certification as a law enforcement officer.

Psychologists can also encourage honesty by adding that the applicant may simply not answer a couple of the questions if they don't understand, or if the question is objectionable for religious or personal reasons. However, they are also cautioned to not do this more than a couple of times or else the test may be deemed invalid because the applicant was too evasive. The present author has given this instruction to more than 1,000 applicants and only one of them abused it to the point where a test was found to be invalid because of too many unanswered items. To further buttress the need for the applicant to be honest the psychologist can emphasize that the police officer job description and oath requires the officer to have integrity, to be honest, and to be a person whose word can be trusted in court. My own anecdotal data and research by others reveal that applicants who try to fake good are oftentimes those officers who get in trouble in their careers. A draft copy of the Police Integrity Study Manual (Timm, Boes, & Chandler, 1997) presented at the Society of Police and Criminal Psychology Conference in Portland, OR (9/8/97) suggests that MMPI Lie and Psychopathic Deviancy scales, the

CPI Social Presence scale, and the information available from the background data can reveal potential indicators of psychopathology which could reasonably be predicted to interfere with their intended duties. Hence, it is vital to gather relevant information from as many different sources as possible, especially the background data gathered by the referring department.

When the psychologist shares this kind of knowledge with the examinees and police executives, it facilitates procedures that make examinees feel compelled to be more honest and self-disclosing during the examination process. During the individual interview, the applicant is again given an opportunity to ask questions about the Statement of Understanding form. This is all part of a well-implemented procedure for administering informed consent in an honest and sensitive way to applicants and other examinees who are most likely feeling stressed by the psychological assessment process. It is fundamental to cover all the bases where implementing informed consent, not just get the form signed. Applicants should feel the psychologist sincerely cares that all the examinees understand the informed consent procedures, and that their honesty is important.

Fundamentals of Personality Assessment

In order to adequately assess the personality characteristics best suited for police work, police psychologists must go beyond simply administering one or two tests. In fact, what appear to be relevant personality characteristics are actually discernable only through a comprehensive battery of tests and procedures. This should include a review of the background data (from the department's background investigation and from the psychologist's own social history forms), reading and intelligence tests, written and verbal communication tests, and an interview.

Some psychologists believe it is fundamental to administer a reading test to ensure that applicants are reading well enough to take the psychological exams. Further, they can help psychologists diagnose any relevant learning disabilities, which might suggest academy failure or difficulties learning new information while on the job. Other psychologists may argue that a reading test is not necessary because their department only hires applicants with Associate degrees or higher and in their experience, reading disabilities have not been a problem. Similarly, some psychologists believe it is fundamental to test the applicant's cognitive abilities with an I.Q. test or other type of test. Other psychologists may disagree with this.

The New Mexico Law Enforcement Academy and some other academies recommend a 10th-grade level for successful matriculation. If an applicant does not achieve a 10th-grade level on one test, it is recommended that a second test, which may tap different reading abilities, be administered. Similarly, if an examinee appears to have difficulties with the problem-solving tasks on an intelligence test, a second instrument is recommended. An examinee's verbal and written communication skills can be seen by examining the applicant's writing sample, the application forms filled out by the applicant, and verbal behavior during the interview. When rating an applicant's overall verbal ability, some psychologists give extra credit for applicants who state they are bilingual on their application forms. This may reduce the adverse impact of reading and intelligence tests for individuals whose first language is not English.

The most important aspect of using all these different sources of data is that the examiner can see the interplay of the examinee's education, work history, intelligence, problem-solving skills, communication skills, interview behavior, and other information to determine whether or not the examinee can do the job. The interplay of all these skills, attitudes, abilities, and personality test results should reveal some consistency across measures. The following sections explore the separate elements and how they might reveal important personality variables which impact the psychologist's assessment of the examinee, no matter what the referral question may be.

Personality Tests

In most law enforcement evaluations, it is fundamental to administer two personality inventories, one for abnormal behavior (like the MMPI-2, the Personality Assessment Inventory (PAI), or another test to detect psychopathology) and a second one for normal behavior (such as the CPI). This is actually mandated in the POST study manuals and is highly recommended and practiced by many police psychologists. Administering two personality inventories is useful no matter what the legal criteria may be in a given jurisdiction. A further benefit of two or more personality instruments is that the psychologist can compare and contrast multiple validity indicators. Frequently, those who appear to be "faking good" on one instrument will be described as "less than candid" on the second instrument also. Importantly, the psychologist may also find out from the background data that the examinee may have been suspected of being dishonest with the background investigators and/or prior supervisors.

As was noted earlier, the POST studies have demonstrated that many of the essential job functions are related to personality variables that can be suggested by various scales and sub scales on a variety of personality tests. Following some ridealongs, police psychologists will be able to see how certain personality characteristics can either help or hinder a police officer to fulfill the essential job functions.

Interview Fundamentals

There are many good reasons to administer an interview, no matter what the referral question may be. The IACP guidelines state that interviews "should" be conducted, most states and departments expect it or mandate it, and a well-structured interview can provide important job-relevant information in many areas. A structured interview should be used to evaluate an applicant's social skills, communication skills, and problem-solving ability. Interview questions are most effective when they are related to the performance of employment duties and are based on the department's job analysis (Aamodt, 2004).

A consistent, standardized interview format should be employed in a generally friendly, but professional way. To help applicants feel at ease they could be initially asked relatively simple questions. The first time they respond, "I don't know" they should be complimented by the examiner for being willing to admit their lack of knowledge. This should have the effect of helping the examinee relax, at least somewhat. They can then be reminded to be honest and if they do not know the answer to any question they can simply say "I don't know," but to not do this too often (and instead ask for clarification of the question). They should also be asked it they have any condition that might require a "reasonable accommodation" under the Americans with Disabilities Act (ADA), if they have ever failed a previous psychological exam, or if they have any condition that might interfere with their ability to do the job.

Initial observations concerning attitude, attention, affect, eye contact, interpersonal presentation, appropriateness, awareness of current events, and informed consent issues should all be documented. Interview items should include procedures to test immediate, recent, and remote recall, judgment for everyday commonsense situations, judgment for potential police dilemmas, and the ability to demonstrate appropriate instincts around taking action and showing restraint. The applicant's ability to accept negative feedback, their ability to change their mind when confronted with new information and their interpersonal sensitivity should all be evaluated through the use of structured questions.

Additionally, some psychologists use the interview to review general test data, specific test responses, social history data, and other personality issues. Frequently, answers to queries about prior jobs may reveal immaturity, impulsivity, or just inexperience. But it may also reveal an applicant's tendency to blame others for their own predicaments and other untoward indicators. By the end of the interview, the psychologist should be able to offer opinions on the applicant's ability to communicate with the public and to demonstrate sensitivity to victims, patience with witnesses, and a command presence with offenders.

There will be further information from the background data, test respons-es, and application forms which can be explored to reveal other personality tendencies which might be predicted to interfere with essential job functions. These may include an inability to plan ahead or understand the conse-quences of one's acts, difficulty in handling life's stresses, gross egocentricity, a history of mental or emotional difficulties, an inability to be sensitive to others, or overt antisocial tendencies. Any of these can have an impact on the applicant's ability to successfully learn in the academy, benefit from field supervision, or fulfill the essential job functions.

It is incumbent on the psychologist to ensure that the interview questions are job-related, the interview is structured or at least semi-structured, and the interviews are consistent. Again, there is value in reviewing the job analysis and using interview items that are consistent with the particular functions described in the job analysis. Finally, the interview can give the psychologist an opportunity to give the applicant feedback about the psychologist's opin-ion as long as that this does not conflict with the agreed upon procedures the psychologist has with the department. To ensure that there is no discrimina-tion against any protected minorities it is fundamental that psychologists track the adverse impact of the total battery and the separate components of the battery, including the interview.

Feedback and Appeals

Psychologists should be willing to advocate for failed applicants and other examinees to have a bona fide appeals procedure. Many believe it is impor-tant to provide verbal feedback to failed examinees. However, some psy-chologists may argue that they screen and reject so many applicants that it would be impractical or impossible or too costly to give each failed applicant a feedback interview (therefore they have the applicant agree to not expect feedback during the Informed Consent procedure). It can also be argued that state law or academy board regulations govern appeals and second opinions, not the individual psychologist.

All of these approaches to feedback and appeals may be correct and justi-fiable, as long as the police psychologist has addressed these issues, dealt with the department(s) concerning their needs and desires, and been honest with the applicants and examinees concerning the procedures the police psy-chologist ultimately decides on regarding these issues.

Departmental Issues

It is fundamental that the psychologist and the department have mutually agreed-upon procedures to manage the referral of an applicant, a former employee who is now suing the department as a litigant, or an incumbent employee. The psychologist must have access to the officer's personnel folder, relevant reports from Internal Affairs, and the officer's supervisors and peers. If the officer is a Sergeant or above, the psychologist may need to gather information from the supervisees as well as from the supervisors. I recommend that the psychologist also gather information from the officer. This is fundamental to developing rapport and credibility with the officer undergoing an evaluation under potentially adversarial conditions.

Even before the psychologist receives a written letter of referral, the psychologist should help the department decide if the referral is justified. At times, certain police executives may be unaware of some of the legal and ethical parameters related to these evaluations. For example, two supervisors ran for sheriff of a small, rural county. The Sheriff who won the election assumed command and almost immediately tried to send the losing candidate (a former peer) to the psychologist for a FFDE. In this case, a phone consult with the newly elected Sheriff convinced him that it would be better to not order a FFDE. A consultation with the County Attorney helped buttress the advice to the Sheriff. Again, many times, police executives may not have the benefit of training attained by psychologists who belong to the relevant police psychology groups (IACP, APA, and SPCP).

The best way to handle an inappropriate request is to use it as an opportunity to educate the police. This may include sharing legal citations and handouts from conferences and speaking with the police executives politely and respectfully. Sometimes a little humor can help, too, if appropriate given the nature of the psychologist's relationship to the police.

It is fundamental to take written notes from the first phone call or the first verbal conversation, and to continue documenting all contacts, collateral conversations, and sources of data throughout the entire evaluation process. The APA Forensic Guidelines may be as important as the FFDE (IACP) guidelines when doing a FFDE or any other type of exam which would be considered adversarial.

Informed Consent for Potentially Adversarial Exams

It is fundamental to have informed consent for any exam which could end up in court such as a FFDE, a request for a disability opinion, or a controversial second or third opinion on any other issue. However, Curran (2008) found that 10 percent of practicing police psychologists sometimes or never obtained a signed consent prior to conducting an FFDE. The FFDE Informed Consent procedure is even more important than others because of the usually adversarial nature of these mandated exams. Most of the officers do not want their careers to end, and most psychologists do not want to end an officer's career. Despite these predispositions, it is still viewed as an adversarial forensic evaluation. For these reasons the psychologist should do everything possible and ethical to let the officer know that the psychologist will make every effort to be fair. To properly administer the Statement of Understanding (SOU) procedure:

• Greet the officer with a warm handshake.
• Sit across a desk, not on a couch or easy chair.
• Invite the officer to call you by your first name (if you are comfortable with that).
• Show the officer the letter received from the department.
• Ask the officer to read the letter, initial and date it, and offer to give the officer a copy.
• Give the officer the SOU but withhold a pen because you want the officer to realize that this is not just another form to be signed, it's a fundamental part of establishing an appropriate relationship.
• Ask the officer to read the SOU aloud so you, the psychologist, can evaluate reading ability, verbal ability, and to make sure it's understandable.
• Ask for any questions or issues the officer may have.
• Once all questions have been answered, have the officer sign and date it and then offer to make a copy for the officer and commence the interview.

Collecting and Using the Data in Adversarial Examinations

During the initial interview (before the personality testing) establish as good a relationship with the officer as possible. Ask the officer to bring in any records, letters of commendation, employee evaluations, medical records, or any other information that may be helpful in answering the referral question. Emphasize the need for telling the truth. Instruct the officer to respond, "I don't know" if they really do not. Then ask them the name of the current Joint Chiefs of Staff. When they reply "I don't know," smile, shake their hand, and compliment them for saying "I don't know." Ask for the names of persons in and out of the department that the officer thinks should be contacted for information. Then let the officer know whether or not you will be able to contact the collaterals, but, if not feasible, the psychologist can at least note these names in the report for the officer. Officers know and understand the importance of including information like this in reports, because they write them all the time at work.

No matter what kind of exam is being administered, it is fundamental to stay within the applicable APA and IACP Guidelines. They carefully outline definitions, threshold issues and considerations, examiner qualifications, identifying the client, informed consent, evaluation procedures, and report recommendations. The psychologist may wish to give a copy of these guidelines to the referring police executive and the department's attorney to let them know what the IACP recommends and how the psychologist intends to proceed. In the psychologist's review of collateral data, it is important to focus on how the data may or may not affect essential job functions. This is especially true when dealing with medical or psychological reports authored by persons unfamiliar with police work.

In one case, a department mandated a FFDE on a dispatcher who had recently been discharged from an inpatient psychiatric facility. The hospital discharge summary described the officer as "capable of returning to work" even though his discharge diagnosis revealed a Global Assessment of Functioning (GAF) score of 30 on Axis V of the *Diagnostic and Statistical Manual of Mental Disorders*, 4th edition (*DSM-IV*). According to the *DSM-IV*, a GAF of 30 indicates the person's: "Behavior is considerably influenced by delusions or hallucinations OR serious impairment in communication or judgment" (APA, 2000, p. 32). The GAF and the recommendation to return the dispatcher to full, unrestricted duty seemed to be a mistake, or, if true, inconsistent with the GAF descriptors. In this situation, I obtained the necessary release of information from the examinee and consulted with the physician who authored the discharge summary. The physician stated the GAF was not a mistake and if the department wanted the dispatcher to work, he (the physician) was not going to say no. The physician had no understanding of the duties of a dispatcher, had never seen the job description or the job analysis, and indicated that he cleared the dispatcher to return to work because the dispatcher said he wanted to return. Thus, it was necessary to examine the basis for the physician's conclusion and to then commence an independent evaluation as to the dispatcher's fitness for duty.

It is fundamental for the psychologist to seek out and utilize multiple sources of data in order to reach the most defensible opinions. When writing the report, the psychologist must specify all sources of data, all appointments, tests and procedures administered, and any relevant information consistent with IACP guidelines. No irrelevant information which might unnecessarily violate an examinee's privacy should be included, the report should answer the questions raised in the referral letter, which may or may not include a request for diagnosis or clinical recommendations.

In a pre-employment case, an applicant was described in the testing as a "high risk for future performance difficulty" on the IPI because he had honestly admitted to a number of youthful misbehaviors. The validity scales of both personality tests indicated that he was very honest in the testing and he had been willing to admit to a number of minor faults and problems. The social history data revealed that the applicant had been fired from a job in the past year. On the face it appeared that this applicant might be an antisocial or impulsive person who had a recent history of job failure. However, further examination revealed that since his youthful indiscretions the applicant had served honorably in the Army for 4 years, he'd been a Mounted Patrol Officer for over a year (with excellent references), and was living a stable life until he was fired from his delivery job. His employer fired him because he had reported to the police some suspicious activities indicating possible drug manufacturing at one of his delivery locations. Hence, the total circumstances of the applicant's recent work and life history seemed to weigh against the initial impression from the testing. Furthermore, during interview he demonstrated excellent judgment, good common sense, and none of his answers to the police dilemmas revealed any indications of impulsivity or immaturity. The applicant was cleared for certification and upon last report he was still performing well as an officer.

The important lesson here is that the police psychologist must use the available information from a variety of sources to make the most defensible and equitable decision for the department and for the examinee. This may require going beyond the tests and interviews and checking with the officers who completed the background investigation, or double checking with a collateral source to verify or refute a prior opinion.

Occasionally, in an adversarial situation, an officer may not allow certain background data to be released, or the officer may refuse to answer so many questions that the referral issue could not be adequately addressed. They might also refuse to undergo further testing such as a urinalysis, neuropsychological testing or another medical test.

If the officer is so uncooperative, or if there is a gap in the data which is vitally important, the psychologist may have to describe the gaps and their significance, and refer the examinee back to the department with a report stating why the question could not be answered. In these cases, the department may choose another psychologist or terminate the officer for lack of cooperation, if that was the reason for the gap in data.

It is necessary that the psychologist have sufficient training, experience, credibility with the department and the officers, and confidence in himself or herself to actually perform fitness-for-duty evaluations. Some psychological and medical personnel who might be lacking some of the above characteristics may be unable to author a report that might remove a person from a job they have been doing.

Specialty Assignment Evaluations

There is currently a committee within IACP examining the role of police psychologists who administer exams for special assignments. It is aptly named Psychological Evaluations for Police Specialty Assignments (PEPSA). The Committee has stated that there is not a large, published body of historical or research data on PEPSAs. Despite this lack, police executives have frequently requested psychologists' input when making these kinds of specialty selections and assignments. According to the IACP-PPS Committee on PEPSA, 77.4 percent of the 53 IACP members responding to a survey "indicated they have performed or participated in formal psychological evaluations of law enforcement candidates for specialty assignments" (Harden, 2008). PEPSAs are most often requested for SWAT and hostage negotiators, and less often for undercover, K9 units, bomb teams, crisis intervention teams, dive teams, interviewers of child sex abuse victims, and others. While there may be job descriptions for many of these positions, there are not necessarily detailed job analyses for all of them.

Three-quarters of the psychologists who perform these evaluations "report reservations about the practice in the absence of adequate, empirically-validated methods and specific practice guidelines for PEPSA screenings" (Harden, 2008). Based on this report, consultations with other police psychologists, and personal experience in this area the present author makes the following recommendations:

- If asked to perform a PEPSA, immediately inform the executive of the lack of a good research basis and other reservations and limitations.
- Obtain the job description and request a job analysis (if available).
- Interview current officers performing the specialty function and attempt to develop specific psychological and personality factors which could reasonably be predicted to facilitate or hinder an applicant's ability to perform the essential job functions.
- Observe training, meetings, and on-the-job experiences with those who currently have the specialty assignments.
- Consult with other psychologists.
- Decide if screening in or screening out would be more appropriate given the laws, rules, court decisions, department desires, and other factors.
- Avoid being the ultimate decision maker in these cases, but offer to provide psychological data that may aid the ultimate decision maker.
- Stay abreast of the literature and the IACP Committee's work in this area which should provide some guidance now and more in the future.

Of course, all the other fundamentals of police psychology would still apply to PEPSAs: Honesty with all parties, adherence to applicable laws, regulations, and informed consent procedures, and documentation.

CONCLUSION

There are many different ways that psychologists can fulfill their obligations to their departments and their examinees as long as they are following the laws, rules, regulations, ethics, and guidelines which apply to the many different types of assessment functions police psychologists engage in. The fundamentals described above are meant to be an invitation for the reader to consider some different ways of fulfilling the mandates of both law enforcement and psychology.

The most important lesson here is that the learning can never stop. Ethical codes, practice guidelines, and new research will continue to change and affect the field. The only constant is continual change. Hence, it is fundamental for police psychologists and the law enforcement executives who hire and supervise them to stay abreast of the changes and to integrate the newer methods into their practices. When one does not know something, it should be easy to honestly acknowledge it. When one does know something, it should be easy to implement it. Finally, the following quote (author unknown) may aid the reader in his or her efforts to perform as a competent police psychologist (or even a police executive who supervises police psychologists): "It is easy to forgive incomplete knowledge but difficult to overlook uninformed pomposity." Hopefully this chapter and book will encourage the reader to stay abreast of the literature, involved in the professional organizations, and humble in the face of the challenges police psychology presents to all of us.

REFERENCES

Aamodt, M.G. (1996). *Applied industrial/organizational psychology* (2nd ed.). Pacific Grove, CA: Brooks/Cole Publishing.

Aamodt, M.G. (2004). *Research in law enforcement selection.* Boca Raton, Fl: Brown Walker Press.

American Educational Research Association, American Psychological Association, and National Council on Measurement in Education. (1999). *Standards for educational and psychological testing.* Washington, D.C.: American Educational Research Association.

American Psychiatric Association. (2000). *Diagnostic and statistical manual of mental disorders* (4th ed. Text revision). Washington, DC: Author.

American Psychological Association. (2002). Ethical principles of psychologists and code of conduct. *American Psychologist, 57*(12), 76–89.

American Psychological Association. (2007). Record keeping guidelines. *American Psychologist, 62,* 993–1004).

54   *Personality Assessment in Police Psychology*

American Psychological Association. (1993). Guidelines for providers of psychological services to ethnic, linguistic, and culturally diverse populations. *American
Psychologist, 48*, 45–48.

American Psychological Association (2003). Guidelines on multicultural education,
training, research, practice, and organizational: Change for psychologists. *American Psychologist, 58*, 377–402.

American Psychological Association Practice Organization. (2002, March). Getting
ready for HIPPA: What you need to know now. *The Trust,* 1–16.

American Psychological Association-Committee on Psychological Tests and
Assessment (1996). Statement on the disclosure of test data. *American Psychologist,
51*, 644–48.

American Psychology and Law Society. (1991). Specialty guidelines for forensic psychologists. *Law and Human Behavior, 15*, 655–665.

Auld, P.J., & Ryan, A.H., Jr. (1995). A study of the Nelson-Denny reading test as a
predictor of law enforcement training academy performance. Unpublished manuscript, South Carolina Department of Public Safety Criminal Justice Training
Academy.

Bersoff, D.N. (2008). *Ethical Conflicts in Psychology* (4th ed.). Washington, DC: American Psychological Association.

Bohl, N. (nd). Gaining departmental acceptance. In J.T. Reese & R.M. Solomon
(Eds.), *Organizational Issues in Law Enforcement* (pp.129–134). Washington, DC:
U.S. Department of Justice, FBI.

Clark, D. W., & White, E. K. (2008, November). Ethics for Police Psychologists.
Paper presented at the annual meeting of The International Association of Chiefs
of Police: Police Psychological Services Section, San Diego, CA.

Commission on Peace Officer Standards and Training. (1977). *Background investigations manual: Guidelines for the investigation.* State of California: California
Commission on Peace Officer Standards and Training.

Commission on Peace Officer Standards and Training. (1984). *Psychological screening
manual.* State of California: California Commission on Peace Officer Standards
and Training.

Curran, S. (2008, November). Results and implications from a 2007 survey of
police/forensic psychologists: Fitness-for-duty assessment procedures. Paper presented at the annual meeting of the International Association of Chiefs of Police:
Police Psychological Services Section, San Diego, CA.

Dietz, P.E., & Reese, J.T. (1986). The perils of police psychology: 10 strategies for
minimizing role conflicts when providing mental health services and consultation
to law enforcement agencies. *Behavioral Sciences & the Law, 4*(4), 385–400.

Haas, L.J. (2008). Competence and quality in the performance of forensic psychologists. In D.N. Bersoff (Ed.), *Ethical conflicts in psychology* (4th ed.) (pp. 459–464).
Washington, DC: American Psychological Association.

Harden, S.L. (2008, November). "Report of the IACP police psychological services
committee on psychological evaluations of police specialty assignments." Paper
presented at the Annual Meeting of the International Association of Chiefs of
Police: Police Psychological Services Section, San Diego, CA.

IACP Police Psychological Services. (2004). *Pre-employment psychological evaluation services guidelines.* Retrieved April 5, 2009, from http://www.theiacp.org/psych_services_section/

IACP Police Psychological Services. (2004). *Officer-involved shooting guidelines.* Retrieved April 5, 2009 from http://wwwtheiacp.org/psych_services_section/

IACP Psychological Services Section. (2007). Guidelines for consulting police psychologists. *The Police Chief, 124*(8), 88.

IACP Psychological Services Section. (2007). Peer support guidelines. *The Police Chief, 124*(8), 90.

International Association of Chiefs of Police. (2004). *Fitness-for-duty evaluation guidelines.* Retrieved April 5, 2009, from http://www.theiacp.org/psych_services_section/ Inwald, R. (1982). *Inwald Personality Inventory technical manual.* Kew Gardens, NY: Hilson Research, Inc. Reprinted, 2008, Chicago: IPAT, Inc.

London, M., & Bray, D.W. (2008). Ethical issues in testing and evaluation for personnel decisions. In D.N. Bersoff (ed.), *Ethical conflicts in psychology* (4th Ed.) (pp. 283–286). Washington, DC: American Psychological Association.

Moreland, K.L., Eyde, L.D., Robertson, G.J., Primoff, E. S., & Most, R. B. (1995). Assessment of test user qualifications: A research-based measurement procedure. *American Psychologist, 60,* 14–21.

New Mexico Law Enforcement Academy. (1991). *New Mexico Law Enforcement Academy basic law enforcement job/task analysis project.* Unpublished manuscript, New Mexico Department of Public Safety.

Ostrov, E. (1986). Use of multiple sources of information when doing mandatory psychological evaluations of police officers. In J.T. Reese & H.A. Goldstein (Eds.), *Psychological services for law enforcement* (pp. 291–298). Washington, DC: U.S. Department of Justice: Federal Bureau of Investigation.

Rostow, C.R.. & Davis, R.D. (2004). *A handbook for psychological fitness-for-duty evaluations in law enforcement.* Binghamton, NY: Haworth Press.

Serafino, G. (1990). Informed Consent for Police Officers Undergoing Psychological Evaluation. *Journal of Police and Criminal Psychology, 6*(1), 2–6.

Spilberg, S. (2002). *Personality-based requirements questionnaire for entry-level patrol officers.* Unpublished manuscript, California Commission on Peace Officer Standards and Training.

Timm, H.W., Boes, J.O., & Chandler, C. (1997). *Police integrity study manual.* Monterey, CA: Defense Personnel Security Research Center.

Younggren, J.N. (2008). *American psychological association insurance trust.* Retrieved February 1, 2009, from http://www.apait.org

Part II

MAJOR ASSESSMENT INSTRUMENTS
USED IN POLICE PSYCHOLOGY

Chapter 3

USING THE MMPI-2 IN POLICE PSYCHOLOGICAL ASSESSMENT

PETER A. WEISS and WILLIAM U. WEISS

The Minnesota Multiphasic Personality Inventory-2, or MMPI-2 (Butcher, Graham, Ben-Porath, Tellegen, Dahlstrom, & Kaemmer, 2001), is a 567-item personality inventory oriented towards identifying psychopathology. Respondents to the test are asked to answer each of a series of statements in a True-False manner. The test is interpreted by examining a series of validity scales to determine if the individual is responding honestly to the test items, and then examining a series of ten clinical scales which mainly (although not exclusively) relate to personal reports of psychopathology. A comprehensive series of content and supplementary scales have been developed to aid the clinical psychologist with interpretation, as the original clinical scales are fairly multidimensional. Interpretive approaches to the MMPI-2 are changing with the publication and development of the MMPI-2 Restructured Clinical (RC) Scales (Tellegen, Ben-Porath, McNulty, Arbisi, Graham, & Kaemmer, 2003) and the related MMPI-2 Restructured Form (RF) (Ben-Porath & Tellegen, 2008). The implications of these new scales and the new RF format for practice in police psychology will be discussed in this chapter, along with interpretive guidelines for the original MMPI-2.

Use of the MMPI-2 in Police Psychology

The MMPI has been investigated as a screening device for law enforcement personnel for many years. A comprehensive literature search by the present authors revealed that the original MMPI was first investigated as a selection device by King, Norrell, and Erlandson (1959), who attempted to use this device to predict police academy grades. A perusal of Weiss and

Inwald (Chapter 1, this volume) will show that the MMPI was extensively validated for use with law enforcement officers, particularly for purposes of selection. Numerous articles on its usefulness for law enforcement applications were published during the 1970s and 1980s.

The MMPI was restandardized in 1989. While the current (MMPI-2) version is similar in many ways to the original MMPI, the MMPI-2 has several important differences which were designed to improve it. In particular, it has a more representative standardization sample, updated items which have removed more archaic language, and several items which were found objectionable by many individuals were deleted. Since its publication in 1989, several new scales have also been developed for the test. This restandardization resulted in the 567-item, True-False format test which is used today. The test has several validity scales, most notably L (Lie), which measures deliberate faking-good, K (Correction) which measures subtle positive impression management, and F (Infrequency) which indicates responses that are not typically endorsed by most people, which can be a rough indicator of faking-bad. The test also has ten basic scales which mainly focus on psychopathology. The test is interpreted using standard (T) scores, which have a mean of 50 and a standard deviation of 10. Any score of T ≥ 65 is considered clinically significant and therefore noteworthy. Several of the basic scales have subscales (Harris-Lingoes subscales) to aid in interpretation of the overall scale. The test also has multiple Content and Supplementary Scales which measure other aspects of personality. Interpretation of the MMPI-2 is currently changing with the development of the Restructured Clinical (RC) scales, which will be discussed later in this chapter.

Test Use in Police Psychology

The MMPI-2 is fundamentally oriented towards the detection of psychopathology. Therefore, in accordance with the Americans With Disabilities Act, it is considered a "medical test." It is only appropriate for use in police selection after all other factors, such as interviews, background checks, strength and fitness tests, and reading tests are considered. The MMPI-2 may be appropriate for use in other kinds of evaluations, such as Fitness-For-Duty-Evaluations (FFDE). While it has not been widely written about, the success of the MMPI-2 for treatment planning purposes in outpatient therapy (Graham, 2006) suggests that it may also be useful for the treatment planning of law enforcement officers seeking counseling or therapy.

The purpose of this chapter is as a "how-to" primer for using the MMPI-2 in law enforcement work. Since the MMPI-2 was revised in 1989, the present will focus mainly on sources which reflect this revision. Since the majority of research has focused on using the MMPI-2 in the selection of law enforcement officers, the present chapter will survey the use of different scales of the MMPI-2 for this purpose. As a conclusion, other applications of the MMPI-2 in law enforcement work, such as FFDE, will then be discussed.

Using the MMPI-2 in Police Selection

As stated earlier, the MMPI-2 is appropriate for the post-offer pre-employment screening of law enforcement officers. Its use should be combined with the appropriate procedures for post-offer screening and evaluation (see Weiss, Chapter 12, this volume). For example, this procedure includes a review of the prospective officer's record, and interview, mental status examination, and other tests. It is not recommended that the MMPI-2 be used as the sole screening measure. Super (2006) recommends that, at a minimum, a test of normal personality and a test of problem solving ability be included as well. This provides an appropriate multimethod approach to assessment. This system avoids an overreliance on a test of psychopathology, which can be used to select individuals out, but not select them in. Tests of psychopathology often do not show clinically significant results due to the fact that police officer applicants tend to be psychologically healthier than the general population (Weiss, Hitchcock, Weiss, Rostow, & Davis, 2008). Therefore, other measures, including the interview, must be used. However, the MMPI-2 can be an integral part of the post-offer battery. It has been successfully used for many years in police selection (Graham, 2006).

Using the MMPI-2 Scales in Police Selection

Validity Scales-L Scale

Considerable research exists supporting the use of the validity scales for use in police selection. The use of the L (Lie) scale as a tool in police selection has been investigated by Weiss, Davis, Rostow, and Kinsman (2003). Their study is based on earlier work by Herndon (1998) and Boes, Chandler, and Timm (1997) which suggested that individuals who obtain elevated (T $\geq$65) scores on the L scale engage in problem behaviors later on when hired as police officers.

An examination of the description of high L scale scorers given in Graham (2006) shows why individuals with high scores on the L scale may not make good law enforcement officers. These individuals claim to be excessively virtuous and deny any problems. They do not admit to even minor shortcomings and, essentially, are not truthful in responding to the MMPI-2 items. They therefore may be attempting to hide negative characteristics or they may be relatively dishonest people.

In the Weiss et al. (2003) study, data from 1,347 officers who had completed the MMPI-2 were used to explore the relationship between the L scale and several measures of police performance. It was discovered that higher L scale scores were associated with a variety of performance problems, including knowledge mistakes, termination for cause, failure to complete the requirements for conditional hire, and insubordination. The conclusion of the investigators in this study is that their generally poor stress tolerance, overevaluation of their own worth, and rigid attitudes, as exemplified by the high L scale scores (Weiss et al., 2003) made them poor candidates for police work even though on the surface they appear normal. Weiss et al. (2003) recommended a raw score cutoff of 8 (T = 70 for males and 71 for females) as indicating a questionable candidate.

One difficulty in interpreting the L scale with police officer candidates is that the pre-employment situation "pulls" for an overly positive, fake good profile (Graham, 2006; Weiss, Weiss, Cain, & Manley, 2009). The study by Weiss et al. (2009) showed that individuals asked to answer the MMPI-2 as if they were applying for a job as a law enforcement officer achieved mean L scale T scores of 65. These were significantly higher than what these individuals achieved when they took the MMPI-2 and were asked to respond normally. Therefore, it is suggested by Weiss et al. (2009) that slightly elevated scores should not be judged too harshly. This is confirmed by Graham's (2006) interpretive guide to the MMPI-2. Therefore, the suggestion of Weiss et al. (2003) that a raw score cutoff of 8 be used still appears to be in order. This allows for slight elevations produced by the test setting, but requires that individuals with extreme scores be examined more closely and should possibly be eliminated from the applicant pool.

Validity Scales–K scale

The role of the K scale in predicting law enforcement performance has been less well researched. This measures a more subtle defensiveness or positive self-presentation than the L scale. According to Aamodt's (2004) meta-analysis of MMPI-2 variables, it is of limited usefulness in predicting future law enforcement performance. Sellbom, Fischler, and Ben-Porath (2007) state that other investigators have found that high K scores are associated with poor performance, but the data they cite was not published in peer-reviewed form. It may well be that high K scores are associated with poorer

outcomes, but this may be a result of the defensiveness accounted for by the
L scale.

Validity Scales–F scales

A series of (F) infrequency scales exist on the MMPI-2 which are mainly
oriented around measuring negative impression on the MMPI-2. These are
the F (Infrequency), Fb (Back Infrequency–this measures infrequent responses to the last part of the test), and Fp (F Psychopathology), which consists of
items rarely endorsed by actual psychiatric patients. Essentially, individuals
with elevated (T > 65) scores on these scales are either reporting psychopathology or engaging in some kind of "faking bad" report. Given the
pull on the MMPI-2 towards positive impression management in police
applicant samples, it seems unlikely that post-offer applicants would elevate
on these scales. If so, they may also elevate on one or more of the clinical
scales, which would provide cause for concern, as described below. It should
be noted that some studies of the MMPI and MMPI-2 have found that the
F (Infrequency) scale is predictive of poor performance as a law enforcement
officer in conjunction with other scales (Detrick, Chibnall, & Rosso, 2001).

Using the MMPI-2 Clinical Scales in
Pre-Employment Assessment

The MMPI-2 has several clinical scales oriented towards measuring psychopathology. These were developed on the original MMPI using empirical
criterion keying, which means that items on these scales are indicative of the
normal population when answered one way and indicative of psychopathology if answered in the other direction. On the MMPI-2, any standard (T)
score of 65 or greater is considered clinically significant. While these scales
do not directly measure psychological disorders according to DSM-IV, and
while there is considerable collinearity between scales (Tellegen et al., 2003),
the MMPI-2 basic scales are useful in identifying and describing personality
characteristics related to psychopathology (Graham, 2006). The MMPI-2
basic scales are the following, listed in order along with their numbers and
abbreviations:

1 Hypochondriasis (Hy)
2 Depression (D)
3 Hysteria (Hy)
4 Psychopathic Deviate (Pd)
5 Masculinity/Femininity (Mf)

6 Paranoia (Pa)
7 Psychasthenia (Pt)
8 Schizophrenia (Sc)
9 Hypomania (Ma)
0 Social Introversion (Si)

These scales are multidimensional and elevated scores on each scale can be indicative of different sets of personality characteristics. Therefore, exacting interpretations of elevations on each scale cannot be given here as this is beyond the scope of this chapter; readers are referred to the interpretive guide to the MMPI-2 by Graham (2006) for more information on interpretation of the Basic Scales.

Considerable research exists on using the MMPI-2 Basic Scales in the pre-employment screening of law enforcement officers. This research will be briefly summarized here. At one time or another, studies of the MMPI and MMPI-2 have shown that higher scores on scales 1, 2, 4, 6, 7, 8, 9, and 0 are indicative of poorer future performance as a law enforcement officer. Curiously, lower scores on Scale 3 (Hysteria) are also associated with performance problems (Sellbom, Fischler, & Ben-Porath, 2007). Studies have not shown levels of Scale 5 (Mf) that are associated with performance problems. In fact, one study (Weiss et al., 2009) has shown that scores on Scale 5 tend to drift towards the "masculine" end of the spectrum as a part of the pre-employment assessment process, most probably because policing is still viewed as a stereotypically male profession.

Beyond these general findings described by Sellbom, Fischler, and Ben-Porath (2007), a few studies have focused on specific clinical scales or small groups of clinical scales on the MMPI-2, most notably with scales 4 (Pd), 6 (Pa), and 9 (Ma). For example, both Bartol (1991) and Costello, Schneider, and Schoenfeld (1996) found that an "immaturity index" composed of Scales 4 and 9 plus F were predictive of terminations and disciplinary suspensions among officers who were eventually hired. Weiss, Serafino, Serafino, Willson, and Knoll (1998) extensively researched Scale 6 (Pa) and discovered that high scores on the Pa Scale of the MMPI-2 were predictive of both removal from the police force and low supervisory ratings after a period of one year. Aamodt (2004) in his meta-analysis of MMPI studies, found that Scale 9 (Ma) was the most important predictor of supervisor ratings of performance (see also Aamodt, Chapter 9, this volume). Although Aamodt's overall correlations are low, this is still a significant result, and may be at least partially accounted for by the fact that most law enforcement applicants produce low clinical scale scores when given the MMPI-2 (see for example Detrick, Chibnall, & Rosso, 2001).

Brewster and Stoloff (1999) investigated the so-called Good Cop/Bad Cop profile developed by Blau, Super, and Brady (1993) for the MMPI-2. This profile takes into account scores on four MMPI-2 scales: 1 (Hs), 3 (Hy), 4 (Pd), and 9 (Ma). An applicant whose T-scores are less than 60 on these scales and less than 65 on the other clinical scales is considered a "good cop" and if any of the clinical scales was above 65 or all of the four relevant scales was greater than 60, they are considered potentially to be a "bad cop." If one to three of the relevant scales were above 60, but no clinical scales are above 65 they are considered "borderline." This study correctly classified 46 percent of the sample based on supervisor ratings of performance, considerably greater than chance. While Blau, Super, and Brady (1993) had a considerably higher hit rate, they also used the original version of the MMPI and only used two as opposed to three rating categories. Brewster and Stoloff (1999) make the recommendation that anyone achieving clinical scale scores in excess of T = 65 be considered for removal from the applicant pool. Considering the history of MMPI and MMPI-2 validity studies, this appears to be a potentially sound recommendation with the exception of Scale 5 (Mf) which may be biased in the Masculine direction due to the "pull" of the screening process. Certainly in pre-employment selection work, any applicant obtaining significant (T=65) scores on these Clinical Scales should be scrutinized carefully prior to hire.

Other Scales-Harris–Lingoes, Supplementary, and Content

The additional scales (Harris-Lingoes, Supplementary, and Content) on the MMPI-2 have not been investigated as extensively, although a few studies do exist using these scales. The Harris-Lingoes subscales have not been the subject of peer-reviewed journal articles, although a recent presentation by Weiss, Rostow, and Davis (2009) shows that they do have some promise as predictors of law enforcement performance, as a number of significant correlations were obtained between these scales and a scale of law enforcement officer performance which included a variety of performance criteria. However, in most cases, this sample showed that *low* scores on the Harris-Lingoes scales were correlated with problem performance. Further investigation showed that high L scale scores were correlated with problem performance, which seemed to account for the correlations between the Harris-Lingoes scales and performance criteria–individuals who were very invested in denying psychological difficulty seemed to perform the worst as officers. Certainly, this result indicates that perhaps the Harris-Lingoes subscales should be investigated further.

More data exist supporting the use of some of the Supplementary Scales in law enforcement selection, particularly the MAC-R (alcoholism) scale and the O-H (Overcontrolled Hostility) scales. Two studies exist which investigated the usefulness of the Overcontrolled Hostility (O-H) scale in police selection. Weiss, Johnson, Serafino, and Serafino (2001) found correlations between the O-H scale and poor performance as a police officer. However, Castora, Brewster, and Stoloff (2003) did not find a relationship between poor performance and the O-H scale, and, in fact, found that higher O-H scorers were less likely to receive citizen complaints. Both of these studies were relatively small N designs, so it appears that more research is required to determine whether or not O-H is a predictor of future police performance. The Castora et al. (2003) study also investigated the role of Hostility (HO), Manifest Hostility (HOS), and the Anger (ANG) supplementary scales in predicting citizen complaints and supervisory ratings of officers. In this study, elevated HO predicted the number of justified complaints that the officer received from citizens, but neither HOS nor ANG were indicative of performance problems.

More noteworthy with regard to the use of the Supplementary Scales are the positive findings on scales involving substance abuse. Sellbom, Fischler, and Ben-Porath (2007) found that the MacAndrew Alcoholism Scale–Revised (MAC-R) was predictive of sustained Internal Affairs complaints in their sample. The authors of this study also note that the original MAC for the MMPI has also been predictive of poor law enforcement performance. In addition, the Addiction Admission Scale (AAS) was also associated with Internal Affairs complaints in this study. Therefore, elevated scores on these scales may be sufficient to eliminate an individual from the applicant pool in a post-offer evaluation.

The Content Scales have also not been widely investigated as to their predictive power regarding law enforcement performance. Daniels and King (2002) investigated the predictive power of the MMPI-2 Content scales on a sample of 96 law enforcement officers. The Content Scales did not differentiate between their groups of "successful" and "unsuccessful" officers. At the time of this publication, no data exist supporting the use of the Content Scales in the pre-employment selection of law enforcement officers.

New Developments–RC Scales and Restructured Form (RF)

MMPI-2 interpretation has been undergoing significant changes in recent years due to the development of the Restructured Clinical (RC) scales (Tellegen et al., 2003) and their associated Restructured Form (MMPI-2 RF) (Ben-Porath & Tellegen, 2008). The RC scales were originally published in 2003 because of the well-known problem of high intercorrelations between most of the MMPI-2 Basic Scales. The RC scales used items that in the view of their developers accounted for the uniqueness of the original Basic Scales.

The major factor that appeared to account for the high intercorrelations between the basic scales, referred to by Tellegen et al. (2003) as Demoralization, is measured as a separate scale in the RC format. This Demoralization factor measures a general unpleasant affective feeling. In addition to Demoralization (RCd), the RC scales are:

RC1–Somatic Complaints
RC2–Low Positive Emotions
RC3–Cynicism
RC4–Antisocial Behavior
RC6–Ideas of Persecution
RC7–Dysfunctional Negative Emotions
RC8–Aberrant Experiences
RC9–Hypomanic Activation

These scale numbers correspond to the scale numbers in the Basic Scales of the MMPI-2. No RC scales were developed for Scale 5 or Scale 0 as those scales are considered independent of traditional measures of psychopathology.

The MMPI-2 Restructured Form (RF) (Ben-Porath & Tellegen, 2008) is a new revised version of the MMPI-2 that is largely oriented around the RC Scales. However, a number of additional scales have been added, in addition to revised versions of the MMPI-2 validity scales. Not all of the original 567 MMPI-2 items have been used; in fact, the RF version has 338 items, making it a more manageable test in many ways than the original MMPI-2. It should be noted that many of the items have been re-numbered on the MMPI-2 RF.

While the MMPI-2 RF has not yet been fully validated for use in pre-employment selection of police officers, preliminary results appear promising. In their recent study of the MMPI-2 and police performance, Sellbom, Fischler, and Ben-Porath (2007) concluded that several of the RC scales, in particular RC3, RC4, RC6, and RC8, exhibited predictive validity about law enforcement officer performance. These scales were significantly correlated with various performance problems. Moreover, the MMPI-2 RF Technical Manual (Tellegen & Ben-Porath, 2008) has a set of personnel screening norms for law enforcement officers (988 men, 337 women, as well as a combined male/female sample of 674 officers). It is noteworthy that in this sample the T-scores are considerably below average, except for the revised L and K scores, as expected from previous research on the MMPI-2. While norms for personnel screening are not in themselves sufficient for use in screening out post-offer applicants, these norms are nonetheless useful for making comparisons when doing evaluations. While the MMPI-2 RF appears to have considerable promise in the area of pre-employment screening, more research is needed for sufficient validation of the new form.

Summary for Use of the MMPI-2 in Pre-Employment Evaluations

- The validity scales are useful in the pre-employment screening of officers. In particular, high L (Lie) scale scores are a concern. Individuals with raw scores of 8 or above may be candidates for removal from the applicant pool.
- The Basic Scales are also useful. Although unusual, an applicant with an elevated (T > 65) score may be a candidate for removal from the applicant pool.
- Elevations on a few Supplementary Scales (MAC-R, AAS, and possibly H-O and O-H may be significant in pre-employment screening.
- Little evidence exists for the use of the Harris-Lingoes or Content scales.
- The RC Scales and MMPI-2 Restructured Form have considerable potential, but have not yet been fully validated for law enforcement screening.

Other Applications Within Police Psychology

Fitness-for-Duty Evaluations (FFDE)

Next to pre-employment screening evaluations, FFDE's are an area where personality assessment may be used in police psychology, and some peer-reviewed literature on using the MMPI and MMPI-2 for this purpose exists. Rostow and Davis (2004), while providing not specific guidelines for the use of the MMPI-2 in FFDE evaluations, call the MMPI-2 and its predecessor, the MMPI, the "workhorses of police psychology." They describe its usefulness for the identification of psychopathology. However, guidelines for its use in FFDE situations are narrow. Grossman, Haywood, Ostrov, Wasyiliw, and Cavanaugh (1990) showed that most officers wanting to be returned to duty being evaluated for FFDE minimized their symptoms on the MMPI.

Therefore, most evaluees will minimize symptoms on the MMPI in FFDE. It is likely that, while testing is important, other issues be used as well in FFDE evaluations.

Treatment Planning

Use of the MMPI-2 in treatment planning has been well documented. While there is not a large literature on using personality testing for treatment planning of law enforcement officers, the use of the MMPI-2 in treatment planning of outpatients is well documented (Graham, 2006). Therefore, using the MMPI-2 for treatment planning of troubled officers may be useful. The MMPI-2 is a useful test for identifying psychopathology and as such may be helpful for treatment planning, but research is required for this application. In the treatment planning process, the psychologist must be aware of the issue of conflict of interest.

In their discussion of Fitness-for-Duty Evaluations (FFDE), Rostow and Davis (2004) state that the police psychologist in the FFDE situation is a protector of the public interest. This is also true of the selection process. The client of the police psychologist in the selection process is the agency or the police department and not the police officer candidate. It is difficult to reconcile the role of protecting the public interest and providing treatment to a candidate who may be psychologically impaired and is therefore unsuitable for the work of a police officer. Serving both constituencies represents a conflict of interest and can be construed as a boundary problem according to the American Psychological Association Ethics Code (American Psychological Association, 2002). If deemed appropriate in prior negotiation by the city or police agency, the psychologist may recommend involvement in a treatment or remedial program. But using the MMPI-2 to assist in planning a treatment or remedial program for a police officer candidate who has been seen by the psychologist as a part of the selection process represents a conflict of interest.

Conclusion

In summary, the MMPI-2 has much to offer the police psychologist. It has been widely used particularly in the selection of law enforcement candidates, where as a test of psychopathology it is appropriate as a post-offer measure. In addition, its popularity and the development of the MMPI-2 RF (with the new research that will undoubtedly be done on the new form) make it an easily defensible instrument for decision making in this setting. As with other instruments, it is not recommended as a stand-alone for screening, but it can be used in conjunction with one or more of the other instruments described in this book, or with other validated instruments. Less is known about using the MMPI-2 for other purposes within police psychology. More research is needed in these areas. However, as with any forensic evaluation, it is important to remember to use the applicable decision rules when using the MMPI-2 for these purposes.

REFERENCES

Aamodt, M.G. (2004). *Research in law enforcement selection.* Boca Raton: Brown Walker Press.

American Psychological Association. (2002). Ethical principles of psychologists and code of conduct. *American Psychologist, 57,* 1060–1073.

Bartol, C.R. (1991). Predictive validation for small-town police officers who fail. *Professional Psychology: Research and Practice, 22,* 127–132.

Ben-Porath, Y.S., & Tellegen, A. (2008). *Minnesota Multiphasic Personality Inventory-2 Restructured Form: Manual for administration, scoring, and interpretation.* Minneapolis: Pearson.

Blau, T.H., Super, J.T., & Brady, L. (1993). The MMPI Good Cop-Bad Cop Profile in identifying dysfunctional law enforcement personnel. *Journal of Police and Criminal Psychology, 9* (1), 2–4.

Boes, Chandler, & Timm, H.W. (1997). *Police integrity: Use of personality measures to identify corruption prone officers.* Monterey, CA: Defense Personnel Security Research Center.

Brewster, J., & Stoloff, M.L. (1999). Using the Good Cop/Bad Cop profile with the MMPI-2. *Journal of Police and Criminal Psychology, 14*(2), 29–34.

Butcher, J.N., Graham, J.R., Ben-Porath, Y.S., Tellegen, A., Dahlstrom, W.G., & Kaemmer, B. (2001). *MMPI-2 manual for administration and scoring.* Minneapolis: University of Minnesota Press.

Castora, K., Brewster, J., & Stoloff, M.L. (2003). Predicting aggression in police officers using the MMPI-2. *Journal of Police and Criminal Psychology, 18* (1), 1–8.

Costello, R.M., Schneider, S.L., & Schoenfeld, L.S. (1996). Validation of a preemployment MMPI index correlated with interdisciplinary suspension days of police officers. *Psychology: Crime and Law 2,* 299–306.

Daniels, S., & King, E. (2002). The predictive validity of the MMPI-2 Content scales for small-town police officer performance. *Journal of Police and Criminal Psychology, 17* (2), 54–62.

Detrick, P., Chibnall, J.T., & Rosso, M. (2001). Minnesota Multiphasic Personality Inventory-2 in police officer selection: Normative data and relation to the Inwald Personality Inventory. *Professional Psychology: Research and Practice, 32,* 484–490.

Graham, J.R. (2006). *MMPI-2: Assessing personality and psychopathology* (4th ed.). New York: Oxford University Press.

Grossman, L.S., Haywood, T.W., Ostrov, E., Wasyliw, O., & Cavanaugh, J.L. (1990). Sensitivity of MMPI validity scales to motivational factors in psychological evaluations of police officers. *Journal of Personality Assessment, 55,* 549–561.

Herndon, J. (1998, October). *Correlates of the MMPI-2 L Scale: Elevations in an LEO selection test battery.* Paper presented at the 27th annual meeting of the Society for Police and Criminal Psychology, Portland, OR.

King, P., Norrell, G., & Erlandson, F.L. (1959). The prediction of academic success in a police administration curriculum. *Educational and Psychological Measurement, 19,* 649–651.

Rostow, C.D., & Davis, R.D. (2004). *A handbook of fitness-for-duty evaluations for law enforcement.* Binghamton, NY: Haworth.

Sellbom, M., Fischler, G.L., & Ben-Porath, Y.S. (2007). Identifying MMPI-2 predictors of police officer integrity and misconduct. *Criminal Justice and Behavior, 34,* 985–1004.

Super, J.T. (2006). A survey of pre-employment psychological evaluation tests and procedures. *Journal of Police and Criminal Psychology, 21*(2), 83–90.

Tellegen, A., Ben-Porath, Y.S., McNulty, J.L., Arbisi, P.A., Graham, J.R., & Kaemmer, B. (2003). *MMPI-2 Restructured Clinical (RC) Scales: Development, validation, and interpretation.* Minneapolis: University of Minnesota Press.

Weiss, P.A., Davis, R.D., & Rostow, C.D. (2009, March). Predicting overall performance of police officers using the MMPI-2. In P.A. Weiss (Chair) *Criterion-related validity in self-report assessment.* Symposium presented at the annual meeting of the Society for Personality Assessment, Chicago, IL.

Weiss, W.U., Davis, R., Rostow, C., & Kinsman, S. (2003). The MMPI-2 L scale as a tool in police selection. *Journal of Police and Criminal Psychology, 18* (1), 57–60.

Weiss, P.A., Hitchcock, J.H., Weiss, W.U., Rostow, C., & Davis, R. (2008). The Personality Assessment Inventory borderline, drug, and alcohol scales as predictors of overall performance in police officers: A series of exploratory analyses. *Policing and Society, 18,* 301–310.

Weiss, W.U., Johnson, J., Serafino, G., & Serafino, A. (2001). A three-year follow-up of the performance of a class of state police academy graduates using the MMPI-2. *Journal of Police and Criminal Psychology, 16,* 51–55.

Weiss, W.U., Weiss, P.A., Cain, S., & Manley, B. (2009). Impression management in police officer candidacy on the MMPI-2. *Journal of Police and Criminal Psychology, 24,* 120–125.

Chapter 4

THE USE OF THE PERSONALITY ASSESSMENT INVENTORY IN POLICE AND SECURITY PERSONNEL SELECTION

WILLIAM U. WEISS and PETER A. WEISS

INTRODUCTION

In the test battery administered to police officer candidates, a general measure of psychopathology is often included by the psychologist evaluator. The MMPI-2 (Butcher, Graham, Ben-Porath, Tellegen, & Kaemmer, 2001) and its prior edition, the MMPI, have been used for this purpose extensively. These tests have been the bulwark of objective psychopathological assessment for about 70 years. Their place is rightfully earned because the tests come closer to an empirically structured test of psychopathology than does any other. They do have some structural weaknesses, however. One of these is the True-False format. An all-or-nothing format is not one that allows the client to realistically report psychopathology. Simple presence or absence of psychopathology does not reflect real world conditions. Most psychopathology is variable in its presentation. Another of the problems of the MMPI-2 is the names of some of the variables on the test. Psychasthenia and Hysteria are terms that essentially date from the 1930s. Further, the number of items on the MMPI-2 is 567, which represents a task whose completion tends to be problematic for some individuals with psychopathology. For these reasons, other options for the general psychopathology instrument are being investigated and brought into use in police selection.

Description of the PAI

A relatively new test of psychopathology is the Personality Assessment Inventory developed by Leslie Morey (2007). The PAI does address many disadvantages cited by test users about the MMPI-2. The Personality Assessment Inventory (hereafter the PAI) ratings are done on a four-point scale. The True-False all-or-none format of the MMPI-2 is not used. Terminology used in scale construction is modern, according to more recent nomenclature in the field of psychopathology. Finally the PAI contains only 344 items, far fewer than does the MMPI-2. It does, however, use the statistical decision rule theory of the MMPI-2. It uses a T-score format with a mean of 50 and a SD of 10. In general, a T-score of 70, two standard deviations above the mean, represents the presence of psychopathology. The manual by Morey describes the scales of the PAI, and the descriptions below are taken directly from the manual (2007). The scales are divided into four areas. These are Validity Scales, Clinical Scales, Treatment Scales, and Interpersonal Scales.

VALIDITY SCALES. The four validity scales are Inconsistency (ICN), Infrequency (INF), Negative Impression (NIM), and Positive Impression (PIM).

CLINICAL SCALES. The 11 clinical scales are Somatic Complaints (SOM), Anxiety (ANX), Anxiety-Related Disorders (ARD), Depression (DEP), Mania (MAN), Paranoia (PAR), Schizophrenia (SCZ), Borderline Features (BOR), and Antisocial Features (ANT). All of these scales contain subscales. Alcohol Problems (ALC) and Drug Problems (DRG) are the other two scales in this group.

TREATMENT SCALES. The five treatment scales are Aggression (AGG), Suicidal Ideation (SUI), Stress (STR), Nonsupport (NON), and Treatment Rejection (RXR). Interpersonal Scales The two interpersonal scales are Dominance (DOM) and Warmth (WRM).

Psychological Screening

Law enforcement applicants are required by law in most jurisdictions to undergo psychological screening. According to ADA guidelines (Americans with Disabilities Act, 1990), the psychological evaluation cannot be performed until there has been a conditional offer of employment. Increasingly, the PAI has been used as a tool in police selection. For example, Super (2006) noted that 42 percent of police agencies that he polled in his selection procedure study were using the PAI as a part of their selection process. In view of the advantages of the PAI—the smaller number of items, the four-point answer scale, and the more up-to-date construct language—it is not surprising that it is being more frequently encountered as a part of the selection process. The PAI is a general measure of psychopathology often replacing the MMPI-2 in the selection process. It is frequently used with the Inwald Personality Inventory (Inwald, 1982) or the M-PULSE (Davis & Rostow,

2008), which are measures more specifically directed toward security personnel.

The next sections involve discussions of the PAI profile and the scales of the PAI. Relevant research is presented. Discussion centers upon the four groups of scales, Validity Scales, Clinical Scales, Treatment Scales, and Interpersonal Scales. Discussion of the scales proceeds with an emphasis upon the selection of security and police officer candidates.

Validity Scales

Inconsistency (ICN) and Infrequency (INF)

The Inconsistency (ICN) and Infrequency (INF) scales on the PAI were constructed largely to determine whether or not the examinee is paying appropriate attention to item content when taking the test. Elevated scores on ICN indicate an individual who has not been answering similar test items in a consistent fashion due to problems with attention, reading comprehension, or carelessness. A T-score of 73 or higher on this scale indicates an invalid protocol that should not be interpreted because the individual was, for one of the above reasons, unable to attend appropriately to the test items (Morey, 2003, 2007). In the experience of the author with security personnel, the ICN scale is almost never elevated but the INF occasionally is. The INF scale consists of a series of items which are designed to be answered in a similar fashion by all examinees regardless of their diagnosis or the purpose of the test administration. These statements are nearly always answered in the same way by all examinees because they either indicate unusual personal characteristics or express commonsense attitudes. Typically, security personnel candidates who obtain elevated scores on this scale do so because they are behaving defensively and in so doing overinterpret the items. They are attempting to hide problems from the examiner by trying to guess what the "hidden agenda" of an item is. Regardless of the reason, scores of $T \geq 75$ mean that the individual did not attend appropriately to test items or overinterpreted them and therefore, the profile should be considered invalid (Morey, 2003, 2007).

Morey (2007) in the most recent edition of the PAI manual discusses interpretation of the INC and INF scales. In the case of security candidate personnel selection, profiles with elevated scores on these two scales are invalid and the clinical scales should not be interpreted. Hiring decisions therefore cannot be made on the basis of the clinical scales and other information must form the basis of the conclusion of the psychological evaluation. However, extremely elevated scores on ICN and INF would be unusual in a personnel screening situation because individuals applying for jobs which involve psychological screening, particularly law enforcement positions, tend to be relatively high functioning and report less psychopathology than the general population (Roberts et al., 2004; Weiss et al., 2003). Research on elevated ICN and INF profiles may ultimately show that high scores on these scales are suggestive of poor employee performance in one or more occupations due to the overinterpretation or the lack of attention indicated by such scores, but up to the present no systematic exploration of INC or INF has been performed with a police candidate sample.

Negative Impression (NIM)

The Negative Impression (NIM) scale is designed to measure the degree to which an individual is presenting himself or herself in a more negative manner than would be expected. Elevations on this scale can be found for a variety of reasons, such as malingering, exaggeration of genuine symptoms, or careless/random responding. Individuals with severe emotional problems can also obtain elevated scores on NIM (Morey, 2007).

It is very unusual to obtain elevated scores on NIM in police candidate selection settings (see, for example, Roberts et al., 2004). Psychologists who are faced with interpreting a profile that has even a slight (approximately T = 73) elevation on NIM in a pre-employment setting should first attempt to find out the reason for the elevation on this scale, as that information will be important in making the final recommendation to the employer. Sometimes obsessive-compulsive characteristics are involved with a high NIM. The individual is endorsing forms of psychopathology on the basis of subtle nuances in the items. This will also sometimes occur as a result of attentional factors, so the scores for INC and INF should be closely examined and the appropriate conclusion drawn (see previous discussion on INC and INF). If these scores are in the normal range, elevations on one or more of the clinical scales are likely to be noted, as the individual is trying to exaggerate some sort of emotional difficulty. While this is an unusual finding in police officer candidate selection evaluations, conclusions may then be made on the basis of clinical scale scores as the elevation is likely to be related to the individual's psychological functioning. It should be noted, however, that studies by Weiss, Rostow, Davis, and Decoster-Martin (2004) and Weiss, Zehner, Davis, Rostow, and Decoster-Martin (2005) showed that elevated NIM scores are modestly correlated with problem performance as a police officer, including behaviors such as neglect of duty, conduct mistakes, and reprimands by supervisors, so elevated NIM (T ≥ 73) may be sufficient to exclude a job candidate from the applicant pool in law enforcement settings.

Positive Impression (PIM)

Scales related to response style in security personnel selection evaluations have been the subject of considerable research in the last few years. For example, Weiss et al. (2003), Herndon (1998), and Boes, Chandler, and Timm (1997) all investigated the L scale of the MMPI-2 as a selection device in police candidate assessment. Unfavorable behavior outcomes were associated with elevations on the L scale. Results of PAI studies show that PIM is also an important variable in predicting future performance for some occupations that typically involve a psychological evaluation as part of the screening process.

An important issue in interpreting PIM with job applicants is that the job application situation leads to the presentation of an overly positive self-image on the instrument. This leads to elevated scores on the validity scales related to positive self-presentation (Roberts et al., 2004; Weiss, Weiss, Cain, & Manley, 2009). Such applicants will tend to obtain higher scores on measures of defensiveness and positive impression management, such as the PAI PIM scale, and the L and K scales on the MMPI-2, than will individuals given the test for other purposes. Therefore, higher cutoff scores should be used to determine levels of defensiveness (see for example Weiss et al., in press). Roberts and associates (2004) make the point that elevated scores on PIM (T = 70 in one of the sample cases presented) are within the normal range for law enforcement and public safety applicants. The evaluating psychologist should not label a profile as extremely defensive or deceptive unless the PIM score is extraordinarily elevated.

Numerous recommendations exist for eliminating applicants from employment consideration due to elevated L-scale scores when the MMPI-2 is given in personnel selection situations (Weiss et al., 2003; Weiss et al., in press) but this is not the case with PIM when the PAI is administered, because research in employment settings suggests that PIM and L measure somewhat different forms of impression management (Weiss, Serafino, & Serafino, 2000). In their factor analytic study of validity indexes used in law enforcement selection, Weiss et al. (2000) identified two main factors measured by personality assessment instruments administered to 42 state police officer candidates. These were a Guardedness/Defensiveness factor represented primarily by the Guardedness scale of the Inwald Personality Inventory and a Social Desirability factor reflected primarily in PIM. While PIM is strongly related to Social Desirability, or a need to present oneself in a positive light, this study suggests that the MMPI-2 L scale measures a different aspect of impression management, one that is not only related to Social Desirability but also to Guardedness and Defensiveness. Confirmation that these scales are measuring different personality characteristics in job applicants is confirmed in the study by Weiss et al. (2004) which showed that PIM was in fact positively correlated with good performance as a police officer on some outcome variables. Therefore, it should not be assumed that a job applicant is lying or being deliberately deceptive on the PAI unless his or her score on PIM is extraordinarily elevated. Unlike with the MMPI-2 L scale, a high score on PIM is not necessarily interpreted as meaning that the individual is a poor candidate for jobs that involve considerable personal risk or responsibility, such as that of police officer.

Other Validity Indicators

The PAI has several supplemental validity indicators that have been developed to help examiners better understand examinee response style. Two of these, the Malingering Index (MAL) and Rogers Discriminant Function (RDF) are designed to assist with detecting fake-bad or malingering profiles. The Malingering Index (MAL) is composed of eight configural features that are observed more frequently in the profiles of individuals simulating mental disorder. Rogers Discriminant Function (RDF) was developed using bona fide clinical patients and those simulating psychiatric disorder. These are unlikely to be factors in security and police candidate selection due to the kinds of impression management issues found in this type of selection. MAL and RDF have not been investigated in police officer candidate selection.

The other supplemental validity indicators measure positive impression management and may be of more interest to personnel selection settings because impression management attempts in police officer candidate selection tend to be in the positive direction. The Defensiveness Index (DEF) and Cashel Discriminant Function (CDF) are the two supplemental indices designed to detect fake-good profiles. DEF is composed of nine configural features of the PAI profile that tend to be observed in greater frequency in individuals instructed to present a positive impression as compared to clinical patients. CDF is a discriminant function that was designed to distinguish between defensive and honest responding. While the PIM scale seems to measure something different for police officer selection than the MMPI-2 L scale, DEF and CDF have potential for use in personnel settings because high scores on them may allow examiners to screen out applicants, whereas high PIM is actually predictive of good performance. It is noteworthy that the DEF correlates significantly with the MMPI-2 L Scale (Morey, 2003), which has frequently been used to screen out applicants in law enforcement personnel selection because of the connection between high scores and poor job performance. The CDF may also be important for investigation because the CDF score appears to be relatively independent of actual mental health status (Morey, 2003). It therefore may be the best indicator of the kind of deliberate impression management that is sometimes associated with future poor job performance in some studies. These supplemental indicators have not yet been validated for use in police candidate selection, but they appear to be an exciting avenue for future research.

Clinical Scales

Axis I: Clinical Psychopathological Scales

Research evidence exists supporting the use of the Obsessive-Compulsive (ARD-O) subscale in the selection of law enforcement officers (Decoster-Martin, Weiss, Davis, & Rostow, 2004). This study showed a small but significant correlation between ARD-O, part of the Anxiety- Related Disorders cluster, and improved performance as a law enforcement officer. This study noted that law enforcement officers with modest elevations (T = 55 to 65) on ARD-O were less likely to have been involved in on- or off-duty motor vehicle accidents, engaged in undesirable off-duty conduct, or to have been the subject of citizen complaints. However, DeCoster-Martin et al. (2004) note that candidates with T ≥ 75 are not likely to make good law enforcement officers because of intrusive thoughts and the belief that their impulses are out of control. Decoster-Martin et al. go on to state that such individuals with T ≥ 75 would be very unusual in a personnel selection sample because they are usually eliminated from the applicant pool very early in the process.

What this means for the psychologist doing personnel selection in the law enforcement arena is that individuals with "high normal" ARD-O scores may be good candidates for law enforcement positions provided the results of their clinical interview, file review, and any other tests administered are satisfactory. However, as Decoster-Martin et al. (2004) state, individuals with extreme scores on ARD-O are probably not satisfactory candidates.

Axis I: Drug and Alcohol Problem Scales

Research also exists connecting the Drug Problems (DRG) Scale with problematic performance as a police officer. Weiss, Hitchcock, Weiss, Rostow, and Davis (2008) performed a comprehensive assessment of the predictive power of the DRG and ALC scales on police performance. This analysis included 632 police officers who had taken the PAI as part of their pre-employment screening; a questionnaire was then completed by each officer's supervisor after the officer had been employed for a period of one year.

This questionnaire contained 32 items, and was scored by the investigators by giving each officer one "point" for each question answered in the direction of poor performance. Each officer therefore obtained a score ranging from 0 to 32. While the initial regression analyses in that study did not show a relationship with job performance, significant results were obtained when the analyses were performed with the 132 poorest performing officers in the sample (score $\geq$ 3). Significant correlations with poor performance were found for this subsample of officers with DRG. In addition DRG was found to be a significant predictor of performance when used in an exploratory stepwise regression with an N=123 subsample. Results of this study show that the DRG scale may be modestly predictive of who will be a poor law enforcement officer.

Elevations (T $\geq$ 70) on DRG would suggest eliminating that individual from the applicant pool in a law enforcement setting based on currently available research. The DRG seemed to be the most predictive of this group of scales in the Weiss, Hitchcock, et al. (2008) study of police officer candidates. Those with more elevated scores on DRG are likely to be individuals who are relatively unconcerned with legal violations (due to the illegality of drug use), and for whom violating police department norms and rules is also less of a concern than for most officers. ALC was not a predictor of problem performance in that study, most likely due to the greater social acceptability of alcohol use. It is likely that somewhat elevated scores on this scale are probably less of a concern in a pre-employment setting than are elevations on DRG, even though high scores on ALC (especially those above T > 84) should obviously be considered carefully before making a hiring decision. It is well known that alcohol is often a disinhibitor and that it is often a factor in violence and crime.

Axis II Scales

Some of the most significant empirical research supporting the use of the PAI in the personnel selection of law enforcement applicants has been performed on the scales measuring Axis II disorders. As far as the Axis II disorders are concerned, the use of the Antisocial (ANT) scale and its subscales for law enforcement selection has been well researched by William Weiss and colleagues (2004, 2005). In these two studies, Weiss and colleagues assessed the relationship between the ANT subscales and a number of performance criteria provided by the officers' supervisors after a period of one year of employment. The two studies showed significant relationships between elevated scores on all three Antisocial subscales (ANT-A/Antisocial Behaviors, ANT-E/Egocentricity, ANT-S/Stimulus Seeking) and problem performance characteristics for law enforcement officers, notably insubordination, excessive citizen complaints, and neglect of duty. In addition, high scores on ANT-E and ANT-S were predictive of other future performance issues, such as conduct mistakes and termination for cause. Further investigation of these scales using a multiple regression format (Weiss et al., 2005) showed that these scales can collectively be used to predict poor performance in law enforcement personnel.

It is clear from these results that the ANT scale and its subscales are important predictors of future performance in law enforcement officers when used as part of a pre-employment process. This finding makes sense when the nature of the ANT scales is examined—these individuals tend to get themselves into trouble due to antisocial behavior or impulsivity, and would not make good law enforcement officers because they create ethical problems and the kind of difficulties that make bad press for law enforcement agencies. In addition, the lack of empathy seen in individuals with high scores on ANT-E is likely to cause problems for them in policing, which is an interpersonally oriented and frequently help-focused occupation.

Because of the prior research on the PAI and law enforcement, it is recommended that individuals who obtain elevated scores $(T \geq 70)$ on either the ANT scale or any of its individual subscales be removed from the applicant pool. These individuals appear to be a significant risk for problem performance based on prior research, and represent a liability for law enforcement agencies due to their impulsivity, lack of empathy, and tendency for trouble. While published data for other professions do not currently exist in the assessment literature, it appears likely because of the characteristics of high ANT scorers that these are people who would not succeed in any kind of sensitive occupation such as that of police officer.

Research also exists connecting the Borderline scale (BOR) and Borderline-Negative Relationship (BOR-N) subscale with problematic performance as a police officer. Weiss, Hitchcock, et al. (2008) performed a comprehensive assessment of the predictive power of the BOR scale and subscales. This study has been described earlier under Alcohol and Drug Problems. To repeat, this analysis included 632 police officers who had taken the PAI as part of their pre-employment screening; a questionnaire was then completed by each officer's supervisor after the officer had been employed for a period of one year. This questionnaire had 32 items on it, and was scored by the investigators by giving each officer one "point" for each question answered in the direction of poor performance. Each officer therefore obtained a score ranging from 0 to 32. While the initial regression analyses in that study did not show a relationship with job performance, significant results were obtained when the analyses were performed with the 132 poorest performing officers in the sample (score ≥ 3). Significant correlations with poor performance were found for this subsample of officers with BOR and BOR-N. In addition BOR-N was found to be a significant predictor of performance when used in an exploratory stepwise regression with an N=123 subsample. Results of this study show that the BOR scale may be modestly predictive of who will be a poor law enforcement officer.

Elevations (T ≥ 70) on BOR, BOR-N would suggest eliminating that individual from the applicant pool in a law enforcement setting based on currently available research. The previously discussed research findings are not surprising given that individuals with elevated BOR scores tend to be individuals with severe personality disorders (Morey, 2007). The BOR-N seemed to be the most predictive of this group of scales in the Weiss, Hitchcock et al. (2008) study. Policing is a fundamentally interpersonal occupation and those with high scores on BOR-N (Negative Relationships) most likely lack the interpersonal skills needed to be a successful police officer.

Treatment Scales

Significant findings also exist for the use of the Aggression (AGG) scale and its subscales in the pre-employment selection of police officers. Weiss et al. (2004) found relationships between elevated scores on the AGG subscales and a number of negative performance characteristics in their sample of hired police officers who had taken the PAI as part of a pre-employment screening process. High scores on Physical Aggression (AGG-P) were associated with reports of insubordination and excess citizen complaints from police supervisors, as well as the number of times that an officer has discharged his or her weapon in the line of duty (using a firearm multiple times in the line of duty over the course of one year is often indicative of performance problems). Scores on Verbal Aggression (AGG-V) were associated with voluntary resignation, while Aggressive Attitude (AGG-A) was associated with officers being more likely to receive suspensions or written reprimands. It is not surprising that the Aggression scale and its subscales are associated with poor performance in law enforcement officers. Officers must use force at times. However, force is to be used judiciously and minimally. Self-control in the area of aggression is an important characteristic of good police officers. Moreover, AGG-V and AGG-A tap into problematic interpersonal styles, and successful law enforcement officers must possess good interpersonal skills. Officers who exhibit overly aggressive behavior or interpersonal styles are thus more likely to encounter on-the-job trouble. Elevated scores (T ≥ 70) on AGG or any of its subscales would therefore justify removing an officer from the applicant pool prior to hire.

While evidence supporting the use of AGG exists, research on the role of the other Treatment Scales does not exist at present in the area of police officer selection. Therefore, it may be difficult to make hiring decisions on the basis of these scales, which include Suicidal Ideation (SUI), Stress (STR), Nonsupport (NON), and Treatment Rejection (RXR). These scales would be interesting to investigate in future research, because, with the exception of SUI, which because of pre-selection is very unlikely to be elevated in populations of police officer candidates, these scales tap into dimensions of personality not directly related to psychopathology and which therefore will have less restriction of range in police officer candidate selection settings. Because of the stressful nature of police work, the Stress (STR) scale does have significant potential for police selection. These scales may ultimately be quite useful in determining suitability for employment, and researchers are encouraged to investigate these scales on the PAI.

Interpersonal Scales

Dominance (DOM) and Warmth (WRM) are two interpersonal scales of the PAI. These are characteristics which are certainly important for the work of security personnel. It would seem that the Yerkes-Dodson Law (Yerkes & Dodson, 1908) that is, a curvilinear relationship with moderate levels of the characteristics being associated with successful police work, would be relevant. Too much of these characteristics and too little of them are likely to have negative outcomes. Even though criterion validity data do not exist for using these scales, clinical acumen would suggest that a curvilinear relationship between these variables and successful police work is a valid approach to their application. Further investigation is needed.

Interpretation of the PAI in Security Personnel Selection

The author of this chapter recommends that interpretation of the PAI involve two processes, (1) Empirically-based interpretation, and (2) Validity Generalization. In interpreting the PAI and making personnel decisions empirically validated information takes precedence. Information that has been gleaned from empirically-based validity studies is the cornerstone of interpretation. The validity scales of the PAI have proven to be important for police selection, as they have been with the MMPI-2. For example, much information about the use of the L scale as predictor of problematic performance (Weiss et al., 2003; Herndon, 1998; Boes et al., 1997) has been developed. Certain Axis I scales, Axis II scales and Treatment scales also have been empirically validated. The following is a summary of information that has been empirically validated using the PAI.

- **The Negative Impression Scale (NIM):** Weiss et al. (2004) and Weiss et al. (2005) showed that elevated NIM scores are modestly correlated with problem performance as a police officer, including behaviors such as neglect of duty, conduct mistakes, and reprimands by supervisors.
- **The Positive Impression Scale (PIM):** Weiss et al. (2004) showed that PIM was in fact positively correlated with good performance as a police officer on some outcome variables.
- **The Anxiety- Related Disorder-Obsessive-Compulsive (ARD-O):** Research evidence exists supporting the use of the Obsessive-Compulsive (ARD-O) subscale in the selection of law enforcement officers (Decoster-Martin et al., 2004). A small but significant correlation between ARD-O and improved performance as a law enforcement officer has been identified. This study noted that law enforcement officers with modest elevations (T = 55 to 65) on ARD-O were less likely to have been involved in on- or off-duty motor vehicle accidents, engaged in undesirable off-duty conduct, or to have been the subject of citizen complaints. However, DeCoster-Martin et al. (2004) note that candidates with $T \geq 75$ are not likely to make good law enforcement officers because of intrusive thoughts and the belief that their impulses are out of control.
- **Antisocial Behaviors (ANT-A), Egocentricity (ANT-E), Stimulus Seeking (ANT-S):** These subscales predicted problematic performance characteristics for law enforcement applicants. William Weiss and colleagues (2004, 2005) identified significant relationships between elevated scores on all three Antisocial subscales (ANT-A/Antisocial Behaviors, ANT-E/Egocentricity, ANT-S/Stimulus Seeking) and problem performance characteristics for law enforcement officers, notably insubordination, excessive citizen complaints, and neglect of duty. In addition, high scores on ANT-E and ANT-S were predictive of other future performance issues, such as conduct mistakes and termination for cause. Further investigation of these scales using a multiple regression format (Weiss et al., 2005) showed that these scales can collectively be used to predict poor performance in law enforcement personnel.
- **Borderline (BOR) and Borderline-Negative Relationships (BOR-N):** Significant correlations with poor performance were found in a subsample of officers with the BOR scale. In addition, BOR-N was found to be a significant predictor of performance when used in an exploratory stepwise regression with a subsample. Results of this study show that the BOR scale may be modestly predictive of who will be a poor law enforcement officer. Because policing is a fundamentally interpersonal occupation, those with high scores on BOR-N most likely lack the interpersonal skills needed to be a successful police officer.

- **Drug Problems (DRG):** Weiss, Hitchcock et al. (2008) found significant correlations with poor performance for a subsample of officers with DRG. In addition DRG was found to be a significant predictor of performance when used in an exploratory stepwise regression. Results of this study show that the DRG scale may be modestly predictive of poor performance as a law enforcement officer.
- **Physical Aggression (AGG-P), Verbal Aggression (AGG-V) and Aggressive Attitude (AGG-A):** Weiss et al. (2004) found relationships between elevated scores on the AGG subscales and a number of negative performance characteristics in their sample of hired police officers who had taken the PAI as part of a pre-employment screening process. High scores on Physical Aggression (AGG-P) were associated with reports of insubordination and excess citizen complaints from police supervisors, as well as the number of times that an officer has discharged his or her weapon in the line of duty (using a firearm multiple times in the line of duty over the course of one year is often indicative of performance problems). Scores on Verbal Aggression (AGG-V) were associated with voluntary resignation, while Aggressive Attitude (AGG-A) was associated with officers being more likely to receive suspensions or written reprimands.

Secondarily, validity generalization (Kaplan & Saccuzzo, 2005) may be employed as an interpretive strategy. It has been previously noted that job applicants, particularly police and public safety candidates who have been studied extensively by psychologists, typically obtain scores on the clinical scales that are lower even than those individuals in the national norming sample. For example, in one recent study of the PAI in law enforcement selection that involved a large sample, applicants obtained PAI clinical scale scores that were, on average, one-half standard deviation lower than the average for a nonclinical population (Weiss, Hitchcock et al., 2008), most likely due to a combination of psychological health and the testing situation in the pre-employment setting. Basically, police officers tend to be psychologically healthier than the average person in the American population. One could even argue that they are more "normal" than the average person. They do not as a group have more psychological problems than the average individual. Therefore it would appear appropriate to use the PAI normative data available with the Professional Manual (Morey, 2007) in decision-making with police officer candidates.

In order for an instrument to be used in effective pre-employment screening, that instrument should first be validated for that purpose (Weiss, Weiss, & Gacono, 2008). Multiple validation studies have been conducted for the PAI with regard to personnel selection in the last several years, and the present interpretation section focuses on scales of the PAI that have been empirically validated for personnel selection purposes. These have been summarized above. However, in the absence of criterion validity information, validity generalization is an appropriate tool in the armamentarium of the psychologist doing police selection.

In continuing the argument for the use of validity generalization in police officer candidate selection, virtually no peer-reviewed research exists at present for decision making based on the results of the Somatic Complaints (SOM), Depression (DEP), Mania (MAN), Paranoia (PAR), or Schizophrenia (SCZ) scales in personnel selection. This lack of published research appears to stem from the fact that these scales are indicative of serious psychopathology, and individuals with these complaints are, as mentioned earlier, typically eliminated from the applicant pool long before the psychologist becomes involved. The police applicant pool is a pre-selected group. All studies done with police officer candidates represent concurrent validity studies (Kaplan & Saccuzzo, 2005) rather than predictive validity studies. In fact, few if any predictive validity studies exist in the literature. However, finding an individual with a T score much above the mean on these clinical scales in a police officer candidate selection sample would be unusual, indeed. A psychologist evaluating an individual who obtains an elevated (T ≥ 70) score on any of the above scales should carefully consider his or her hiring recommendation and also integrate other sources of data to strengthen the case for the decision. While data showing an association between poor performance and elevations on these scales have not yet been published, such data exist for similar scales on the MMPI-2. Brewster and Stoloff (1999) make a case for eliminating anyone from law enforcement applicant pools who obtains an elevated score on any of the MMPI-2 clinical scales (with the possible exception of scales 5 and 0). Considering the significant correlations between many of the PAI clinical scales and the MMPI-2 clinical scales in law enforcement and public safety personnel selection samples (Roberts et al., 2004), this may be an appropriate recommendation for psychologists using the PAI as well. However, more research with these scales is needed to further validate the PAI for police candidate selection. Nevertheless, these scales are useful in the selection procedure provided that the guidelines of the Professional Manual are followed.

Use of the PAI in Employment Screening

Structure of the Candidate Psychological Screening Process

Elsewhere in this book, the structure of the police candidate selection process is discussed. Minimally, the process should consist of a mental status exam and at least two tests, one a general measure of psychopathology and the other a test assessing problematic behavioral potential specifically geared toward law enforcement candidates. The PAI can be used as a general measure of psychopathology. Traditionally the MMPI-2 has been used for this purpose. The PAI, as mentioned previously, represents a replacement for the MMPI-2, in fact in some ways improving the assessment of psychopathology. However, this author does not recommend the use of the PAI as a standalone measure in police candidate selection. A general measure of psychopathology does not provide sufficient information for adequate decision making. A measure specifically geared to law enforcement selection such as the Inwald Personality Inventory (Inwald, 1982) or the M-PULSE (Davis & Rostow, 2008) adds an important and necessary dimension to the police candidate selection process because these instruments assess significant criterion behaviors associated with success as a security officer. Multiple sources of information are recommended for conducting psychological evaluations in police candidate employment situations. Super (2006) in his survey of the practices of psychologists performing pre-employment law enforcement screenings, noted the value of multiple sources of information. Super stated that an effective pre-employment evaluation (in addition to interviews) will include, *at a minimum*, a test of psychopathology, a test of normal personality functioning, and a test of cognitive or problem-solving ability. Certainly more information at the disposal of the psychologist assists in more accurate predictions. However, the use of a mental status exam, the PAI, and a measure geared toward identifying problematic law enforcement behavior would meet ADA requirements since the purpose of the police candidate evaluation is to identify the presence of psychopathology and the potential for problematic behavior as a police officer. Normal personality variables, although useful, are less helpful in making these decisions.

Another reason for using other measures in addition to the PAI is the current emphasis on multimethod assessment in clinical psychology. Erdberg (2008) states that for purposes of psychological assessment, interviews, self-report measures, performance-based personality tests (for example, the Rorschach and Thematic Apperception Test), and behavioral measures all provide different types of information. The standard of practice in police officer candidate assessment is also moving in the multimethod direction, perhaps because of this overall trend. Roberts et al. (2004) and Super (2006) provide examples of a variety of instruments used together in security personnel selection, citing the importance of multiple instruments because they all provide different kinds of information to the evaluating psychologist.

Scoring, Software and Interpretive Report

One advantage of the PAI is that it can be both hand scored and computer scored (Morey, 2007). Another recent development which makes the PAI advantageous for use in personnel selection is the PAI Law Enforcement, Corrections, and Public Safety Selection Report service, available from Psychological Assessment Resources (Roberts et al., 2004). This is a computerized report service which compares PAI scores for applicants to norms for law enforcement and other occupations (corrections officers, firefighters, EMT's, and communications dispatchers) that frequently involve pre-employment psychological evaluations as part of the hiring process. In addition to making this norm comparison, the program evaluates critical items and makes a statement about the applicant's risk level and suitability for the job being applied for. While, like all computerized interpretation aids, this report service should not operate as a stand-alone, it does provide a valuable and exciting aid to the psychologist who routinely conducts pre-employment evaluations.

Further Validation Research

The PAI appears to have sufficient validity to be used in selecting law enforcement officers based on the published studies discussed above. The PAI has been shown to be effective at predicting future performance of a law enforcement officer when administered as part of the hiring process. However, much research remains to be done in this area as well. While some of the clinical scales have still not been investigated in criterion validity studies (see above), the Interpersonal and Treatment scales also appear to have considerable potential and, with the exception of the Aggression (AGG) scales, have not been systematically investigated at present. The potential of the Dominance (DOM) and Warmth (WRM) scales in the area of police selection has been discussed earlier. Law enforcement researchers are therefore encouraged to attempt to establish the criterion validity of these as yet unexplored scales for purposes of personnel selection in law enforcement.

The PAI Report in Police Candidate Selection

Weiss, elsewhere in this book, discusses the structure of the police selection process and the communication of findings to the city or police agency. Reference is made to this chapter. Weiss also discusses the important issue of Informed Consent. It is important for the candidate to realize that for sensitive, high-risk occupations like that of police officer the privilege lies with the agency, not the candidate. While a release of information is obtained, it is also important for the candidates to realize that they may not have access to the original report of the psychologist. In psychological evaluations for police officer candidates, communication of findings is done in a report directly to the hiring agency. These evaluations are only done for sensitive, high-risk occupations such as that of police officer or firefighter, which often involves a government agency. In most cases, the applicant signs a form waiving privilege and confidentiality prior to testing, so that the results of the evaluation can be given directly to the referring agency by the psychologist. Usually, the applicant will not have direct access to the report. The report, of course, is based upon the findings of the evaluation and all information provided to the psychologist. The psychologist is asked to make a pass-fail decision. In most cases, the psychologist will make a positive recommendation, because most individuals with problems or potential for problematic behavior are eliminated from the applicant pool at earlier stages than the psychological evaluation (for reasons elaborated earlier in this chapter). Usually the opinion of the psychologist is taken very seriously by the agency. If the psychologist deems the individual unacceptable, the agency will not hire because, should any negative event occur, the agency is subject to lawsuits from those claiming injury from the occurrence. If the applicant is deemed unacceptable after participating in the psychological evaluation, he or she is often able to appeal the finding. In the case of an appeal, the results of the initial evaluation are usually forwarded to a second psychologist who conducts an independent evaluation, which may involve re-administering the PAI. A full explanation of this process can be found elsewhere in this book in the chapter by Khadivi. While infrequent, applicants who fail a second opinion evaluation may at times seek legal action if they feel that they have been treated unfairly in the hiring process. This may result in lawsuits against the employer, department, or government agency that requested the original evaluation for hiring purposes. In such circumstances, the PAI data and results may need to be presented in court. The PAI has been demonstrated to meet current standards for admissibility as evidence in court (Morey, Warner, & Hopwood, 2007; Weiner & Greene, 2008).

Conclusion

The PAI is an important instrument in the armamentarium of psychologists who do police officer candidate selection. Its advantages have been described. They are up-to-date nomenclature, a four-point answer scale and fewer items than the MMPI-2. In the area of personnel selection, the primary validation studies have been with police and security personnel and therefore psychologists can proceed with confidence in using the PAI with police officer candidates. It has not been as well validated with other types of jobs. However, the focus of this chapter has been upon the selection of police and security personnel. The MMPI-2 is still used more frequently than the PAI, according to Super (2006). Of course, in some jurisdictions, the MMPI-2 is mandated by law. However, the PAI is being used more as time goes on and additional empirical research data are being collected and developed and become more extensive, use of the PAI in police officer candidate selection will continue to grow.

REFERENCES

Americans with Disabilities Act, 42 U.S.C. §12112© (3) and (4) (1990).

Boes, J.O., Chandler, C.J., & Timm, H.W. (1997). *Police integrity: Use of personality measures to identify corruption-prone officers.* Monterrey, CA: Defense Personnel Security Research Center.

Brewster, J., & Stoloff, M.L. (1999). Using the good cop/bad cop profile with the MMPI-2. *Journal of Police and Criminal Psychology, 14*(2), 29–34.

Butcher, J.N., Graham, J.R., Ben-Porath,Y.S., Tellegen, A., Dahlstrom, W.G., & Kaemmer, B. (2001). *MMPI-2 (Minnesota Multiphasic Personality Inventory-2): Manual for administration, scoring, and interpretation, revised edition.* Minneapolis, University of Minnesota Press.

Davis, R.D., & Rostow, C.D. (2008). *Matrix-Predictive Uniform Law Enforcement Selection Evaluation Inventory (M-PULSE): Technical manual.* Toronto: MHS.

Decoster-Martin, E., Weiss, W.U., Davis, R.D., & Rostow, C.D. (2004). Compulsive traits and police officer performance. *Journal of Police and Criminal Psychology, 19*(2), 64–71.

Erdberg, P. (2008). Multimethod assessment as a forensic standard. In G.B. Gacono & F.B. Evans (eds.), *The handbook of forensic Rorschach assessment* (pp. 561–566). New York: Routledge.

Herndon, J. (1998, Oct.). *"Correlates of MMPI-2 L scale: Elevations in an LEO selection test battery."* Paper presented at the 27th annual meeting of the Society for Police and Criminal Psychology, Portland, OR.

Inwald, R.E. (1982). *Inwald Personality Inventory (IPI) technical manual.* New York: Hilson Research.

Kaplan, R.M., & Saccuzzo, D.P. (2005). *Psychological testing: Principles, applications, and issues.* (6th Ed.). Belmont, CA: Wadsworth/Thomson.

Morey, L.C. (2003). *Essentials of PAI assessment.* New York: Wiley.

Morey, L.C. (2007). *Personality Assessment Inventory: Professional manual* (2nd ed.) Odessa, FL: Psychological Assessment Resources.

Morey, L.C., Warner, M.B., & Hopwood, C.J. (2007). Personality Assessment Inventory: Issues in legal and forensic settings. In A.M. Goldstein (Ed.), *Forensic psychology: Emerging topics and expanding roles* (pp.97–126). Hoboken, NJ: Wiley.

Roberts, M.D., Thompson, J.A., & Johnson, M. (2004). *PAI law enforcement, corrections, and public safety selection report: Manual.* Odessa, FL: Psychological Assessment Resources.

Super, J.T. (2006). A survey of pre-employment psychological evaluation tests and procedures. *Journal of Police and Criminal Psychology, 21*(2), 83–90.

Weiner, I.B., & Greene, R.L. (2008). *Handbook of personality assessment.* Hoboken, NJ: Wiley.

Weiss, P.A., Hitchcock, J.H., Weiss, W.U., Rostow, C., & Davis, R. (2008). The Personality Assessment Inventory borderline, drug, and alcohol scales as predictors of overall performance in police officers: A series of exploratory analyses. *Policing and Society, 18*, 301–310.

Weiss, P.A., Weiss, W.U., & Gacono, C.B. (2008). The use of the Rorschach in police psychology: Some preliminary thoughts. In C.B. Gacono & F.B Evans, (eds.) *The handbook of forensic Rorschach assessment* (pp. 527–542). New York: Routledge.

Weiss, W.U., Davis, R., Rostow, C., & Kinsman, S. (2003). The MMPI-2 L scale as a tool in police selection. *Journal of Police and Criminal Psychology, 18*(1), 57–60.

Weiss, W.U., Rostow, C., Davis, R., & Decoster-Martin, E. (2004). The Personality Assessment Inventory as a selection device for law enforcement personnel. *Journal of Police and Criminal Psychology, 19*(2), 23–29.

Weiss, W.U., Serafino, G., & Serafino, A. (2000). A study of the interrelationships of several validity scales used in police selection. *Journal of Police and Criminal Psychology, 15*(1) 41–44.

Weiss, W.U., Weiss, P.A., Cain, S., & Manley, B. (2009). Impression management in police officer candidacy on the MMPI-2. *Journal of Police and Criminal Psychology.*

Weiss, W.U., Zehner, S.N., Davis, R.D., Rostow, C., & Decoster-Martin, E. (2005). Problematic police performance and the Personality Assessment Inventory. *Journal of Police and Criminal Psychology, 20*(1), 16–21.

Yerkes, R.M., & Dodson, J. (1908). The relation of strength of stimulus to rapidity of habit forming. *Journal of Comparative Neurology and Psychology, 18*, 459–482.

Chapter 5

USE OF THE INWALD PERSONALITY INVENTORY, HILSON TESTS, AND INWALD SURVEYS FOR SELECTION, "FITNESS-FOR-DUTY" ASSESSMENT, AND RELATIONSHIP COUNSELING

ROBIN INWALD

The Inwald Personality Inventory (IPI) was the first comprehensive personality inventory to focus on admitted behavior patterns, such as drug and alcohol use, reckless driving behavior, and trouble with the law, as well as personality characteristics and clinical indicators of psychopathology (Inwald, 1982, 1988, 2008). Used by police psychologists and law enforcement/security departments as an industry standard and key component in the psychological evaluation of public safety officer candidates (U.S. Congress, 1990; Super, 2006), IPI prediction equations were developed to screen candidates in a number of high risk occupational groups (see Appendix A for IPI scale names). High IPI scale t-scores (usually those over 59t or 69t) point to areas of concern for psychologists to consider when evaluating individuals for public safety officer positions. One IPI-generated performance predictor, defined as the combination of more than 10 "IPI Critical Items" combined with a positive "Prediction of Termination" (based on a discriminant function analysis provided in the IPI results), has consistently identified "high risk" candidates (Inwald, 1988). Other predictions, such as Absence, Lateness and Disciplinary Actions also are included in IPI results. A benchmark for newer tests in the selection field, research on the IPI has demonstrated that it identifies antisocial behavior patterns and is a useful predictor of police and public safety officer job performance (Cortina et al., 1992, Detrick & Chibnall, 2002; Inwald et al., 1984, 2008; Ones et al., 1993; Mufson & Mufson, 1998; Scogin et al., 1995, Shusman et al., 1984, 1987).

Following the IPI, the Hilson Personnel Profile/Success Quotient (HPP/SQ) was the first published inventory focusing on characteristics associated with "emotional intelligence" (Inwald & Brobst, 1988). The Hilson Career Satisfaction Inventory (HCSI) was the first instrument developed specifically for police/public safety officer "fitness-for-duty" evaluations (Inwald & Kaufman, 1989). The Inwald Survey 5 (IS5) was developed to focus on integrity issues and antisocial attitudes/behaviors (Inwald & Gebbia, 1992), while the Hilson Safety/Security Risk Inventory (HSRI) was developed as an instrument focusing on risk-taking behavior and attitudes after police administrators expressed concerns about increased accidents and driving incidents involving officers (Inwald, 1995). The Inwald Survey 2 (IS2) was the first comprehensive inventory developed for employee selection and "fitness-for-duty" evaluations that focused on characteristics associated with violent behavior (Inwald et al., 1994). The Hilson Life Adjustment Profile (HLAP) was developed to focus on the identification of psychopathology, with additional scales measuring levels of social and family functioning to indicate its severity (Inwald, 1998).

These tests, along with the Hilson Background Investigation Inventory-Revised (HBI-R, a combination of the Inwald Survey 5-Revised [IS5R], IS2 and HSRI) and the Hilson Management Inventory (a combination of the HPP/SQ and the Hilson Management Survey, HMS) combine to form the Hilson Tests or various Hilson Test Batteries (Inwald et al., 1998). High t-scores (over 59t or 69t) for scales on all Hilson tests, with the exception of the HPP/SQ, HMS and HMI, suggest areas of potential difficulty for job candidates or incumbents. For the HPP/SQ, HMS and HMI, high scores are indicative of positive qualities, with low t-scores (below 40t or 30t) indicating possible lack of those described qualities. A detailed description of the rationale, development, and validation of the Hilson Tests is available in a recent publication (Inwald, 2008) and, therefore, is not within the scope of this chapter (see Appendix A for Hilson Test scale names).

The Inwald Research Relationship Surveys, including the Inwald Couples Compatibility Questionnaire (ICCQ), Inwald Partner's Personality Inventory (IPPI), Inwald Personality Survey (IPS), Inwald Attitude Survey (IAS) and Inwald Trauma Recovery Inventory (ITRI), are used for the purpose of public safety officer relationship assessment and couples counseling in employee assistance programs (Inwald, 2006). The IPS and IAS are derivatives of the HPP/SQ and IS5, respectively, and are used for self-assessment with regard to relationship issues. The ICCQ and IPPI are surveys completed by individuals about their partners/spouses. The ICCQ focuses on relationship compatibility while the IPPI focuses on the partner's behavior patterns that may negatively affect relationships, such as antisocial attitudes and substance abuse tendencies (see Appendix B for Inwald Research

Relationship Survey scale names and descriptions). These inventories were developed after a series of conferences sponsored by the FBI revealed that relationship problems are often the triggers for police officer suicides and violent behavior.

The Inwald Research Relationship Surveys are the first partner/spouse-oriented surveys to be developed for use as a "preventative" approach, providing actuarial relationship "checkups" to assist public safety officers (Inwald, 2007). An employee assistance counselor or family psychotherapist can interpret narrative results to couples, as well as comparative profile graphs, showing each individual how his/her admitted behavior patterns and personality characteristics may be affecting the relationship. Providing and explaining survey results with the aid of a tangible graph format to officers, who may be defensive about admitting to their shortcomings, can help them better understand how their behavior patterns might be improved. In addition, the therapist can use the visual documentation of the profiles, along with the printed individual item endorsements, to develop a treatment plan with the direct involvement of each couple. Finally, public safety agencies can offer the use of accessible online surveys, such as these relationship surveys, as a way to demonstrate their commitment to maintaining a preventative approach to domestic violence in police families.

Selected case studies are presented in this chapter that best demonstrate the use of this author's inventories for public safety officer selection and fitness for duty (the Hilson Tests/Batteries) as well as for self-development/relationship counseling in an employee assistance context (the Inwald Research Relationship Surveys). Guidelines for conducting selection, "fitness-for-duty," and other types of employee evaluations can be found in the appropriate chapters in this volume.

SELECTION AND "FITNESS-FOR-DUTY" CASES

Four Inwald Personality Inventory (IPI) Case Studies

Inwald Personality Inventory (IPI) Case 1

This public safety officer candidate was given the IPI along with other tests and an interview (see Figure 1). He was not recommended by the author for the job. Within five months, he was accepted by a large neighboring police department that did not administer the IPI. A few weeks before his hiring date, he became "deranged," attacked ten people in an office building and, after struggling with six officers called to the scene, died on the way to the hospital in police custody. His unusually high scores on Depression (DE), Anxiety (AN), Alcohol Use (AL), Drug Use (DG) and Family Conflicts (FC) should be noted. This individual also had a Prediction of Termination that, along with more than 10 Critical Items, is a standard marker for the prediction of poor job performance (Inwald, 1988). This combination of scores, indicating depression/anxiety along with substance abuse admissions, raises the possibility that this individual's unusual outburst represented a "suicide by cop" event (or that the person was actively suicidal and may have intentionally provoked the officers rather than committing suicide himself).

Inwald Personality Inventory (IPI) Case 2

This police officer candidate was evaluated using the IPI (see Figure 2) and was not recommended for employment by the author's staff. Several months later, he entered a police station, slammed a phone against the wall, tried to enter an off-limits area of the police station and then attacked an officer. His IPI profile is typical of the profiles found for 16 other officer candidates studied who later became violent, with Driving Violations (DV) as the highest score, followed by Trouble with the Law (TL).

Inwald Personality Inventory (IPI) Case 3

Five years after being hired, this public safety officer shot his son twice with a .25 caliber automatic and was charged with attempted murder. In his department, he also had been charged with using excessive force on the job, including menacing and fighting with a police officer. In reviewing his pre-employment IPI (see Figure 3), it can be seen that this officer's highest scores had been in the areas of admitted antisocial behavior patterns and attitudes, beginning with Antisocial Attitudes (AS), and followed by elevations on Driving Violations (DV), Substance Abuse (SA), Hyperactivity (HP) and Alcohol Use (AL). Again, the combination of admitted antisocial attitudes with antisocial behavior patterns (such as the admission here of excessive alcohol use) were predictive of serious adjustment problems for an officer candidate.

Inwald Personality Inventory (IPI) Case 4

This public safety officer's pre-employment screening evaluation revealed that he had been involved in a fistfight while in the service. After being hired, he later was charged with beating his wife. His pre-employment IPI (see

Figure 4) showed relative elevations on the Loner Type (LO) scale, followed by Guardedness (GD), Unusual Experiences (UE) and Driving Violations (DV). Based on other profiles studied after the occurrence of officer-involved domestic violence incidents, it has been this author's observation that limited social orientation (or a "Loner Type" personality) coupled with a lack of insight (GD) and some tendencies towards "road rage" (as may be implied by elevations on DV) help to identify people with limited social tools during times of stress or confrontation. It is these individuals who may be least suited for public safety work as they may tend to resort to violence as their primary way to handle conflict.

Four Hilson Personnel Profile/Success Quotient (HPP/SQ) Cases of Public Safety/Security Candidates/Personnel

Hilson Personnel Profile/Success Quotient (HPP/SQ) Case 1

A successful public safety administrator completed the HPP/SQ (see Figure 5). Note that both his Social Ability (SA) and Initiative (IN) scales are elevated over 59t. In addition, Popularity (PO) and Sensitivity (SE) content area scores are over 69t (see Figure 6). As frequently found for successful managers, the high scores on these scales suggest the presence of excellent communication skills and social sensitivity.

Hilson Personnel Profile/Success Quotient (HPP/SQ) Case 2

A juvenile detention officer who was rated as "excellent" by his supervisor completed the HPP/SQ. His supervisor also described him as the "one person I'd want to back me up in a crisis" and as someone who knows how to handle difficult adolescents. Note that this individual's SA scale is above 69t (see Figure 7). He shows strong work ethic on Anxiety about Organization (AX) as well (60t – see Figure 8).

Hilson Personnel Profile/Success Quotient (HPP/SQ) Case 3

An applicant who had been ranked as the best of four candidates for Assistant State Police Chief completed the HPP/SQ. His scores over 59t on four of the five HPP/SQ scales (see Figure 9) as well as elevations on five of the ten HPP/SQ content areas suggest a candid (Candor – CA at 67t), charismatic personality (PO at 69t – see Figure 10), with competitive drive (Competitive Spirit – CO at 70t) and strong work orientation (IN at 67t).

Hilson Personnel Profile/Success Quotient (HPP/SQ) Case 4

The director of security of a large bank completed the HPP/SQ. He admitted that he is "burned-out" now and that he would have "answered the questions differently ten years ago." While candor (CA at 70t – see Figure 11) and social skills (see PO and SE on Figure 12) are his relative strengths, his initiative (IN) is very low by comparison.

Two Hilson Test Battery Case Studies

Hilson Test Battery for Fitness-for-Duty Evaluation–Case Study 1

A Hilson Test Battery for Public Safety Officer Fitness-for-Duty Evaluation (see Figures 13 to 19) was completed by a 23-year-old Caucasian male police officer prior to his interview with the police psychologist for a "fitness-for-duty" assessment. Tests taken included the Hilson Career Satisfaction Index (HCSI), Hilson Life Adjustment Profile (HLAP), Inwald Survey 5 (IS5 – note that this test version, now replaced with the IS5-R, does not contain the newest scale focusing on domestic violence issues, Domestic Concerns [DC]), Inwald Survey 2 (IS2) and Hilson Personnel Profile/Success Quotient (HPP/SQ). This candidate had been removed from duty after his department received a call from his girlfriend charging him with slapping and threatening her. The officer was undergoing this assessment in order to regain his position in the department. Without a "pass" on the fitness-for-duty evaluation from the police psychologist, this officer would not be able to return to duty.

The psychologist called the author for a consultation on the results since he was concerned about the fact that a different police psychologist had "passed" this individual during the pre-employment screening phase and had given him at least one of the Hilson Research tests at that time, the Inwald Personality Inventory (IPI). These original IPI test results were not made available to the evaluating psychologist and he wished to interpret the current test results in as accurate a manner as possible. Other than the negative report from this officer's girlfriend, the officer had shown no other indications of interpersonal adjustment difficulties or any evidence of job adjustment difficulties since he had been working for this department.

When reviewing the HCSI results (see Figures 2–3), it can be seen that the Excusing Attitudes (EA) scale is elevated on both the standard and promotional norms graphs (66t and 70 t, respectively). This, along with the slight elevation on the Defensiveness (DN) scale, similar to the Candor (CA) scale of the HPP/SQ, suggests a defensive individual who has difficulty admitting his limitations/shortcomings and also believes that it is acceptable to break rules. Although not clinically elevated (over 60t), the Anger Patterns (AP) score is the third highest score, suggesting that had this officer not answered the test questions in a defensive manner, he may have shown significant anger control problems compared with other officers tested.

The HLAP shows slight elevations on the Concerns about Health (CH) and Obsessive-Compulsive Personality (OC) scales. Some evidence of stress symptoms and a tendency to become obsessive over details is indicated by these results. The IS5 results include an elevation of the Work Efforts Concerns (WE) scale as well as elevations on Lack of Insight/Candor (LC) and Lack of Sensitivity (LS). This combination suggests that this person may lack judgment and social sensitivity related to relationships at work and should be evaluated in conjunction with results on the HPP/SQ to determine if there is consistency between these two test results. The IS2 shows the unusually high t-score of 88 on Firearms Interest (FI) and a t-score of 69 on Reckless Driving/Safety Patterns-RD. This pattern matches the profile related to poor job performance and serious adjustment difficulties, including other profiles where officers have engaged in non-job-related violent behavior.

Finally, although the HPP/SQ main scales are typical for a police candidate, the Content Areas show a profile that suggests future job performance difficulties. First, it can be seen that Extroversion (EX) is higher than Popularity (PO). This indicates that the person may "try too hard" and may not be as well-liked as he is extroverted. Although this individual's scores on this test indicate good work ethic, drive and self confidence, the t-score of 70 on the Sensitivity (SE) scale raises concerns and is similar to the scores of some working public safety officers who have serious performance problems. This person's oversensitivity to social rejection or criticism may result in overreactions that are inappropriate and dangerous.

Assuming that the department's investigation can verify the truthfulness of the report of physical abuse filed by his girlfriend, it is not recommended that this individual continue in the position of police officer at this time. This recommendation is made based on a comprehensive test battery whose results are similar to those of other officers who have demonstrated serious adjustment difficulties and problems serving as a law enforcement officers. While the pattern of test results raising concern on this Hilson Research Test Battery may not have been noted previously, recent evidence suggests that this battery presents a "high risk" profile compared to those of successful public safety officers tested.

Hilson Test Battery for Pre-Employment Selection—Case Study 2

The full Hilson Test Battery for Public Safety Officer Screening (see Figures 20 to 28) were completed by a 32-year-old Caucasian male police officer candidate prior to his interview with the police psychologist at the post-conditional offer phase of the pre- employment process. These tests included the IPI, HLAP, HBIR, and HMI. This candidate had "passed" the standard background investigation and the police psychologist was "leaning towards passing him" on the psychological. The department he had applied to was interested in hiring him, provided that the psychologist "OK'd" him after the psychological interview. The psychologist called the author for a consultation on the results since he was concerned about the fact that his office manager had complained that she had found the candidate to be "nervous and creepy" while sitting in the office with her. She told the psychologist that she had overheard a negative interaction between the candidate and his wife, who was sitting outside in their car, and had a poor impression of the applicant.

In interview, it was discovered that this individual had come from a troubled home where he had lived with friends, dropped out of school and ran away from home after being raised by different relatives. At the age of 23, he was charged with driving with a suspended license. He had been picked up by the police after they discovered three guns and a knife in his car. Despite this unstable background, both the department and the psychologist had a generally positive impression of this candidate.

When reviewing the IPI results (see Figures 9–10), it can be seen that the candidate was predicted to be terminated (discriminant function equations) and also had 10 Critical Items. The recommended "cut point," based on the occurrence of a "hit" for termination and more than 10 Critical Items, was missed by only one Critical Item here, making this a borderline IPI result (or close to a "high risk IPI" for hiring). It is interesting to note the relative elevations on the IPI profile graph. The highest scale is Driving Violations (DV), matching the profile of the violent officers in Figure 1. With the second high scores of Trouble with the Law (TL) and Depression (DE), there is concern that this person might be both depressed and impulsive. While there are no "terrorist" profiles on the IPI to date, the combination of chronic depression and recklessness seems more likely to lead to potential trouble than other profiles.

The HLAP for this individual (Figure 11) shows relative elevations on the Low Activity Level (LV) and Lack of Satisfaction with Life (SL) scales, suggesting lack of activities/hobbies or other pursuits compared with others tested along with a general dissatisfaction with life. This profile corroborates the IPI regarding the possibility of depression. There are no unusual elevations on the HBIR (Figures 12–14), but both Candor (CA) and Sensitivity (SE) are less than 60t on the HMI's Hilson Personnel Profile/Success Quotient (HPP/SQ). This is coupled with the low score on Self Worth (SW = 40t) and the relatively low score on the Hilson Management Inventory's Admission of Shortcomings (AD) score. The HPP/SQ and HMS profiles suggest that this person may tend to be insensitive socially, may not know his own limits and has low self esteem. Based on these results and the results of the study of other candidates who later have performed poorly, this individual was not recommended for hire by the psychologist. The office manager's view that he was "nervous and creepy" was a helpful verification of the more subtle, yet troublesome, scores on the Hilson Test Battery.

EMPLOYEE ASSISTANCE COUNSELING CASE

Inwald Research Relationship Surveys–Couple Case Study

The Inwald Research Relationship Surveys were administered to a 28-year-old male public safety officer, Jeff, and his live-in girlfriend, Rita, a 36-year-old public safety officer in the same agency. Instruments completed included the Inwald Couples Compatibility Inventory (ICCQ), Inwald Partner's Personality Inventory (IPPI), Inwald Personality Survey (IPS), and Inwald Attitude Survey (IAS). These two officers began counseling due to admitted problems in their relationship, such as arguments over money. They received their voluntary referral to the psychologist after they requested counseling through the Employee Assistance Program (EAP) provided by their department. The psychologist reported that there were clear class and background differences that were contributing to their difficulties in getting along. Rita was described as a middle-class woman, whose father was a member of the clergy. In contrast, Jeff's father had been incarcerated and his mother had a known substance abuse problem. Rita was described as thoughtful and rigid, while Jeff was described by the psychologist as "loose about things" and a person who tended not to "think in advance and learn about mistakes he's made and their consequences." After one year of therapy, the couple still was living together and the therapist reported that Rita had "toned down her opinions" and Jeff was "more thoughtful, using self-talk" to control his anger. The psychologist reported that Rita and Jeff were proud of each other's accomplishments at work and were not jealous of each other. However, he felt that Jeff needed to learn to control his expressions of anger better in the relationship.

On the Inwald Couples Compatibility Quotient (ICCQ - see Figure 29), Jeff described his relationship with Rita as having difficulties in all areas tested (t-score of 40 on Bottom Line – BL), except for Social Compatibility (SN) and Lack of Jealous Behavior (JE – see Figure 30). It should be noted that low scores on the ICCQ suggest the presence of difficulties in the tested areas. Jeff was particularly concerned about his lack of background compatibility with Rita (low BC score), financial compatibility (low FD score) and his partner's lack of temper control (low TE t-score of 20). Rita's ICCQ showed a greater overall satisfaction with the relationship (BL t-score of 60 – see Figure 31), with similar concerns about lack of background compatibility (BC), and some relative concerns about Jeff's controlling behavior (CB) and lack of temper control (TE t-score of 50).

On the Inwald Partners Personality Inventory (IPPI), where high scores suggest a partner's difficulties in tested areas, Jeff's responses suggest that he believed Rita had a history of legal problems (LP) and past employment problems (EP – see Figure 33). Rita's IPPI relating to Jeff also suggests that he had some legal difficulties (LP – see Figure 34). This may be the result of several endorsed individual items indicating that this couple had difficulties with their finances and with bill collectors.

On the Inwald Personality Survey (IPS – see Figure 35), Jeff showed strong empathy and interest in helping others (Empathy – EM) as well as excellent academic ability (Academic Interest – AI). It should be noted that high IPS scores suggest positive characteristics. Average social skills were shown here with limited interest in gaining the social approval of others (Social Approval Concerns – SC) and lower, though average, willingness to admit faults (Admission of Faults – AF). Not overly driven, Jeff showed average self-confidence (SB) and average willingness to make extra efforts to meet his responsibilities (Effort towards Responsibilities – ER).

Rita's IPS suggests that she was willing to admit her faults more readily than Jeff (high AF score – see Figure 36). She, too, showed a strong interest in helping others (EM). Unlike Jeff, she was not academically inclined (low AI score), showed average social skills, but above average self-confidence (SB). Not driven to work excessively (EF), Rita showed limited concerns about meeting her responsibilities (SR t-score of 34) and admitted to procrastinating more than most people (TR t-score of 24).

On the Inwald Attitude Survey (IAS), where high scores suggest antisocial behavioral tendencies, Jeff's profile showed no t-score elevations over 59 (see Figure 37). Likewise, Rita's profile was similar, with no elevations indicating antisocial difficulties (see Figure 38). Since these were two working public safety officers attending therapy sessions due to an interest in maintaining their relationship, "clear" IAS profiles (containing few individual scale elevations) were expected.

Finally, each of the Inwald Research Relationship Survey reports contains a set of Critical Items that provide counselors with specific items for follow up. A sample of one of Jeff's ICCQ pages, showing some of his endorsed critical items regarding his relationship with Rita, is found on Figure 39. With these, and other endorsed items on the surveys, the therapist/counselor can begin to work with couples using their own words and statements as points for discussion and problem resolution. In this case, the need for an anger management program was suggested by survey results and its need later was verified by the treating psychologist.

In summary, the tests described in this chapter have proved useful for screening out troubled job candidates, not predicted to perform well in public safety officer positions, as well as for assisting working officers in the maintenance of key relationships that help to sustain them at home and in their careers.

Personality Assessment in Police Psychology

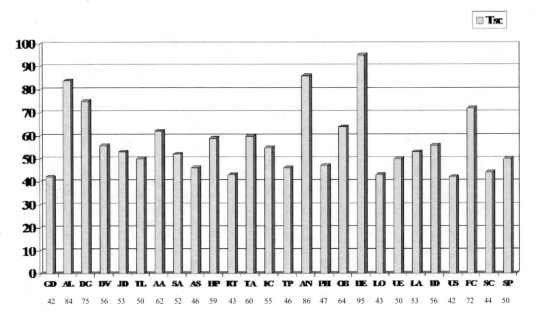

Figure 1. Inwald Personality Inventory (IPI) Profile for Violent Police Officer Candidate.

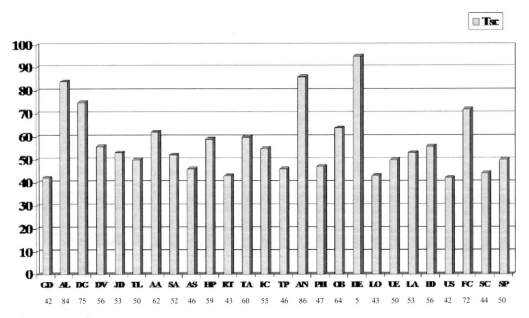

Figure 2. IPI Profile for Rejected Police Officer Candidate who Attacked Police Officer.

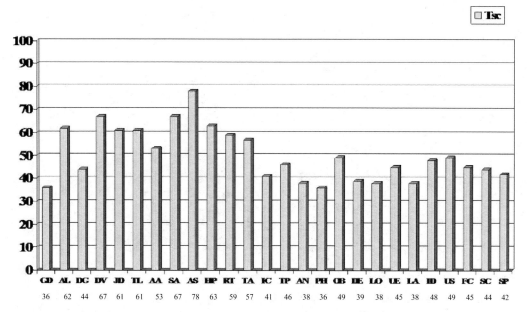

GD	AL	DG	DV	JD	TL	AA	SA	AS	HP	RT	TA	IC	TP	AN	PH	OB	DE	LO	UE	LA	ID	US	FC	SC	SP
36	62	44	67	61	61	53	67	78	63	59	57	41	46	38	36	49	39	38	45	38	48	49	45	44	42

Figure 3. IPI Profile for Public Safety Officer Charged with Attempted Murder of his Son.

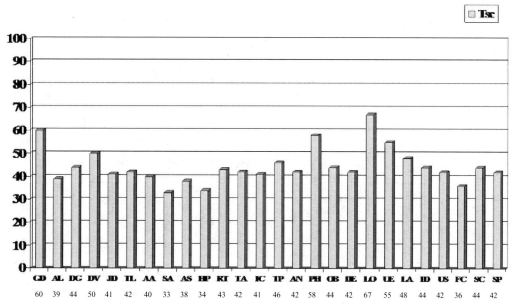

GD	AL	DG	DV	JD	TL	AA	SA	AS	HP	RT	TA	IC	TP	AN	PH	OB	DE	LO	UE	LA	ID	US	FC	SC	SP
60	39	44	50	41	42	40	33	38	34	43	42	41	46	42	58	44	42	67	55	48	44	42	36	44	42

Figure 4. IPI Profile Graph for Public Safety Officer Charged with Beating his Wife.

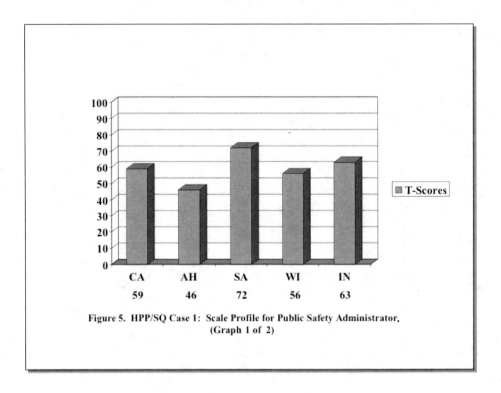

Figure 5. HPP/SQ Case 1: Scale Profile for Public Safety Administrator.
(Graph 1 of 2)

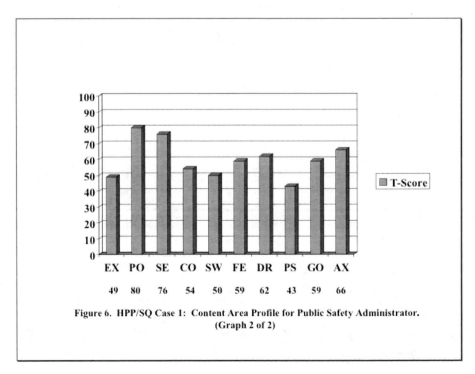

Figure 6. HPP/SQ Case 1: Content Area Profile for Public Safety Administrator.
(Graph 2 of 2)

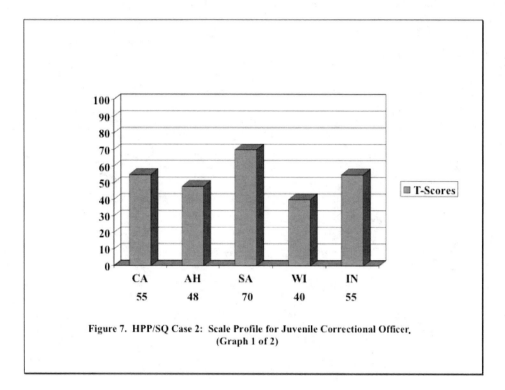

Figure 7. HPP/SQ Case 2: Scale Profile for Juvenile Correctional Officer.
(Graph 1 of 2)

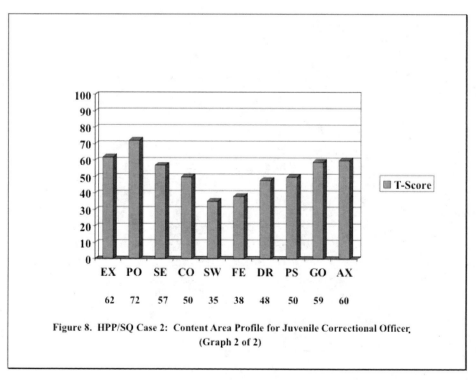

Figure 8. HPP/SQ Case 2: Content Area Profile for Juvenile Correctional Officer.
(Graph 2 of 2)

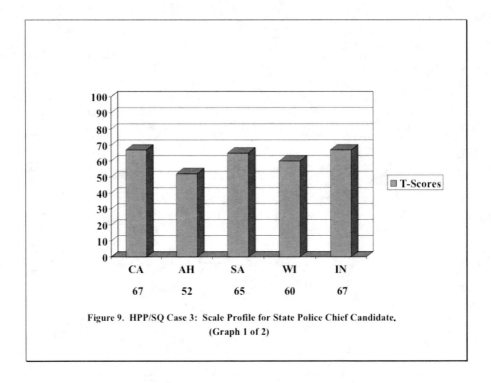

Figure 9. HPP/SQ Case 3: Scale Profile for State Police Chief Candidate.
(Graph 1 of 2)

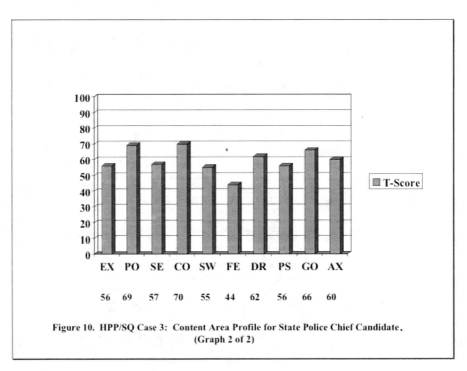

Figure 10. HPP/SQ Case 3: Content Area Profile for State Police Chief Candidate.
(Graph 2 of 2)

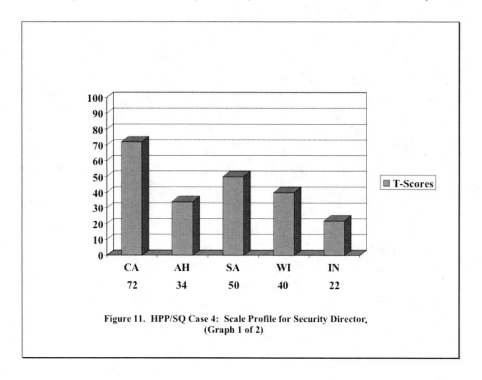

Figure 11. HPP/SQ Case 4: Scale Profile for Security Director.
(Graph 1 of 2)

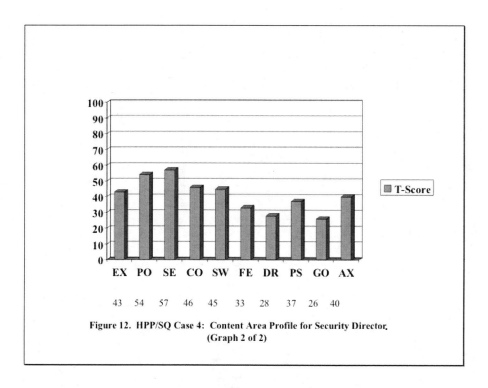

Figure 12. HPP/SQ Case 4: Content Area Profile for Security Director.
(Graph 2 of 2)

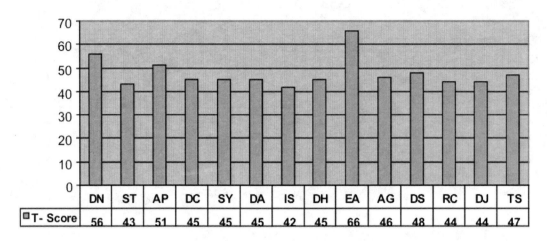

Figure 13. Hilson Career Satisfaction Inventory (HCSI) for Case Study 1.

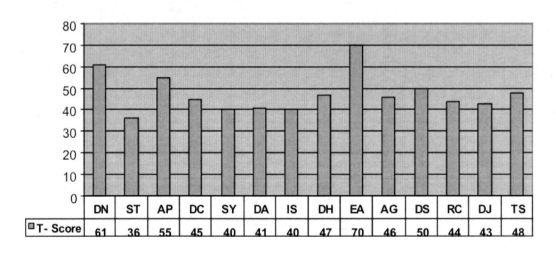

Figure 14. Hilson Career Satisfaction Inventory (HCSI) Promotional Norms for Case Study 1.

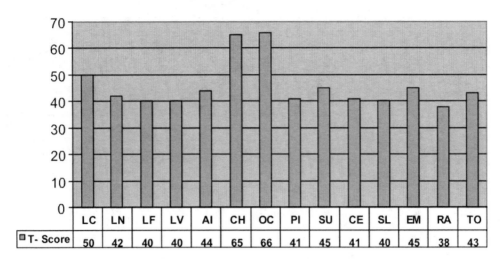

Figure 15. Hilson Life Adjustment Profile (HLAP) for Case Study 1.

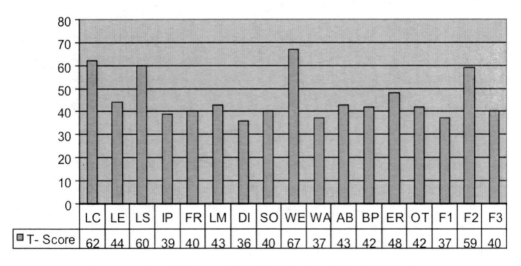

Figure 16. Inwald Survey 5 (IS5) Profile Graph for Case Study 1.

Inwald Survey 2 (IS2) - Case Study 1

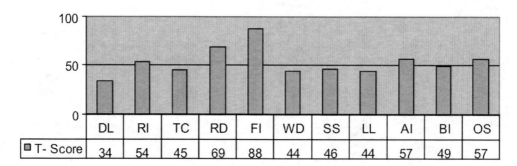

	DL	RI	TC	RD	FI	WD	SS	LL	AI	BI	OS
▣ T- Score	34	54	45	69	88	44	46	44	57	49	57

Figure 17. Inwald Survey 2 (IS2) Profile Graph for Case Study 1.

Hilson Personnel Profile/Success Quotient - HPP/SQ for Case Study 1

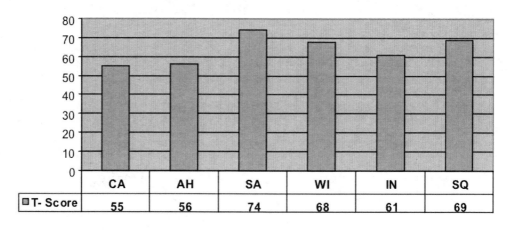

	CA	AH	SA	WI	IN	SQ
▣ T- Score	55	56	74	68	61	69

Figure 18. Hilson Personnel Profile/Success Quotient (HPP/SQ) for Case Study 1.

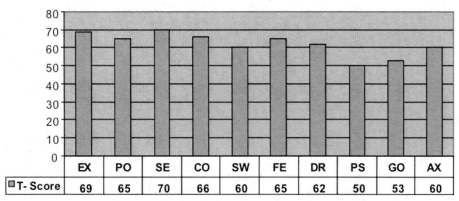

Figure 19. Hilson Personnel Profile/Success Quotient (HPP/SQ)
Content Areas for Case Study 1.

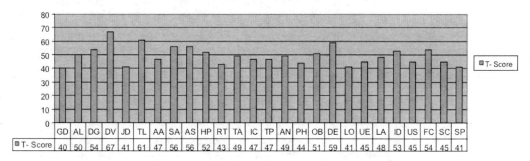

Figure 20. Inwald Personality Inventory (IPI) Graph for Case Study 2.

Critical Items for IPI for Follow-up Evaluation, Case 2

Critical Item Total = 10 T-Score = 56

Predictions of Performance (all present)

Prediction of Absence – greater than 3 times
Prediction of Disciplinary Actions
Prediction of Termination

Figure 21. IPI Critical Items Total for Follow-up Evaluation of Case Study 2.

Hilson Life Adjustment Profile (HLAP) for Case Study 2

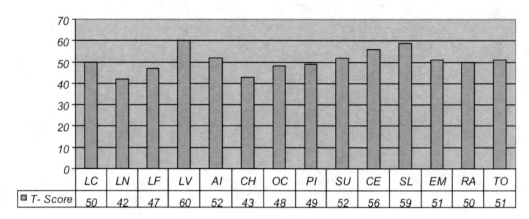

T- Score	LC	LN	LF	LV	AI	CH	OC	PI	SU	CE	SL	EM	RA	TO
	50	42	47	60	52	43	48	49	52	56	59	51	50	51

Figure 22. Hilson Life Adjustment Profile (HLAP) for Case Study 2.

Inwald Survey 5 (IS5) Profile Graph of the Hilson Background Investigation Inventory (HBI-R) for Case Study 2

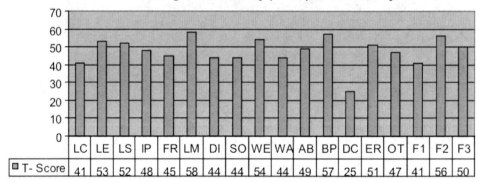

T- Score	LC	LE	LS	IP	FR	LM	DI	SO	WE	WA	AB	BP	DC	ER	OT	F1	F2	F3
	41	53	52	48	45	58	44	44	54	44	49	57	25	51	47	41	56	50

Figure 23. Inwald Survey 5 (IS5) Profile Graph for the Hilson Background Investigation Inventory (HBIR) for Case Study 2.

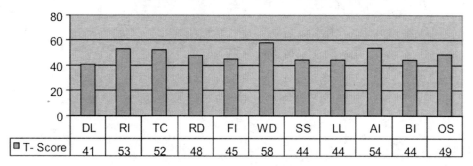

Figure 24. Inwald Survey 2 (IS2) Profile Graph of the Hilson Background Investigation Inventory (HBIR) for Case Study 2.

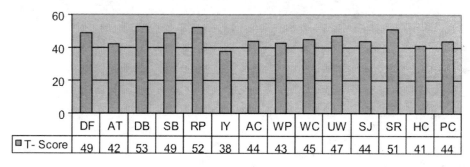

Figure 25. Hilson Safety/Security Risk Inventory (HSRI) Profile Graph of the Hilson Background Investigation Inventory (HBI-R) for Cast Study 2.

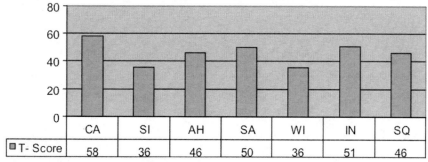

Figure 26. Hilson Personnel Profile/Success Quotient (HPP/SQ) Scales from the Hilson Management Inventory (HMI) for Case Study 2.

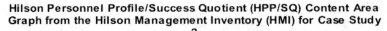

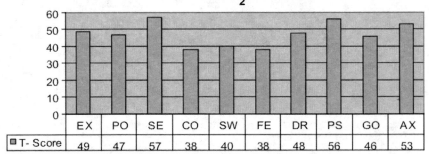

Figure 27. Hilson Personnel Profile/Success Quotient (HPP/SQ) Content Area Graph from the Hilson Management Inventory (HMI) for Case Study 2.

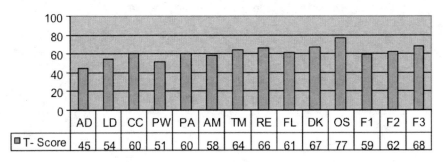

Figure 28. Hilson Management Survey (HMS) Graph for Case Study 2.

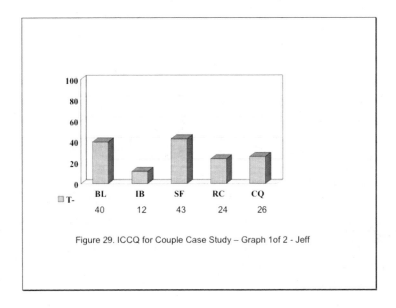

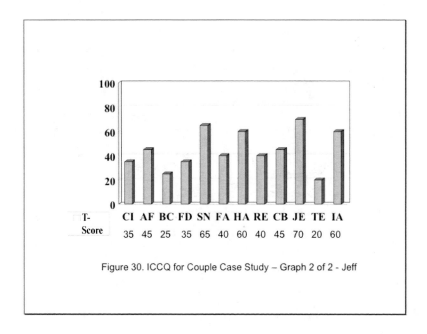

Figure 30. ICCQ for Couple Case Study – Graph 2 of 2 - Jeff

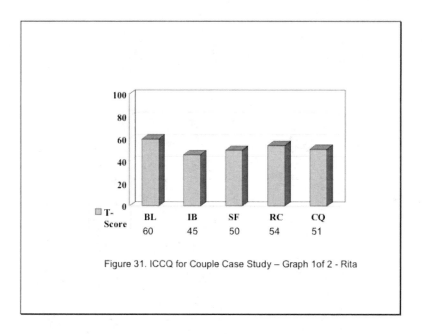

Figure 31. ICCQ for Couple Case Study – Graph 1of 2 - Rita

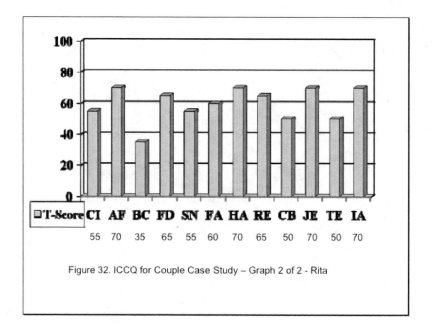

Figure 32. ICCQ for Couple Case Study – Graph 2 of 2 - Rita

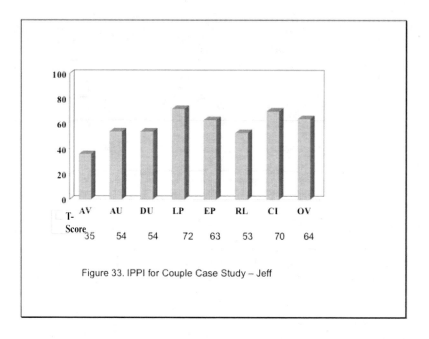

Figure 33. IPPI for Couple Case Study – Jeff

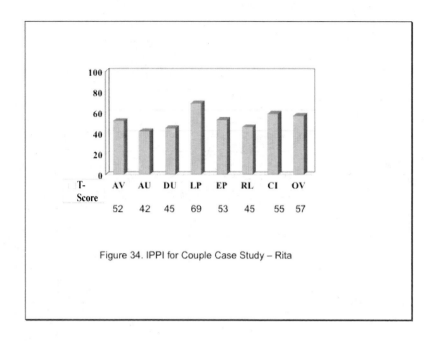

Figure 34. IPPI for Couple Case Study – Rita

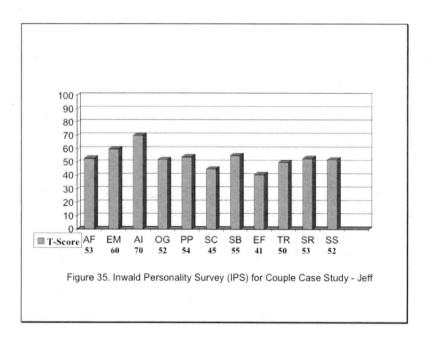

Figure 35. Inwald Personality Survey (IPS) for Couple Case Study - Jeff

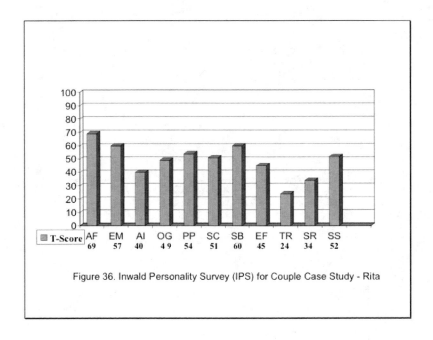

Figure 36. Inwald Personality Survey (IPS) for Couple Case Study - Rita

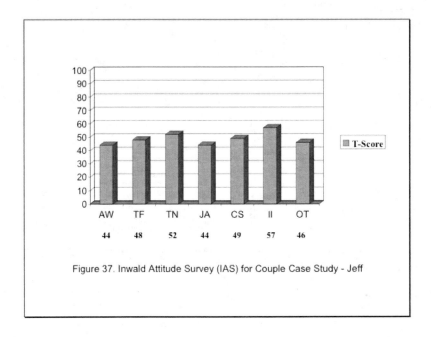

Figure 37. Inwald Attitude Survey (IAS) for Couple Case Study - Jeff

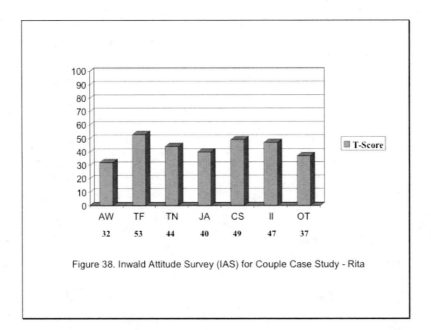

Figure 38. Inwald Attitude Survey (IAS) for Couple Case Study - Rita

---

117. I believe that he/she respects my opinion most of the time.   (F)

124. I think that he/she speaks nicely to me at least 80% of the time. (F)

141. Sometimes I have felt that he/she punishes me with his/her moods. (T)

22. I think that I only will be able to live happily with this person if he/she makes some major changes. (T)

137. I think about the possibility of breaking off with this relationship at least once a month. (T)

Critical Item Total = 20   T-score = 65

Figure 39. ICCQ Selected Critical Items for Couple Case Study - Jeff

Appendix A

IPI SCALE NAMES

Inwald Personality Inventory (IPI)

26 Scales

Guardedness-GD
Rigid Type-RT
Alcohol Use-AL
Drug Use-DG
Substance Abuse-SA
Driving Violations-DV
Job Difficulties-JD
Trouble with Law & Society-TL
Antisocial Attitudes-AS
Hyperactivity-HP
Absence Abuse-AA
Illness Concerns-IC
Treatment Programs-TP
Anxiety-AN Type "A"-TA
Phobic Personality-PH
Lack of Assertiveness-LA
Obsessive Personality-OB
Depression-DE
Loner Type-LO
Interpersonal Difficulties-ID
Family Conflicts-FC
Sexual Concerns-SC
Spouse/Mate Concerns-SP
Undue Suspiciousness-US
Unusual Experiences/Thoughts-UE

Hilson Management Inventory (HMI)

Including the HPP/SQ and HMS
31 Scales

Hilson Personnel Profile/Success Quotient (HPP/SQ)

Candor-CA
Sales Interest-SI
Achievement History-AH
Social Ability-SA
"Winners Image"-WI
Initiative-IN
Extroversion-EX
Popularity/"Charisma"-PO
Sensitivity-SE
Competitive Spirit-CO
Self Worth-SW
Family Achievement History-FE
Drive-DR
Preparation Style-PS
Goal Orientation-GO
Anxiety about Organization-AX
Success Quotient-SQ

Hilson Management Survey (HMS)

Admission of Shortcomings-AD
Leadership-LD
Coaching/Counseling Orientation-CC
Positive Work Attitudes-PW
Performance Appraisal Ability-PA
Assertive Management Style-AM
Teamwork Orientation-TM
Realistic Expectations of Others-RE
Flexibility-FL
Delegation Skills-DK
Overall Score-OS
Factor 1: Leadership Potential-F1
Factor 2: Employee Performance Mgmt Skills-F2
Factor 3: Team-Oriented Style-F3

Hilson Background Investigation Inventory - Revised (HBI-R)
Including the IS5-R, IS2, and HSRI
43 scales

Inwald Survey 5- Revised (IS5-R)

Lack of Insight/Candor-LC
Leadership Avoidance-LE
Lack of Sensitivity-LS
Introverted Personality Style-IP
Frustration/Anger Patterns-FR
Lack of Competitive Motivation-LM
Distrust of Others-DI
Total Score: Lack of Service
Orientation-SO
Work Effort Concerns-WE
Work Adjustment Difficulties-WA
Attitudes: Antisocial Behaviors-AB
Behavior Patterns: Integrity Concerns-BP
Total Score: Lack of Employee Reliability-ER
Factor 1: Lack of Conscientiousness/
Reliability-F1
Factor 2: Lack of Work Ethic-F2
Factor 3: Lack of Social Initiative-F3
Overall Total Score-OT
Domestic Concerns-DC

Inwald Survey 2 (IS2)

Denial of Shortcomings-DL
Risk-Taking/Reckless Behavior-RI
Lack of Temper Control-TC
Reckless Driving/Safety Patterns-RD
Firearms Interest-FI
Work Difficulties-WD
Lack of Social Sensitivity-SS
Lack of Leadership Interest-LL
Attitudes: Antisocial Behaviors-A1
Behavior Patterns: Integrity Concerns-B1
IS2 Overall Score-OS

Hilson Safety/Security Risk Inventory (HSRI)

Preparation Concerns-PC
Defensive Responses: Validity Style-DF
Lack of Work Ethic Concerns-WC
Undue Worry-UW
Lack of Social Judgment-SJ
Safety Risk-SR
Safety Attitudes-AT
Driving Behaviors-DB
Safety Behaviors-SB
Risk-Taking Patterns-RP
Lack of Hostility Control-HC
Lack of Integrity Concerns-IY

Hilson Career Satisfaction Inventory (HCSI)

14 Scales

Defensiveness-DN
Stress Patterns-ST
Stress Symptoms-SY
Drug/Alcohol Abuse-DA
Lack of Interpersonal Support-IS
Anger/Hostility Patterns-AP
Disciplinary History-DH
Excusing Attitudes-EA
Aggression/Hostility-AG
Dissatisfaction with Career-DC
Dissatisfaction with Supervisor-DS
Relationship with Co-workers-RC
Dissatisfaction with Job-DJ
Total Score on the HCSI-TS

Hilson Life Adjustment Profile (HLAP)

14 Scales

Lack of Candor-LC
Lack of Social Network-LN
Lack of Family Support-LF
Low Activity Level-LV
Anxiety-AI
Concerns about Health-CH
Obsessive-Compulsive Personality-OC
Paranoid Ideation-PI
Suicidal/Depressive Thoughts-SU
Critical Events-CE
Lack of Satisfaction with Life-SL
Factor 1: Emotional Adjustment
Difficulties/ Psychopathology-EM
Factor2: Recent Activity Level/
General Functioning-RA
HLAP Total Score-TO

Appendix B

INWALD RESEARCH RELATIONSHIP SURVEYS –
SCALE DESCRIPTIONS

Inwald Couples Compatibility Questionnaire (ICCQ) Scale Descriptions

Interests/Background Compatibility (IB = CI + AF + BC + FD)

Interests Compatibility - CI
Identifies compatibility in the area of common interests such as hobbies, shared activities, time spent together, daily routines, and friends. Elevated scores indicate that, as far as the person answering the questionnaire is concerned, there is compatibility in this area.

Affection/Physical Compatibility - AF
Identifies the level of physical attraction the person answering this questionnaire feels towards his/her mate. High scores also measure the level of satisfaction with affection received from the other person. Low scores suggest that there may not be as much affection and/or physical attraction in the relationship as the person answering the questionnaire would like.

Background Compatibility - BC
Identifies cultural, political, religious and age similarities for this couple. High scores suggest that both people in this relationship come from similar backgrounds and age groups. Low scores suggest potential difficulties in the relationship based on different cultural, religious, and/or political backgrounds.

Financial/Functional Compatibility - FD
Identifies areas of conflict regarding financial matters, including concerns that the other person in the relationship has had financial difficulties and/or career problems that have caused difficulties for the couple.

Social/Family Compatibility (SF = SN + FA)

Social Network Compatibility - SN
Identifies the compatibility of this couple with regard to each member's friends and social network. Low scores suggest that there are serious concerns about the other person's friends and/or the amount of time spent socializing with them.

Family Compatibility - FA

Identifies the compatibility of this couple with regard to family members. Low scores suggest that there are problems getting along with certain relatives and/or concerns about this relationship by relatives that may be a source of conflict for this couple.

Relationship Compatibility ($RC = HA + RE + CB + JE + TE + IA$)

Habits/Issues Compatibility - HA

Designed to measure concerns about the other person's habits, such as use of alcohol, drugs, personal care, and overeating. Low scores suggest that some habitual behaviors of this nature may be causing friction in the relationship.

Respectful Treatment - RE

Scale results indicate whether or not the person answering this questionnaire believes that his/her mate is respectful and sensitive. High scores suggest that there are concerns about the way he/she is treated by the other person.

Lack of Over-Controlling Behavior - CB

Identifies the presence of over-controlling behavior on the part of the other person. Low scores suggest problems in the relationship due to the other person's overly critical, moody, or assertive nature.

Lack of Jealousy - JE

Documents a pattern of jealous behavior on the part of the other person. A low score on this scale indicates that jealous behavior is causing some discomfort for the person answering this questionnaire.

Temper Control - TE

Measures concerns about the other person's ability to control his/her temper. Low scores indicate that the other person may tend to overreact, may lose his/her temper, and may be unpleasant and complaining when there are conflicts in the relationship.

Interpersonal Assertiveness - IA

Documents the respondent's concerns regarding the other person's level of assertiveness. Low scores suggest that the respondent believes his/her partner lacks assertiveness and may let others take advantage of situations.

Bottom Line Summary - BL

Identifies doubts or insecurities about the relationship. Serious differences about the level of commitment or staying together may be expressed. Low scores suggest that the person answering the questionnaire is unsure about the other person and the possibility of a future together.

Compatibility Quotient - CQ

The Compatibility Quotient is the total score that indicates overall compatibility in the relationship. High scores suggest high compatibility in most areas for this couple.

Inwald Partners Personality Inventory (IPPI) Scale Descriptions

Avoidance of Criticism (AV)

A high score on this scale indicates that the test-taker believes his/her partner often is not candid about feelings and behaviors. He/she feels that this partner has limited insight and judgment about personal shortcomings. Individuals with high scores feel their partners may tend to give "socially-acceptable" responses to questions.

Alcohol Use Patterns (AU)

High scores suggest that the test-taker believes his/her partner has been a habitual user of alcohol.

Drug Use Patterns (DU)

A positive score indicates that the test-taker believes his/her partner has some admitted use of drugs. A high score indicates the partner may be a habitual drug user.

Legal Problems (LP)

A high score on this scale indicates the test-taker believes his/her partner has had a history of brushes with the law and/or with societal norms. This may include arrests and/or convictions.

Employment Problems (EP)

A high score on this scale indicates the test-taker believes his/her partner has had difficulties holding a job. The partner may have had a spotty employment record and may have a history of interpersonal difficulties at work.

Reliability (RL)

A high score here indicates that the test-taker believes his/her partner has a tendency to contract minor illnesses that may keep the partner from working. The partner also may have difficulty meeting job responsibilities and may have a history of abusing sick leave privileges at work.

Critical Items (CI)

A list of critical items for further evaluation and discussion.

Overall Score (OV)

A combination of all IPPI scales measuring overall potential for difficulties in relationships due to a lack of "conscientiousness" and/or the presence of antisocial behavior patterns. High scores are suggestive of such patterns.

Inwald Personality Survey (IPS) Scale Descriptions

Admission of Faults (AF)

Measures degree of defensive responding on this survey. Low scores suggest a desire to appear unusually virtuous and without fault. Low scores on this scale indicate that the other test scores may be inflated due to "socially-desirable" responses.

Empathy/Helping Others (EM)

Individuals with high scores on this scale may be skilled in counseling and coaching others. Such individuals enjoy making suggestions and giving people advice regarding their problems and/or goals.

Academic Interest/New Skills Development (AI)

Measures achievement in past jobs and school. High scores suggest excellence in academic/work history as well as past recognition for special skills and/or talents. General level of academic ability may be reflected in this scale.

SA - Social Ability Content Areas (OG, PP, SC)

"Out-going" Personality (OG)

Measures tendency to be "outgoing" and talkative. High scores suggest an extroverted, "outer-directed" individual.

Popularity with Peers (PP)

Measures degree of "popularity" this person has enjoyed in the past. High scores suggest a charismatic individual who is well-liked by others and may have been frequently chosen as a leader or spokesperson.

Social Approval Concerns (SC)

Measures degree of sensitivity regarding social approval. High scorers are particularly aware of how their behavior is being judged by others and strive to gain other peoples' approval. High scorers may become upset when they feel they have said the "wrong thing" or hurt someone else's feelings.

Self-Belief (SB)

Measures self-confidence and general sense of mastery over obstacles in the world. High scorers are sure of themselves and feel they can do most things well.

IN - Initiative Content Areas (EF, TR, SR)

Effort towards Responsibilities (EF)
Measures the tendency to "go the extra mile" and strive for completion of tasks and excellence. High scorers may tend to work harder than their peers and may demonstrate qualities of "workaholism." They may also show the ability to focus or concentrate on tasks for long periods of time.

Timeliness about Responsibilities (TR)
Measures the tendency to avoid procrastination. High scorers tend to complete work on time, to organize work when it is assigned, and to meet responsibilities in a timely fashion. Low scorers may complete their work on or close to schedule, but they tend to put it off until the last minute.

Sensitivity about Responsibilities (SR)
Measures level of concern regarding completing assigned tasks in a correct and/or timely manner. Anxiety over incomplete or unsatisfactory work is common for high scorers, who try to meet responsibilities so that they will not feel guilty or pressured.

Adaptability Quotient (AQ) Total Score
Measures potential for "success" and "emotional intelligence." High scores on the combination of all IPS scales suggest higher overall potential.

Inwald Attitude Survey (IAS)

Lack of Self Awareness (AW)
Measures the degree to which the individual has been honest or candid about his/her feelings and behaviors. High scores suggest a denial of minor shortcomings in an effort to appear unusually virtuous and without fault. Elevated scores on this scale also may indicate that other tests scores may be deflated due to socially-desirable responses.

Limited Tolerance of Frustration (TF)
Identifies individuals with impulsive behavior patterns and low frustration tolerance. High scores indicate patterns of impulsive, restless behavior. High scorers on this scale may be outspoken and/or impatient with others. Elevated scores also may identify those who express hostility and anger more frequently than others who face similar situations.

Lack of Trusting Nature (TN)
High scorers may tend to distance themselves from others and may show distrust regarding the behavior of others. These individuals may be more content in situations that do not require extensive teamwork.

Job/Career Adjustment Difficulties (JA)
High scorers on this scale may tend to have job adjustment difficulties and/or difficulties holding jobs. Elevated scorers may have a history of being disciplined for counterproductive behavior.

Composure Under Stress Difficulties (CS)
Elevated scores on this scale suggest antisocial attitudes. High scorers may have more relaxed attitudes towards theft when compared with others. These individuals may feel that taking risks, or bending the rules in order to "beat the system," is justified.

Integrity Issues (II)
Elevated scores on this scale suggest a history of brushes with the law and societal norms, especially with regard to theft from employees and/or other parties. The backgrounds of these individuals may include incidents where personal integrity has been questioned.

Overall Total (Risk Score - OT)
A combination of all IAS scales measuring overall conscientiousness/reliability. Low scores suggest lower levels of overall conscientiousness/reliability.

REFERENCES

Cortina, J.M., Doherty, M.L., Schmitt, N., Kaufman, G., & Smith, R. (1992). Big five personality factors in the IPI and MMPI. *Personnel Psychology, 45*, 119–139.

Detrick, P. & Chibnall, J.T. (2002). Prediction of police officer performance with the Inwald Personality Inventory. *Journal of Police and Criminal Psychology, 17*, 9–17.

Inwald, R.E. (1982). *Inwald Personality Inventory (IPI) Technical Manual.* New York: Hilson Research, Inc., acquired by OPP Ltd. in 2007, Reprinted (2008), Illinois: IPAT, Inc., a subsidiary of OPP Ltd.

Inwald, R.E. (1988). Five year follow-up study of departmental terminations as predicted by 16 pre-employment psychological indicators. *Journal of Applied Psychology, 73*, 703–710.

Inwald, R.E. (1995). *Hilson Safety/Security Risk Inventory (HSRI) Technical Manual.* New York: Hilson Research, Inc., acquired by OPP Ltd. in 2007, Reprinted (2009), Illinois: IPAT, Inc., a subsidiary of OPP Ltd.

Inwald, R.E. (1998). *Hilson Life Adjustment Inventory (HLAP) Technical Manual.* New York: Hilson Research, Inc., acquired by OPP Ltd. in 2007, Reprinted (2009), Illinois: IPAT, Inc., a subsidiary of OPP Ltd.

Inwald, R.E. (2007. September). *The Inwald Couples Battery: From Selection to Treatment Using Assessment Tools.* Paper presented at the meeting of the Society for Police and Criminal Psychology, Springfield, MA.

Inwald, R.E. (2008). The Inwald Personality Inventory (IPI) and Hilson Research inventories: Development & rationale. *Journal of Aggression and Violent Behavior, 13*, 298–327.

Inwald, R.E., & Brobst, K.E. (1988). *Hilson Personnel Profile/Success Quotient (HPP/SQ) Technical Manual.* New York: Hilson Research, Inc., acquired by OPP Ltd. in 2007, Reprinted (2008), Illinois: IPAT, Inc., a subsidiary of OPP Ltd.

Inwald, R.E., & Gebbia, M.I. (1992). *Inwald Survey 5 (IS5) Technical Manual.* New York: Hilson Research, Inc., acquired by OPP Ltd. in 2007, Reprinted (2008), Illinois: IPAT, Inc., a subsidiary of OPP Ltd.

Inwald, R.E., & Kaufman, J.C. (1989). *Hilson Career Satisfaction Index (HCSI) Technical Manual.* New York: Hilson Research, Inc., acquired by OPP Ltd. in 2007, Reprinted (2009), Illinois: IPAT, Inc., a subsidiary of OPP Ltd.

Inwald, R.E., & Shusman, E.J. (1984). The IPI and MMPI as predictors of academy performance for police recruits. *Journal of Police Science and Administration, 12*, 1-11.

Inwald, R.E., Resko, J.A., & Favuzza, V.A. (1994). *Inwald Survey 2 (IS2) & Inwald Survey 8 (IS8) Technical Manual.* New York: Hilson Research, Inc., acquired by OPP Ltd. in 2007, Reprinted (2009), Illinois: IPAT, Inc., a subsidiary of OPP Ltd.

Inwald, R.E., Resko, J.A., & Favuzza, V.A. (1996). *Hilson Life Adjustment Profile (HLAP) Technical Manual.* New York: Hilson Research, Inc., acquired by OPP Ltd. in 2007, Reprinted (2009), Illinois: IPAT, Inc., a subsidiary of OPP Ltd.

Inwald, R.E., Traynor, B., & Favuzza, V.A. (2004). *Use of the Hilson Background Investigation Inventory (HBI) and Hilson Management Inventory (HMI) to Predict Community-Oriented Law Enforcement Officer Job Performance, US Department of Justice "Hiring in the Spirit of Service"* Project Grant, New York: Hilson Research, Inc.

Inwald, R.E., Traynor, B., & Favuzza, V.A. (1998). *Hilson Management Survey (HMS) Technical Manual*, New York: Hilson Research, Inc., acquired by OPP Ltd. in 2007, Reprinted (2009), Illinois: IPAT, Inc., a subsidiary of OPP Ltd.

Mufson, D.W., & Mufson, M. (1998). Predicting police officer performance using the IPI: An illustration from Appalachia. *Professional Psychology Research and Practice, 29,* 59–62.

Ones, D.S., Viswesvaran, C. & Schmidt, F.L. (1993), Comprehensive meta-analysis of integrity test validation: Findings and implications for personnel selection and theories of job performance. *Journal of Applied Psychology, 78,* 679–703.

Scogin, F., Schumacher, J., Gardner, J., & Chaplin, W. (1995). Predictive validity of psychological testing in law enforcement settings. *Professional Psychology Research and Practice, 26,* 68–71.

Shusman, E.J., Inwald, R.E., & Landa, B. (1984). Correction officer job performance as predicted by the IPI and MMPI: A validation and cross-validation study. *Criminal Justice and Behavior, 11,* 310–327.

Shusman, J.E., Inwald, R.E., & Knatz, H.F. (1987). A cross-validation study of police recruit performance as predicted by the IPI and MMPI. *Journal of Police Science and Administration, 15,* 162–168.

Super, J.T. (2006). A survey of pre-employment psychological tests & procedures. *Journal of Police and Criminal Psychology, 21,* 83-90.

U.S. Congress, Office of Technology Assessment. (1990). *The use of integrity tests for pre-employment screening,* OTA-SET-442. Washington, D.C.: Government Printing Office.

AUTHOR NOTE

Special thanks to Dr. Ed Reisfeld, a psychologist whose private practice focuses on police psychology in Ft. Lauderdale, FL, for his participation in the couples project.

All Hilson test profiles and graphs included in this chapter, including the IPI, HPP/SQ, IS5, IS2, HSRI, HCSI, HBI-R and HMI, were reprinted with kind permission of OPP Ltd. Institute for Personality and Ability Testing, Inc. (IPAT) is a wholly-owned subsidiary of OPP Ltd. and distributes the complete line of Hilson assessments.

Inquiries about the Hilson tests, including the IPI, HPP/SQ, IS5, IS2, HSRI, HCSI, HBI-R and HMI, should be addressed to: Institute for Personality and Ability Testing, Inc. (IPAT), PO Box 1188, Champaign, IL 61824-1188, email: custserv@IPAT.com, Phone: 800-926-2258 or 217-356-3402

Inquiries about the Inwald Research tests, including the ICCQ, IPPI, IAS, IPS and ITRI for use with couples, should be addressed to: Inwald Research, Inc., PO Box 73, Cleverdale, NY 12820, email: info@CA-CI.com, Phone: 800-228-2258 or 917-757-9063

Chapter 6

THE USE OF THE M-PULSE INVENTORY IN LAW ENFORCEMENT SELECTION

ROBERT D. DAVIS and CARY D. ROSTOW

The Matrix-Predictive Uniform Law Enforcement Selection Evaluation (M-PULSE) Inventory (Davis & Rostow, 2008), though fifteen years in development, is a new test designed specifically for the law enforcement candidate population. Published by MHS, Inc. in 2008, the M-PULSE Inventory was intentionally designed to represent a significant paradigm shift in Law Enforcement Officer (LEO) selection. Most instruments or tests that have traditionally been, and continue to be, used in LEO selection were designed for other purposes, applications, or populations and retrofitted or re-normed for the LEO population. As such, many of these instruments or tests were originally designed to measure the presence or absence of psychopathology or personality and character traits and styles (both along the spectrum of normalcy, and those of a disordered intensity). A consequence of this approach has necessarily involved the development and measurement of constructs that required inferential leaps of judgment on the part of the police psychologist to determine the degree to which a given construct (e.g., anxiety, extroversion, defensiveness, etc.) relates to future LEO job performance for a given candidate. The M-PULSE Inventory was designed to remove that "inferential leap" by directly predicting LEO job performance liabilities, and giving the police psychologist a better, more relevant tool for the demands placed upon them by Federal Laws and professional ethical mandates as they relate LEO selection.

It is important for the reader to understand the context within which the foundation of the M-PULSE Methodology, and ultimately the M-PULSE Inventory, were conceived and developed. Approximately fifteen years ago, the authors were approached by a representative of the risk management insurance pool for the State's Municipal Association that, at that time, served about 185 small to medium-sized municipalities. The problem was simply stated: Millions of dollars annually were being lost in litigation costs related to officer misconduct and allegations of officer misconduct despite the fact that post-conditional offer psychological evaluations were required. The question was also simply stated: Is there a better way to identify the bad actors before they are hired and a better way to defend the law enforcement executive, agency, and municipality in order to minimize these costs?

The authors' investigation into the pertinent issues related to the question revealed, quite surprisingly, that the role of the police psychologist in the selection of law enforcement officers had already been clearly delineated by the demands of Federal Law, Case Law, Federal Rules, and professional ethical mandates.

Federal Law

As it regards selection, it was learned that law enforcement executives, agencies, and municipalities were primarily being sued on three fronts:

- The Civil Rights Act of 1871 had become the cornerstone of Federal Law Enforcement Civil Litigation (known as 42 USC 1983 cases). This Federal Law, and its associated case law, clearly mandate the demonstration of *due diligence* (avoiding the claim of *deliberate indifference*) by foreseeing the risk of injury or predicting the liabilities that a candidate brings to the table of public safety and security, and acting to mitigate that risk or liability.
- The Americans with Disabilities Act (the ADA) that essentially requires that any information or data that it used to make hire-no hire decisions must be demonstrated to be job-related (particularly "no hire" decisions).
- The Equal Employment Opportunity Commission (EEOC) and its extensively broad-based regulations that essentially require "fairness" and the avoidance of adverse impact on protected groups in the selection process.

It became obvious that the mandates imposed on administrators and policymakers in law enforcement were necessarily shared responsibilities for the Police Psychologist. That is to say, any selection methodology developed by the Police Psychologist, in order to meet the mandates of federal law, must assist law enforcement executives, agencies, and municipalities in demonstrating their due diligence to predict the liabilities a candidate may demonstrate under the unique demands and stressors of the job, must be able to demonstrate that the information used to make decisions are job-related, and must be able to demonstrate that the methodology developed has no adverse impact.

Federal Rules

While meeting such mandates represent a step in the right direction for defending agencies, it was also learned that any selection methodology developed must conform to the mandates of the Federal Rules of Evidence 702 (FRE 702) and the case laws that further defined and delineated this rule. FRE 702 relates to the Admissibility of Evidence by experts. The essential case laws in this regard (i.e., *Daubert v. Merrill Dow Pharmaceuticals, G.E. v. Joiner,* and *Kumho Tire v. Carmichael*) have placed the Judge in the role of "gatekeeper" to determine the admissibility of evidence and provided guidance for the Judge to determine if the testimony of the expert is based on the scientific method by determining:

- If the methodology is standardized in its data collection and decision-making
- If the methodology is testable or replicable
- If the methodology is peer reviewed and/or published
- If the methodology has known probabilities and error rates
- (NB: A fifth prong has been interpreted by some to suggest that there should be some degree of general acceptance (i.e., the Frye Standard) of the methodology in the relevant scientific community)

These criteria fall squarely on the shoulders of the police psychologist to develop a selection methodology that guarantees the admissibility of his/her testimony in order to better defend the agency in allegations of negligent hiring litigation (but are no less relevant in the event of ADA complaints of job-relatedness or EEOC complaints of adverse impact).

Professional Ethical Mandates

For ten years, psychologists have been governed by (although largely ignored) the practice changes mandated by "The Standards for Educational and Psychological Testing" (1999) that declared there were no longer valid tests, only valid uses of tests, and burdened the psychologist with the responsibility validating his/her methodology for the purpose it is used, as well as the development of local and regional normative data.

The authors, pulling together these issues, reached the conclusion that the role of the police psychologist in selection had already been defined. Any methodology for selection required the above component demands. Further, the core demands of any methodology (i.e., **Predicting the Discrete Liabilities, Demonstrating Job-Relatedness, Demonstrating No Adverse Impact, Demonstrating Known Probabilities and Error Rates, Validating the Methodology, and Developing Local and Regional Norms**), from the authors' perspective, clearly required a statistical or actuarial (i.e., purely mathematical) approach to decision-making, as opposed to one of impressionistic decision-making, simply because the core demands called for mathematical answers. The M-PULSE Methodology has been described in much more detail in other publications and presentations for the interested reader (Davis & Rostow, 2001; Davis & Rostow, 2002; Rostow et al., 2001; Rostow et al., 2002; Rostow & Davis, 2002; Rostow et al., 2005; Rostow et al., 2006; Toldson et al., 2005; Toldson et al., 2004).

Development of the M-PULSE Inventory

The development of the actuarial M-PULSE Methodology was, in part, designed to ultimately construct the M-PULSE Inventory. The M-PULSE Methodology initially began with the standardized collection of numerous forms of data and information from law enforcement candidates including, but not limited to, demographics, background/historical data, structured interview data, observational data, verbal knowledge, verbal abstraction ability, and at least two psychometric instruments for each candidate. Each candidate was followed with Supervisory Rating Forms, tracking 58 variables of conduct on the job, at six-month intervals to determine if the officer demonstrated the presence or absence of any of the eighteen liabilities, as well as number of times those liabilities occurred.

The core psychometric instrument utilized was the MMPI-2, but the second (and in some cases, the third) psychometric instrument varied (e.g., PAI, 16PF, MCMI-III, etc.). After sufficient data collection, analyses were conducted to determine which secondary instrument accounted for the most variance in law enforcement job performance liabilities. That instrument turned out to be the PAI, which was subsequently used as the secondary instrument for all candidates in the M-PULSE Methodology. The total battery for M-PULSE Methodology, along with continued job performance follow-up, was collected on several thousand candidates. An analysis of the items and scales from each of psychometric instruments identified those that best correlated with job performance liabilities. Three or four analog items were then constructed for each of the original items, resulting in a total item population that was ultimately reduced to 600 items.

Concomitant with the above undertaking, the authors were engaging in an extensive review of the sociological literature, utilizing their own experiences in law enforcement, and conducting interviews with law enforcement executives (from every conceivable aspect of policing) to develop an item population that reflected the attitudes, values, and beliefs of LEO's regarding the unique culture of law enforcement. This process resulted in an item population of 500 statements directly related to the law enforcement profession.

The original 1100-item pool underwent further analyses, examination, and expert review to produce a beta version of the M-PULSE Inventory involving 621 items. This test version was given as the second psychometric instrument in the M-PULSE Methodology battery for the next 400 LEO candidates, which was analyzed by Dr. Robert Leark of Alliant International University to further reduce the size of the instrument.

The initial data collection was expanded to include several thousand LEO candidates, whose job performance was tracked over several years. Numerous analyses were conducted on these data to identify potentially problematic items with poor psychometric value or features. Along with standard analyses determining internal consistency for scale construction, and analyses to determine and maximize predictive validity (i.e., the relationship to actual job performance liabilities), items were externally reviewed for various legal criteria (e.g., privacy concerns under Title VII).

Current Version of the M-PULSE Inventory

The analyses of the initial data focused on looking at item intercorrelation, eliminating redundant items. About half of the items on the current M-PULSE Inventory involve content that is specifically related to the attitudes, values, and beliefs about the culture of law enforcement, police work, and police officers. The other half of the items are more generalized attitudinal items. Items that were deemed to potentially be inconsistent with legal standards in some states for pre-offer usage (i.e., ADA, EEOC, and Title VII) were eliminated. (NB: This was done to maximize the application of the M-PULSE Inventory, rather than limit its use to the post-conditional offer phase only.) Results of all these analyses identified 166 problematic items, resulting in a final version of 455 M-PULSE Inventory items. A four-choice response set of "Strongly Agree," "Agree," "Disagree," and "Strongly Disagree."

The M-PULSE Inventory is easily administered and scored. Administration is directly available online through the publisher (MHS, Inc.) or can be administered in the paper and pencil format with separate item booklet and response sheets. Scoring with the online administration is an automatic process when the candidate finishes. Scoring the paper and pencil version simply requires scanning the response sheet to the publisher's scoring organizer and (with an established account) immediately printing the report. A sample report is appended to this chapter for the reader's review.

The M-PULSE Inventory consists of Validity Scales, Liability Scales, Empirical Scales, and the California POST Psychological Screening Dimensions. These scales each serve critical purposes depending upon the instrument's application at the pre-offer or post-conditional offer phases of hiring. The reader is referred to the M-PULSE Inventory technical manual of the publisher (MHS, Inc., 2008) for an in-depth review of these scales, their development, and rationale. Validity scales obviously assess a candidate's response style or approach to the testing process. The M-PULSE Inventory consists of two validity scales:

• Impression Management
• Test Attitude

These scales were initially rationally derived, then correlated with similar scales from other instruments, and establishing scale reliability.

Liability Scales are the essential core and uniqueness of the M-PULSE Inventory. Both regression analyses and predictive discriminant function analyses were utilized for the construction of these scales and develop strong statistical relationships between the M-PULSE Inventory items and scales and the liabilities (i.e., actual job performance liabilities) derived from very large data sets. There are eighteen Liability Scales:

• Interpersonal Difficulties
• Chemical Abuse/Dependency
• Off-Duty Misconduct
• Procedural and Conduct Mistakes
• Property Damage
• Misuse of Vehicle
• Motor Vehicle Accidents
• Discharge of Weapon
• Inappropriate Use of Weapon
• Unprofessional Conduct
• Excessive Force
• Racially Offensive Conduct
• Sexually Offensive Conduct
• Lawsuit Potential

• Criminal Conduct
• Reprimands/Suspensions
• Potential for Resignation
• Potential for Termination

The following tables, reprinted with permission of the publisher from the technical manual, give the reader a sense of the overall classification accuracy for the 18 liabilities in law enforcement as measured by the M-PULSE Inventory:

Interpersonal Difficulties

	Predicted Outcome from the M-PULSE Inventory		
Actual Outcome	Liability Predicted Not to Occur	Liability Predicted to Occur	Percent Correctly Classified
Liability Did Not Occur	1,738	298	85.4
Liability Occurred	47	73	60.8
Overall Classification Accuracy	84.0%		

Off-Duty Misconduct

	Predicted Outcome from the M-PULSE Inventory		
Actual Outcome	Liability Predicted Not to Occur	Liability Predicted to Occur	Percent Correctly Classified
Liability Did Not Occur	1,786	279	86.5
Liability Occurred	32	59	64.8
Overall Classification Accuracy	85.6%		

Chemical Abuse/Dependency

	Predicted Outcome from the M-PULSE Inventory		
Actual Outcome	Liability Predicted Not to Occur	Liability Predicted to Occur	Percent Correctly Classified
Liability Did Not Occur	2,042	89	95.8
Liability Occurred	4	21	84.0
Overall Classification Accuracy	95.7%		

Motor Vehicle Accidents

	Predicted Outcome from the M-PULSE Inventory		
Actual Outcome	Liability Predicted Not to Occur	Liability Predicted to Occur	Percent Correctly Classified
Liability Did Not Occur	1,645	397	80.6
Liability Occurred	33	80	70.2
Overall Classification Accuracy	80.0%		

Procedural and Conduct Mistakes			
	Predicted Outcome from the M-PULSE Inventory		
Actual Outcome	**Liability Predicted Not to Occur**	**Liability Predicted to Occur**	**Percent Correctly Classified**
Liability Did Not Occur	1,087	567	65.7
Liability Occurred	169	337	66.6
Overall Classification Accuracy	65.9%		

Property Damage			
	Predicted Outcome from the M-PULSE Inventory		
Actual Outcome	**Liability Predicted Not to Occur**	**Liability Predicted to Occur**	**Percent Correctly Classified**
Liability Did Not Occur	1,777	331	84.3
Liability Occurred	11	39	78.0
Overall Classification Accuracy	84.2%		

Discharge of Weapon			
	Predicted Outcome from the M-PULSE Inventory		
Actual Outcome	**Liability Predicted Not to Occur**	**Liability Predicted to Occur**	**Percent Correctly Classified**
Liability Did Not Occur	2,055	87	95.9
Liability Occurred	6	14	70.0
Overall Classification Accuracy	95.7%		

Inappropriate Use of Weapon			
	Predicted Outcome from the M-PULSE Inventory		
Actual Outcome	**Liability Predicted Not to Occur**	**Liability Predicted to Occur**	**Percent Correctly Classified**
Liability Did Not Occur	2,097	44	97.9
Liability Occurred	1	16	94.1
Overall Classification Accuracy	97.9%		

Misuse of Vehicle

Actual Outcome	Predicted Outcome from the M-PULSE Inventory		
	Liability Predicted Not to Occur	Liability Predicted to Occur	Percent Correctly Classified
Liability Did Not Occur	1,827	277	86.8
Liability Occurred	11	47	81.0
Overall Classification Accuracy	86.7%		

Excessive Force

Actual Outcome	Predicted Outcome from the M-PULSE Inventory		
	Liability Predicted Not to Occur	Liability Predicted to Occur	Percent Correctly Classified
Liability Did Not Occur	1,941	175	91.7
Liability Occurred	9	31	77.5
Overall Classification Accuracy	91.5%		

Unprofessional Conduct

Actual Outcome	Predicted Outcome from the M-PULSE Inventory		
	Liability Predicted Not to Occur	Liability Predicted to Occur	Percent Correctly Classified
Liability Did Not Occur	1,676	368	82.0
Liability Occurred	32	80	71.4
Overall Classification Accuracy	81.4%		

Criminal Conduct

Actual Outcome	Predicted Outcome from the M-PULSE Inventory		
	Liability Predicted Not to Occur	Liability Predicted to Occur	Percent Correctly Classified
Liability Did Not Occur	1,988	141	93.4
Liability Occurred	7	22	75.9
Overall Classification Accuracy	93.1%		

Racially Offensive Conduct

Actual Outcome	Predicted Outcome from the M-PULSE Inventory		
	Liability Predicted Not to Occur	Liability Predicted to Occur	Percent Correctly Classified
Liability Did Not Occur	2,130	18	99.2
Liability Occurred	0	13	100.0
Overall Classification Accuracy	99.2%		

Sexually Offensive Conduct

Actual Outcome	Predicted Outcome from the M-PULSE Inventory		
	Liability Predicted Not to Occur	Liability Predicted to Occur	Percent Correctly Classified
Liability Did Not Occur	1,947	178	91.6
Liability Occurred	11	23	67.6
Overall Classification Accuracy	91.2%		

Reprimands/Suspensions

Actual Outcome	Predicted Outcome from the M-PULSE Inventory		
	Liability Predicted Not to Occur	Liability Predicted to Occur	Percent Correctly Classified
Liability Did Not Occur	1,461	521	73.7
Liability Occurred	51	124	70.9
Overall Classification Accuracy	73.5%		

Potential for Resignation

Actual Outcome	Predicted Outcome from the M-PULSE Inventory		
	Liability Predicted Not to Occur	Liability Predicted to Occur	Percent Correctly Classified
Liability Did Not Occur	373	147	71.7
Liability Occurred	90	245	73.1
Overall Classification Accuracy	72.3%		

Lawsuit Potential			
	Predicted Outcome from the M-PULSE Inventory		
Actual Outcome	**Liability Predicted Not to Occur**	**Liability Predicted to Occur**	**Percent Correctly Classified**
Liability Did Not Occur	2,108	44	98.0
Liability Occurred	1	8	88.9
Overall Classification Accuracy	97.9%		

Potential for Termination			
	Predicted Outcome from the M-PULSE Inventory		
Actual Outcome	**Liability Predicted Not to Occur**	**Liability Predicted to Occur**	**Percent Correctly Classified**
Liability Did Not Occur	424	135	75.8
Liability Occurred	57	159	73.6
Overall Classification Accuracy	75.2%		

Empirical Scales provide an understanding of a candidate's attitudes, values, and beliefs about the culture of law enforcement. These scales and subscales were derived or constructed through factor analyses in such a manner as to have no overlap among the primary scales. There are four empirical scales, and twelve associated subscales:

- NEGATIVE SELF-ISSUES
    1. Negative Emotions
    2. Egocentrism
    3. Inadequate Views of Police Work
    4. Poor Emotional Controls
- NEGATIVE PERCEPTIONS OF LAW ENFORCEMENT
    1. Inappropriate Attitudes About the Use of Force
    2. Overly Traditional Officer Traits
    3. Suspiciousness
- UNETHICAL BEHAVIOR
    1. Lack of Personal Integrity
    2. Negative Views of Department/Leadership
    3. Amorality
- UNPREDICTABILITY
    1. Risk Taking
    2. Novelty Seeking

The California POST Psychological Screening Dimensions were included in the M-PULSE Inventory to acknowledge the historical power and influence of the California POST Commission as leaders in the profession of police psychology. Some years ago, Dr. Shelley Spilberg, Chief Psychologist for the California POST Commission, undertook to daunting task of revising its manual for police psychological services. As part of that task, Dr. Spilberg commissioned the most comprehensive meta-analysis to date of all research and databases related to LEO selection. This task was conducted by Dr. Deniz Ones et al. (2004a, 2004b) and identified ten basic dimensions of personality or character traits that research and other data, through the meta-analysis, were found to be relevant to law enforcement job performance. It should be noted that these ten dimensions were not constructs or scales that were available from any single test or instrument, but rather came from several different tests being used in law enforcement research and other data. It should further be noted that the new California POST Manual will impose requirements on those police psychologists involved in selection to consider these ten dimensions as part of their overall decision-making process. For these reasons, the California POST Psychological Screening Dimensions were included in the M-PULSE Inventory, and provide the police psychologist involved in selection a single source for these constructs. The dimensions (which are termed negatively in keeping with the Liability focus of the Inventory, the Methodology, and Federal Law) include:

• Social Incompetence
• Lack of Teamwork
• Unreliability
• Reckless-Impulsivity
• Rigidity
• Lack of Integrity/Ethics
• Emotional Instability-Stress Intolerance
• Poor Decision-Making and Judgment
• Passivity-Submissiveness
• Substance Abuse

Summary and Discussion

It should be readily evident to the experienced police psychologist that the M-PULSE Inventory is a significant departure from the tests and instruments of the past on many fronts: Modern psychometric construction developed and normed on law enforcement candidates (rather than re-norming tests designed for other purposes on incumbent officers), scales that are actually relevant (and statistically tied) to law enforcement job performance liabilities, and items related to the attitudes, values, and beliefs regarding the culture of law enforcement. These features make the M-PULSE Inventory invaluable to the police psychologist, and readily understandable to the law enforcement executive.

The M-PULSE Inventory was specifically designed to have utility at both the pre-offer and post-conditional offer phases of the hiring or selection process. The M-PULSE Inventory may be used by human resource personnel during the 5 to 7 step pre-offer phase in order to rank-order those candidates in whom to invest the enormous time and economic costs of the application process, criminal background checks, driving checks, credit checks, former employment checks, personal references and the development of secondary sources, the interview panel or process, and polygraphy. Such an application of the M-PULSE Inventory early in the process (to rank-order candidates when the number of applicants exceed the number of positions) can greatly streamline efficiency and costs.

At the post-conditional offer phase, the M-PULSE Inventory is an invaluable new tool for the police psychologist with his/her own battery of tests that utilize the impressionistic decision-making approach to selection. The M-PULSE Inventory provides actuarially-based predictions of the liabilities or vulnerabilities a candidate brings to the table of public safety and security. It is no longer necessary for the police psychologist to make that "leap of inference" from a given level of endorsement on personality construct or dimension to its actual job performance implications for that given candidate. Additionally, knowing the liabilities or vulnerabilities of a given candidate greatly facilitates an understanding on the part of the police psychologist of the degree to which his/her pattern of responding to other psychometrics and historical/background information may enhance or mitigate such potential under the demands of the job.

Of course, the M-PULSE Inventory was also designed to be an integral part of the actuarial M-PULSE Methodology (a post-conditional offer phase evaluation), which statistically combines all evaluative data to provide the most accurate prediction of the discrete liabilities in law enforcement, conform to the mandates of federal law and case law, Federal Rules of Evidence, and professional ethical demands. It should also be noted that because the M-PULSE Methodology is an actuarial decision-making process (as opposed to an impressionistic decision-making methodology), psychologists and police psychologists are freed from the ethical burden of providing other police psychological services that might otherwise be forbidden (e.g., individual psychotherapy, FFDE's, etc.). In other words, since the psychologist or police psychologist is not making the selection decision (i.e., unacceptable risk or liability is determined mathematically), there is no ethical conflict in later providing another clinically-based service to the given candidate/officer, as is the case with impressionistic decision-making according to IACP (Police Psychological Services) Guidelines in this regard.

It should be noted, that because the M-PULSE Inventory is a new instrument to the police psychology armamentarium, there has been limited research on the instrument. Obviously, the psychometric soundness of the instrument has been the subject of scientific presentations (Rostow et al., 2005; Davis et al., 2005; Sitarenios & Davis, 2005; Williams et al., 2008a; Williams et al., 2008b; Davis et al., 2008). There have also been numerous studies and presentations conducted by Catanese et al. (2009, 2007), Githua et al. (2007), Kadin-Hoestra et al. (2007), Leark (2008), Leark et al. (2009, 2008, 2008), Topchyan et al. (2008, 2007), and Trytten et al. (2007) researching many aspects of the instrument. Thus far, there has been dissertation research by Werner (2008) looking at the POST Dimensions related to law enforcement job performance, and Trytten (2009) related to the M-PULSE Inventory Unpredictability Scales and the MMPI-2 Content Scales. Obviously, much more research, apart and separate from the authors, is needed as this critical instrument becomes the standard in police psychology selection.

Robert D. Davis, Ph.D., M.P., and Cary D. Rostow, Ph.D., M.P.

Profile Report

Client's Name: **Joe Sample**

Age: 33
Gender: Male
Test Duration: N/A - QuikEntry
Administration Date: April 07, 2008 (Online)
Assessment Number: 447353

Cautionary Note: Use and interpretation of this report is the responsibility of the user; the authors and publisher are not responsible for the misuse of this tool, or for any misinterpretations made.

M-PULSE Inventory Report for Joe Sample

Validity Scales

The following graph shows the results for the M-PULSE Inventory Validity Scales.

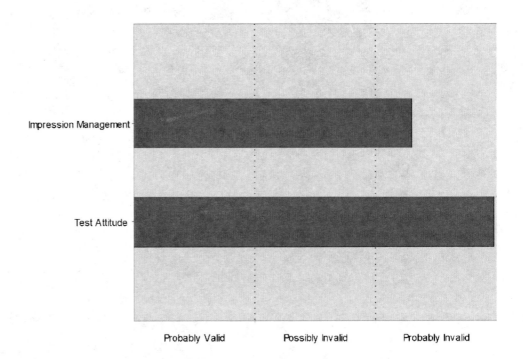

Validity Summary

Significant elevations were noted for the following Validity Scale(s):

Test Attitude
Impression Management

The validity of the administration may be questionable.

M-PULSE Inventory Report for Joe Sample

Liability Scales

The following graph shows the results for the M-PULSE Inventory Liability Scales.

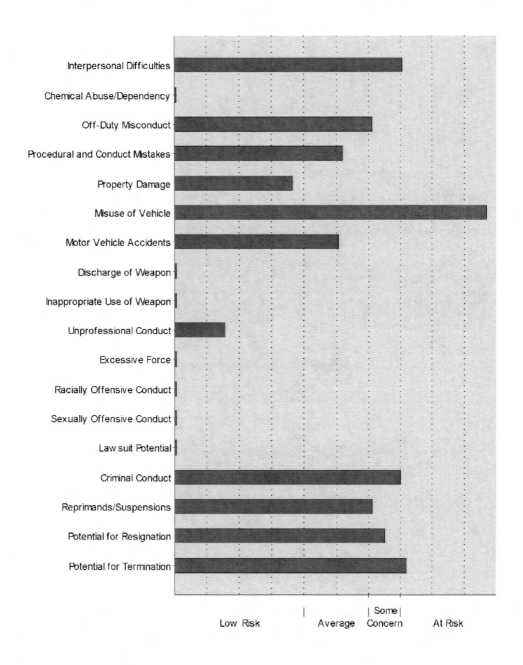

M-PULSE Inventory Report for Joe Sample

Empirical Scales

The following graph shows the results for the M-PULSE Inventory Empirical Scales.

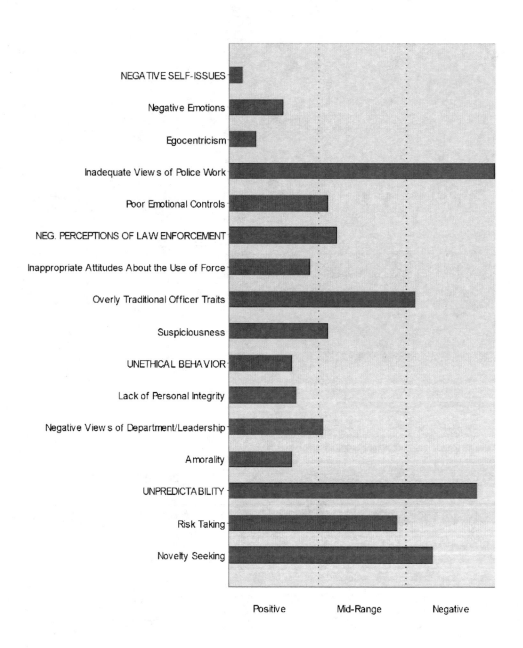

M-PULSE Inventory Report for Joe Sample

California POST Psychological Screening Dimensions

The following graph shows the results for the M-PULSE Inventory California POST Psychological Screening Dimensions.

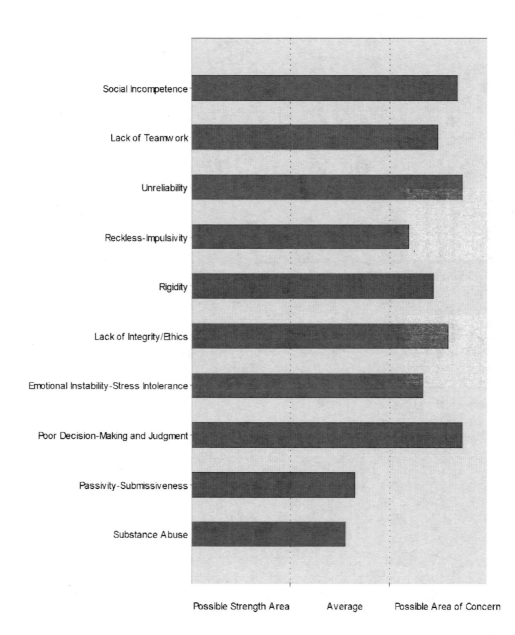

M-PULSE Inventory Report for Joe Sample

Administrative Section

The remainder of this report provides the raw and standard scores for each M-PULSE Inventory Scale, as well as the responses to each item. This information is useful if you want to further explore the candidate's scores.

Validity Scales

Scale	Raw Score	T-Score	Interpretation
Impression Management	45	73	Probably Invalid
Test Attitude	10	81	Probably Invalid

Liability Scales

Scale	Raw Score	T-Score	Interpretation
Interpersonal Difficulties	2.05	74	At Risk
Chemical Abuse/Dependency	-6.08	49	Low Risk
Off-Duty Misconduct	1.10	67	Some Concern
Procedural and Conduct Mistakes	0.21	53	Average
Property Damage	-1.34	51	Low Risk
Misuse of Vehicle	4.70	79	At Risk
Motor Vehicle Accidents	0.07	58	Average
Discharge of Weapon	-8.71	44	Low Risk
Inappropriate Use of Weapon	-16.90	27	Low Risk
Unprofessional Conduct	-3.42	36	Low Risk
Excessive Force	-8.61	34	Low Risk
Racially Offensive Conduct	-16.04	43	Low Risk
Sexually Offensive Conduct	-5.81	42	Low Risk
Lawsuit Potential	-10.75	46	Low Risk
Criminal Conduct	2.01	71	At Risk
Reprimands/Suspensions	1.10	60	Some Concern
Potential for Resignation	1.50	57	Some Concern
Potential for Termination	2.18	63	At Risk

M-PULSE Inventory Report for Joe Sample

Empirical Scales

Scales	Raw Score	T-Score	Interpretation
NEGATIVE SELF-ISSUES	350	23	Positive
Negative Emotions	99	32	Positive
Egocentricism	137	26	Positive
Inadequate Views of Police Work	89	80	Negative
Poor Emotional Controls	25	42	Mid-Range
NEG. PERCEPTIONS OF LAW ENFORCEMENT	172	44	Mid-Range
Inappropriate Attitudes About the Use of Force	65	38	Positive
Overly Traditional Officer Traits	49	62	Negative
Suspiciousness	51	42	Mid-Range
UNETHICAL BEHAVIOR	87	34	Positive
Lack of Personal Integrity	28	35	Positive
Negative Views of Department/Leadership	29	41	Mid-Range
Amorality	30	34	Positive
UNPREDICTABILITY	60	76	Negative
Risk Taking	16	58	Mid-Range
Novelty Seeking	20	66	Negative

California POST Psychological Screening Dimensions

Scale	Raw Score	T-Score	Interpretation
Social Incompetence	87	74	Possible Area of Concern
Lack of Teamwork	78	70	Possible Area of Concern
Unreliability	74	75	Possible Area of Concern
Reckless-Impulsivity	72	64	Possible Area of Concern
Rigidity	119	69	Possible Area of Concern
Lack of Integrity/Ethics	125	72	Possible Area of Concern
Emotional Instability-Stress Intolerance	100	67	Possible Area of Concern
Poor Decision-Making and Judgment	29	75	Possible Area of Concern
Passivity-Submissiveness	31	53	Average
Substance Abuse	17	51	Average

M-PULSE Inventory Report for Joe Sample

Item Response Table

This table lists Joe's individual responses to each item. Omitted items are identified with a question mark.

Item #	Response	Item #	Response	Item #	Response	Item #	Response	Item #	Response
1.	1	41.	3	81.	2	121.	2	161.	3
2.	1	42.	1	82.	2	122.	2	162.	2
3.	2	43.	2	83.	2	123.	2	163.	1
4.	4	44.	2	84.	1	124.	2	164.	2
5.	3	45.	3	85.	3	125.	2	165.	1
6.	4	46.	1	86.	2	126.	2	166.	3
7.	2	47.	2	87.	2	127.	3	167.	2
8.	3	48.	4	88.	2	128.	2	168.	4
9.	2	49.	3	89.	3	129.	3	169.	2
10.	4	50.	2	90.	2	130.	1	170.	3
11.	4	51.	3	91.	2	131.	2	171.	2
12.	3	52.	1	92.	1	132.	4	172.	2
13.	2	53.	2	93.	1	133.	4	173.	1
14.	4	54.	3	94.	1	134.	2	174.	2
15.	2	55.	4	95.	2	135.	3	175.	2
16.	1	56.	3	96.	3	136.	2	176.	4
17.	2	57.	1	97.	4	137.	2	177.	4
18.	3	58.	3	98.	2	138.	3	178.	3
19.	2	59.	2	99.	3	139.	2	179.	2
20.	1	60.	4	100.	1	140.	4	180.	3
21.	2	61.	3	101.	2	141.	2	181.	2
22.	3	62.	3	102.	2	142.	3	182.	1
23.	2	63.	1	103.	3	143.	1	183.	2
24.	1	64.	2	104.	2	144.	3	184.	3
25.	1	65.	4	105.	3	145.	2	185.	2
26.	1	66.	3	106.	4	146.	2	186.	1
27.	2	67.	2	107.	2	147.	2	187.	3
28.	4	68.	1	108.	1	148.	4	188.	2
29.	2	69.	3	109.	2	149.	4	189.	2
30.	4	70.	1	110.	3	150.	3	190.	4
31.	2	71.	2	111.	1	151.	2	191.	3
32.	2	72.	4	112.	2	152.	1	192.	2
33.	2	73.	3	113.	3	153.	3	193.	1
34.	1	74.	2	114.	3	154.	3	194.	3
35.	1	75.	1	115.	2	155.	2	195.	2
36.	2	76.	2	116.	2	156.	2	196.	4
37.	3	77.	2	117.	3	157.	3	197.	3
38.	4	78.	3	118.	2	158.	4	198.	2
39.	4	79.	3	119.	1	159.	2	199.	3
40.	3	80.	2	120.	1	160.	2	200.	1

M-PULSE Inventory Report for Joe Sample

Item Response Table (continued)

Item #	Response	Item #	Response	Item #	Response	Item #	Response	Item #	Response
201.	3	241.	4	281.	3	321.	2	361.	3
202.	3	242.	1	282.	1	322.	4	362.	1
203.	2	243.	1	283.	2	323.	3	363.	4
204.	4	244.	2	284.	4	324.	2	364.	4
205.	4	245.	4	285.	4	325.	1	365.	3
206.	1	246.	3	286.	4	326.	2	366.	4
207.	3	247.	1	287.	4	327.	4	367.	4
208.	1	248.	3	288.	2	328.	3	368.	4
209.	2	249.	1	289.	3	329.	4	369.	2
210.	4	250.	2	290.	2	330.	2	370.	3
211.	3	251.	4	291.	4	331.	3	371.	2
212.	2	252.	4	292.	4	332.	4	372.	1
213.	3	253.	3	293.	1	333.	4	373.	1
214.	1	254.	1	294.	2	334.	4	374.	1
215.	2	255.	4	295.	4	335.	2	375.	1
216.	1	256.	4	296.	3	336.	1	376.	2
217.	2	257.	4	297.	2	337.	1	377.	3
218.	4	258.	3	298.	2	338.	3	378.	2
219.	3	259.	1	299.	2	339.	2	379.	1
220.	4	260.	3	300.	3	340.	4	380.	2
221.	2	261.	2	301.	2	341.	2	381.	3
222.	3	262.	2	302.	3	342.	1	382.	3
223.	2	263.	3	303.	4	343.	1	383.	2
224.	2	264.	4	304.	3	344.	2	384.	3
225.	4	265.	4	305.	1	345.	3	385.	2
226.	3	266.	2	306.	2	346.	1	386.	2
227.	2	267.	3	307.	4	347.	2	387.	2
228.	1	268.	4	308.	3	348.	4	388.	1
229.	1	269.	2	309.	2	349.	4	389.	1
230.	2	270.	4	310.	3	350.	4	390.	2
231.	2	271.	4	311.	2	351.	2	391.	3
232.	2	272.	2	312.	4	352.	3	392.	2
233.	3	273.	1	313.	4	353.	1	393.	2
234.	1	274.	3	314.	2	354.	2	394.	1
235.	2	275.	4	315.	4	355.	4	395.	2
236.	2	276.	2	316.	3	356.	4	396.	2
237.	2	277.	3	317.	4	357.	2	397.	2
238.	3	278.	4	318.	4	358.	4	398.	2
239.	4	279.	2	319.	1	359.	4	399.	3
240.	4	280.	4	320.	1	360.	2	400.	1

Item Response Table (continued)

Item #	Response	Item #	Response	Item #	Response	Item #	Response	Item #	Response
401.	2	412.	2	423.	2	434.	4	445.	4
402.	1	413.	2	424.	1	435.	4	446.	4
403.	3	414.	2	425.	1	436.	3	447.	1
404.	4	415.	2	426.	2	437.	2	448.	2
405.	4	416.	4	427.	2	438.	1	449.	3
406.	4	417.	4	428.	4	439.	2	450.	1
407.	2	418.	2	429.	3	440.	4	451.	2
408.	1	419.	4	430.	4	441.	4	452.	4
409.	3	420.	2	431.	2	442.	3	453.	2
410.	3	421.	1	432.	3	443.	2	454.	4
411.	2	422.	1	433.	4	444.	4	455.	3

REFERENCES

American Educational Research Association, American Psychological Association, & National Council on Measurement in Education. (1999). *Standards for Educational and Psychological Testing.* American Educational Research Association. Washington, D.C.

Catanese, S., Leark, R.A., & Topchyan, A. (2009, June). "Relationship of Measured Personality Disorders to Fitness for Duty Evaluations: Referrals and Decisions." Paper presentation at the International Associaton for Forensic Mental Health Annual Conference. Edinburgh, Scotland.

Catanese, S., Leark, & Skidmore, S. (2007, July). "Validation of the M-PULSE Scales to Detect Random Responding." Paper presentation at the 3rd International Congress of Psychology and Law. Adelaide, Australia.

Davis, R.D. & Rostow, C.D. (2008). *M-PULSE Inventory: Matrix-Predictive Uniform Law Enforcement Selection Evaluation Inventory. Technical Manual:* MHS, Inc. Toronto, Ontario, Canada.

Davis, R.D., Rostow, C.D., & Sitarenios, G. (2005, September). "To Select and Protect: Innovations in Law Enforcement Hiring." Research presentation at the 112th Annual Conference of the International Association of Chiefs of Police. Miami, Florida.

Davis, R.D. & Rostow, C.D. (2002). The M-PULSE: Matrix-Psychological Uniform Law Enforcement Selection Evaluation. *The Forensic Examiner, 11*(12), 19–25.

Davis, R.D. & Rostow, C.D. (2001, October). "An Actuarial Model for Police Selection: Meeting the Demands of Law Enforcement, Federal Rules of Evidence, and Professional Standards of Police Psychology." Research Paper/Presentation at the 30TH Annual Conference of the Society of Police and Criminal Psychology. Austin, Texas.

Githua, O., Leark, R.A. & Skidmore, S. (2007, July). "Predictive Ability of the M-PULSE to Detect Fitness-for-Duty Decisions." Paper presentation at the 3rd International Congress of Psychology and Law. Adelaide, Australia.

Kadin-Hoestra, J., Leark, R.A., & Skidmore, S. (2007, July). "Correlation of Male Gender Role Identification to M-PULSE Scale and Officer Selection." Paper presentation at the 3rd International Congress of Psychology and Law. Adelaide, Australia.

Leark, R. A., Snyder, A., Farrand, K. & Thebus, K. (2009, June). "Construct Validity of the M-PULSE: Comparison with Personality Measurements." Paper presentation at the International Associaton for Forensic Mental Health Annual Conference. Edinburgh, Scotland.

Leark, R. (2008, October). "Advances in Matrix-Psychological Uniform Law Enforcement Selection Evaluation (M-PULSE) Research." Research presentation at the 37th Annual Conference of the Society for Police and Criminal Psychology. Walnut Creek, California.

Leark, R.A., Catanese, S., Topchyan, A., & Githua, O. (2008, October). "Research on the M-PULSE Inventory." Paper presentation at the Society for Police and Criminal Psychology Annual Conference. Walnut Creek, California.

Leark, R.A., Kafka, A., Lindemann, L., Catanese, S., Trytten, H. (2008, July). "Derivation & Validation of an Empirically Derived Measure of Police Applicant Screening." Paper presentation at the International Associaton for Forensic Mental Health Annual Conference. Vienna, Austria.

Ones, D.S., Viswesvaran, C., & Dilchert, S. (2004a, April). The Development of Pre-Employment Psychological Screening Procedures for California Peace Officers: An Arranged Marriage with No Pre-Nup. In J. Weiner (Chair), *Selection Research for Public Safety-Related Positions – Contributions and Challenges.* Symposium conducted at the Annual Conference of the Society for Industrial and Organizational Psychology. Chicago, Illinois.

Ones, D.S., Viswesvaran, C., & Dilchert, S. (2004b, November). Personality and Police Officer Work Performance: A Construct-Based, Comprehensive Meta-Analysis and Implications for Pre-Offer Screening and Psychological Evaluations. In S. Spilberg (Chair), *California Commission on POST Pre-Employment Psychological Evaluation Guidelines for Entry-Level Peace Officers, Revision Project Update.* Symposium conducted at the Annual Conference of the International Association of Chiefs of Police. Los Angeles, California.

Rostow, C.D., Davis, R.D., & Brennan, A.M. (2006). Psychological Police Officer Selection. Part I: History and Forensic Implications, Part II: The M-PULSE Methodology and Inventory, *Law Enforcement Executive Forum, Vol. 6*(1), 27–38.

Rostow, C.D., Davis, R.D., & Wheldon, H. (2005, October). "M-PULSE: Introduction to Matrix-Psychological Uniform Law Enforcement Selection Evaluation." Presentation at the 34th Annual Conference of the Society for Police and Criminal Psychology. Scottsdale, Arizona.

Rostow, C.D., Davis, R.D., & Levy, J.P. (2002). Police Psychology: The Influence of Daubert and Its Progeny. *The Journal of Police and Criminal Psychology, 17*(2), 1–8.

Rostow, C.D. & Davis, R.D. (2002). Psychological Screening. *Law and Order, 50*(5), 100–106.

Rostow, C.D., Davis, R.D., Levy, J.P., & Brecknock, S. (2001). Civil Liability and Psychological Services in Law Enforcement Administration. *The Police Chief, 68*(6), 36–43.

Sitarenios, G. & Davis, R.D. (2005, September). *Psychometric Prediction of Police Misconduct.* Research presentation at the 112th Annual Conference of the International Association of Chiefs of Police. Miami, Florida.

Toldson, I.A., Davis, R.D., & Rostow, C.D. (2005). Profiling Police: Evaluating the predictive and structural validity of an actuarial method for screening civil liabilities among police officer candidates. Grant number 02-523702 awarded by the National Institute of Justice, Office of Justice Programs, US Department of Justice.

Toldson, I.A., Rostow, C.D., & Davis, R.D. (2004, July). "Evaluating the Predictive and Structural Validity of an Actuarial Method for Screening Law Enforcement Candidates." Paper Presentation at the 2004 Annual Convention of the American Psychological Association. Honolulu, Hawaii.

Topchyan, Avetis, Leark, R.A., & Skidmore, S. (2008, March). "Validity of the M-PULSE Validity Scales: Correlation to MMPI-2 Validity Scales." Paper presentation at the American Psychology-Law Society Annual Meeting. Jacksonville, Florida.

Topchyan, A., Leark, R.A. & Skidmore, S. (2007, July). "Cross-Validation of M-PULSE Validity Scales to MMPI-2 and PAI Validity Measures." Paper presentation at the 3rd International Congress of Psychology and Law. Adelaide, Australia.

Trytten, H.L. (2009). "Relationship of Measures of the Unpredictability Scales of the M-PULSE to the Content Scales on the MMPI-2." Doctoral Dissertation for Alliant International University. Los Angeles, California.

Trytten, H., Leark, R.A., & Skidmore, S. (2007, July). "Relationship of Impulsive Behavior, Aggression and Negative Beliefs of Police Officers on the M-PULSE." Paper presentation at the 3rd International Congress of Psychology and Law. Adelaide, Australia.

Werner, L.M. (2008). "The M-PULSE Inventory POST Scales and Police Officer Performance: Liabilities, Termination, and Resignation." Doctoral Dissertation for Alliant International University. San Diego, California.

Williams, K., Sitarenios, G., Davis, R.D., & Rostow, C.D. (2008a, October). "Assessing Future Job Performance in Law Enforcement with the Matrix-Predictive Uniform Law Enforcement Selection Evaluation (M-PULSE) Inventory." Research presentation at the 37th Annual Conference of the Society for Police and Criminal Psychology. Walnut Creek, California.

Williams, K., Sitarenios, G., Davis, R.D., & Rostow, C.D. (2008b, October). "Predicting Actual Liability Outcomes of Law Enforcement Personnel Via the Matrix-Predictive Uniform Law Enforcement Selection Evaluation (M-PULSE) Inventory." Research presentation at the 37th Annual Conference of the Society for Police and Criminal Psychology. Walnut Creek, California.

Chapter 7

PRE-OFFER POLICE INTEGRITY TESTING: SCIENTIFIC FOUNDATION AND PROFESSIONAL ISSUES

JOHN W. JONES, MICHAEL R. CUNNINGHAM, and KELLY D. DAGES

The public entrusts its safety and security to its police officers. To meet that responsibility, police officers are given substantial discretionary authority, including the power to stop, to search, to arrest, and to use deadly force (Delattre, 2002). Because police officers often operate with minimal direct supervision, they also have the opportunity to engage in antisocial conduct, such as theft, extortion/shakedowns, harassment, abuse, providing false testimony, and unauthorized violence (Claussen-Rogers, & Arrigo, 2005).

Need for Pre-Hire Assessment of Police Officer Candidates

Extreme acts of police crime and dishonesty are on record, such as the officer who committed robbery and murder (Gwynne, 1995), and the officer who was convicted for stealing bank robbery money and computer equipment from an evidence unit, to name a few (Leventis, 2008). Police officer theft exposures have historically included the temptation to steal seized drugs (Silver, 2008; Johnson, 2008). In a nationwide research study (Samuels, 2000), the following types of police officer dishonesty were rated as being serious and worthy of immediate reporting and discipline:

- Stealing personal cash and/or property from a crime scene and blaming the theft on the burglar(s).

- Taking bribes from suspects and offenders by accepting "personal gifts," and then not issuing a citation.
- Recovering lost property but keeping a portion of the retrieval for personal gain (e.g., finding a wallet with money but only turning in the wallet).
- Allowing businesses in one's jurisdiction to violate community laws and ordnances, oftentimes receiving "gifts" in the process.
- Receiving kickbacks for inappropriately referring customers to local businesses and professionals.
- Engaging in "time theft" by conducting personal, nonpolice work while on the clock.

To be worthy of the trust and authority that they are given, and reduce the likelihood of dishonest and deviant on-the-job behavior, prospective police officers must be carefully selected. When selecting potential police officers, three questions arise:

- Which individual qualities are most important for effective performance as a police officer?
- Which of the necessary individual qualities should the applicant possess prior to pre-employment selection, and which can be taught during training?
- Of the qualities that a prospective police officer should possess, which qualities can be assessed before a conditional offer of employment has been made (i.e., pre-offer), and which can only be assessed after such an offer?

Pre-offer vs. Post-Offer Assessments

Questions about the qualities that are most essential for a police officer to possess can be answered by a job analysis, therefore this chapter reports the results of one component of a job analysis, a competency model, below. Police training generally is of limited duration, and focuses on teaching relevant laws and police procedure to the recruits. The necessary elements of character, aptitude, and psychological makeup should be present before the police recruit begins training. But, not all personal dimensions can be assessed in the initial screening of applicants to the police force. The International Association of Chiefs of Police (IACP) Police Psychological Services Section (2004) made a clear distinction between pre-offer and post-offer assessments, with the latter occurring after a conditional offer of employment has been made:

The pre-employment psychological evaluation must be conducted in accordance with the Americans with Disabilities Act [ADA]. A psychological evaluation is considered 'medical' if it provides evidence that could lead to identifying a mental or emotional disorder or impairment as listed in the DSM-IV, and therefore must only be conducted after the applicant has been tendered a conditional offer of employment. . . . Personality tests and other methods of inquiry that are not medical by the above definition and that do not include specific prohibited topics or inquires may be conducted at the pre-offer stage. However, these assessments alone are not capable of determining a candidate's emotional stability and therefore would not constitute an adequate pre-employment psychological evaluation. (p. 2)

Corey (2008) recently reported that the bifurcation between nonmedical pre-offer assessments, and medical/psychiatric post-offer assessments was affirmed in court rulings (*Griffin v. Steeltek*, 1998; *Karraker v. Rent-A-Center*, 2005; see Mook, 2008). Thus, those post-offer tests that are designed to measure a police applicant's emotional maladjustment and presence of psychopathology, such as the Minnesota Multiphasic Personality Inventory (MMPI), would be classified as medical tests and would only be appropriate following a conditional offer of employment.

CLINICAL ASSESSMENTS. Obtaining in-depth clinical assessments of officer candidates, using the MMPI or another clinical battery, accompanied by a clinical interview conducted by a psychologist or psychiatrist, are important due-diligence steps. Some investigators have also sought to use MMPI and other clinical tests to predict nonclinical outcomes, such as positive versus negative outcomes during training, completion versus failure to complete probation, long-term loyalty to the job versus voluntary turnover, remaining in good standing versus termination for cause, and promotions to higher rank versus remaining patrolman. Use of clinical assessments for this purpose has produced mixed results. Some investigators have reported predictive success using the MMPI (Brewster & Stoloff, 2003; Weiss, Davis, Rostow, & Kinsman, 2003), others reported predictive success in some police departments but not in others (Castora, Brewster, & Stoloff, 2003), and a few reported that the MMPI did not measure the individual dimensions that were most relevant to high levels of success in the police departments studied (Cortina, Doherty, Schmitt, Kaufman, & Smith, 1992; Inwald, 1992). For further details, consult the MMPI chapter in this volume.

The MMPI is a valuable clinical instrument that has demonstrated its value over more than half a century, and has allowed the development of many scales unimagined by the original authors. To enhance the assessment of work-related attitude, behavior and personality dimensions, and to remain compliant with the law, however, many police departments have begun to

employ nonclinical, pre-offer tests as the first step in screening police applicants, while reserving the use of the MMPI and other clinical evaluations for
post-offer assessments. Pre-offer attitude, behavior and personality tests that
measure an applicant's job-relevant qualities, but do not produce a medical
diagnosis, are legitimate under EEOC and ADA laws (Befort, 1997). Pre-
offer assessments are important tools for selecting in qualified public safe-
ty/protective services officers for the following reasons, at a minimum:

IMPROVED COST CONTROL. Post-offer assessments should be conducted
only by licensed or certified psychologists who are trained and experienced
in psychological test interpretation for public safety organizations. Although
the elimination of inappropriate police candidates before training is a wise
investment, Corey (2008) reported that the applicant rejection rate of post-
offer-only psychological evaluations averaged 25 percent across the United
States. By contrast, Corey (2008) reported that the applicant rejection rate for
post-offer psychological evaluations that were preceded by valid and reliable
pre-offer assessments averaged only 5 percent. Consequently, tremendous
cost savings can be realized by a bifurcated testing approach that involves
pre-screening applicants in order to produce more rejections of unsuitable
individuals earlier in the process and thereby reduce the number of job candidates who receive the more elaborate and costly post-conditional offer psychological assessments. For example, suppose a police department receives
1,000 job applicants per year, and conducts clinically-oriented post-offer
assessments that cost $400 per applicant, for a total expense of $400,000. If
the police department implemented a pre-offer screening program that cost
$20 per applicant, the cost would be $20,000. Yet, that cost would be more
than offset by the $80,000 savings that follows from the 20 percent reduction
in the number of applicants who receive the expensive post-offer assessments, producing a net savings of $60,000, and a Return on Investment
(R.O.I) of 3:1. The R.O.I. likely will increase further as a result of savings in
training and discipline costs associated with selecting in higher caliber officer
candidates.

BROADER ASSESSMENT FOCUS. Typically, the post-conditional-offer assessment phase focuses more on the clinical/medical issues (e.g., emotional instability, mental illness, and/or learning disorders) that could lead to
unsafe/unreliable on-duty police behaviors. By contrast, the pre-offer assessment phase can include job-related measures of integrity, and job relevant
knowledge, skills, abilities and other nonclinical competencies (KSAOs).
Such assessments provide broader and deeper information about the applicants' competencies, and ensure that the overall assessment process is not
overly skewed toward clinical/medical testing.

INCREASED RELIABILITY & VALIDITY. Police psychology assessment experts recognize that more comprehensive assessment batteries and screening

programs that clearly measure job-relevant constructs are always more reliable and valid than "narrower" assessment programs that only rely on one test battery and a follow-up interview. The use of a strong pre-offer/post-offer comprehensive test battery increases the odds of selecting in potentially safe/reliable/competent candidates, while screening out potentially unsafe/unreliable/ incompetent candidates.

Pre-employment Assessments

This chapter focuses on pre-employment assessments, including both integrity tests and general personality tests, for pre-offer police candidate screening. Both preemployment integrity tests and general personality tests can be administered both pre-offer and post-conditional offer, if they comply with the IACP's Guidelines. This chapter will share some perspectives related to using these types of tests during the pre-offer (i.e., nonmedical) phase of the selection process.

Competency Model: Patrol Officer Position

The IACP's Pre-employment Psychological Evaluation Services Guidelines (2004) clearly require that the selection of assessments for police applicant screening be based on job analytic and related data: "Data on attributes considered important for effective performance in a particular position should be obtained from job analysis, interview, surveys, or other appropriate sources" (p. 1). Therefore, as part of this chapter, results from an illustrative competency model are presented for the generic position of patrol officer.

Competency models are summaries of the job-related personal attributes required for successful performance within a position, a set of positions, and/or an organization. The patrol officer position is classified within Vangent's Security occupational module. While the purpose of this chapter is not to review the entire set of competency modeling results (see Jones & Dages, 2008a for a review of the complete model), a comparison of the results as they pertain to both pre-employment integrity tests and general personality assessments will be summarized.

All Vangent competency modeling projects include a standard survey consisting of 140 competencies, which is completed online by subject matter experts (SMEs) (Vangent, Inc., 2008). The competency survey includes demographic questions addressing the SMEs' relationships to the position(s), tenure with their company, tenure in their position, and tenure in their field. The definition and behavioral indicators are presented for each competency in the survey. SMEs rate the importance, and the frequency of use, of each competency. A nine-point rating scale is used with anchors of Very Low to Very High. Higher scores are associated with more importance and higher frequency of use. Vangent analyzes the aggregate SME responses for identifying the competency model.

For the current competency model, five (5) SMEs rated the patrol officer position. The SMEs that completed the survey were all I/O psychologists who were familiar with the requirements of police and protective services positions, including several with long engagements with police departments. Two of the raters were also licensed clinical psychologists, one of whom was involved with clinically oriented police testing, and the other was involved with police promotion examinations. The product of the importance rating and frequency of use rating averaged across raters was used to calculate the criticality index (CI) of each competency. The range for the CI, based on two dimensions using nine-point rating scales, is 1–81. While there is no absolute cut-off on the CI for a competency to be considered critical to a position, Vangent suggests the evaluative categories presented in Table 1, and that criticality scores over 49.00 should be given special consideration:

Table 2 provides the competencies with the highest criticality ratings, and

Table 1
INTERPRETATION OF A COMPETENCY'S CRITICALITY INDEX (CI)

Criticality Range	Interpretation
1–20	Not Critical
21–48	Slightly Critical
49–63	Highly Critical
64–81	Extremely Critical

reveals that the integrity/honesty competency is the number one patrol officer competency, followed by ethics. Although this ranking could change somewhat based on different SMEs, few would argue that the need for police officers to be honest and trustworthy, while avoiding the temptation to steal, accept bribes, or engage in related corruption, is a top priority (cf. Samuels, 2000). After all, police officers have exceptional access to businesses, homes, cars, and to confiscated money, drugs, and other evidence seized during their investigations. They must routinely resist the temptation to purloin valuable items, and to otherwise misuse their authority. In addition, police officers come into frequent contact with criminals, who may offer money, drugs, event tickets, and other goods and services in exchange for inappropriately favorable treatment. Based on these results, we will consider the question of how can a public safety department best screen their candidates for job-related integrity and honesty.

Table 2
TOP 5 PATROL OFFICER COMPETENCIES CORE COMPETENCIES CRITICALITY INDEX (IMPORTANCE X FREQUENCY)

Integrity/Honesty: Recognizing the consequences of making a dishonest decision or exhibiting deviant behavior that goes against commonly held values.
79.20

Business Ethics & Practices: Demonstrates knowledge of and adherence to ethical business standards and practices.
77.60

Drug Avoidance: Not selling, using, or tolerating illegal drugs on the job.
71.00

Non-Violence: Not engaging in unsanctioned violent behavior at work.
71.00

Stress Tolerance: Maintaining stable performance and emotional control when faced with conflict, pressure, hostility, and stressful conditions
68.80

Five-Factor Model Assessments vs. Integrity Tests

Once it is recognized that pre-offer assessments provide many benefits to the police recruiting agency, and that integrity and ethics are important dimensions to assess, the question becomes one of selecting the most relevant test, or battery of tests, to screen the police officer candidates. There are two leading classes of assessments for pre-offer screening, Five-Factor Model batteries, and integrity tests.

Five-Factor Model (FFM) Personality Assessments

Over the last two decades, personality psychologists became increasingly interested in the Five-Factor Model (FFM) of general personality, also known as the "Big-5" (Digman, 1994; Saucier & Goldberg, 2002). The FFM was originally created based on descriptive terms found in the dictionary that were used to describe normal aspects of personality. The idea was that common language would mirror the basic distinction that people made about other people. Factor analyses and other measures of internal consistency of those terms suggested five broad personality dimensions. The FFM dimensions of neuroticism (a.k.a. emotional instability or emotional stability), extraversion, openness to experience, conscientiousness, and agreeableness seemed like commonsensical ways to describe some basic individual differences, and involved fewer dimensions than earlier personality batteries. Many academic psychologists chose to embrace the FFM of general personality traits, both because such researchers like to study a wide variety of personality traits in both work and nonwork settings, and also due to the fact that many FFM personality assessments and scoring keys are freely available on the Internet (see Goldberg, Johnson, Eber, Hogan, Ashton, Cloninger, & Gough, 2006). It should be noted, however, that the fact that a given set of personality terms is routinely used to describe people does not mean that the descriptions are job-relevant or predictive of success. Such physical terms as tall and short, and blond and brunette, also are used to describe people, but those qualities are typically unrelated to job performance.

How relevant is the Five-Factor Model to pre-offer police officer selection and performance? Data has been published suggesting that the conscientious dimension of the FFM is a good predictor of on-the-job success (Barrick, & Mount, 1991). Employees with a high level of conscientiousness tend to be "organized, reliable, hard-working, scrupulous, and persevering" (Claussen-Rogers & Arrigo, 2005, p. 30). The data is mixed concerning the other FFM dimensions. Extraversion, Agreeableness, Openness to Experience, and Emotional Stability are not consistently related to success across industries and jobs (Barrick, Mount, & Judge, 2001).

Some writers on the topic of police selection have suggested that FFM measures of conscientiousness could serve as a measure of integrity and honesty (Claussen-Rogers, & Arrigo, 2005). Integrity is related to conscientiousness, such that individuals with a high level of honesty also tend to possess conscientiousness, and are dependable, diligent, and well-structured. Yet, it does not follow that everyone who is conscientious is honest, or that a measure of conscientiousness can serve the same purpose as a pre-offer honesty test. Supporting this point, statistically removing the effect of conscientiousness out of integrity was found to have only a small effect on integrity test validity, but removing the effects of integrity from conscientiousness reduced the criterion-related validity of conscientiousness to near zero (Murphy & Lee, 1994a).

Integrity tests are offered in two forms. Overt, or clear purpose, integrity tests have items that ask job applicants about their attitudes and behaviors involving honesty, theft, workplace standards, law enforcement, and on-the-job misbehavior. Personality-based, or disguised purpose, integrity tests ask about worker reliability, dependability, and self-control (Berry, Sackett, & Weimann, 2007). Overt integrity tests and personality-based integrity tests tap into some of the same underlying constructs, but the two types of tests also show some divergence in the pattern of their relations with other attitude and personality dimensions. For example, a measure of conscientiousness correlated more strongly with a personality-based measure of integrity than with an overt integrity test (Murphy & Lee, 1994b). Investigators also found that honesty/humility items formed a sixth factor, beyond the familiar Five-Factor Model dimensions (Lee, Ashton, & deVries, 2005); an overt integrity test was reported to correlate more with this sixth dimension than did a personality-based integrity test (Marcus, Lee, & Ashton, 2007). Taken together, such results suggest that overt and personality-based integrity tests may assess the related constructs of honesty and conscientiousness to differing degrees. This issue will be revisited in Table 4.

THE FFM DIMENSION OF EMOTIONAL INSTABILITY. The Emotional Instability dimension of the FFM poses additional challenges. Jones and Arnold (2008) reported that certain FFM personality tests still use clinical terminology as labels for the Big 5 "Emotional Instability" global construct. For example, the first dimension on the NEO-PI R Big Five measure (Costa & McCrae, 1992) is labeled "Neuroticism", and provides subscales assessing "Anxiety," "Depression," "Self-Consciousness," "Anger/Hostility," and "Vulnerability to Stress." Jones and Arnold reported that other FFM tests rely on items that apparently relate to depression (e.g., "Often feel blue"), anxiety (e.g., "Panic easily"), and possibly even bipolar disorders (e.g., "Change my mood a lot."). In addition, certain FFM tests also have been used to generate clinical reports and their scale scores have been used to generate overall clinical composite scores. As a consequence, the assessment of Emotional Instability/Neuroticism would be appropriate for post-offer testing, but it could raise ADA issues for pre-offer screening. Therefore, police department human resource directors need to make sure that no clinical items or scales or scores are included in the pre-offer assessment. More specifically, if any Five-Factor Model measure of personality, or any general measure of personality, is used for pre-offer assessment, it is prudent to ask the test publisher the following questions:

- Does the Big-5 or other assessment generate any clinical reports?
- Does the test manual recommend using the FFM assessment or other assessment in any form of clinical/counseling application?
- Are the five-factor model scales combined with any clinical scales to generate any clinical composite score?
- Are there any clinical items (e.g., items that clearly assess self-reported anxiety and/or depression, for example) that are included in any of the FFM subscales that are used to compute the Global FFM factor commonly referred to as "Emotional Instability," "Neuroticism," or "Anxiety," to name but a few labels?
- Are any of the FFM or other assessment norms based on clinical samples?

• Are any FFM special equations and/or cut-scores based on clinical samples?

If the publisher answers "yes" to any of the foregoing questions, it might be unwise to use the FFM or other assessment as a pre-offer test (Jones & Arnold, 2008).

FFM COMPETENCY CRITICALITY ANALYSIS. Data from the competency modeling job analysis described above was also analyzed to provide additional insight into the relevance of FFM tests to police selection (see Jones & Dages, 2008a for a complete set of analyses). Three to five personality-oriented competencies related to each of the standard FFM global dimensions were averaged to determine the criticality of each one for the position of patrol officer. The selection of items was based on SMEs with extensive experience with the FFM and with the patrol officer position. Constructs that are explicitly measured on integrity tests, such as Integrity/Honesty, Business Ethics, Drug Avoidance, and Non-Violence were excluded. The competencies of Stress Tolerance, Chaos Management and Self-Confidence were averaged to compute a proxy criticality index for the *Emotional Stability* global factor. *Extraversion* was defined by averaging the Assertiveness, Directiveness, and Energy competencies. Competencies including Responsibility, Policy Compliance, Safety Orientation, Safety Promotion, Driving Ability, and Impression Management were combined to form the *Conscientiousness* Big-5 factor. The *Agreeableness* global factor was computed by averaging the Teamwork, Supervisory Relations, Patience, and Diversity Tolerance competencies. Finally, the *Openness* global factor was defined by averaging the Questioning, Curiosity, Adaptability/Flexibility, and the Cross-Cultural Adaptability competencies.

Table 3 reports the criticality scores for each of the FFM dimensions constituted using the competency measures described above. Inspection of Table 3 reveals that while all five of the targeted competencies would be deemed "Highly Critical" for the Patrol Officer position using the competency modeling interpretive guidelines listed in Table 1 that accompany the Vangent Competency Modeling System (Vangent, 2008), none of the global Big-5 factors in Table 3 would be classified as "Extremely Critical." Additionally, none of the Big-5 factors have criticality scores as high as those constructs typically measured with integrity tests (see Table 2). The top competency was "Emotional Stability" which, we suggest, should be assessed in a post-offer clinical test, especially if any of the primary factor scores that are used to compute the global factor are arguably clinical in nature. The other dimensions, such as Extraversion and Conscientiousness, could be assessed in a pre-offer assessment along with the "Extremely Critical" integrity competency. Again, care should be taken to ensure that assessments of any components of the FFM are appropriate for pre-offer.

Table 3
FIVE-FACTOR MODEL ANALOGUES

Five Factors Model Dimensions	Criticality Index (Importance * Frequency)
Emotional Stability	60.93
Extraversion	60.80
Conscientiousness	59.10
Agreeableness	58.50
Openness	53.40

Vangent Reid Report Integrity Test

After describing the rationale for pre-offer integrity tests, it is appropriate to look at one in more detail. Information on various Vangent integrity tests is presented in the following sections, including: validity (criterion, construct, and content), reliability, and comparison to other instruments, noninvasiveness, and comparing test performance of a police sample with security and general samples. The Vangent Reid Public Safety Report is an attitude and behavior assessment of employee integrity that includes an overt integrity test that was developed by John E. Reid in 1947, initially marketed in 1951, and continuously refined and updated through psychometric analysis and field testing since the 1960s. Hence, this integrity test has over a 60-year legacy. John Reid was an attorney and consultant to the Chicago Police Department, so the Reid integrity test was based on firsthand observations of individuals who displayed honest and dishonest behavior (Reid & Inbau, 1977).

The Vangent Reid Report, now in its 29th edition, measures job-related integrity through a series of questions on attitudes toward honesty and employee theft, as well as work history and past productive and counterproductive behaviors, including illicit drug use and interpersonal aggressiveness. The Reid Report was developed for pre-offer screening, a dominant theoretical underpinning of which is the attitude-behavior congruence theory (Jones, 1991). This assessment has never been used for any form of clinical assessment. The Reid Report has consistently been found to yield no adverse impact as a function of sex or race (Ash, 1971; Brooks & Arnold, 1989a). Vangent's Reid Public Safety Report (RPSR) contains the following five sections. It was also designed to accept add-on modules to measure additional dimensions:

PART 1. REID INTEGRITY ATTITUDE SCALE (RIAS). Contains 83 noninvasive questions that allow applicants to reveal their attitudes about integrity and conscientiousness versus dishonesty and counterproductivity. Reid began with several hundred items, which were reduced to 114, and then refined by Dr. Philip Ash (1970, 1971, 1986) to the present 83 items using a sample of 1,853 applicants for a variety of jobs. Abbreviated and Express versions of the Reid integrity scale use even fewer items. The applicant receives a *Recommend, Qualified Recommend,* or *Not Recommend* evaluation based on the number of questions answered in the direction favored by honest employees. A percentile rank score indicates how the applicants' attitudes about integrity compare to others who have taken the test. Research, which is described in more detail below, has shown that the Reid Integrity Attitude Scale, both alone, and in junction with the full RPSR, predicts work motivation, psychological balance, service orientation and overall job performance.

PART 2. ANTISOCIAL HISTORY. Involves 73 questions that directly probe the applicants' experiences at work and elsewhere, including commission of criminal acts and criminal convictions. Admissions of criminal convictions or to the commission of serious criminal actions can produce a *Not Recommend* evaluation on this part. Admissions of lesser but jobrelevant dishonest acts can result in a *Qualified Recommend* evaluation.

PART 3. SUBSTANCE USE. Consists of 46 questions that evaluate the applicant's prior use of illegal drugs at work and elsewhere. This can earn a *Not Recommend* evaluation or a *Qualified Recommend* evaluation, depending on the nature and use of the illicit substance.

PART 4. PUBLIC SAFETY ATTITUDES AND ADMISSIONS. This section contains 59 questions that measure applicants' attitudes about public safety work and that inquire into prior public safety work experience. Poor attitudes or admissions of dutyrelated misconduct can produce a *Not Recommend* or *Qualified Recommend* evaluation on this section.

PART 5. WORK HISTORY AND PERSONAL ACHIEVEMENTS. Compiles a concise record of the applicants' education, employment history, job performance, attendance, and circumstances of termination.

Parenthetically, other scales also may be added to the Reid Public Safety Report including the (a) Risk Avoidance Scale (i.e., a 40-question attitude test that identifies applicants who are likely to use illicit drugs or take inappropriate risks on the job) and (b) the Service Relations Scale (i.e., a 50-item scale that selects applicants with the ability to establish effective and helpful relationships with supervisors, coworkers and the public). Applicants who score reliably higher on the Service Relations Scale are typically described by their supervisors as helpful, self-controlled, and pleasant. Conversely, research has demonstrated that low scoring applicants who receive a High Risk evaluation do not perform well with the public, and are described as moody, defensive, and irritable.

RPSR – Reliability, Validity and Norms

Reid integrity assessment instruments have been used in job selection for hundreds of occupations and within multiple industries, including police and security testing (Cunningham, 1997). The Reid Integrity Attitude Scale, a major component of the RPSR, was found to possess a coherent factor structure (Cunningham & Ash, 1988). The internal consistency of this Integrity Attitude Scale was tested in several samples of over 1,000 individuals, and produced Cronbach alphas = .91. Reliability was further evaluated with 113 individuals who took the test twice, with one to six months between administrations; the testretest correlation was r = .69. The mean of the Integrity Attitude Scale for a sample of 1,230 was 48.2, with a standard deviation of 11.8, and a standard error of measurement of 3.97. (Brooks & Arnold, 1989a). (Parenthetically, the Public Safety Attitude scale, Part 4 of the RPSR, has a Cronbach alpha = .85 [Brooks & Arnold, 1989b].) In addition, the Integrity Attitude Scale was resistant to faking (Cunningham & Ash, 1989). Cunningham, Wong & Barbee (1994) reported three experiments in which subjects were coached to obtain high scores on the Integrity Attitude Scale, and even offered a monetary incentive, but failed to achieve exceptional scores.

To establish convergent validity, 91 applicants for various positions at a major southeastern police department completed the Reid Public Safety Report, the Inwald Personality Inventory, and the Minnesota Multiphasic Personality Inventory (MMPI). Applicants who performed well on the Reid Integrity Attitude Scale had significantly lower scores on the Inwald scales measuring Trouble with the Law and Society (r = .56), Antisocial Attitude (r = .45), Interpersonal Difficulties (r = .47), Substance Abuse (r = -.53), and Rigidity (r = .43). High scorers on the Reid Integrity Attitude Scale also had lower MMPI scores on Depression (r = .51), Paranoia (r = .42), and Mania (r = .58) (Arnold & Brooks, 1988). Note that it is permissible for a pre-offer scale to demonstrate favorable correlations with mental health assessments provided that it was not developed or used for that purpose (Berry, Sackett & Weiman, 2007).

The predictive validity of the Reid Integrity Attitude Scale was assessed using 39 applicants for security guard positions at a radio and television manufacturer who were hired without reference to their Reid scores. Between six months and one year later, the relation between Reid scores and continued employment was investigated. Whereas half of those who received *Recommend* evaluations on the Reid Report remained in service, all of those whose scores merited a *Not Recommend* evaluation had been terminated, with "theft verified or suspected for each" (Ash, 1971, p. 986). A subsequent study used the Reid Report to predict time theft two months after hiring in a retail setting (Kamp, 1989). Employees were assured of anonymity, and offered a small monetary incentive to complete a questionnaire at their homes. The confidential survey was completed by 144 employees. Nearly half (48.4%) of the employees whose scores on the Reid Report would have merited a *Not Recommend* evaluation admitted to engaging in time theft at least once a month, while only 19.4 percent of the *Recommended* employees admitted to any time theft.

The concurrent validity of the Reid instruments have been established, and crossvalidated, in a variety of settings. One study focused on 1,300 public safety job applicants for a variety of police, fire, and security agencies across the county. Scores on the Reid Public Safety Report Part 1 (i.e., the Integrity Attitude Scale), were significantly correlated in the predicted direction with admissions of Past Criminal Behavior (r = -.43) and with Illicit Substance Abuse (r = -.21) (Brooks & Arnold, 1989c.). Another study examined the relationship of scores on the RIAS at the time of application to job performance of 53 employees in a large retail chain about 6 months later (Brooks, 1990a). Higher entry scores on the RIAS were associated with higher subsequent supervisor evaluations in the areas of Overall Performance (r = .35), Honesty (r = .33), Customer Relations (r = .45) and Coworker Relations (r = .57). Using an experimental approach, Cunningham et al. (1994) had employees in a variety of jobs complete the Reid Integrity Attitude Scale and several other measures. After the testing, individual employees were overpaid for their participation. The overpayment occurred in private, was apparently due to a counting error, and seemed to have no chance of detection by the supervisor. Reid Integrity Attitude scores were significantly correlated with subsequent decisions to return versus retain the undeserved money, r = .33, p <.01. Finally, The Asset Protection (security and investigation) department of a major retail chain deployed a test battery designed to assess 12 competencies, including honesty. The test battery included a shortened version of the Reid Integrity Attitude Scale as part of its screening for new hires. In this company, 1,700 new hires passed the test battery including the Reid Integrity Attitude Scale, and 1,194 did not take the test battery. Across the span of a year, the turnover rate of the screened hires was 7.7 percent lower than that of the unscreened hires, saving the company hundreds of thousands of dollars in recruitment and training costs (Billings, 2006).

Although most research has focused on the Reid Integrity Attitude Scale, Brooks and Arnold (1989b) examined the Public Safety Attitude Scale (Part 4), which is a separate section of the Reid Public Safety Report from the Reid Integrity Attitude scale (Part 1). The Public Safety Attitude scale was found to be a valid predictor (r = -.34) of such organizational criteria as admissions of criminal history, substance abuse, and prior problems in previous public safety positions. In addition, Brooks (1990b) examined the relationship of the

Antisocial Behavior history component (Part 2) with managers' performance ratings. That study found that favorable performance on Part 2 was associated with following safety procedures (r = .30), ease of supervision (r = .23), and overall evaluation of employee performance (r = .53). Finally, Brooks (1992) used the summary recommendation of the Reid Public Safety Report, which was based on all 5 parts, as a predictor of screening outcomes using other methods by a major metropolitan police department. The summary recommendation produced by the Reid Public Safety Report produced an 81.2 percent rate of agreement with the overall results of the department's traditional selection procedures. The RPSR had a 65 percent rate of agreement with biochemical drug tests results and a 73.3 percent rate of agreement with department background investigations of past counterproductive behaviors.

Vangent instruments, such as the RPSR, are designed to be used as one job-related and scientific component of a comprehensive employee selection system. It is expected that some job applicants who perform well on Reid instruments will be rejected for employment because of poor fit with the skill requirements of the position. Poor performers on the Reid Public Safety Report may also be appropriate for positions that involve a high level of supervision, or who do not require integrity and conscientiousness. As a consequence, the Reid Public Safety Report was designed to initially screenin the best two-thirds of the applicant pool for enhanced consideration, and to identify the bottom third for more intensive investigation.

The norms used for the Reid integrity assessment instruments are researched on a continuing basis, and currently are based on over 200,000 cases selected across a variety of job classifications. All norms are based on job candidates. Police candidate and related protective services norms are available.

OTHER INTEGRITY MEASURES. A variety of other pre-offer integrity tests are available in the market, with varied levels of scientific support, and demonstrated validity and reliability. Vangent's Law Enforcement Applicant Inventory (LEAI) is multidimensional integrity test that contains separate scales to measure Honesty, Non-Violence, Drug Avoidance, Safety, Risk-Avoidance, and Criminal Justice Orientation, among other supplemental scales as needed (see Peirce & Martin, 1997).

As noted earlier, in addition to overt integrity tests such as the RPSR and the LEAI, there are personality-oriented or disguised-purpose integrity tests that measure such constructs as reliability, dependability, and conscientiousness (see Berry, Sackett, & Weimann, 2007). Both overt and personality-based integrity tests reliably predict employee theft, especially when coefficients are corrected for the low base rate of theft. Cunningham and Jones (2008) reviewed the literature comparing overt and personality-based integrity tests, and FFM conscientiousness, in terms of their capacity to predict employee deviance and overall work performance. Table 4 presents the figures from that review. The results indicate that overt integrity tests provide the strongest means of predicting employee deviance, followed by personality-based integrity tests. Conscientiousness runs third in terms of predicting employee deviance.

Overt integrity tests also predict counterproductive work behaviors (CWB) other than theft, such as violence and substance abuse, a bit better than do personality-based tests (Ones, Viswesvaran, & Schmidt, 1993), whereas personality-based tests may be a bit better than overt integrity tests in predicting absenteeism (Ones, Viswesvaran, & Schmidt, 2003). Thus, a police department that was concerned with officer violence and substance abuse might be well-advised to deploy an overt integrity test, whereas a department that was concerned with absenteeism might select a personality-based integrity test as a pre-offer screening instrument.

Table 4
COMPARISON OF INTEGRITY TESTS AND FIVE-FACTOR MODEL
DIMENSIONS TO PREDICT EMPLOYEE DEVIANCE AND OVERALL
JOB PERFORMANCE

Meta-analytic Investigations:	Employee Deviance Uncorrected/Corrected*	Overall Job Performance Uncorrected/Corrected
Integrity tests		
Overall Integrity	-.31/-.44[a]	.20/.34[a]
Overt	-.39/-.55	.18/.30
Personality-based	-.22/-.32	.22/.37
Five-Factor Model		
Overall FFM	-.18/-.22[c]	.06/.16[b]
Conscientiousness only	-.16/-.26[d]	N/A

[a]Ones, Viswesvaran & Schmidt, 1993.
[b]Barrick & Mount, 1991; Tett, Jackson & Rothstein, 1991; Barrick, Mount & Judge, 2001.
[c]Berry, Ones, & Sackett, 2007.
[d]Salgado, 2002.
Note: All correlations in Table 4 were presented so that higher scores, or more integrity, were associated with less deviance. Conversely, with the job performance criteria, all correlations were presented where higher integrity was associated with stronger performance. Ones, Dilchert, Viswesvaran & Judge (2007) suggested a somewhat higher correlation between conscientiousness and deviancy than that reported by Salgado (2002), accounting for 14% of the variance. But, questions about the Ones et al. (2007) analyses were raised by Morgeson et al. (2007), including issues about the deviancy criteria and the assumptions underlying their multiple regression and meta-analytic correction procedures. We believe that employee attitude and behavior assessments will continue to show higher predictive validity than FFM conscientiousness when tested with comparable samples, criteria, and correction procedures.

Content Validity of Integrity vs. Conscientiousness Items

The SMEs who contributed to the competency modeling study described above were also asked by Dages and Jones (2008) to rate the relevance of each item, or individual question, on the Reid Integrity Attitude Scale in terms of its relevance to predicting employee theft and counter-productivity in Police/Security, Retail, and Hospitality positions. The same five SMEs also rated the relevance of items from a universal FFM measure of conscientiousness available in the public domain (Goldberg et al., 2006). The measure of content validity was reflected in an index that ranged from -1.0 to +1.0. Higher Content Validity Index (CVI) values reflect a high degree of relevance and "fit" between the item set's content and the types of on-the-job behaviors they were designed to predict in the Police/Security field. Table 5 reports that CVI value for the Reid Integrity Attitude Scale was .70 for Police/Security positions, and was only .02 for the FFM measure of conscientiousness.

This pattern of results is arguably one of the reasons why general measures of conscientiousness are not strong predictors of employee theft and deviance, and it supports the attitude-behavior congruence theory as one of the major theoretical foundations for overt integrity tests (Ajzen, 1991; Ajzen & Fishbein, 1977; Jones, 1991). Two sample Reid Integrity Attitude Scale items with high content validity that help demonstrate the relatedness of the Reid scale to employee deviance are: "Do you think taking damaged goods from a company without asking is all right?"; "Do you think a person should be fired if it is found that he or she helped employees cheat their company out of overtime once in a while?" On the other hand, the conscientiousness measure included the following items: "Get chores done right away" and "Am always prepared." Such results suggest that if police departments want to screen out job applicants at the highest risk to engage in on-the-job theft and dishonesty, then they should seriously consider including overt preem-

Table 5
CONTENT VALIDITY INDEX (CVI) VALUES FOR OVERT INTEGRITY AND
CONSCIENTIOUSNESS ASSESSMENTS

	Reid Report CVI (Overt Integrity)		Conscientiousness Scale CVI		t-Value
Market Sector	Mean (range)	Std Dev	Mean (range)	Std Dev	
Police/Security	.70 (0.0 - 1.0)	.32	.02 (-0.6 - 1.0)	.44	7.19*

*The CVI values for the Reid Report and conscientiousness scale are significantly different (p < .01).

ployment integrity tests as part of their assessment battery, ideally during the pre-offer phase.

Outcomes of Pre-Offer Screening for Integrity

There are a wide variety of case studies on police officer theft and corruption in the literature (Samuels, 2000; Sellbom, Fischler, & Ben-Porath, 2007). At the same time, there also is a widespread belief that individuals self-select into occupations based on their personalities. Such reasoning suggests that, because police officers must take an oath to uphold the law, individuals who are attracted to the law enforcement profession usually are honest and law-abiding. Thus, police specialists may claim that police officers exhibit significantly higher levels of job-related honesty and integrity than security guard candidates, who are presumed to be more honest than job applicants to private sector businesses.

To test this assumption, Jones and Dages (2008b) conducted a field study of pre-offer integrity testing results in three employment domains. During the 2007 and 2008 recruitment periods, there were 5,874 job candidates applying to: (1) Police Departments (N = 3 mid-size departments in cities with populations ranging from 26,000 to 300,000), (2) Security Firms (N = 2; including a global Security firm, although only applicants applying for jobs in the United States were studied) and (3) General Business companies (N = 4; i.e. Retail & Manufacturing firms). The main focus of this applied research was on the passing rates of the applicants on the Vangent Reid Report. Cut-scores to determine passing rates were kept constant across the employment domains.

Table 6 summarizes the results for the 5,874 job applicants as a function of organizational type. Overall results revealed that 15.6 percent of the total applicants were *Not Recommended* (NR) due to both their tolerant attitudes toward employee theft and their self-reported admissions of deviance. In addition, 3% received *Qualified Recommend* (QR) status, which means their attitudes toward theft were probably acceptable but they made a troubling admission, and 81.5% were *Recommended* (R), which means that they had both favorable attitudes and past histories. It is interesting to note that significantly more police applicants were classified as *Not Recommend* (NR) or received a *Qualified Recommend* (QR) outcome compared to the other two groups of job candidates. Such results indicate that police departments may receive many applications from individuals who are theft-prone and lack integrity, indicating that departments should not deny or minimize this type of risk exposure.

Table 6
REID REPORT ASSESSMENT EVALUATION CATEGORIES BY SAMPLE

Organization X2	NR	QR	R	Total
Police Departments	45 (38.5%)	6 (5.1%)	66 (56.4%)	117 100.0%
Security Firms	449 (14.2%)	104 (3.3%)	2603 (82.5%)	3156 100.0%
General Business	420 (16.1%)	64 (2.5%)	2117 (81.4%)	2601 100.0%
Total	914 (15.6%)	174 (3.0%)	4786 (81.5%)	5874 100.00%
58.28**				

**Value is significant at the 0.01 level. NR Not Recommend; QR Qualified Recommend; R Recommend

Reid Report Profile Analysis

The Reid Integrity Attitude Scale is the primary predictor of overall integrity potential, but, as indicated above, the Reid integrity assessment instruments also assesses job-related admissions. Figure 1 shows the report of an applicant to a police department who was *Not Recommended* by the RPSR, with the name redacted. This applicant had extremely low integrity attitudes suggesting a high likelihood of engaging in on-the-job dishonesty and mis-behavior. This impression was confirmed by the applicant's admissions of misbehaviors on past jobs, including: theft of merchandise from employer in the past and providing unauthorized discounts at work. Moreover, this job candidate had an extremely low Service Relations score, indicating that s/he would act more abrasively in the community and would more than likely have interpersonal conflicts with his superiors and peers, among others. Finally, follow-up interview questions were generated to both better under-stand and to confirm such admissions of deviance.

The police applicant in Figure 1 who was assessed pre-offer was not unique in his/her pattern of misbehaviors. Table 7 summarizes actual admis-sions of misbehaviors made by job applicants applying to both the police (N = 117) and security (N = 3,156) positions. Again, both groups of protective services applicants who were assessed in the pre-offer phase made significant job-related admissions.

Assessment Results: NOT RECOMMEND

The Reid Report with Service (RR-SR)

Scales

Attitudes	Description	Value	10	20	30	40	50	60	70	80	90	100
Integrity	%	7										
Service Relations	%	8										

Significant Admissions | Number

Social Behavior	2
Substance Use	0
Work Background	0
Service Relations Admits	0
Total Count	2

Significant Indicators

Significant Admissions

Social Behavior

Applicant has taken $10 or less in merchandise from employers in the past three years.

Applicant has given unauthorized discounts at work once or twice in the last three years.

Additional Information

Work Background

Applicant has sometimes ignored safety rules at work in the past three years.

Applicant has left a job because of difficulties in getting along with coworkers or managers.

Service Relations Admits

Applicant has shouted at a supervisor once or twice in the past year.

Applicant has shouted at a fellow worker once or twice in the past year.

Interview Questions

Integrity

You said you've been tempted to take company merchandise. What were you tempted to take and what stopped you from taking it?

You said you don't believe you are too honest to steal. What kind of situation at work do you think might tempt you to steal?

How much money do you think a person would have to take before he or she should be fired?

What do you think an employer should do, if anything, if an employee cheats him or her out of overtime?

You reported that most workers have cheated their employers out of something. What have you cheated an employer out of?

Social Behavior

You reported having taken merchandise without permission from past employers. What did you take, how often and why did you do it?

What products, free services or discounts have you given away without permission? How often and why did you do it?

Work Background

You reported ignoring safety rules at work in the last three years. Why was that?

Please tell me more about when you left a job because you didn't get along with a coworker, supervisor or manager.

Service Relations

You indicated that you keep calm even when someone is mad at you. Tell me about a time you kept calm when someone was mad.

You responded that you probably enjoy making people feel better. Why do you enjoy it and how do you do it?

You indicated you get tremendous satisfaction out of serving others. Why does serving others satisfy you and when were you most satisfied?

Service Relations Admits

You reported shouting in anger at a supervisor in the past year. Please tell me about the circumstances regarding that situation.

You reported shouting in anger at a fellow worker in the past year. Please tell me about the circumstances regarding that situation.

Figure 1. Reid Report Police Pre-Offer Applicant.

Table 7

PRE-OFFER ADMISSIONS OF COUNTERPRODUCTIVE BEHAVIOR (PARTIAL LISTING)

Assessment Category

Police	Security	Specific Behavioral Admission Item

Theft, Fraud, & Dishonesty

Police	Security	Specific Behavioral Admission Item
6.84%	3.64%	Gave unauthorized discounts to others in the past three years
5.13%	0.98%	Took merchandise from work without permission in the past three years
2.56%	1.62%	Committed a crime involving theft, fraud, or dishonesty in the past five years
0.85%	1.14%	Convicted of a crime involving theft, fraud, or dishonesty in the past five years
4.27%	1.87%	Took something from a store without paying for it in the past five years
0.85%	0.35%	Took money from work without permission in the past three years

Social Behavior

Police	Security	Specific Behavioral Admission Item
23.08%	12.67%	Engaged in shouting matches at work
4.27%	5.13%	Committed or were disciplined for sexual harassment at work
0.85%	1.65%	Engaged in shoving matches or fistfights at work

Work Background

Police	Security	Specific Behavioral Admission Item
6.84%	12.10%	Was fired from past jobs
14.53%	11.41%	Quit jobs because didn't get along with co-worker, supervisor, or manager
0.00%	2.72%	Quit 3 or more jobs in the past 3 years
14.53%	5.99%	Ignored safety rules at work
3.42%	2.28%	Had multiple unexcused absences from work in the past year
0.00%	2.60%	Plans to work for the company less than one year
0.85%	1.84%	Were late without permission two times a month or more

Additional analyses revealed that Integrity Attitude scale scores correlated significantly with a composite measure of the admitted employee theft and deviance behaviors shown in Table 7, along with some additional admissions of illicit substance abuse. For police applicants the correlation was r = -.54, p < .01, and for the security applicants the correlation was r = -.36, p < .01. These correlations further demonstrate the job relevance of the Reid Integrity Attitude Scale as an attitudinal measure that can be used for identifying both police and security applicants likely to engage in dishonest or theft-related behaviors at work. The more admissions an individual makes, the lower he/she typically scores on the Reid Integrity Attitudes scale, thus documenting the criterion-related validity of this attitudinal measure of integrity. These validity coefficients are consistent with previous test validation research on Vangent assessments (cf. Cunningham, 1997; Cunningham & Jones, 2008).

Applicant Acceptance of Pre-Offer Integrity Tests

When Vangent research teams first started developing and validating pre-employment integrity tests, both professionals and practitioners speculated that pre-employment integrity tests would be perceived as being overly offensive by job applicants. Therefore, Vangent research teams conducted a series of studies on test invasiveness, which yielded a consistent pattern of results. For example, to assess the invasiveness of the Reid Report, a random sample of 9,022 applicants were asked to rate their acceptance or resentment toward the instrument. Based on these responses, 92 percent of the sample perceived the test as being nonintrusive. Only 1.5 percent indicated that they "very much resented" answering any test part (Cunningham, 1997).

AVOID UNJUSTIFIABLE INVASIVENESS. When tort attorneys who specialized in privacy invasiveness in the workplace examined a pool of scrambled test items, follow-up statistical analyses showed that the most offensive items came from clinical tests like the MMPI, which at the time included items that asked about sexual, religious, and other highly private behaviors that were not job-relevant. The second most offensive items came from general personality tests that asked overly personal questions that were not clearly related to work. Finally, the least offensive items were from job related integrity tests that asked straightforward questions about attitudes toward workplace theft (Jones, Ash, Soto, & Terris, 1991).

AVOID A ONE-SIZE-FITS-ALL BATTERY. Personality-oriented measures of responsibility are most likely to be packaged in a battery of tests, which may contain other scales that create problems. As noted earlier, *Conscientiousness* is most likely to be assessed with other FFM global measures, some of which may be unrelated to work performance, and others, such as *Emotional*

Instability, which may be inappropriate for pre-offer screening. Even when a FFM assessment is advertised as a measure of "normal personality" that can be administered pre-offer caution is warranted (see Jones & Arnold, 2008). Similar care should be exercised when considering other test batteries which might contain invasive items that were developed prior to the ADA.

UNDERSTAND WHO COMPLAINS. Finally, it was discovered that anywhere from 1–2 percent of general population job applicants felt somewhat offended at having to take preemployment integrity tests (cf. Cunningham, 1997). However, a follow-up statistical analysis revealed that the offended applicants made significantly more admissions of past theft and deviance that the majority of applicants who were not offended. That is, admitted thieves were significantly more likely to be offended!

The foregoing indicates that pre-offer measures of integrity would typically be experienced as inoffensive and noninvasive unless a job applicant with a history of theft and deviance became agitated and upset while taking the exam (cf. Rosse, Miller, & Ringer, 1996). Thus, any FFM or other general measure of personality that is being considered for pre-offer assessment should be excluded if it includes offensive clinical or general personality items that ask questions about one's family, health status, or emotional maladjustment. The bottom line is that the most offensive test items should always be administered as part of the post-offer clinical assessments.

Summary

This chapter compared and contrasted pre-employment integrity tests versus Five-Factor Model personality assessments as possible tools to use during pre-offer police applicant testing. Pre-offer integrity tests are critically important due to the high value placed on police officer integrity, one of the most important competencies in police work. Special attention was given to the Five-Factor model measures of conscientiousness, which suggested the following conclusions:

JOB-RELEVANCY. Job analyses and competency modeling exercises conducted with police departments would surely document the importance of police officer honesty and integrity, but too few police departments use targeted pre-employment integrity tests to optimally control for theft exposures (cf. Cochrane, Tett & Vandercreek, 2003).

VALIDITY. Measures of conscientiousness that are commonly provided as part of a Five-Factor Model test battery typically do not predict employee theft potential at the same degree of magnitude as pre-employment integrity tests (cf. Cunningham & Jones, 2008).

RISK EXPOSURE. Despite common misperceptions, police officer candidates do need to be screened for integrity attitudes since they are placed in positions of trust with high theft exposure. Moreover, data reviewed in this paper revealed that a sample of police officer candidates scored significantly poorer on a standardized measure of integrity–the Reid Report–than did both general business applicants and security applicants (cf. Jones & Dages, 2008).

ADA COMPLIANCE. There is a greater risk that a few inappropriate and medically oriented test items will be included in a FFM general personality questionnaire compared to a job-related measure of integrity, especially those five-factor model items that load onto the Emotional Instability/Neuroticism global factor. This issue will become even more important in the near future with the 2008 passage of the new Americans with Disabilities Amendment Act (cf. Jones & Arnold, 2008). Moreover, for those police psychologists advocating a "bifurcated" assessment model (cf. Corey, 2008), only pre-offer tests, scales, and items that comply fully with the ADA and related amendments to the ADA can be administered pre-offer.

NONINVASIVENESS. Lastly, the most invasive test items typically come from test questionnaires and inventories that measure clinical/medical issues and general personality traits, respectively, as opposed to either measures of integrity or conscientiousness (cf. Jones, Ash, Soto, & Terris, 1991).

Finally, it is also worth noting that clinically-oriented police psychologists must realize that psychopathology is not the only "trigger" for employee theft and other forms of corruption among police officers. That is, one can also use a nonclinical pre-employment integrity test in the pre-offer phase to determine with a relatively high degree of accuracy if a police officer job candidate is cognitively endorsing attitudes, values, beliefs, and perceptions that make on-the-job theft and deviance a high probability occurrence (cf. Jones, 1991). However, one must also remember that FFM measures of conscientiousness, which were never originally developed and validated to predict on-the-job theft and related counterproductive behaviors, will yield more misclassifications when it comes to psychometrically identifying potentially theft-prone and dishonest job candidates. Whether administered pre-offer or post-offer, it is our position that pre-employment integrity tests can only strengthen a comprehensive psychological evaluation of police officer candidates.

REFERENCES

Ajzen, I. (1991). The theory of planned behavior. *Organizational Behavior and Human Decision Processes. 50*, 179–211.

Ajzen, I. & Fishbein, M. (1977). Attitude-behavior relations: A theoretical analysis and review of empirical research. *Psychological Bulletin. 84*, 888–918.

Arnold, D. & Brooks, P. (1988). Personality correlates of honesty in a public safety setting, *RPS Research Abstract Number 14.* Chicago: Reid Psychological Systems.

Ash, P. (1970). Validation of an instrument to predict the likelihood of employee theft. Proceedings of the 78th Annual Convention of the American Psychological Association, 579–580.

Ash, P. (1971). Screening employment applicants for attitudes toward theft. *Journal of Applied Psychology, 55,* 161–164.

Ash, P. (1986). Test prediction versus hiring without testing: False positives and false negatives. *Research Memorandum Number 10.* Chicago: Reid Psychological Systems.

Association of Test Publishers. (2009). *Model Guidelines for Preemployment Integrity Testing.* Washington, DC: ATP.

Barrick, M.R. & Mount, M.K. (1991). The Big Five personality dimensions and job performance: A meta-analysis. *Personnel Psychology. 44,* 1–25.

Barrick, M.R., Mount, M.K. & Judge, T.A. (2001). Personality and performance at the beginning of the new millennium. What do we know and where do we go next? *Personality and Performance. 9,* 9–28.

Befort, S.F. (1997). Pre-offer screening and investigation. Navigating between a rock and a hard place. *Hofstra Labor Law Review. 14,* 365–422.

Berry, C.M., Ones, D.S. & Sackett, P.R. (2007). Interpersonal deviance, organizational deviance, and their common correlates: A review and meta-analysis. *Journal of Applied Psychology. 92,* 410–424.

Berry, C.M., Sackett, P.R. & Weimann, S. (2007) A review of recent developments in integrity test research. *Personnel Psychology, 60,* 271–301.

Billings, S. (2006). Summary of 2006 API use at a major retail chain. *Vangent Technical Report.* Vangent, Inc.: Chicago.

Brewster, J. & Stoloff, M.L. (2003). Using MMPI Special Scale Configurations to Predict Supervisor Ratings of Police Officer Performance. *Applied H.R.M. Research. 9,* 53–56.

Brooks, P. (1990a). Predictive relationship of the Reid Report to measures of employee work performance in a retail setting. *Research Memorandum Number 36.* Chicago: Reid Psychological Systems.

Brooks, P. (1990b). Relationship of the Reid Report to performance ratings in a retail environment. *Research Memorandum Number 34.* Chicago: Reid Psychological Systems.

Brooks, P. (1992). Classification accuracy of the Reid Public Safety Report. *Research Abstract Number 54.* Chicago: Reid Psychological Systems.

Brooks, P., & Arnold, D. (1989a). *Reid Report Examiner's Manual (3rd Ed.).* Chicago: Reid Psychological Systems.

Brooks, P. & Arnold, D. (1989b). Public Safety attitudes as predictors of public safety organizational criteria, *Research Memorandum Number 30.* Chicago: Reid Psychological Systems.

Brooks, P. & Arnold, D. (1989c). Integrity attitudes as predictors of public safety organizational criteria. *Research Memorandum Number 29.* Chicago: Reid Psychological Systems.

Castora, K., Brewster, J. & Stoloff, M. (2003). Predicting aggression in police officers using the MMPI-2. *Journal of Police and Criminal Psychology, 18,* 1–18.

Claussen-Rogers, N.L. & Arrigo, B.A. (2005). *Police corruption and psychological testing.* Durham, NC: Carolina Academic Press.

Cochrane, R.E., Tett, R.P. & Vandecreek, L. (2003). Psychological testing and the selection of police officers: A national survey. *Criminal Justice and Behavior, 30,* 511–537.

Corey, D. (2008, Oct). Bifurcation Implications. *Annual Conference of the Society of Police and Criminal Psychology.* Walnut Creek, California.

Cortina, J.M., Doherty, M.L., Schmitt, N., Kaufman, G. & Smith, R.G. (1992). The "Big Five" personality factors in the IPI and MMPI: Predictors of police performance. *Personnel Psychology, 45,* 119–130.

Costa, P.T. Jr. & McRae, R.R. (1992). *Revised NEO personality inventory and new five factor inventory: Professional manual.* Psychological Assessment Resources, Odessa, Fl.

Cunningham, M.R. (1997). The Reid Public Safety Report. *Security Journal. 8,* 151–155.

Cunningham, M.R. & Ash, P. (1988). The structure of honesty: Factor analysis of the Reid Report. *Journal of Business and Psychology. 3,* 54–66.

Cunningham, M. R. & Ash, P. (1989). Testtaking motivations and outcomes on a standardized measure of onthejob integrity. *Journal of Business and Psychology, 4,* 119–127.

Cunningham, M.R. & Jones, J.W. (2008). *Impacting key business indicators in the United States: Why attitude and behavior assessments are better predictors of effective hiring decisions than personality tests.* Chicago: Vangent Human Capital Sciences White Paper.

Cunningham, M.R., Wong, D.T. & Barbee, A.P. (1994). Self-presentation dynamics on preemployment integrity tests: Experimental studies of the Reid Report Inventory. *Journal of Applied Psychology. 79,* 643–658.

Dages, K.D. & Jones, J.W. (2008). "Content validity of occupational personality measures." Paper presented at Midwestern Psychological Associates, Annual Conference, Chicago, IL, May 2009, Chicago: Vangent Human Capital Sciences Technical Report.

Delattre, E.J. (2002). *Character and Cops: Ethics in Policing.* Washington, D.C.: The AEI Press.

Digman, J.M. (1994). Historical antecedents of the five-factor model. In P.T. Costa & T.A. Widiger (Editors), *Personality Disorders and the Five-Factor Model of Personality.* Washington, D.C.: American Psychological Association, pp. 13-18.

Goldberg, L.R., Johnson, J.A., Eber, H.W., Hogan, R., Ashton, M.C., Cloninger, C.R. & Gough, H.G. (2006). The international personality item pool and the future of public-domain personality measures. *Journal of Research in Personality. 40,* 84–96.

Griffin v. Steeltek, Inc., 160 F.3d 591 (10th Cir. 1998).

Gwynne, S.C. (1995). Cops and robbers. *Time.* New York: March 20, Vol. 145, Issue 11, pg. 45.

International Association of Chiefs of Police (IACP) Police Psychology Services Section. (2004). *Pre-employment psychological evaluation services guidelines.* Los Angeles, CA: IACP. (Available on IACP's website)

Inwald, R. (1992). *IPI: Inwald Personality Inventory technical manual.* New York: Hilson Research, Inc.

Johnson, O. (2008). Boston officers eyed in drug thefts. *Internal Affairs News,* http://www.officer.com/Internal-Affairs-News/Boston-Officers-Eyed-in-Drug-Thefts/5$33257. July 8th Updated Version.

Jones, J.W. (1991). Attitude-behavior relations: A theoretical and empirical analysis of preemployment integrity tests. In J.W. Jones (Editor), *Preemployment honesty testing: Current research and future directions.* Westport, CT: Greenwood/Quorum Books.

Jones, J.W. & Arnold, D.W. (2008). Protecting the legal and appropriate use of personality testing: A practitioner perspective. *Industrial and Organizational Psychology: Perspectives on Science and Practice. 1,* 296–298.

Jones, J.W., Ash, P., Soto, C. & Terris, W. (1991). Protecting job applicants' privacy rights when using preemployment honesty tests. In J.W. Jones (Editor), *Preemployment honesty testing: Current research and future directions.* Westport, CT: Greenwood/Quorum Books.

Jones, J.W. & Dages, K.D. (2008a, Oct.). "Integrity Testing versus the Five-Factor Model Personality Assessments for Pre-Offer Police Selection: A Practitioner's Perspective." Paper presented at The Annual Conference of the Society for Police and Criminal Psychology, Walnut Creek, California, 2008.

Jones, J.W. & Dages, K.D. (2008b). *Performance analysis summary: Impact of Vangent's Reid Report in the Security Industry.* Chicago: Vangent Human Capital Sciences Technical Report.

Kamp, J. (1989). Relationship of the Reid Report to time theft in a retail setting. *Research Memorandum Number 24.* Chicago: Reid Psychological Systems.

Karraker v. Rent-A-Center, 411 F.3d. 831 (7th Cir. 2005).

Lee, K., Ashton, M.C. & deVries, R.E. (2005). Predicting workplace delinquency and integrity with the HEXACO and five-factor models of personality structure. *Human Performance, 18,* 179–197.

Leventis, A. (2008). Ex-officer is found guilty of theft. *St. Louis Post – Dispatch.* St. Louis, MO, September 13, pg. A.8.

Marcus, B. Lee, K. & Ashton, M.C. (2007). Personality dimensions explaining relationships between integrity tests and counterproductive behavior: Big Five, or one in addition? *Personnel Psychology, 60,* 1–34.

Mook, J.R. (2008). Psychological testing and the ADA. *LexisNexis Expert Commentaries.* Jan., 1–13.

Morgeson, F.P., Campion, M.A., Dipboye, R.L., Hollenbeck, J.R., Murphy, K., & Schmitt, N. (2007). Are we getting fooled again? Coming to terms with limitations in the use of personality tests for personnel selection. *Personnel Psychology. 60,* 1029–1049.

Murphy, K.R. & Lee, S.L. (1994a). Does conscientiousness explain the relation between integrity and job performance? *International Journal of Section and Assessment, 2,* 226–233.

Murphy, K.R. & Lee, S. L. (1994b). Personality variables related to integrity scores: The role of conscientiousness. *Journal of Business and Psychology, 8,* 413–424.

Ones, D.S., Dilchert, S., Viswesvaran, C. & Judge, T.A. (2007) In support of personality assessment in organizational settings. *Personnel Psychology. 60,* 995–1027.

Ones, D.S., Viswesvaran, C. & Schmidt, F.L. (1993). Comprehensive meta-analysis of integrity test validities: Findings and implications for personnel selection and theories of job performance. *Journal of Applied Psychology. 78,* 679–703.

Ones, D.S, Viswesvaran C., & Schmidt, F.L. (2003). Personality and absenteeism: A meta-analysis of integrity tests. *European Journal of Personality, 17,* S19–S38.

Peirce, W.G. & Martin, S.L. (1997). The Law Enforcement Applicant Inventory. *Security Journal. 8,* 85–89.

Reid, J. E., & Inbau, F. E. (1977). *Truth and deception* (2nd Ed.). Baltimore, MD: Williams and Wilkins.

Rosse, J.G., Miller J.L., & Ringer, R.C. (1996) The deterrent value of drug and integrity testing. *Journal of Business and Psychology, 10,* 477–485.

Salgado, J.F. (2002). The big five personality dimensions and counterproductive behaviors. *International Journal of Selection and Assessment. 10,* 117-125.

Samuels, J.E. (2000). *The measurement of police integrity.* Washington, DC: U.S. Department of Justice "Research in Brief."

Saucier, G. & Goldberg, L.R. (2002). Assessing the big five: Applications of 10 psychometric criteria to the development of marker scales. In B. de Raad & M. Perugini (Editors), *Big Five assessment.* Ashland, Ohio: Hogrefe & Huber Publications. pp. 30–54.

Sellbom, M., Fischler, G.L. & Ben-Porath, Y.S. (2007). Identifying MMPI-2 predictors of police officer integrity and misconduct. *Criminal Justice and Behavior. 34,* 985–1003.

Silver, J.DE. (2008). Ex-police officer charged with theft of seized drugs. *Pittsburgh Post-Gazette.* October 29th Edition.

Tett, R.P., Jackson, D.N. & Rothstein, M. (1991). Personality measures as predictors of job performance: A meta-analytic review. *Personnel Psychology. 44,* 703–742.

Vangent, Inc. (2008). *The Vangent Competency Modeling System Information Guide.* Chicago: Vangent Human Capital Sciences.

Weiss, W.U., Davis, R., Rostow, C. & Kinsman, S. (2003). The MMPI-2 L scale as a tool in police selection. *Journal of Police and Criminal Psychology. 18,* 57–60.

Chapter 8

USING THE RORSCHACH COMPREHENSIVE SYSTEM IN POLICE PSYCHOLOGY

JoAnne Brewster, Phillip W. Wickline and Michael L. Stoloff

The Rorschach is used infrequently in police psychology today, particularly when compared with self-report personality inventories, such as the Minnesota Multiphasic Personality Inventory-2 (MMPI-2; Butcher, Dahlstrom, Graham, Tellegen, & Kaemmer, 1989), the California Psychological Inventory (CPI; Gough, 1996), and the Inwald Personality Inventory (IPI; Inwald, 1992). It was used more frequently in the past; in 1979 Spielberger reported that it was one of the most commonly used tests in police departments. In contrast, only 4.4 percent and 5.8 percent of police departments reported using the Rorschach in 1990 and 2003, respectively (Ash, Slora, & Britton, 1990; Cochrane, Tett, & Vandercreek, 2003). A recent survey of 20 psychologists who perform pre-employment psychological screenings of police officer candidates revealed that none of them reported using the Rorschach as part of their assessment battery (Super, 2006).

There are few published studies that describe the use of the Rorschach with police officers. Kates (1950) administered the Rorschach to 25 New York City patrolmen in a study of job satisfaction in police. This study was conducted before the development of the Rorschach Comprehensive System (RCS), making it difficult to compare the results to current studies. Rankin (1959) noted that the Rorschach was one of the most valuable tests that he used to screen police recruits, however, he did not describe how he scored or used his data, and his group administration method would not be used today. Matarazzo, Allen, Saslow, and Wiens (1964) administered the Rorschach to successful applicants for the positions of police officer or firefighter. They reported that, using the Beck method of scoring the protocols, the police and fire applicants did not differ from each other on any

Rorschach variable. Peterson (1997) presented a case study of the Rorschach profile of a police officer who had sought outpatient treatment at a facility for Vietnam veterans. Zacker (1997) published descriptive statistics on a number of RCS variables for 53 police applicants. He noted that some of his results called into question the appropriateness of the candidates for police work. He did not report data on hire rates for the applicants, or subsequent performance data. All of these studies have drawbacks that reduce their contribution to an understanding of the current value of the Rorschach in police psychology.

Recently, some psychologists have suggested that the Rorschach might be a useful tool for police psychologists involved in pre-employment psychological evaluations, fitness-for-duty evaluations, and the selection of officers for promotions or special duty assignments (Brewster, 1995; Weiss, 2000; Weiss, 2002; Weiss, Weiss, & Gacono, 2008). Weiss et al. (2008) have additionally suggested that the Rorschach might be useful in treatment planning for police officers who are experiencing emotional difficulties. There have been no published data on the utility of the Rorschach for any of these uses, although some preliminary data have been presented on the predictive validity of the Rorschach in pre-employment screenings (Wickline, Brewster, & Stoloff, 2002, 2007, 2008; Brewster, Wickline, Williams, & Stoloff, 2007).

Criticisms, Misperceptions, and Drawbacks of the Rorschach

The Rorschach is often poorly understood, even by psychologists. Many psychologists who are unfamiliar with its current use believe that it is a projective test whose reliability and validity have not been adequately established, and that it is inadmissible in court. These issues have been comprehensively addressed by other authors, and have been resolved to the satisfaction of assessment psychologists and the courts, but we will discuss them briefly. We will also address the issue of the time that it takes to properly administer and interpret the Rorschach.

Reliability and Validity of the Rorschach

There is evidence that the Rorschach is reliable and valid for assessing personality traits in a wide variety of populations, when it is administered, scored, and interpreted according to the principles of the Rorschach Comprehensive System (RCS; Exner, 2003). Studies of interrater reliability among graduate students, expert raters, practicing clinicians, and researchers have reported reliability coefficients largely in the excellent range (i.e. $> .74$;

Cicchetti, 1994) for primary interpretive variables. Meyer and his colleagues (2002) reported a range of intraclass correlation coefficients (ICC) from .82 to .95 across these four groups, with a mean pooled ICC of .91. Similar results have been found for the temporal stability of RCS variables. Gronnerod (2003) reported correlation coefficients ranging from .55 for variables over a five-year period to .84 over 21 days. The results of several meta-analyses have revealed that RCS scores possess validity coefficients generally equivalent to those for scores on other commonly used assessment instruments such as the WAIS, MMPI, and MMPI-2 (Hiller, Rosenthal, Bornstein, Berry, & Brunell-Neuleib, 1999; Meyer & Archer, 2001; Rosenthal, Hiller, Bornstein, Berry, & Brunell-Neuleib, 2001; Mattlar, 2004; Parker, Hanson, & Hunsley, 1988).

Admissibility in Court

Because the results of pre-employment psychological evaluations may be challenged legally (Ho, 2001), the RCS must meet legal standards for admissibility in expert witness testimony (Weiss, 2002; Weiss et al., 2008). Several authors (Hamel, Gallagher, & Soares, 2001; Hilsenroth & Stricker, 2004; McCann & Evans, 2008; Ritzler, Erard, & Pettigrew, 2002) have detailed how the RCS meets relevant professional and legal standards, including the *Federal Rules of Evidence* (1992), the *Frye test (United States v. Frye, 1923),* and the *Daubert* standard *(Daubert v. Merrell Dow Pharmaceuticals, Inc.,* 1993) and its clarifications (i.e., *General Electric Co. v. Joiner,* 1997; *Kumho Tire Co. Ltd. V. Carmichael,* 1999) regarding the use of psychological tests in court. Surveys of assessment psychologists (Weiner, Exner, & Sciara, 1996) and U.S. case law (Meloy, Hansen, & Weiner, 1997) have revealed that testimony based on the results of RCS data is rarely challenged, and even less frequently excluded. Meloy's (2008) recent review of 150 appellate cases that included the Rorschach between 1996 and 2005 noted that there had been no Daubert challenge to the scientific status of the Rorschach in any appellate court during that time period.

Usability of the Rorschach

There are potentially legitimate criticisms that the Rorschach is not cost-effective for routine personnel screening. The Rorschach must be individually administered by an examiner who is well-trained in administration, coding, and interpretation. Administration typically takes 30–60 minutes. Time spent coding and interpreting the data varies with the length of the record and the experience of the examiner, and takes at least another hour (Camara, Nathan, & Puente, 2000). This may not be justified for many personnel decisions, since other personality tests, such as self-report personality inventories, may provide sufficient information with less investment of expensive professional time. We believe that the additional cost is justified for law enforcement and other high risk occupations, because the Rorschach may be more resistant to defensiveness than self-report inventories, and it may provide information about personality functioning that would be difficult to obtain using the inventories.

Potential Benefits of the Rorschach in Police Psychology

Rorschach Resilience Against Defensiveness

Psychological evaluation in police selection usually consists of administration of one or more self-report inventories. The MMPI-2 and the IPI are two of the most commonly used (Super, 2006). Newer inventories have also been developed to aid in police selection, such as the M-PULSE (Davis & Rostow, 2008). These tools include items that may be "transparent" in intent to a police candidate. Of course, each of these instruments has validity scales. Blatant or unsophisticated "faking good" can often be identified, and the candidate might be rejected or subject to additional screening. However, it is likely that a significant amount of subtle impression management occurs when police officer candidates respond to self-report inventories, which can distort the accuracy of the information generated.

Any MMPI-2 clinical scale elevation over 65 T has been shown to be associated with poorer performance in police officers (Brewster & Stoloff, 1999), so psychological examiners and police administrators should be cautious about accepting such candidates. Every police psychologist probably also has examples of officers whose MMPI-2 validity and clinical scales were within acceptable ranges, who subsequently performed poorly because of undetected personality problems. Weiss and his colleagues (Weiss, Weiss, Cain, & Manley, 2009) demonstrated that individuals asked to take the MMPI-2 while imagining that they were applying for a position as a police officer produced significantly higher scores on scales L and K and significantly lower scores on most of the clinical scales than they had when taking the test under standard conditions. They suggest that the pre-employment evaluation for police officers is likely to produce a fake-good response set in which candidates will not report existing psychological problems. For screening high risk occupations, we need an assessment tool that is not as vulnerable to attempts at impression management as self-report inventories. We agree with others (Zacker, 1997; Weiss, 2002; Weiss et al., 2008) that the Rorschach might be that tool.

It may be difficult for subjects to fake good on the Rorschach. In two studies, alleged sex offenders, who had strong motivation to deny psychological problems and were in legal situations almost guaranteed to produce distress, produced MMPI profiles within the normal range. Nevertheless, they still showed evidence of distress and psychopathology on the Rorschach that was consistent with what would be expected in view of their legal problems (Grossman, Wasyliw, Benn, & Gyoerkoe, 2002; Wasyliw, Benn, Grossman, & Haywood, 1998). This suggests that in spite of their ability to produce a positive impression on the MMPI-2, they were not able to do so on the Rorschach. Ganellen (1994) reported RCS results for a sample of airline pilots undergoing fitness-for-duty evaluations following treatment for drug and alcohol problems. Although all of the pilots produced defensive MMPI profiles, results from the Rorschach revealed significant problems in functioning that were consistent with their histories and stressors at the time of testing. Singer, Hoppe, Lee, Olesen and Walters (2008) reported Rorschach findings of 728 child custody litigants, a group that would be expected to attempt to create a positive impression and to minimize or deny psychological problems. Their Rorschach protocols still contained features that suggested difficulties in their psychological functioning.

Ganellen (2008) recently reviewed the literature regarding attempts to consciously manipulate Rorschach findings. He concluded that some individuals do appear to be able to produce defensive Rorschach protocols that reveal little, and an evaluator should not draw firm conclusions from those protocols about the presence or absence of psychological problems. However, many individuals who are motivated to produce a favorable impression, and who succeed in doing so on the MMPI, still produce valid and interpretable Rorschach protocols that reveal evidence of psychological difficulties. If an individual who is motivated to portray himself in a positive light still produces a valid and interpretable Rorschach protocol, any existing psychological problems may be revealed. This would potentially make the Rorschach an ideal tool to use in police selection.

Incremental Validity of the Rorschach

The Rorschach provides information about some of the same characteristics as self-report personality inventories, and the data from the different types of instruments can be compared. If inconsistencies are found, particularly if there are indications of defensiveness on the self-report inventories, perhaps more weight should be given to the Rorschach findings, because it may be relatively easy for the average police officer candidate to minimize psychopathology on self-report measures. In contrast, it may be difficult to deliberately create a positive impression on the Rorschach, as described above. Several authors (Blais, Hilsenroth, Castelbury, Fowler, & Baity, 2001; Ganellen, 1996; Weiner, 1999) have suggested that using the Rorschach and the MMPI in conjunction can produce more information than using the MMPI alone. This suggestion is consistent with the current practice of assessment based on the integration of the results of more than one test or method (Mattlar, 2004; Meyer et al., 2001). Zacker (1997) noted that the Rorschach information that he obtained from his police candidates was incremental to the information obtained on the MMPI-2, particularly regarding reality testing and coping deficits. Wickline, Brewster, and Stoloff (2002) also suggested that the Rorschach can provide additional information about coping skills in police officers, beyond what is provided by the MMPI-2. Weiss and his colleagues (Weiss, 2002; Weiss et al., 2008) agreed that a potential benefit of using the RCS in police pre-employment evaluations is the unique information that it can provide above and beyond commonly used self-report inventories.

The Current Investigation

This chapter will focus on the potential contributions of the Rorschach to understanding the police personality, the information that it can provide beyond that obtained on the MMPI-2, and whether that information can be used in police selection. We will describe Rorschach data from 128 police officer candidates obtained during a psychological evaluation performed shortly after they had been offered positions as police officers. Our goal is to provide normative data on the Rorschach responses of individuals who have gone on to become police officers. First, we will describe the MMPI-2 profiles of the officers to compare the data obtained from a self-report inventory with the data obtained from the Rorschach. The officers' Rorschach data will also be compared with a normative non-patient sample (Exner, 2007) and with Zacker's (1997) sample of officers. Finally, we will summarize preliminary analyses of the predictive validity of selected RCS scores for various aspects of police performance.

Method

Participants

The sample of 128 officers consisted of 110 men and 18 women between the ages of 19 and 46 (M = 26.18 years, SD = 4.80). Twenty-five percent had a high school education, 39 percent had up to two years of college, 34 percent had three to four years of college, and 2 percent had more than four years of college (M = 14.09 years, SD = 1.60). Ninety-six percent of the officers were Caucasian, 3 percent were African-American, and 1 percent were Hispanic.

Procedures

The Rorschach was administered as part of a multimethod battery that also included the MMPI-2 and an interview. All of the participants became police officers in one of two small city police departments. Yearly performance ratings completed by each officer's direct supervisor were collected for as long as the individual was employed by the department.

The 128 protocols were collected by the first author between 1992 and 2008 as part of a larger research project designed to validate the use of various psychological tests in police selection. The data were not used to screen out officers, but the officers knew that feedback would be provided to their departments to assist with their supervision. All of the officers seemed to take the evaluation seriously, and appeared to be putting their best foot forward.

All of the officers consented to participate in the evaluation and the research project. At the time of the evaluation, most had never consulted a mental health professional. Two officers had been treated for depression, and one had briefly seen a psychologist as a child, after his parents' divorce. None of the officers reported use of psychotropic medications or recreational drugs, with the exception of one officer who was previously prescribed an antidepressant, and a small number of officers who reported occasional marijuana use when younger.

Each protocol was coded by the examiner who administered the test. Thirty-five percent of the protocols were also coded by another psychologist, and discrepancies were resolved by discussion. To establish interrater reliability, 20 additional protocols were independently coded by the second author. Percent agreement for traditional response code segments ranged from .92 for determinants to .99 for special scores other than those included in the *Sum6* variable. Meyer's (1999) formulas for estimating kappa coefficients were used to correct for chance agreement. Estimated kappa coefficients ranged from .82 for the cognitive special scores to .96 for both location and the frequency of Z scores assigned. Using Cicchetti's (1994) interpretive guidelines, these statistics all fall in the "excellent" range.

RESULTS

MMPI-2 Descriptive Statistics

Profile Validity

Table 1 at the end of this chapter contains descriptive statistics for each of the original MMPI-2 validity and clinical scales. Thirty percent of the officers obtained scores between 56-64 *T* on the *L* scale, and 45 percent obtained scores in this range on the *K* scale. Scores in this range raise the possibility of defensive responding, although the profile can still be interpreted if the defensiveness is taken into account. An additional 31 percent had scores above 64 *T* on the *L* scale and 32 percent had scores above 64 *T* on the *K* scale, suggesting that they were trying to present an unusually favorable impression of themselves. Scores in this range represent a level of defensiveness that seriously limits the utility of the protocol, which should probably not be interpreted (Graham, 2006).

Basic Clinical Scales

There were very few elevations on any of the clinical scales and their means were all within normal limits. For several clinical scales (*D, Hy, Pa, Pt,* and *Sc*), none of the candidates obtained a score above 64 *T*. For scales *Hs, Pd, Ma,* and *Si*, one to three candidates (1-2%) had scores above 64 *T*. Through their responses, none of the candidates acknowledged symptoms of depression, stress, suspiciousness, anxiety, or difficulties in thinking. The vast majority also did not report any rebelliousness, hostility, agitation, emotional lability, or interpersonal difficulties.

On the *Mf* scale, only one male officer ($< 1\%$) scored above 64 *T*, suggesting that he did not identify with a traditional masculine role. On the other hand, 76 percent of the male officers scored below 45 *T*, suggesting that they strongly identified with a traditional masculine role. Fifty percent of the female officers scored above 64 *T* on the *Mf* scale, indicating that they endorsed items in the keyed direction for males, as opposed to the way that females usually respond to the items. This would not be surprising among women who intended to become police officers, a traditionally male occupation. The female officers may have genuinely endorsed more stereotypically masculine beliefs, or they may have been trying to portray themselves as more masculine than the typical female because of their desire to appear suited for law enforcement. Only 11 percent of female officers scored below 45 *T* on the *Mf* scale, indicating that they strongly identified with a traditional female role.

SUMMARY. The MMPI-2 clinical scores of these officers, if taken at face value, would suggest that police officers are a psychologically healthy group, which is consistent with the findings of other authors (Bartol, 1982; Carpenter & Raza, 1987; Gould, 2000; Nowicki, 1966). However, one-third of these candidates might have been disqualified because of validity scale elevations suggesting that they had not responded honestly, and an additional third were moderately defensive. For two-thirds of the officers, we cannot be confident that the MMPI-2 provided us with an accurate picture of their personality functioning.

Rorschach Descriptive Statistics and Personality Organization

The descriptive statistics for the RCS variables are shown in Table 2 at the end of this chapter. Table 3 contains frequency data relevant to some general interpretive variables, ratios, and indices.

The interpretations of the officer data were based on the interpretive principles of the Comprehensive System described by Exner (2000, 2003). As is customary with interpretation according to the principles of the RCS, we will discuss some variables more than once, since they have implications for different areas of functioning. Although we will compare the data from our sample with a nonpatient normative sample (Exner, 2007), and note any obvious differences, we will not do any statistical comparisons between the samples. This is consistent with Exner's (1991) suggestion that statistical comparisons of homogeneous samples, such as a group of police officers, to normative samples that are heterogeneous may be misleading.

Protocol Validity

Ganellen (2008) has suggested that defensive responding on the Rorschach is characterized by, among other things, brief records (i.e., low *R*). It would be reasonable to expect that police officers tested as part of the employment process might use the most obvious strategy to limit the information that they reveal on the Rorschach, which is to restrict the number of responses given to the test stimuli. However, the officers produced a mean number of responses that is consistent with nonpatient normative data. All but three officers produced more than the minimal number of responses required to interpret the test (i.e., 14 responses). For those officers, the test was readministered before the inquiry phase, using standard instructions (Exner, 2003). In all three cases sufficient responses were produced on the second administration.

Information Processing

It is important to consider processing efforts in conjunction with response sets or styles. None of the officers have a positive Obsessive Style Index *(OBS)*, indicating that their processing efforts are not affected by an obsessive response set. Thirteen percent of the officers have a positive Hypervigilance Index *(HVI)*; these individuals invest a lot of energy into scanning the Rorschach stimuli. Although this is far from a majority, it is higher than the 1 percent of adult nonpatients who had a positive *HVI* (Exner, 2003). Gilmartin (1986; 2002) suggests that the hypervigilance that is frequently observed in police officers is a product of their training and experience. These data are consistent with that suggestion, in that only a small percentage of these entry-level officers demonstrate hypervigilance at the beginning of their careers.

Thirty-four percent of the officers are avoidant; an additional 23% are avoidant in combination with one of the *EB* styles (introversive, extratensive or ambient). Although avoidant individuals are typically conservative when processing new information, the officers put an average amount of effort into organizing the Rorschach stimuli, based on their mean *Zf* value. Given that the expected value for *Zf* is lower for avoidant individuals, many of the officers are exhibiting more processing effort than expected. This observation is also supported by their elevated *Dd*, which may reflect a guarded approach to the stimuli. Based on the *W:M* ratio, they may be attempting to accomplish more than their capabilities comfortably allow. The mean *Zd* value suggests that their scanning efficiency is within the expected range, although their mean is somewhat lower than the nonpatient normative sample. Twenty-eight percent of the officers are underincorporators; they tend to neglect critical bits of information in the stimulus field and may ignore environmental cues important to decision-making. Twenty-one percent are overincorporators; they are unusually thorough in their scanning efforts. The slightly elevated mean perseveration score *(PSV)* suggests that they may have some difficulty shifting attention. The quality of their processing, as suggested by *DQ+, DQv/+, and DQv,* tends to be adequate, but is more conservative and economical than is typical of nonpatients.

SUMMARY. In spite of their average *R*, the officers may have approached the test in a careful, perhaps guarded, manner. Most of them invested more energy than would be expected in processing new information, and they tended to set ambitious goals that may exceed their abilities. The efficiency of their scanning and processing is like that of most adults, although they may at times have difficulty shifting attention. The quality of their processing efforts is reasonably adequate, but their approach is more conservative than that of most people.

Cognitive Mediation

The officers' cognitive mediation is generally appropriate to the situation and reflects a basic ability to interpret reality in a conventional way, in view of their *XA%* and *WDA%* and the general absence of *No Form* responses. However, they produced a fair number of minus responses, suggesting that mediational problems sometimes occur. Some of the mediational problems may be due to negativism or anger (S-% = .28). Their mean number of popular *(P)* responses is lower than would be expected, suggesting some reluctance to identify conventional responses. The higher than average number of unusual responses supports the idea that they have a tendency to be overly individualistic or may fail to respond in socially expected ways. In combination with an avoidant style, this may represent social defensiveness.

SUMMARY. The officers' reality testing is appropriate in most circumstances, but is occasionally disrupted by feelings related to anger or hostility. They have a greater tendency than most people to disregard social convention, which may be related to social defensiveness.

Ideation

The most obvious difference between the officers and the nonpatient normative sample is the large number of officers (56%) with a high *Lambda* (>.99). An elevated *Lambda* can represent defensiveness regarding taking the test, but given that the mean number of responses is within normal limits and the mean *EA* is greater than 3.5, it is more likely to represent an avoidant style. Thirty-four percent of the officers are avoidant, 9 percent are avoidant-introversive, 5 percent are avoidant-extratensive, and 9 percent are avoidant-ambitent. When the avoidant style is present, it tends to be dominant. Such individuals avoid complexity or ambiguity in the environment and simplify their perceptions of situations, in order to avoid being overwhelmed. However, if a situation is inherently complex or ambiguous, and recognition of that is important for accurate responding, the tendency to ignore the complexity may result in faulty responding.

Eighteen percent of the officers are introversive. People with this problem-solving style like to think things through, are not reliant on external feedback or emotions to assist in decision-making, and prefer not to engage in trial-and-error behavior. Most of the introversive officers (91%) have a pervasive style, and cannot switch to a more intuitive approach even when that would be more appropriate. They strongly prefer to deal with their experience through ideation, without paying attention to feelings. If they need to deal with emotionally charged situations, they may feel anxious or overwhelmed, and may cling rigidly to their ideational approach. They may behave in a manner that is consistent with the public impression that police officers are often aloof, indifferent to the feelings of citizens, or concerned with "just the facts, ma'am."

Five percent of the officers are extratensive, and all of them have a pervasive style. Emotions strongly influence their decision-making, even in situations where this might not be the best approach. They are more action-oriented, preferring a trial-and-error problem-solving strategy. The remaining 17 percent of the officers are ambitents. The decision-making of ambitents is not consistent; sometimes their thinking resembles an introversive and sometimes an extratensive. This lack of consistency generally reduces efficiency and accuracy.

None of the officers had a positive *OBS*, indicating that their thinking is not impacted by an obsessive style. Thirteen percent had a positive *HVI*, which may reflect a mistrusting attitude toward the environment. The number of Morbid *(MOR)* responses given by the officers is similar to that of nonpatients. The presence of a pessimistic set (i.e., three or more *MOR* responses) occurred in 9 percent of their records, compared with 4 percent of nonpatients (Exner, 2003).

The amount of peripheral mental activity experienced by the officers that is provoked by unmet internal need states is lower than that of the nonpatient normative sample. The expected value for *FM* is three to five; 63 percent of the protocols had fewer than three *FM* responses. A possible explanation for the lower values may be that the officers act quickly to reduce their need states. In terms of current situational stress reflected by *m*, the officers' protocols were similar to the nonpatient normative sample. Given that we obtained the data as part of the employment process, the existence of some situational stress at the time of testing would be expected. The officers' Intellectualization Index is not elevated; they do not have a tendency to overuse intellectualization as a defense. Twenty-four percent tend to retreat into fantasy as a defense when faced with stressful situations ($Mp > Ma$, where $M > 1$). Such individuals appear to operate under the assumption that unpleasant realities will somehow be resolved if they can be denied and avoided long enough for others to do something about the situation.

None of the officers suffered from any serious psychiatric disorders at the time of the evaluation, and only two officers had a score of three on the Perceptual Thinking Index *(PTI)* or a score of four on the Schizophrenia Index *(SCZI)*. The *WSum6* for the officer group is lower than for the nonpatient normative sample, suggesting that overall the officers experience no significant disruption in the clarity of their thinking. Eighty-four percent of the officers obtained a *WSum6* score of less than 6, suggesting that their experiences of cognitive slippage or faulty judgment are within normal limits.

Seven percent have a *WSum6* score of 7 to 10, suggesting that their thinking is less sophisticated than is ideal, although they do not necessarily have a significant thinking problem. The remaining 9 percent have a *WSum6* score greater than 11, suggesting that they have an increased probability of flawed decision-making. The officers' *WSum6* consists primarily of Level 1 scores; only 7 percent of the officers produced responses with Level 2 scores. There were no *DR2*, one *DV2*, five *INCOM2*, four *FABCOM2*, one *ALOG*, and no *CONTAM*. The mean number of *M-* responses is slightly elevated, suggesting some ideational difficulties not picked up by the special scores. One *M-* response was found in 20 percent of the records, 7 percent had two *M-* responses, and 1 percent had three or four *M-* responses. With two exceptions, the *M-* responses were not given by the same officers who had elevated *WSum6*.

SUMMARY. Over half of the officers have a dominant style that involves simplifying a stimulus field and ignoring complexity or ambiguity. This might be manifested as a tendency to engage in "black and white thinking." They are not obsessive or perfectionistic, and most of the officers are not impacted by hypervigilant or pessimistic sets. They appear to be relatively untroubled by the type of peripheral mental activity generated by unmet need states that tends to affect attention and concentration, although they exhibit normal levels of situational stress. They do not overuse intellectualization as a defense process, but one-quarter of the officers tend to overuse fantasy and denial to deal with stress. The majority display no clinically significant disruption in the clarity of their thinking, although the data suggest some immaturity in thinking.

Controls and Stress Tolerance

The officers' mean *AdjD* is approximately zero, which would suggest that their stress tolerance and capacity for control are similar to other people. However, 14% had an *AdjD* of -1, suggesting a potential for becoming disorganized when under stress. Five percent had an *AdjD* of -2, suggesting a more serious and chronic vulnerability to stress.

The officers' mean Coping Deficit Index *(CDI)* is elevated compared to the nonpatient normative sample, and 42% of the officers have a positive *CDI*. This suggests that a significant number of the officers have an immature personality organization that makes them prone to interpersonal and affective difficulties.

The officers' mean *EA* is lower than that of the nonpatient normative sample, suggesting more limited coping resources than would be ideal. The *EA* is impacted by the high *Lambda*, which probably represents an avoidant style. The avoidant style is relevant to capacity for control in that the tendency to simplify limits the impact of stimulation from the environment, reducing the possibility of being overwhelmed. The *AdjD* suggests that the majority of the officers successfully manage the stress in their lives, probably because they interact with the environment in such a way as to keep stress to a minimum. However, their limited resources make them vulnerable to stressors that cannot be managed through an avoidant strategy.

SUMMARY. As a group, the officers have a capacity for control and stress tolerance that is within normal limits, although there are individual officers who do have the potential for becoming disorganized under stress. There is a significant subset of officers who appear to be particularly vulnerable to interpersonal stressors. The officers tend to have more limited resources available for coping with stress than the nonpatient normative sample, but they maintain adequate control by avoiding complexity and acting quickly to resolve any need states that they experience. Their coping resources may not be sufficient to handle the stress generated by complex or ambiguous situations.

Affect

Forty percent of the officers had a positive Depression Index (DEPI). In 15 percent of the sample the *DEPI* score was high enough to suggest a vulnerability for a significant affective problem. The remaining 25 percent with a positive *DEPI* are probably susceptible to episodes of moodiness, but they may not identify these feelings as depression. In the interview, only 2 officers reported having experienced depression. Of the 51 officers with a positive *DEPI*, 24 (19% of the full sample) also had a positive *CDI*. People who are positive on both the *DEPI* and *CDI* experience episodes of distress similar to depression. However, their distress is socially reactive and indicative of difficulties with adjustment in interpersonal relationships. No other unusual sources of distress were noted from inspection of the variables on the right side of the *eb* or the *SumC':WSumC* ratio.

To evaluate the influence of emotions on decision-making, it is important to again consider *EB* styles. Only 5 percent of the officers are extratensive. These individuals tend to be influenced by emotion and are more willing to display feelings openly. They are more likely to use trial-and-error as a problem-solving strategy. All of the extratensive officers had a pervasive style, indicating that most of their decision-making is influenced by emotion. An additional 5 percent of the officers are avoidant-extratensive. These individuals demonstrate the extratensive style, but because of their avoidance of complexity they do not process emotions very effectively.

As discussed previously, 18 percent of the officers are introversive and an additional 9 percent are avoidant-introversive. These individuals tend to ignore feelings during decision-making. They avoid using a trial-and-error approach, and are not very tolerant of making errors. They are concerned with carefully controlling their expression of emotions. Almost all of the introversive officers demonstrate a pervasive style, suggesting an inflexible use of the introversive strategy. Emotions have very little influence on their decision-making, even when such an approach would be adaptive. The avoidant-introversive officers demonstrate a basic introversive style but tend to be less effective because the avoidant tendency results in more simplistic thinking.

Seventeen percent of the officers are ambitents. Sometimes their decision-making is influenced by emotions, and sometimes emotions play only a peripheral role. Because ambitents handle feelings inconsistently, they may be confused by them, and may not use them effectively in decision-making. Ambitents also display feelings inconsistently, sometimes carefully controlling them and other times displaying them in less modulated ways. An additional 9 percent of the officers are avoidant-ambitents. They are even more inefficient in the way that emotions impact problem-solving and in the way emotions are expressed, and they experience more difficulty in handling complexity. As a result, their behaviors tend to be less adaptive.

As a group, the officers have a lower than expected Affective Ratio *(Afr)*, suggesting that they experience discomfort in dealing with emotion and are less willing to confront and process the emotional components of situations. Such individuals often attempt to avoid situations where they might have an emotional response that they fear they would have difficulty handling. An inspection of the *FC:CF + C* ratio also suggests that the officers control their emotional displays more than most people, given that the left side of the ratio is three times the value of the right side. Consistent with this interpretation, the majority of the officers (80%) gave no pure *C* responses, which represent a relatively unmodulated display of emotion. Only 4 percent of the officers gave more than one pure *C* response. However, their pure *C* responses did not appear to represent impulsivity or a loss of control, but rather a choice to display emotion in an unmodulated fashion; in each case, the officer's *D* score was zero or above.

SUMMARY. A significant number of the officers have difficulty dealing with emotions. In general, they are less willing to process emotional stimuli than would be expected in adults. They may be confused by emotions and may experience discomfort when confronted by them. They tend to ignore the influence of emotions when they are involved in decision-making. When they do express emotions, they attempt to carefully control that expression. Their efforts to simplify and to avoid emotion might actually prove to be an asset in traditional police work, where the majority of decisions should be unaffected by emotion. However, this strategy probably puts them at a disadvantage in their personal lives, where the negotiation of emotional exchanges is important for successful relationships.

Self-Perception

The officers' mean reflection frequency is elevated, although 72 percent did not have any reflection responses. Twenty-eight percent gave reflection responses, suggesting a narcissistic self-absorption that may interfere with interpersonal relationships. The group's mean egocentricity ratio is within normal limits, although slightly low, suggesting that the officers are no more or less self-involved than other people. However, this interpretation actually applies to only 23 percent of the officers, whose egocentricity ratio is between .33 and .44. The mean obscures the fact that 52 percent have an egocentricity ratio less than .33, suggesting that they have unfavorable images of themselves. The remaining 25 percent have an egocentricity ratio greater than .44, indicating that they are more self-absorbed than average. Of the officers with a high egocentricity ratio, 18 (14% of the total sample) have one or more reflection responses, suggesting that their self-absorption may be self-serving and entitled. The 11 percent of officers with a high egocentricity ratio but no reflections are also self-absorbed, but with an underlying sense of inadequacy with possible depressive features.

The officers' mean *FD* frequency is similar to the nonpatient normative sample, while their mean *SumV* is slightly higher. Thirty-two percent of the officers, whose *SumV* is zero and *FD* is one or two, may engage in self-inspecting behavior routinely, which is generally a positive feature if it leads to reevaluation of the individual's self-view. Another 26 percent, whose *SumV* and *FD* equal zero, are less self-aware than is usual, and may have somewhat naive views of themselves. The remaining 42 percent have an unusual degree of self-focus or concern for their self-image, which may include painful feelings. Almost half of these officers have elevated *MOR* responses, further suggesting that they harbor negative impressions of themselves.

The officers, a relatively young, healthy group, appear to have no unusual body concerns; their *An+Xy* value is similar to the nonpatient normative sample. Fifty-two percent gave no *An* or *Xy* responses, and 23% gave only one such response. Ten percent had three or more such responses. Since they reported no health problems, these responses are more likely to reflect a preoccupation with their self-image, or a sense of vulnerability.

The ratio of pure *H* to other human contents is in the opposite direction than would be expected, suggesting that the officers' self-image and/or self-value are not necessarily based on accurate perceptions of their social inter-actions with other people. Rather, they may be based on experiences that they have fantasized or distorted.

SUMMARY. At first glance, the most surprising finding in these data is that more than half of the officers have negative self-perceptions. But this may not be so surprising in view of data presented earlier that suggest that many of them are lacking in the skills needed to effectively navigate interpersonal relationships. Data from other variables in the self-perception cluster suggest that the many of the officers have some awareness of their difficulties, and that it is troublesome to them. A total of 77 percent of the sample is either self-absorbed in a narcissistic way, or has a negative self-image. These find-ings may have more implications for the officers' personal relationships than they do for vocational functioning, but the more narcissistic officers may have a tendency to be rigid and authoritarian in their interactions with citi-zens. Officers with low self-esteem may have more difficulty making deci-sions, or may be less confident in interactions with citizens. Depending on other features of their personality, they may also overcompensate by becom-ing more rigid and authoritarian.

Interpersonal Perception and Behavior

Forty-two percent of the officers have a positive *CDI*, suggesting that they are less socially mature than ideal. This is likely to lead to difficulties in social interactions and more superficial relationships. They are also likely to be less sensitive to others. Thirteen percent are hypervigilant, indicating that they may be mistrusting, cautious and guarded in their relationships with other people. They may have difficulty with close relationships unless they are in control.

The officers do not appear to assume a passive role in interpersonal rela-tionships; their *a:p* ratio favors active movement responses. The majority are no more dependent than other people, based on their Food responses. No Food responses are expected in adults, and 80 percent of the officers had none. The 20 percent who did have a Food response may be more inclined to rely on others for support, or may naively expect others to be tolerant of their needs.

Texture responses are related to needs for closeness and emotional rela-tionships; the expected value for *SumT* is one. The mean *SumT* of the officers is half that of the nonpatient normative sample. In fact, only 27 percent of the officers had the expected value of *SumT* equal to 1; those officers may be amenable to close relationships in a manner similar to most people. Forty-five percent had no *T* responses, but did give other shading or achromatic color responses. People with this pattern of responses take a conservative approach to close relationships, and may not be open to close emotional ties. An additional 17 percent had no *T* responses, but also had no other achromatic color or shading responses. In these cases it is difficult to determine whether the absence of *T* is a valid finding. When *T* is greater than 1, as it was in 10 percent of the officers, it suggests strong unfulfilled needs for closeness, and loneliness.

The sum of human contents and pure *H* responses is a gauge of interest in other people and the extent to which impressions of other people are based on real interactions. Although the sum of human contents is lower in the officers than in the nonpatient normative sample, it is consistent with the large percentage of avoidant officers in the group. The officers are probably interested in other people, but may not understand them very well, given that pure *H* responses constitute less than half of the *SumH* for 48 percent of the officers. Of the officers for whom data were available (n = 78), 33 percent have *PHR* equal to or greater than *GHR*, suggesting that their interpersonal behaviors are not generally regarded positively by others.

The expected frequency for both cooperative *(COP)* and aggressive (AG) movement scores is one. The mean frequency of *COP* was lower in the officer group than in the nonpatient normative sample. Forty-one percent of the officers had one or two *COP* responses; they may routinely anticipate having positive interactions with others. An additional 3 percent who had three or more *COP* may be gregarious and outgoing and may seek out relationships with others. The 56 percent who did not have any *COP* responses may lack interest in engaging with other people in collaborative interactions, may not routinely anticipate positive interactions between people, and may feel uncomfortable in interpersonal situations. In addition, the officers also gave fewer *AG* responses than expected. The 84 percent of the officers who had no *AG* responses may not expect aggressiveness or competitiveness to be a normal part of interpersonal relationships.

The officers' mean value for personalized responses *(PER)* is not different from the nonpatient sample. One *PER* response is not unusual; more than half of adult nonpatient protocols contain at least one. Fourteen percent of the officers gave two or three *PER* responses, suggesting that they do not feel secure in situations that involve interpersonal challenges and they may rely on displays of personal knowledge as a way of maintaining a sense of security in such situations. An additional 6 percent gave more than three *PER*, suggesting that they become defensively authoritarian in situations that involve perceived challenges to their sense of personal integrity. They are probably seen by others as rigid and may insist that others react submissively toward them. Thus, a total of 20 percent of the officers had a sufficient number of *PER* responses to suggest that they have the potential to act in ways that may be perceived as mildly to moderately authoritarian. This finding, in conjunction with the large number of officers who may react defensively because of their self-absorption or negative self-image, may explain the perception that some citizens have of police officers as arrogant or authoritarian.

The officers' mean Isolation Index is similar to the nonpatient normative sample. The majority (71%) had values that suggest that they participate in social interactions as frequently as most people. A small number (13%) had values that suggest that they are less active socially. This should not be taken to mean that they are socially maladjusted; it simply indicates that they are less likely to participate in social interactions. An additional 16% of the officers had scores that do suggest social isolation. They do not relate well to others, and find it hard to establish rewarding relationships.

SUMMARY. The variables in the Interpersonal Perception cluster support the developing hypothesis that many of the officers have difficulty relating to others in a comfortable way. They have poorly developed social skills and take a conservative approach to relationships. A minority are additionally hampered by hypervigilant sets, or tendencies to become stubbornly defensive of their personal integrity, which may be perceived as authoritarianism. Most of the officers continue to be interested in relationships with others, although a small number are socially isolated.

Comparisons with Other Police Samples

The only published RCS data on Rorschach responses of police applicants of which we are aware is Zacker's (1997) sample of 53 applicants to suburban police departments. Zacker reported descriptive statistics for those variables on which his sample differed from Exner's (1995) sample of 700 nonpatients. For every reported variable, the deviation from the normative sample was in a less desirable direction. We compared Zacker's applicants' mean scores to our sample. With very few exceptions, our sample had a strong resemblance to Zacker's, although in many cases our sample did not deviate quite as much from the normative sample as did Zacker's. His interpretations of the data also did not differ significantly from ours.

Zacker concluded that the applicants had a potential for behaviors that do not coincide with social expectations. He also stated that the applicants tended to be hyperalert, although in our sample only 13 percent had a positive *HVI*. Zacker concluded that his applicants had tendencies to oversimplify and to interpret stimuli unconventionally, which may lead to ignoring or distorting significant features of situations. He also concluded that the officers in his sample were more vulnerable to becoming disorganized by stress than the nonpatient sample, and would function most effectively in well-structured settings with minimal ambiguity. Our data are consistent with these assertions.

Zacker's sample differed from the normative sample on many affective variables, as did ours. For most of the affective variables, our sample did not differ as much as Zacker's, although the frequency of S responses in our data is identical to Zacker's. He noted that half of his applicants were ambitents, whereas 17 percent of our officers were ambitents, and 9 percent were avoidant-ambitents.

On self-perception variables, Zacker's applicants differed from the normative sample in the same direction as ours, although he found a decreased *FD* frequency and we did not. He noted that his protocols suggested that the officers experienced a conflict between elevated self-value and depressed self-image, which is consistent with the description of some officers in our sample. As was the case with our sample, he suggested that their self-perceptions tend to be based largely on imaginary experiences, indicating possible immaturity.

In terms of interpersonal perception, Zacker suggested that his applicants were socially immature, would have difficulty interacting with others, seemed less interested in others, and seemed not to anticipate positive interactions between people. Our interpretations of these data for our sample were quite similar, although we noted that the officers are probably interested in other people, but do not understand them very well. Interestingly, Kates (1950), using a different method of administering and scoring the Rorschach, also concluded that police officers with high police interests tended to have difficulty establishing positive social relationships.

This comparison of two police applicant samples, from suburban and semi-rural areas, provides initial support for the consistency of RCS scores in this population. Unfortunately, Zacker's study is hampered by several drawbacks; he did not provide interrater reliability statistics for his RCS data, he did not report which applicants went on to become police officers, and he did not present data on their subsequent job performance.

The Rorschach and Prediction of Police Job Performance

As was the case with Zacker's sample, our police officer candidates had many discrepancies between their scores on Rorschach variables and the scores of the nonpatient normative sample. In many instances, the scores of the officers were in a less psychologically healthy direction, but are these scores actually predictive of relevant aspects of police performance? A full exploration of this question is beyond the scope of this chapter, but we will present some preliminary data to begin to address this issue and to encourage others to investigate the utility of the Rorschach in police psychology.

EB Style as a Predictor of Police Performance

People who demonstrate the introversive and extratensive styles are considered equally effective in reaching appropriate decisions, although they approach problems in different ways. If we need officers to work in a traditional policing environment that focuses on maintenance of law and order, which is probably best performed in an objective manner, it might be appropriate to choose introversive officers because they use a problem-solving strategy that is not overly impacted by emotional factors. The extratensive style would seem to be less advantageous for traditional police work, however, extratensive officers might be a good choice to spearhead efforts in community- and/or problem-oriented policing, because they would be willing to process and use emotional information, and might be more attuned to the concerns of citizens.

At first glance, avoidant individuals might appear to be not well-suited for police work, given their preference for ignoring complexity. Police officers are routinely confronted with highly complex situations, with many variables that could be considered as part of the decision-making process. However, it is possible that many of these situations can be reduced to common denominators that can be handled with standard operating procedures, perhaps reducing any liability that might result from an avoidant style. In fact, one might argue that some police training procedures actually encourage officers to use what is essentially an avoidant strategy. For example, officers in some departments are taught to decide whether or not they are going to write a ticket for a traffic infraction before even talking to the motorist, so that they are not influenced by extraneous interpersonal variables. The avoidant style may allow officers to ignore variables that might complicate problem-solving, allowing fairly straightforward decision-making, such as whether or not to make an arrest. Any complexity or ambiguity inherent in the situation can be dealt with later by the courts. We expect that the ambient style would be the least appropriate for police work, given the general loss of problem-solving effectiveness typically found in these individuals.

We attempted to empirically determine which style is most effective for police work. We sorted the officers for whom we had adequate performance data into four groups based on *EB* style: avoidant ($n = 32$), introversive (including avoidant-introversive, $n = 27$), extratensive (including avoidant-extratensive, $n = 10$), and ambient (including avoidant-ambitent, $n = 25$). As our measures of officer effectiveness, we used supervisors' ratings for two performance items: overall performance and whether the supervisor would rehire the officer knowing his or her performance. Ratings on these two questions were averaged across the number of years each officer had worked for the department (up to 10 years). We performed an ANOVA to determine whether officers with different *EB* styles were rated differently. On both questions, there were no significant differences in supervisors' ratings of the four groups, $F(3, 90) = 1.21$, $p = .312$; $F(3,90) = 1.76$, $p = .161$. The supervisors were consistent in how they rated the groups on both of these items: introversives received the highest overall rating and were the most likely to be rehired, followed by extratensives, then avoidants, then ambitents.

Another way of judging whether a candidate is suitable for police work is to note which officers remain on the job over time. Admittedly, this is an imprecise measure. Officers who were terminated were clearly unsuitable. Officers who resigned might have left for a number of reasons, which might include a mismatch of the officer with the job, but could also include leaving for career advancement. Table 4 at the end of this chapter illustrates the job status of the officers at the end of 2008, according to problem-solving style. The groups were defined as above. We did a chi-square test to determine whether *EB* style differed among officers who were terminated, resigned, or were still on the job; it was not significant, $x^2(6, N = 123) = 4.7$, $p = .58$.

It seems unlikely that each of these problem-solving strategies is equally effective for police work, but the small sample sizes of our groups and the relative imprecision of these measures of police performance may have prevented us from ascertaining the most effective *EB* style. We do not believe that these data have settled the issue of the preferred problem-solving style for police work. It should be explored further with larger groups of officers, and more sensitive measures of effective performance.

Control Variables as Predictors of Police Performance

Police work is a stressful profession, making capacity for control and stress tolerance variables relevant to police selection. *AdjD* is a measure of the potential for becoming disorganized under stress. Officers who have an *AdjD* of 0 would be expected to have a stress tolerance similar to other people. Officers with an *AdjD* of -1 or less would be expected to have a lower stress tolerance than is ideal, and possible problems with behavioral control. Officers with an *AdjD* greater than 0 may have better stress tolerance and control than most people. We predicted that officers with an *AdjD* of -1 ($n = 18$) would have lower overall performance ratings than officers with an *AdjD* of 0 ($n = 73$) or an *AdjD* of 1 ($n = 11$). We eliminated officers with an *AdjD* of -2 and an *AdjD* greater than 1 from the analysis due to the small number of officers in those groups. Some subjects were also lost because of missing performance data. For this analysis, our performance measure was the overall performance rating, calculated as described above. An ANOVA indicated no significant differences between the groups; the officers who had an *AdjD* of -1 were not rated as performing more poorly overall than officers whose stress tolerance is better, $F(2, 99) = .90$, $p = .410$.

This is not to say that supervisors did not notice any differences among the officers. We performed an ANOVA using an additional performance item that asked supervisors to rate the officers' emotional and psychological maturity. The results of this analysis revealed significant differences among the groups, $F(2, 68) = 4.07$, $p = .02$. Post-hoc tests (Scheffe) revealed that officers with an *AdjD* of -1 were not rated as less mature than officers with an *AdjD* of 0 (officers with "normal" stress tolerance and capacity for control), but they were rated as less mature than officers with an *AdjD* of 1 (officers with high stress tolerance and capacity for control), $p = .08$ and $p = .03$, respectively. Apparently, the recognition of some emotional immaturity in the officers with an *AdjD* of -1 was not heavily weighted by supervisors when they rated overall performance. Even people with an *AdjD* of -1 may function adequately in structured situations where there are well-established procedures for many situations, such as police work.

Although officers with an *AdjD* of -1 are apparently capable of performing police tasks in an acceptable manner, their poorer stress tolerance may cause them to function less adequately in their personal lives. We had current marital status data for 46 officers who had been tested 4 to 16 years earlier. At the time of the current investigation these officers were 23 to 47 years old, an age range where the majority of working adults might be expected to have married. Table 5 (see end of chapter) illustrates the marital status of officers with an *AdjD* of -1, -2 and zero or above. Of the officers who had an *AdjD* of zero or greater, 28% had never married or had divorced or married multiple times. Of the officers who had an *AdjD* of -1 and -2, 70% and 75%, respectively, had never married or had divorced or married multiple times. We did a chi-square test to determine whether marital status differed among the *AdjD* groups. The chi-square was significant, $x^2(4, n = 46) = 14.3$, $p = .006$. These data are consistent with the suggestion that as *AdjD* falls below zero, difficulties in sustaining personal relationships increase. A personal vulnerability to stress that is present at the time of hiring, combined with a stressful occupation, may account for some of the marital difficulties reported in police officers.

Interpersonal Variables as Predictors of Police Performance

Another striking finding is the high percentage of officers with a positive *CDI*. When the *CDI* is positive, the individual has limited social skills and may experience difficulty interacting with others. In a previous pilot study (Wickline, Brewster, & Stoloff, 2002), we looked at *CDI* scores for 43 of these officers, and found that those who had a positive *CDI* (42%) were rated more poorly by their supervisors with regard to emotional functioning than officers who did not have a positive *CDI*. In spite of the fact that the supervisors had observed more emotional difficulties in the officers with a positive *CDI*, they stated that they still would have been willing to rehire those officers if they had it to do over again. Apparently, the emotional difficulties identified by the supervisors did not preclude acceptable performance as a police officer.

For the current investigation, we divided the officers into two groups, CDI positive ($n = 60$) and *CDI* negative ($n = 35$). Using *t*-tests, we compared supervisors' ratings of the officers on their social skills with the public and their overall performance; ratings were averages as described above. There was a significant difference between the two groups on ratings of social skills with the public; the *CDI* positive group was rated as having significantly poorer social skills with the public than the *CDI* negative group, $t(93) = -2.69$, $p = .009$. There was no difference between the groups on ratings of overall performance, $t(93) = -1.16$, $p = .25$. Again, although supervisors did recognize differences between officers on seemingly important skills, that did not impact overall performance ratings.

Rorschach Variables as Predictors of Hostility in Police Officers

In an attempt to predict hostility in the officers, we focused on the use of Space *(S)* responses and *S-%*. As the number of responses that include *S* increases, it becomes more likely that the individual experiences episodes of negativism, oppositionalism, or anger. If these episodes affect the individual's judgment, *S-%* will increase. We predicted that increases in these variables would be correlated with negative affective experiences related to hostility that might affect an officer's interactions with colleagues and the public.

We calculated Pearson's correlations between *S* frequency and *S-%*, and supervisors' ratings of the officers' ability to get along with fellow officers, social skills with citizens, and overall performance. There were no significant correlations between S frequency and any of these items. However, as *S-%* increased, officers were rated as having more problems getting along with fellow officers, $r = .224$, $n = 95$, $p = .029$, and as having poorer social skills with the public, $r = .205$, $n = 95$, $p = .046$. There was no significant correlation of *S-%* with overall performance, $r = .191$, $n = 95$, $p = .06$. Although *S-%* was correlated with observable social behaviors, overall performance ratings were not significantly lowered as *S-%* increased.

Summary and Future Directions

We have presented descriptive data on the Rorschach protocols of 128 police officers and a detailed comparison of those data with Exner's (2007) nonpatient normative sample, as well as a brief comparison with Zacker's (1997) sample of 53 police officer candidates. Although the clinical scales of the MMPI-2 profiles of the officers in our sample were generally within normal limits, the Rorschach variables were different from the nonpatient normative sample in a number of ways. The Rorschach data of the officers in Zacker's sample also differed from a normative nonpatient sample in a similar manner to ours. The data presented here may provide useful comparisons with information obtained on the police personality using other instruments. The data may also be useful to examiners who are considering using the Rorschach for the evaluation of candidates in pre-employment and/or fitness-for-duty situations, or who need to develop treatment plans for officers in distress.

On the positive side, the officers appear to have taken the test seriously, and they made an ambitious effort to process the stimuli. Their processing was of adequate quality, although their approach was conservative. They appear to be relatively free from serious disruptions in their thinking. They are not overly obsessive, perfectionistic, or pessimistic. They tend to be relatively unaffected by pressure from unmet need states, and they are not experiencing significant levels of external stress. For the majority of the officers their capacity for control and stress tolerance is similar to that of most people.

There are a number of differences between the officers and the nonpatient normative sample that are in a less psychologically healthy direction. They tend to be fairly emotionally constricted. They avoid dealing with complexity in their environment, particularly emotional complexity. They tend not to use emotional information when making decisions, and they are quite controlled in their expression of emotions. They have fewer coping resources than would be ideal, but nevertheless they appear to be maintaining a relatively stable psychological equilibrium, perhaps because they avoid becoming overwhelmed by complexity. However, their limited resources make them vulnerable to intense or unexpected stressors that cannot be easily dealt with through simplification of complexity or avoidance of the emotional aspects of the situation. The majority of the officers are interested in relationships with other people, but they may not be very skilled at interacting with and understanding others, at least in part because of their reluctance to process emotional complexity. These personality features may contribute to the marital instability that we observed in some officers. For a substantial subsample of the group, interpersonal difficulties may result in tension, discouragement, or moodiness. Their interpersonal difficulties may also lead them to have negative self-perceptions.

This summary description of the characteristics of this group of police officers as revealed by their Rorschach protocols suggests that they may fit some of the stereotypes that the public holds of police officers. For example, their avoidant strategy and vulnerability to interpersonal challenges may cause them to be perceived by citizens as aloof, distant, or authoritarian. As Zacker (1997) suggested, they may be attracted to policing because of the structure provided by its paramilitary environment. Their personality characteristics may be compatible with traditional models of policing, but not with community policing and/or problem-oriented policing models that encourage active interaction and collaboration with citizens and community resources (Gaines & Kappeler, 2008; Goldstein, 1990).

These data also have implications for our current conceptualization that the stress of police work leads to high rates of divorce and depression in officers (Miller, 2006). It is undeniably true that law enforcement is a stressful profession. However, the Rorschach protocols of our sample suggest that many of the individuals attracted to law enforcement have personality vulnerabilities that may predispose them to difficulties in interpersonal adjustment that may lead to negative affect states. These findings may help to explain some of the difficulties observed in the police population. Other researchers will need to contribute Rorschach data from police departments of various sizes and locations to establish whether the characteristics of this sample are representative of police officers in general.

Our preliminary analyses also suggest that the Rorschach may be able to provide information that could be useful in police selection. We were unable to demonstrate which *EB* style is preferable for police work, probably due to small samples of each style, and relatively insensitive measures of performance. A Rorschach variable related to capacity for control is correlated with supervisors' ratings of the officers' levels of emotional and psychological maturity. Officers who had a positive *CDI* were rated as having poorer social skills with the public. A Rorschach measure of the degree to which the officers' judgment is impaired by feelings of hostility also appears to have potential for predicting difficulties in relating both to fellow officers and the public. Interestingly, these issues did not lead the supervisors to lower their judgment of the officers' overall performance, suggesting that supervisors are more concerned with other factors when rating overall performance. As long as police officers meet productivity goals and do not create significant problems, they may be rated satisfactorily in spite of the supervisors' recognition that their emotional and social functioning is not ideal.

Our exploration of the ability of the Rorschach to provide information relevant to future performance of police officers is in the very early stages, and much more work needs to be done, but these preliminary analyses suggest that such an exploration could be fruitful. We have not yet demonstrated that Rorschach variables should be used to screen out candidates, because the variables that we explored in our preliminary analyses do not impact over-all performance ratings. However, if we wish to select police candidates who are more likely to exhibit good social skills with colleagues and with the pub-lic, the Rorschach may be able to help us to identify those individuals. In addition, for those candidates who have been defensive on the MMPI-2 or other self-report measures, including the Rorschach in the selection battery may provide important incremental information.

A future goal of our research is to continue to investigate the use of the Rorschach in police selection, including an exploration of how scores from the RCS and scores from other measures, such as the MMPI-2 and the IPI, can be used in combination to best predict police performance. The most appropriate way to use the Rorschach in the evaluation of police officers is to include it as part of a multimethod assessment battery, to provide a more comprehensive picture of an individual's functioning (Meyer et al., 2001). The description of personality functioning provided by the Rorschach may also prove to be useful in fitness-for-duty evaluations and for treatment plan-ning, as Weiss and his colleagues (2008) have suggested.

AUTHOR NOTE

We thank Phil Broadfoot, Doug Davis, Butch Wells, and Jim Williams (Chiefs of Police) for providing us with the opportunity to conduct this research. We thank Jim Williams and Deputy Chief Bill Maki for their com-ments on the manuscript. We also thank James Koepfler, Caitlin Price, Julie Niziurski, and Lauren Krakosky of James Madison University for their assis-tance with manuscript preparation. Finally, we thank the police officers and supervisors who participated in the research. Correspondence concerning this chapter should be addressed to JoAnne Brewster, Department of Graduate Psychology, MSC 7704, James Madison University, Harrisonburg, Virginia, 22807. E-mail: brewstja@jmu.edu

Table 1
MMPI-2 DESCRIPTIVE STATISTICS AND T-SCORES (N = 128)

Scale	M	SD	MIN	MAX	MODE	MEDIAN	SK	KU	#(%)scores>64T
L	59.84	11.02	43	91	52	56	.72	.03	40 (31%)
F	42.95	4.92	36	65	42	42	1.56	4.84	1 (<1%)
K	60.06	8.44	37	75	60	61.5	-0.77	.17	41 (32%)
Hs	48.05	6.68	30	67	54	48	-0.26	.34	1 (<1%)
D	45.84	5.97	30	64	47	47	.27	.30	0 (0%)
Hy	49.54	6.98	31	64	54	50	-0.07	-0.62	0 (0%)
Pd	50.36	6.72	35	67	46	50	.08	-0.53	1 (<1%)
Mf	43.96	10.34	30	84	38	42	1.48	2.12	10 (8%)
Pa	48.23	6.74	32	64	49	49	.06	.03	0 (0%)
Pt	46.55	6.39	31	62	47	47	-0.36	-0.05	0 (0%)
Sc	46.13	5.51	32	58	49	46.5	-0.22	-0.11	0 (0%)
Ma	47.75	7.64	31	75	43	47	.9	1.1	3 (2%)
Si	43.89	6.95	33	66	40	42.5	.77	.59	2 (2%)

Table 2
RORSCHACH DESCRIPTIVE STATISTICS FOR POLICE OFFICER SAMPLE

Variable	M	SD	MIN	MAX	FREQ	MODE	MEDIAN	SK	KU
Age	26.18	4.80	19.00	46.00	128	25.00	26.00	1.38	2.55
Years Educ.	14.09	1.60	12.00	17.00	128	32.00	14.00	36.00	5.00
R	22.84	6.84	14.00	47.00	128	21.00	21.00	1.31	1.79
W	9.88	4.42	2.00	23.00	128	8.00	9.00	0.59	-0.36
D	8.66	4.90	2.00	27.00	128	7.00	7.00	0.94	0.85
Dd	4.23	3.30	0.00	14.00	128	0.00	2.00	1.09	0.65
S	3.00	2.05	0.00	10.00	128	2.00	3.00	0.64	0.45
DQ+	5.80	3.54	0.00	19.00	128	4.00	5.00	1.01	0.95
DQo	16.41	6.65	3.00	40.00	128	14.00	15.00	1.14	1.81
DQv	0.54	0.95	0.00	4.00	128	0.00	0.00	2.04	3.74
DQv/+	0.09	0.31	0.00	2.00	128	0.00	0.00	3.78	14.99
FQx+	0.09	0.57	0.00	4.00	128	0.00	0.00	6.33	39.78
FQxo	11.28	3.19	6.00	22.00	128	12.00	11.00	0.77	0.76
FQxu	7.37	3.85	1.00	19.00	128	7.00	7.00	0.70	0.11
FQx-	3.99	2.88	0.00	16.00	128	2.00	3.00	1.39	2.75
FQxNone	0.22	0.57	0.00	4.00	128	0.00	0.00	3.77	18.31
MQ+	0.05	0.40	0.00	4.00	128	0.00	0.00	8.51	77.55
MQo	2.06	1.66	0.00	6.00	128	2.00	2.00	0.65	-0.14
MQu	0.51	0.86	0.00	4.00	128	0.00	0.00	2.27	5.81
MQ-	0.39	0.72	0.00	4.00	128	0.00	0.00	2.16	5.43
MQNone	0.00	0.00	0.00	0.00	128	0.00	0.00	0.00	0.00
SQual-	1.10	1.22	0.00	6.00	128	0.00	1.00	1.46	2.82
M	2.99	2.43	0.00	13.00	128	2.00	3.00	1.51	3.42
FM	2.29	1.88	0.00	9.00	128	2.00	2.00	1.06	1.29
M	1.40	1.38	0.00	7.00	128	0.00	1.00	1.16	1.77
FM + m	3.69	2.55	0.00	11.00	128	4.00	3.00	0.84	0.30
FC	2.11	1.60	0.00	7.00	128	1.00	2.00	0.67	0.07
CF	0.70	1.04	0.00	5.00	128	0.00	0.00	1.74	3.11
C	0.26	0.58	0.00	3.00	128	0.00	0.00	2.64	7.81
Cn	0.00	0.00	0.00	0.00	128	0.00	0.00	0.00	0.00
SumColor	3.01	2.14	0.00	10.00	128	3.00	3.00	0.75	0.55
WSumC	2.15	1.73	0.00	7.50	128	2.50	2.00	1.07	0.92

Table 2 – *Continued*

Sum C'	1.17	1.36	0.00	6.00	128	0.00	1.00	1.48	2.22
Sum T	0.51	0.79	0.00	5.00	128	0.00	0.00	2.18	7.49
Sum V	0.52	0.81	0.00	4.00	128	0.00	0.00	1.65	2.57
Sum Y	0.49	0.79	0.00	3.00	128	0.00	0.00	1.66	2.15
SumShading	2.69	2.13	0.00	9.00	128	2.00	2.00	0.65	-0.24
Fr + rF	0.55	1.19	0.00	8.00	128	0.00	0.00	3.34	14.26
FD	1.33	1.40	0.00	7.00	128	0.00	1.00	1.50	3.12
F	11.88	5.95	2.00	34.00	128	10.00	10.00	1.02	1.33
(2)	5.89	3.49	1.00	19.00	128	4.00	5.00	1.28	2.48
3r + (2)/R	0.34	0.20	0.05	1.06	128	0.29	0.32	1.08	1.58
Lambda	1.64	2.65	0.11	21.00	128	1.00	1.13	5.93	39.87
EA	5.17	3.08	0.00	18.50	128	5.50	5.00	1.05	2.12
Es	6.38	3.56	0.00	19.00	128	3.00	6.00	0.68	0.31
D Score	-0.23	0.98	-3.00	5.00	128	0.00	0.00	1.04	6.66
AdjD	-0.03	0.89	-2.00	5.00	128	0.00	0.00	1.51	8.89
a (active)	3.89	2.96	0.00	15.00	128	2.00	3.00	1.19	1.70
p (passive)	2.82	2.13	0.00	10.00	128	2.00	2.50	0.86	0.60
Ma	1.56	1.61	0.00	7.00	128	0.00	1.00	1.33	1.83
Mp	1.46	1.43	0.00	7.00	128	1.00	1.00	1.46	2.63
Intellect	1.89	2.07	0.00	12.00	128	0.00	1.00	2.04	6.34
Zf	13.42	4.87	5.00	27.00	128	8.00	13.00	0.58	-0.10
Zd	-0.73	5.04	-16.00	12.00	128	2.00	0.00	-0.39	0.20
Blends	2.89	2.61	0.00	14.00	128	1.00	2.00	1.50	3.02
Blends/R	0.13	0.12	0.00	0.60	128	0.00	0.10	1.51	2.77
Afr	0.47	0.17	0.19	1.13	128	0.5	0.43	1.35	2.78
Populars	4.82	1.77	1.00	10.00	128	4.00	5.00	0.54	0.31
XA%	0.82	0.10	0.53	1.00	78	0.83	0.83	-0.44	0.33
WDA%	0.86	0.10	0.58	1.00	78	1.00	0.87	-0.69	0.39
X+%	0.51	0.14	0.26	0.89	128	0.50	0.50	0.36	0.04
X-%	0.17	0.10	0.00	0.53	128	0.17	0.17	0.91	1.53
Xu%	0.31	0.11	0.07	0.61	128	0.29	0.32	0.05	-0.44
S-%	0.28	0.30	0.00	1.00	128	0.00	0.25	1.02	0.28
Isolate/R	0.20	0.14	0.00	0.71	128	0.00	0.18	0.99	1.15
H	2.39	1.91	0.00	12.00	128	2.00	2.00	1.78	6.65

Table 2 – *Continued*

(H)	0.86	0.92	0.00	6.00	128	1.00	1.00	1.83	6.81
Hd	1.56	1.58	0.00	10.00	128	1.00	1.00	1.93	6.39
(Hd)	0.58	0.90	0.00	4.00	128	0.00	0.00	1.79	3.09
Hx	0.16	0.71	0.00	7.00	128	0.00	0.00	7.62	69.82
All H	5.39	2.73	0.00	15.00	128	5.00	5.00	0.71	1.07
A	8.16	3.34	3.00	26.00	128	6.00	8.00	1.63	5.77
(A)	0.45	0.69	0.00	3.00	128	0.00	0.00	1.54	2.12
Ad	2.11	1.97	0.00	9.00	128	0.00	2.00	1.35	2.44
(Ad)	0.25	0.50	0.00	2.00	128	0.00	0.00	1.90	2.84
An	0.79	1.13	0.00	6.00	128	0.00	0.00	1.81	3.97
Art	0.75	1.13	0.00	5.00	128	0.00	0.00	1.77	3.00
Ay	0.79	0.94	0.00	4.00	128	0.00	1.00	1.31	1.79
Bl	0.19	0.50	0.00	3.00	128	0.00	0.00	3.07	10.56
Bt	1.53	1.51	0.00	7.00	128	0.00	1.00	1.05	0.87
Cg	1.23	1.27	0.00	7.00	128	1.00	1.00	1.58	3.55
Cl	0.12	0.35	0.00	2.00	128	0.00	0.00	2.97	8.67
Ex	0.31	0.62	0.00	2.00	128	0.00	0.00	1.83	2.04
Fi	0.52	0.86	0.00	4.00	128	0.00	0.00	1.78	2.81
Food	0.23	0.54	0.00	3.00	128	0.00	0.00	2.87	10.04
Ge	0.25	0.61	0.00	3.00	128	0.00	0.00	2.89	8.80
Hh	1.25	1.25	0.00	6.00	128	1.00	1.00	1.12	1.22
Ls	0.83	0.92	0.00	4.00	128	0.00	1.00	1.02	0.54
Na	0.81	1.12	0.00	7.00	128	0.00	0.00	1.88	6.07
Sc	1.17	1.45	0.00	8.00	128	0.00	1.00	1.77	4.54
Sx	0.05	0.25	0.00	2.00	128	0.00	0.00	5.82	36.83
Xy	0.13	0.38	0.00	2.00	128	0.00	0.00	3.15	9.99
Idio	0.82	0.98	0.00	4.00	128	0.00	1.00	1.40	1.98
DV	0.41	0.77	0.00	4.00	128	0.00	0.00	2.09	4.57
INCOM	0.34	0.71	0.00	4.00	128	0.00	0.00	2.67	8.21
DR	0.12	0.56	0.00	4.00	128	0.00	0.00	5.36	29.77
FABCOM	0.29	0.60	0.00	3.00	128	0.00	0.00	2.39	6.17
DV2	0.01	0.09	0.00	1.00	128	0.00	0.00	11.31	128.00
INC2	0.05	0.25	0.00	2.00	128	0.00	0.00	5.82	36.83
DR2	0.00	0.00	0.00	0.00	128	0.00	0.00	0.00	0.00

Table 2 – *Continued*

FAB2	0.03	0.17	0.00	1.00	128	0.00	0.00	5.45	28.17
ALOG	0.01	0.09	0.00	1.00	128	0.00	0.00	11.31	128.00
CONTAM	0.00	0.00	0.00	0.00	128	0.00	0.00	0.00	0.00
Sum6SpSc	1.27	1.55	0.00	8.00	128	0.00	1.00	1.70	3.59
Lvl2SpSc	0.09	0.33	0.00	2.00	128	0.00	0.00	4.19	18.32
WSum6	3.09	4.50	0.00	23.00	128	0.00	1.00	2.04	4.27
AB	0.17	0.55	0.00	4.00	128	0.00	0.00	4.15	21.01
AG	0.22	0.59	0.00	4.00	128	0.00	0.00	3.70	17.05
COP	0.66	0.91	0.00	5.00	128	0.00	0.00	1.56	3.23
CP	0.00	0.00	0.00	0.00	128	0.00	0.00	0.00	0.00
GHR	3.58	1.87	0.00	10.00	78	3.00	3.00	0.34	0.63
PHR	2.22	1.80	0.00	9.00	78	2.00	2.00	1.33	2.15
MOR	0.80	1.20	0.00	6.00	128	0.00	0.00	1.98	4.20
PER	0.97	1.48	0.00	8.00	128	0.00	0.00	2.28	6.13
PSV	0.39	0.82	0.00	5.00	128	0.00	0.00	3.41	15.26

Table 3
SELECTED RATIOS, PERCENTAGES, AND DERIVATIONS
(N = 128, UNLESS OTHERWISE NOTED)

$R = 22.84$ (SD $= 6.84$)		$L = 1.64$ (SD $= 2.65$)

EB Style
  Introversive $= 2\%$ Extratensive $= 0\%$
  Pervasive Introversive $= 16\%$ Pervasive Extratensive $= 5\%$
  Avoidant-Introversive $= 9\%$ Avoidant Extratensive $= 5\%$
All Introversive $= 27\%$ All Extratensive $= 10\%$
  Ambitent $= 17\%$ Avoidant $= 34\%$
  Avoidant-Ambitent $= 9\%$ Style not categorized $= 4\%$
All Ambitent $= 26\%$

Processing Variables
  $EB = 3.02{:}2.16$ $L = 1.64$
  $Zf = 13.42$ $Zd = -.73$
  $Zd > +3 = 21\%$ $Zd < -3 = 28\%$
  $W{:}D{:}Dd = 9.88{:}8.66{:}4.23$ $W{:}M = 9.88/2.99$
  HVI positive $= 13\%$ OBS positive $= 0\%$ $PSV = .39$
  $DQ+ = 5.80$ $DQv = .54$ $DQv/+ = .09$

Mediation Variables
  $P = 4.82$ $P < 4 = 23\%$ $P > 7 = 8\%$
  $XA\% = .82$ $WDA\% = .86$ $W + D = 18.54$
  $FQx+ = .09$ $FQxo = 11.28$
  $FQxu = 7.37$ $FQx- = 3.99$
  $FQxNone = .22$ $Xu\% = .31$ $X-\% = .17$
  $S- = 1.1$ $S-\% = .28$

Ideation Variables
  $L = 1.64$ $OBS = $ positive $= 0$ $HVI = $ positive $= 13\%$
  $EB = 3.02/2.16$ $ea = 5.17$
  $A{:}p = 3.89{:}2.82$ $p > a + 1 = 30\%$
  $Ma{:}Mp = 1.56{:}1.46$ $Mp > Ma = 34\%$
  $M = 3.02$ $M- = .39$ $MNone = 0$
  $eb = 3.69{:}2.69$ $m = 1.40$
  $FM = 2.29$ $FM < 3 = 63\%$ $FM > 5 = 7\%$
  Intel. Index $= 1.89$ *Intel. Index* $> 5 = 3\%$ $MOR = .80$

Critical Special Scores
  $DV = .41$ $DV2 = .01$
  $DR = .12$ $DR2 = 0$
  $INC = .34$ $INC2 = .05$
  $FAB = .29$ $FAB2 = .03$
  $ALOG = .01$ $CON = 0$
  $PTI = 0.26$ $SCZI = 1.02$ $Sum6 = 1.27$
  $WSum6 = 3.09$ $WSum6 \geq 6 = 84\%$
  $WSum6 = 7\text{-}10 = 7\%$ $WSum6 > 10 = 9\%$
  Level 2 Sp Sc $= .09$ *Level 2 Sp Sc* $> 0 = 7\%$

Table 3 – *Continued*

Controls
  $EB = 3.02{:}2.16$ $EA = 5.17$ $L = 1.64$
  $D = -.23$ $D < 0 = 30\%$ $CDI = 3.23$
  $AdjD = -.03$ $AdjD = -1 = 14\%$ $AdjD = -2 = 5\%$
  $eb = 3.69{:}2.69$ $es = 6.38$ $Adj\ es = 5.51$
  $FM = 2.29$ $m = 1.40$ $C' = 1.17$
  $T = .51$ $V = .52$ $Y = .49$

Affect
  $EB = 3.02{:}2.16$ $eb = 3.69{:}2.69$ *Intel. Index* $= 1.89$
  $FC{:}CF + C = 2.11{:}0.96$
  $FC > CF + C + 2 = 23\%$ $FC > CF + C + 1 = 35\%$
  $CF + C > FC + 2 = 2\%$ $CF + C > FC + 1 = 9\%$
  Pure C $= .26$ *Pure C* $> 0 = 20\%$ *Pure C* $> 1 = 4\%$
  $DEPI = 4.06$ $DEPI$ positive $= 40\%$
  $CDI = 3.23$ CDI positive $= 42\%$
  $DEPI\ \&\ CDI =$ positive $= 19\%$
  $C' = 1.17$ $SumC'{:}SumC = 1.17{:}3.07$ $SumC'{:}WSumC = 1.17{:}2.15$
  $V = .52$ $Y = .49$ $T = .51$
  $Afr = .47$ $Afr < .4 = 34\%$ $Afr < .5 = 61\%$

Self-Perception
  OBS positive $= 0$ $Fr + rF = .55$
  $3r + (2)/R = .34$ $3r + (2)/R < .33 = 52\%$ $3r + (2)/R > .44 = 25\%$
  $FD = 1.33$ $Sum\ V = .52$
  $An + Xy = .91$ $MOR = .80$
  $H{:}(H) + Hd + (Hd) = 2.39{:}3.0$

Interpersonal Perception
  HVI positive $= 13\%$ CDI positive $= 42\%$ $CDI = 3.23$
  $Food = .23$ $a{:}p = 3.89{:}2.82$
  $Sum\ T = .51$ $Sum\ T = 0 = 63\%$
  $Sum\ T = 1 = 27\%$ $Sum\ T > 1 = 10\%$
  $COP = .66$ $COP = 0 = 56\%$ $COP > 2 = 3\%$
  $AG = .22$ $AG = 0 = 84\%$ $AG > 2 = 2\%$
  $PER = .97$ *Isol. Index* $= .20$
  $Sum\ H = 5.39$ $Sum\ H \geq 3 = 88\%$
  $H = 2.39$ $H = 0 = 15\%$ $H < 2 = 37\%$
  $GHR{:}PHR = 3.58{:}2.22$ (n $= 78$) $GHR > PHR = 41\%$ (n $= 78$) $PHR > GHR = 33\%$ (n $= 78$)

Constellations
  $DEPI = 7 = 1\%$ $DEPI = 6 = 14\%$ $DEPI = 5 = 25\%$
  $CDI = 5 = 14\%$ $CDI = 4 = 28\%$
  $PTI = 5 = 0\%$ (n $= 78$) $PTI = 4 = 0\%$ (n $= 78$) $PTI = 3 = 2\%$ (n $= 78$)
  $SCZI = 6 = 0\%$ (n $= 50$) $SCZI = 5 = 0\%$ (n $= 50$) $SCZI = 4 = 2\%$ (n $= 50$)
  $SCON$ positive $= 2\%$ HVI positive $= 13\%$ OBS positive $= 0\%$

Table 4
EB STYLE AND RETENTION OUTCOME (*N* = 123)

EB Style	Fired	Resigned	Still Employed	Total
		Retention Outcome		
Avoidant	7	10	27	44
Introversivea	5	12	17	34
Extratensiveb	3	3	6	12
Ambitentc	7	13	13	33
Total	22	38	63	123

[a]Includes avoidant-introversive. [b]Includes avoidant-extratensive. [c]Includes avoidant-ambitent.

$x^2(6, N = 123) = 4.7, p = .58$

Table 5
ADJD AND MARITAL STATUS (*N* = 46)

Marital Status	AdjD = -2	AdjD = -1	AdjD > 0	Total
Never married	3	4	3	10
One marriage	0	3	23	26
Divorced or multiple marriages	1	3	6	10
Total	4	10	32	46

$x^2(4, N = 46) = 14.3, p = .006$

REFERENCES

Ash, P., Slora, K.B., & Britton, C.F. (1990). Police agency officer selection practices. *Journal of Police Science and Administration, 17*, 258–269.

Bartol, C.R. (1982). Psychological characteristics of small town police officers. *Journal of Police Science and Administration, 10*(1), 58–63.

Blais, M.A., Hilsenroth, M.J., Castelbury, F., Fowler, J.C., & Baity, M.R. (2001). Predicting DSM-IV Cluster B personality disorder criteria from MMPI-2 and Rorschach data: A test of incremental validity. *Journal of Personality Assessment, 76*, 150–168.

Brewster, J. (1995, October). "Use of the Rorschach in evaluations where deception is a concern." Paper presented at the meeting of the Society for Police and Criminal Psychology. Honolulu, HI.

Brewster, J., & Stoloff, M.L. (1999). Using the Good Cop/Bad Cop profile with the MMPI-2. *Journal of Police and Criminal Psychology, 14*(2), 29–34.

Brewster, J., Wickline, P.W., Williams, J.E., & Stoloff, M.L. (2006, October). "Predicting inappropriate aggression in police officers." Paper presented at the meeting of the Society for Police and Criminal Psychology. Chevy Chase, MD.

Butcher, J.N., Dahlstrom, W.G., Graham, J.R., Tellegen, A., & Kaemmer, B. (1989). *MMPI-2: Manual for administration and scoring.* Minneapolis, MN: University of Minnesota Press.

Camara, W.J., Nathan, J.S., & Puente, A.E. (2000). Psychological test usage: Implications in professional psychology. *Professional Psychology: Research and Practice, 31*, 141–154.

Carpenter, B.N., & Raza, S.M. (1987). Personality characteristics of police applicants: Comparisons across subgroups and with other populations. *Journal of Police Science and Administration, 15*(1), 10–17.

Cicchetti, D.V. (1994). Guidelines, criteria, and rules of thumb for evaluating normed and standardized assessment instruments in psychology. *Psychological Assessment, 6*, 284–290.

Cochrane, R.E., Tett, R.P., & Vandercreek, L. (2003). Psychological testing and the selection of police officers: A national survey. *Criminal Justice and Behavior, 30*, 511–537.

Daubert v. Merrell Dow Pharmaceuticals, Inc., 113 S. Ct. 2786 (1993).

Davis, R.D., & Rostow, C.D. (2008). *Matrix-Predictive Uniform Law Enforcement Selection Evaluation: M-PULSE Inventory. Technical Manua*l. Toronto, Ontario, Canada: Multi-Health Systems, Inc.

Exner, J.E., Jr. (1991). *The Rorschach: A comprehensive system. Vol.2: Interpretations.* NY: Wiley.

Exner, J.E., Jr. (1995). *A Rorschach workbook for the comprehensive system* (4th ed.) Asheville, NC: Rorschach Workshops.

Exner, J.E., Jr. (2000). *A primer for Rorschach interpretation.* Asheville, NC: Rorschach Workshops.

Exner, J.E., Jr. (2003). *The Rorschach: A comprehensive system. Volume 1: Basic foundations and principles of interpretation* (4th ed.). New York: John Wiley and Sons.

Exner, J.E., Jr. (2007). A new U.S. adult nonpatient sample. *Journal of Personality Assessment, 89*, S154–S158.

Federal Rules of Evidence. (1992). Boston: Little, Brown.

Gaines, L.K., & Kappeler, V.E. (2008). *Policing in America* (6th ed.). Newark, NJ: LexisNexis.

Ganellen, R.J. (1994). Attempting to conceal psychological disturbance: MMPI defensive response sets and the Rorschach. *Journal of Personality Assessment, 63*, 423–437.

Ganellen, R.J. (1996). *Integrating Rorschach and MMPI-2 in personality assessment.* Hillsdale, NJ: Lawrence Erlbaum Associates.

Ganellen, R.J. (2008). Rorschach assessment of malingering and defensive response sets. In C. B. Gacono & F. B. Evans (Eds.), *The handbook of forensic Rorschach assessment* (pp. 89–119). New York: Lawrence Erlbaum Associates.

General Electric Co.v. Joiner, 526 U.S. 137 (1997).

Gilmartin, K.M. (1986). Hypervigilance: A learned perceptual set and its conse-quences on police stress. In J. T. Reese & H. A. Goldstein (Eds.), *Psychological ser-vices for Law Enforcement* (pp. 445–448). Washington, DC: U.S. Government Printing Office.

Gilmartin, K.M. (2002). *Emotional survival for law enforcement: A guide for officers and their families.* Tucson, AZ: E-S Press.

Goldstein, H. (1990). *Problem-oriented policing.* New York: McGraw-Hill, Inc.

Gough, H. (1996). *California Psychological Inventory manual.* Palo Alto, CA: Consulting Psychologists Press.

Gould, L.A. (2000). A longitudinal approach to the study of the police personality: Race/gender differences. *Journal of Police and Criminal Psychology, 15*(2), 41–51.

Graham, J.R. (2006). *MMPI-2: Assessing personality and psychopathology.* (5th ed.). New York: Oxford University Press.

Gronnerod, C. (2003). Temporal stability in the Rorschach method: A meta-analyt-ic review. *Journal of Personality Assessment, 80,* 272–293.

Grossman, L.S., Wasyliw, O.E., Benn, A.F., & Gyoerkoe, K.L. (2002). Can sex offenders who minimize on the MMPI conceal psychopathology on the Rorschach? *Journal of Personality Assessment, 78,* 484–501.

Hamel, M., Gallagher, S., & Soares, C. (2001). The Rorschach: Here we go again. *Journal of Forensic Psychology Practice, 1,* 79–87.

Hiller, J.B., Rosenthal, R., Bornstein, R.F., Berry, D.T.R., & Brunell-Neuleib, S. (1999). A comparative meta-analysis of Rorschach and MMPI validity. *Psychological Assessment, 11,* 278–296.

Hilsenroth, M.J., & Stricker, G. (2004). A consideration of challenges to psychologi-cal assessment instruments used in forensic settings: Rorschach as exemplar. *Journal of Personality Assessment, 83,* 141–152.

Ho, T. (2001). The interrelationships of psychological testing, psychologists' recom-mendations, and police departments' recruitment decisions. *Police Quarterly, 4,* 318–342.

Inwald, R. (1992). *Inwald personality inventory technical manual* (revised). New York: Hilson Research.

Kates, S.L. (1950). Rorschach responses, Strong blank scales, and job satisfaction among policemen. *Journal of Applied Psychology, 34,* 249–254.

Kumho Tire Company, Ltd., v. Carmichael, 526 U.S. 137 (1999).

Matarazzo, J.D., Allen, B.V., Saslow, G., & Wiens, A.N. (1964). Characteristics of successful policemen and firemen applicants. *Journal of Applied Psychology, 48,* 123–133.

Mattlar, C.E. (2004). The Rorschach Comprehensive System is reliable, valid, and cost-effective. *Rorschachiana, 26*(1), 158-186.

McCann, J.T., & Evans, F.B. (2008). Admissibility of the Rorschach. In C. B. Gacono & F. B. Evans, (Eds.), *The handbook of forensic Rorschach assessment* (pp. 55-78). New York: Lawrence Erlbaum Associates.

Meloy, J.R. (2008). The authority of the Rorschach: An update. In C. B. Gacono & F. Barton Evans, (Eds.), *The handbook of forensic Rorschach assessment* (pp. 79-87). New York: Lawrence Erlbaum Associates.

Meloy, J.R., Hansen, T.L., & Weiner, I.B. (1997). The authority of the Rorschach: Legal citations during the past 50 years. *Journal of Personality Assessment, 69,* 53–62.

Meyer, G.J. (1997). Assessing reliability: Critical corrections for a critical examination of the Rorschach Comprehensive System. *Psychological Assessment, 9,* 480–489.

Meyer, G.J. (1999). Simple procedures to estimate chance agreement and kappa for the interrater reliability of response segments using the Rorschach Comprehensive System. *Journal of Personality Assessment, 72,* 230–255.

Meyer, G.J., & Archer, R.P. (2001). The hard science of Rorschach research: What do we know and where do we go? *Psychological Assessment, 13,* 486–502.

Meyer, G.J., Finn, S.E., Eyde, L.D., Kay, G.G., Moreland, K.L., Dies, R.R., Eisman, E.J., Kubiszyn, T.W., & Reed, G.M. (2001). Psychological testing and psychological assessment: A review of evidence and issues. *American Psychologist, 56,* 128–165.

Meyer, G.J., Hilsenroth, M.J., Baxter, D., Exner, J.E., Jr., Fowler, J.C., Piers, C.C., & Resnick, J. (2002). Examination of interrater reliability for scoring the Rorschach Comprehensive System in eight data sets. *Journal of Personality Assessment, 78,* 219–274.

Miller, L. (2006). *Practical police psychology: Stress management and crisis intervention for law enforcement.* Springfield, IL: Charles C. Thomas.

Nowicki, S., Jr. (1966). A study of the personality characteristics of successful policemen. *Police, 11,* 39–41.

Parker, K.C., Hanson, R.K., & Hunsley, J. (1988). MMPI, Rorschach, and WAIS: A meta-analytic comparison of reliability, stability, and validity. *Psychological Bulletin, 103,* 367–373.

Peterson, C.A. (1997). A borderline policeman: AKA, a cop with no COP. In J.R. Meloy, M.W. Acklin, C.B. Gacono, J.F. Murray, & C.A. Peterson (Eds.), *Contemporary Rorschach interpretation* (pp. 157–176). Mahwah, NJ: Lawrence Erlbaum Associates.

Rankin, J.H. (1959). Psychiatric screening of police recruits. *Public Personnel Review, 20,* 191–196.

Ritzler, B., Erard, R., & Pettigrew, G. (2002). A final reply to Grove and Barden: The relevance of the Rorschach Comprehensive System for expert testimony. *Psychology, Public Policy, and Law, 8,* 235–246.

Rosenthal, R., Hiller, J.B., Bornstein, R.F., Berry, D.T.R., & Brunell-Neuleib, S. (2001). Meta-analytic methods, the Rorschach, and the MMPI. *Psychological Assessment, 13,* 449–451.

Singer, J., Hoppe, C.F., Lee, S.M., Olesen, N.W., & Walters, M.G. (2008). Child custody litigants: Rorschach data from a large sample. In C.B. Gacono & F.B. Evans (Eds.), *The handbook of forensic Rorschach assessment* (pp. 445–464). New York: Lawrence Erlbaum Associates.

Spielberger, C.D. (1979). *Police selection and evaluation: Issues and techniques.* Washington, DC: Hemisphere.

Super, J.T. (2006). A Survey of pre-employment psychological evaluation tests and procedures. *Journal of Police and Criminal Psychology, 21*(2), 83–90.

United States v. Frye, 293 F. 1013 (DC Cir. 1923).

Wasyliw, O.E., Benn, A.F., Grossman, L.S., & Haywood, T.W. (1998). Detection of minimization of psychopathology on the Rorschach in cleric and noncleric alleged sex offenders. *Assessment, 5*, 389–397.

Weiner, I.B. (1999). What the Rorschach can do for you: Incremental validity in clinical applications. *Assessment, 6*, 327–338.

Weiner, I.B., Exner, J.E., Jr., & Sciara, A. (1996). Is the Rorschach welcome in the courtroom? *Journal of Personality Assessment, 67*, 422–424.

Weiss, P.A. (2000, October). "Potential uses of the Rorschach Comprehensive System in the selection of police officers." Paper presented at the meeting of the Society for Police and Criminal Psychology. Canton, OH.

Weiss, P.A. (2002). Potential uses of the Rorschach in the selection of police officers. *Journal of Police and Criminal Psychology, 17*(2), 63–70.

Weiss, P.A., Weiss, W.U., & Gacono, C.B. (2008). The use of the Rorschach in police psychology: Some preliminary thoughts. In C. B. Gacono & F. B. Evans (Eds.), *The handbook of forensic Rorschach assessment* (pp. 527–542). New York: Lawrence Erlbaum Associates.

Weiss, W.U., Weiss, P.A., Cain, S., & Manley, B. (2009). Impression management in police officer candidacy on the MMPI-2. *Journal of Police and Criminal Psychology, 24*, 120–125

Wickline, P.W, Brewster, J., & Stoloff, M.L. (2002, October). "A Rorschach investigation of the police personality." Paper presented at the meeting of the Society for Police and Criminal Psychology. Orlando, FL.

Wickline, P.W., Brewster, J., & Stoloff, M.L. (2007, March). "Predicting police job performance with the Rorschach and the MMPI-2: A test of incremental validity." Poster presented at the meeting of the Society for Personality Assessment. Arlington, VA.

Wickline, P.W., Brewster, J., & Stoloff, M.L. (2008, March). A qualitative study of the pre- employment personality functioning of 100 police officers using the Rorschach Comprehensive System. In P.A. Weiss (Chair), *Personality assessment in police psychology*. Symposium conducted at the Annual Meeting of the Society for Personality Assessment, New Orleans, LA.

Zacker, J. (1997). Rorschach responses of police applicants. *Psychological Reports, 80*, 523–528.

Part III

RESEARCH METHODS IN POLICE PSYCHOLOGY PERSONALITY ASSESSMENT

Chapter 9

PREDICTING LAW ENFORCEMENT OFFICER PERFORMANCE WITH PERSONALITY INVENTORIES

MICHAEL G. AAMODT

Many of the chapters in this book describe the use of individual personality inventories in a variety of law enforcement contexts. In this chapter, I will review the research investigating whether any of these inventories is consistently successful in predicting police officer performance. I initially reviewed this research in a series of meta-analyses (Aamodt, 2004a) and thus will not repeat all of the findings here. Instead, I will discuss some important research issues, briefly describe meta-analysis, and then provide an update to the 2004 meta-analyses.

Before going further in this chapter, it is important to discuss the term *validity*, when talking about personality inventories. Validity refers to the accuracy of *inferences* made from test scores. There is no such thing as a "valid test" because no test will predict all types of behavior in all situations. Instead, we might say that scores from a given test are valid predictors of supervisor ratings of police performance or are valid predictors of use-of-force incidents. Because test scores that predict supervisor ratings often are different from those predicting commendations or disciplinary problems or traffic accidents, it is important that care be taken when discussing the validity of test scores.

Because most personality inventories have multiple scales that measure a variety of personality dimensions (e.g., extraversion, conscientiousness), when discussing validity, it is essential to be specific about which scales predict which behaviors. That is, it would be inappropriate to say that the California Personality Inventory (CPI) is a valid predictor of police performance. However, on the basis of research findings to be discussed later in the chapter, it might be appropriate to say that research indicates that the *tolerance scale* of the CPI is a valid predictor of *supervisor ratings* of police performance.

KEY ISSUES IN PERSONALITY ASSESSMENT RESEARCH

Prior to discussing the results of decades of research on the validity of personality inventories in law enforcement selection, there are several key issues that need to be addressed so that the research findings can be placed in their proper context.

Personality Constructs versus Individual Tests

In discussing validity research, it is helpful to distinguish whether it is a particular construct (e.g., conscientiousness) measured by a variety of tests or whether it is a scale on a particular test (e.g., conscientiousness scale of the Personal Perspectives Inventory) that predicts performance. For example, in the situation depicted in Table 1 at the end of this chapter, there are three personality inventories, each of which has three similar scales—sensitivity, extraversion, and conscientiousness. Although the publisher of the Test of Personality would like to claim that its test is "valid," it is clear that the personality *construct* of conscientiousness seems to be a valid predictor of disciplinary problems, regardless of which test is used. Likewise, none of the scales on any of the tests predicts the number of commendations received by an officer. Furthermore, only the openness-to-experience scale on the Surrette Inventory predicts academy performance. So, what is the proper conclusion regarding the Test of Personality? It looks to be a useful tool in police selection, as one of its scales predicts discipline problems. However, it is not unique in its ability to predict this one aspect of performance, and in fact, the Surrette Inventory is probably a better choice as its scales predict two relevant aspects of behavior.

Tests of Psychopathology versus Tests of Normal Personality

When discussing the validity of personality inventories, it is important to distinguish between two types of inventories: those designed to assess psychopathology and those designed to assess "normal" personality.

Tests of Normal Personality

Tests of normal personality measure the traits exhibited by normal people in everyday life. Examples of such traits are extraversion, conscientiousness, assertiveness, and friendliness. Although there is some disagreement, psychologists generally agree there are five main personality dimensions (McCrae & Costa, 2003). Popularly known as the *Big Five*, these dimensions are openness to experience (bright, adaptable, inquisitive), conscientiousness (reliable, dependable, rule oriented), extraversion (outgoing, friendly, talkative), agreeableness (works well with others, loyal), and emotional stability (calm, not anxious or tense). Commonly used measures of normal personality in law enforcement research include the California Psychological Inventory (CPI), 16PF, Inwald Personality Inventory (IPI), NEO PI-R, and Edwards Personal Preference Schedule (EPPS). Although not found in the law enforcement literature, there are literally hundreds of other commercially available measures of normal personality. Some of the more commonly used inventories in employee selection include the Hogan Personality Inventory, Personality Employment Test, and the Caliper Profile. The Myers-Briggs Type Indicator is a personality assessment commonly used in training and individual development, but it has no research support for use in personnel selection and should not be used for such purposes.

In the context of law enforcement selection, tests of normal personality are typically administered prior to a conditional offer of hire and are used to *predict* whether an applicant will be an effective officer. For purposes of the Americans with Disabilities Act (ADA), tests of normal personality are not considered to be medical tests.

Tests of Psychopathology

Measures of psychopathology determine if individuals have such serious psychological problems as depression, severe anxiety, and schizophrenia. Commonly used measures of psychopathology used in law enforcement research include the Minnesota Multiphasic Personality Inventory (MMPI; MMPI-2), Personality Assessment Inventory (PAI), Millon Clinical Multiaxial Inventory (MCMI-III), and the Clinical Assessment Questionnaire (CAQ). Such measures are designed to "screen out" applicants who have psychological problems that could cause performance or discipline problems on the job. Measures of psychopathology are not designed to "select in" applicants, and as will be seen in the meta-analysis results, they are seldom predictive of job performance.

Under the ADA, tests of psychopathology are considered to be medical exams. As such, they can only be administered following a conditional offer of employment.

This might be a good point to discuss the role of the clinician in law enforcement selection, especially as it ties into using tests of psychopathology. Law enforcement selection is typically divided into two stages: selecting in and screening out. In the "selecting in" stage, human resource professionals and industrial-organizational psychologists administer a variety of assessments that tap job-related constructs identified in a formal job analysis. In the law enforcement context, such assessments often include cognitive ability tests, structured interviews, assessment centers, tests of normal personality, and biodata. The purpose of these assessments is to determine which applicants have the knowledge, skill, ability, and other characteristics to best perform the job. Such assessments are best developed by industrial-organizational psychologists who have extensive training in job analysis, test development, and test validation.

Once an applicant has been identified as having the necessary competencies to perform the job of a police officer, a series of "screening out" assessments take place. Such assessments include physical ability tests, medical exams, background checks, and psychological exams. It is important to note that when an applicant is sent for a psychological evaluation, it has already been determined that the applicant possesses the competencies needed to perform the job. What then, is the role of the clinician? It is not to predict performance; that has already been done. Instead, it is to use a variety of clinical assessments to determine if the applicant has some type of pathology that would result in the applicant, if put in a law enforcement position, being a danger to himself or to others.

Given this role of the clinician and the tests of psychopathology that will be used, it is not surprising that tests of psychopathology do not predict work performance. Predicting employee performance is not the purpose of these tests nor is it the goal of the psychological evaluation.

Spurious Findings versus Consistency

A particularly troubling pattern that is often seen in the testing literature is that several studies are conducted using a particular personality inventory, a significant validity coefficient is reported in each study, and the resulting claim is that the test is valid. Let's use the hypothetical test shown in Table 2 at the end of this chapter as an example. In each of the six studies, The Test of Personality significantly predicted supervisor ratings of performance. Do these findings suggest that the test is a useful predictor of police performance? Probably not. For the test to be considered a valid predictor of police performance, we need to see consistency in the scales that predict performance. With 20 scales, we would expect at least one to be significant at the .05 level in every study–exactly what was found.

Furthermore, the pattern of results should be consistent across studies. That is, for us to consider the guardedness scale to have potential validity in selecting police officers, that scale should, after controlling for sampling error, have similar levels of validity across studies. In the example shown in Table 2, although each study produced a significant validity coefficient, no scale *consistently* predicted performance across the six studies. Thus, although there are six studies reporting significant validity coefficients, our conclusion regarding the Test of Personality is that neither the test, nor any of its scales, shows potential validity in police selection.

The need for consistency is why it is essential that studies report *all* correlations, not just those that are significant. As will be discussed later in the chapter, such a practice has important implications when conducting meta-analyses.

Incremental Validity

The final key issue to consider in evaluating research on personality assessment is incremental validity: the extent to which a test adds predictability beyond the assessments already being used. That is, will the results of a personality inventory increase the accuracy of predictions based on such assessments as structured interviews, cognitive ability tests, and background checks? If not, there is no reason to include the test in the assessment battery.

RESEARCH METHODS

In reviewing studies investigating the validity of personality inventories, it appears the there are four common ways in which scores from personality inventories have been used to predict law enforcement performance: correlation of individual scales, regression of multiple scales, use of scale patterns, and overall pattern interpretation.

Correlation of Individual Scales

This is the method most commonly found in the research literature. With this method, scores from individual personality scales are correlated with some measure of job performance (e.g., supervisor ratings, disciplinary actions). As previously mentioned, for police psychologists to get excited about a given scale or test, a body of research findings must demonstrate consistency in the scales that significantly predict performance and the size of the correlation coefficient must be high enough to justify the effort and cost that goes into testing applicants. It is important to keep in mind that a statistically significant validity coefficient only means that the results did not occur by chance; it does not mean that the validity coefficient will have utility.

Regressions of Multiple Scales

Rather than looking at the correlations of individual scales with performance, some studies (e.g., Gettys & Elam, 1985; Inwald, 1988; Mufson & Mufson, 1988; Ronan, Talbert, & Mullet, 1977; Scogin, Schumacher, Gardner, & Chaplin, 1995; Swope, 1989; Wilson, 1980) used multiple-regression analysis to determine the *combination* of scales that best predict performance. Studies using this approach have typically found significant validity coefficients for the scale combinations. Unfortunately, there are so few studies using this approach and no consistency in the inventories and scales used, that no conclusions can be drawn regarding the best combination of scales. Unfortunately, studies using regression designs but not reporting individual correlation coefficients cannot be included in meta-analyses.

Test Profiles

A third approach found in the literature is to look at the *pattern* of scores across two or more personality scales. Interestingly, in the law enforcement literature, this approach seems to be limited to the following MMPI-2 profiles.

Good Cop/Bad Cop Profile

The Good Cop/Bad Cop (GCBC) Profile was developed by Blau, Super, and Brady (1993). A prediction of an applicant being a "good cop" is made when the applicant's T scores are less than 60 on the Hy, Hs, Pd, and Ma scales and less than 70 on the other clinical scales. Brewster and Stoloff (1999) modified this technique to include three categories: good cop (no scores above the cutoff), borderline (one score above the cutoff), and bad cop (two or more scores above the cutoff).

Goldberg Index

The Goldberg Index was created in 1965 to assist in discriminating between neurotic and psychotic MMPI profiles. The formula for the Goldberg Index is L + Pa + Sc - Hy - Pt. Applicants with scores below 40 are considered in to be in the neurotic range and those with scores above 49 are considered to be in the psychotic range. It should be noted that although the Goldberg Index was created using the original MMPI, all studies using it to predict police officer performance, with the exception of the Matyas (1980) data, used the MMPI-2.

Huesmann Index

The Huesmann Index is a measure of aggression and impulsivity and is formed by summing the F, Pd, and Ma scales (Huesmann, Lefkowitz, & Eron, 1978).

Aamodt Index

Similar to the Huesmann Index, the Aamodt Index is formed by summing the F and Ma scales. This index was created as the meta-analysis on the validity of the MMPI (Aamodt, 2004a) suggested that these two scales were the most successful MMPI scales in predicting academy grades and supervisor ratings of law enforcement performance. The logic behind this combination is that the F scale represents potential problems and the Ma scale represents the energy needed to act on these potential problems.

Gonder Index

The Gonder Index is created by summing the Pd, Pt, Mf, Ma, Hs, and Hy scales (Gonder, 1998).

Five-Factor Model

Bernstein, Schoenfeld, and Costello (1982) factor-analyzed the MMPI and suggested that there are five basic MMPI factors that can be used in predicting law enforcement performance:

- Factor I (general pathology): Hs + Pd + Pa + Pt + Sc + Ma
- Factor II (bipolar): Hy + Hs + K - Ma
- Factor III (introversion): Si
- Factor IV: Pa + MF - L - K
- Factor V: F-K

Overall Pattern Interpretation

The final way in which personality inventory scores are used is for the testing professional to view the personality scores as a whole and to look for meaningful patterns. The difference between this method and the previous method is that the "meaningful patterns" are idiosyncratic to the individual testing professionals and typically lack consistency. Evaluating the effectiveness of this method has proven to be difficult due to the wide variety of research designs and information available to the evaluator. For example, in some studies (e.g., Baczynska, 2006), clinicians had access only to the test profile, whereas in others (e.g., Cave & Westfried, 2001, 2002), the clinician also had access to cognitive ability scores, background data, and information from a clinical interview. Furthermore, the authors of the studies varied from independent researchers to test users to test vendors.

Meta-Analysis

Prior to discussing the meta-analysis findings on the validity of personality testing in law enforcement, a brief discussion of meta-analysis seems in order. A meta-analysis is a statistical method for combining multiple studies. Most meta-analyses try to answer four questions for the issue in question:

1. What is the typical validity coefficient found in the literature?
2. Is the size of typical validity coefficient practically and statistically significant?
3. If there were no measurement artifacts (e.g., criterion unreliability, range restriction) limiting the size of the validity coefficient, what would be our best estimate of the true validity?
4. Is the validity coefficient consistent across situations (i.e., generalizable), or does the size of the validity coefficient depend on additional variables (moderators)?

Understanding Meta-Analysis Results

Table 3 contains the partial results of a meta-analysis conducted on the relationship between cognitive ability and police performance. The numbers in the table represent the validity of cognitive ability in predicting academy grades and supervisor ratings of performance as a police officer.

NUMBER OF STUDIES AND SAMPLE SIZE. The "K" column indicates the number of studies included in the meta-analysis and the "N" column indicates the number of total subjects in the studies. There is not a magical number of studies we look for but a meta-analysis with 20 studies is clearly more useful than one with 5.

MEAN OBSERVED VALIDITY COEFFICIENT. The "*r*" column represents the mean validity coefficient (correlation) across all studies (weighted by the size of the sample). This coefficient answers our question about the typical validity coefficient found in validation studies on the topic of cognitive ability and police performance. On the basis of our meta-analysis, we would conclude that the validity of cognitive ability in predicting academy grades is .41 and the validity of cognitive ability in predicting supervisor ratings of on-the-job performance is .16.

CONFIDENCE INTERVALS. To determine if the observed validity coefficient is "statistically significant," look at the next two columns that represent the lower and upper limits to our 95 percent confidence interval. If the interval includes zero, we cannot say that our mean validity coefficient is significant. From the data in Table 3, we would conclude that cognitive ability is a significant predictor of grades in the academy (our confidence interval is .33 - .48) and performance as a police officer (our confidence interval is .14 - .18).

Using confidence intervals, we can communicate our findings with a sentence such as, "Though our best estimate of the validity of cognitive ability in predicting academy performance is .41, we are 95 percent confident that the validity is no lower than .33 and no higher than .48." It is important to note that some meta-analyses use 80 percent, 85 percent, or 90 percent confidence intervals. The choice of confidence interval levels is a reflection of how conservative a meta-analyst wants to be: The more cautious one wants to be in interpreting the meta-analysis results, the higher the confidence interval used. I tend to be conservative in my analyses so a 95 percent confidence interval was used in the meta-analyses described in this chapter.

CORRECTIONS FOR ARTIFACTS. The column labeled (rho) represents our mean validity coefficient corrected for such study artifacts as criterion unreliability and range restriction. This coefficient represents what the "true validity" of cognitive ability would be if we had a perfectly reliable measure of academy grades and supervisor ratings of performance and no range restriction. Notice how our observed correlations of .41 and .16 increase to .62 and .25 after being corrected for study artifacts. When encountering ρ, it is important to consider how many artifacts were included in the corrected correlation. That is, two meta-analyses on the same topic might yield different results if one meta-analysis corrected for three artifacts while another corrected only for range restriction.

CREDIBILITY INTERVAL. Credibility intervals are used to determine if the corrected correlation coefficient (ρ) is statistically significant and if there are moderators present. Whereas a standard error is used to compute a confidence interval, the standard deviation is used to compute a credibility interval. As with confidence intervals, if a credibility interval includes zero, the corrected correlation coefficient is not statistically significant. If a credibility interval contains zero or is large, the conclusion to be drawn is that the corrected validity coefficient cannot be generalized and that moderators are operating.

PERCENTAGE OF VARIANCE DUE TO SAMPLING ERROR AND STUDY ARTIFACTS. The next column in a meta-analysis table represents the percentage of observed variance that is due to sampling error and study artifacts. This percentage is used to determine whether one can generalize the results or whether there are moderators. That is, can we say that the finding can be generalized to all departments or does the validity depend on a variable such as the size of the department, the year the study was conducted, or the type of department (i.e., police department vs. sheriff's office)? The accepted rule-of-thumb is that if the percentage of variance due to sampling error and study artifacts is at least 75 percent, the meta-analysis results can be generalized (Hunter & Schmidt, 1990). Notice that in our example, for grades and performance, these percentages are 78 percent and 84 pecent respectively. Because the percentage is greater than 75, we can generalize our findings and do not need to search for moderators. Such a finding is desired, but is unusual.

Rather than using the 75 percent rule, some meta-analyses use a test of statistical significance. The results of these tests are reported as a Q_w or H_w statistic. If this statistic is significant, then a search for moderators must be made. If the statistic is not significant, we can generalize our findings. As shown in Table 3 at the end of this chapter, the Q_w statistic was not significant for either academy grades or supervisor ratings of performance (had the Q_w been significant, there would have been an asterisk). This lack of significance is consistent with the fact that sampling error and study artifacts accounted for at least 75 percent of the observed variance.

Do Personality Inventories Predict Law Enforcement Performance?

In the remainder of the chapter, I will summarize and update the results of a series of meta-analyses investigating the validity of personality inventories in predicting law enforcement performance. I will concentrate on the "big picture" issues. Readers interested in the full validity results for individual tests should refer to Aamodt (2004a).

Validity of Tests of Psychopathology

INDIVIDUAL TEST SCALES. Unfortunately, the MMPI-2 is the only test of psychopathology for which there is a sufficient amount of research to discuss. There are a few published articles using the PAI, but most of these articles drew from the same dataset and most only listed the significant correlations. As a result, PAI studies could not be properly meta-analyzed. Further research using the PAI seems warranted as some studies (e.g., Roberts, Thompson, & Johnson, 2004; Weiss et al., 2004) have found significant correlations between PAI scales and aspects of law enforcement performance whereas others (e.g., Richardson, Cave, & La Grange, 2007) have not. For the IPI, an insufficient number of studies included a correlation matrix for a meaningful meta-analysis to be conducted.

As shown in Table 4, the uncorrected correlations between the individual test scales of the MMPI and measures of police performance tend to be very low. None of the scales significantly predicted commendations or discipline problems.

TEST CONSTRUCTS. To determine the typical validity of personality constructs in predicting law enforcement performance, scales from a variety of tests were grouped on the basis of the personality dimension they purport to measure. For example, the depression construct includes the depression scales from the MMPI, MMPI-2, IPI, Clinical Analysis Questionnaire (CAQ), and the Bipolar Psychological Inventory.

As shown in Tables 5 and 6 at the end of this chapter, measures of psychopathology have not been successful in predicting law enforcement performance. The median correlation between such measures and supervisor ratings of job performance is only -.06 and the median correlation with disciplinary problems is only .01. Personality scales tapping mania were the most successful in predicting supervisor ratings of performance ($r = -.10$) and scales tapping substance abuse ($r = .05$) were most successful in predicting disciplinary problems. Though both are statistically significant, neither is of the magnitude that would render the scales useful.

At first glance, the low correlations for these personality constructs would seem to suggest that tests of psychopathology are not useful in law enforcement selection. This, however, may not completely be the case. Keep in mind that, although many practitioners incorrectly use tests of psychopathology to predict performance, such tests were not designed for use in personnel selection. Rather, they were designed to help clinicians determine the presence of psychopathology. Although the link between psychopathology and police performance seems negligible, it is important to note that most applicants "failing" tests of psychopathology are not hired, and thus, the available research findings are often based on a restricted range in test scores.

SCALE PATTERNS. As mentioned previously, many clinicians use scale patterns rather than individual scale scores to make predictions regarding police performance. As shown in Table 7 at the end of this chapter, some of these special scale patterns do a better job of predicting performance than do the individual scales. On the basis of a small number of studies, the Good Cop/Bad Cop pattern correlates highest with supervisor ratings ($r = -.19$) and the Aamodt Scale correlates highest with disciplinary problems ($r = .18$). Because these special scale patterns have higher validity coefficients than individual scales, more research into these scales seems warranted.

Validity of Tests of Normal Personality

INDIVIDUAL SCALES. The CPI is the only personality inventory with sufficient research to analyze at the scale level. As shown in Table 8 (see end of chapter), several scales do a reasonable job of predicting academy performance and the tolerance scale seems to provide the best combination of predicting supervisor ratings of performance ($r = .19$), disciplinary problems ($r = -.15$), and academy performance ($r = .22$).

PERSONALITY CONSTRUCTS. As shown in Table 9, measures of openness to experience best predict academy performance ($r = .13$), measures of conscientiousness best predict supervisor ratings of performance ($r = .08$), and measures of emotional stability best predict disciplinary problems ($r = -.07$). With the exception of predicting academy performance, the Big 5 dimensions of normal personality, in general, appear to be poor predictors of law enforcement performance ratings and disciplinary problems.

It should be noted that although most of the Big 5 validity coefficients are low, they are at a level consistent with those found in meta-analyses investigating the validity of personality in nonlaw enforcement occupations (Hurtz & Donovan, 2000).

Future Directions

I began the chapter by discussing some research issues that should be considered when reviewing research on the validity of personality inventories and finished with a meta-analytic review of the literature. Where does that leave us?

It seems clear that measures of psychopathology are not good predictors of law enforcement performance. As a result, it would seem that the logical conclusion is to move on to other topics. However, because many state laws require pre-employment psychological evaluations, and some states actually dictate the specific tests to be used, future research should focus on identifying the areas of psychopathology that are related to officers abusing power, violating ethics, and using unjustified levels of force. New tests should then be developed that tap these areas. It is frustrating that most police psychologists agree that psychopathology in general is not a good predictor of violent behavior, yet as a field, we continue to use tests of psychopathology to predict such behavior in law enforcement applicants. It is essential that we rely on evidence-based testing and evidence-based interventions and act as scientist-practitioners.

The use of tests of normal personality is a bit more complicated. Placing all tests into the Big 5 dimensions yields low correlation coefficients. Yet some scales, such as the CPI tolerance scale, show promise. Perhaps the next step is to create a personality inventory based directly on the personality traits identified in law enforcement job analyses. Such an approach seems reasonable as some researchers (e.g., J. Hogan & Holland, 2003, R. Hogan, 2005) have argued that personality inventories are most valid when one uses only the test scales that directly match the results of a job analysis. Although such thinking makes sense, others have argued that content valid tests are no more likely to yield higher criterion validity coefficients than are tests not directly based on job analyses (Murphy, Dzieweczynski, & Yang, in press).

There have been approximately 200 studies conducted on the use of personality inventories in the selection of law enforcement personnel. Although this seems like a high number, there is much more research that needs to be done, especially given the small number of studies conducted since my 2004 meta-analysis.

The bulk of research has focused on the MMPI/MMPI-2, which is not surprising given its extensive use. However, many more studies are needed on other personality inventories and many more studies are needed that study the relationship between personality and such criteria as the use of force, absence abuse, commendations, and discipline problems. It is also important to determine the extent to which personality inventories add incremental validity over other methods normally used to select employees.

It is clear that more research is still needed, but the research must be of high quality. It is essential that the correlations from *all* scales be included in the results tables to provide accurate data for future meta-analyses. When sample sizes are large, researchers must address the magnitude of the correlation coefficient, not just its statistical significance. I can't wait to meta-analyze the next 200 studies.

Table 1

HYPOTHETICAL CORRELATIONS BETWEEN TEST SCORES AND PERFORMANCE

Inventory/Scale	Performance Measure		
	Discipline Problems	Commendations	Academy Performance
Test of Personality			
Sensitivity	.07	.08	.00
Extraversion	.04	.05	.02
Conscientiousness	- .35*	.04	.01
Revised Personality Inventory			
Sensitivity	.04	.02	.03
Extraversion	.05	.01	.04
Conscientiousness	- .31*	09	.02
Surrette Inventory			
Sensitivity	.08	.00	.06
Extraversion	.07	.03	.00
Conscientiousness	- .39*	.04	.01
Openness to experience	.01	.06	.43*

* indicates correlation is statistically significant

Table 2
CORRELATIONS BETWEEN SCORES ON THE TEST OF
PERSONALITY AND SUPERVISOR RATINGS IN SIX STUDIES

Scale	Study					
	Smith (2008)	Jones (2007)	Andrews (2007)	James (2006)	Grimm (2005)	West (2009)
Guardedness	.35*	.00	.00	.00	.00	.00
Extraversion	.00	.41*	.00	.00	.00	.00
Sensitivity	.00	.00	.39*	.00	.00	.00
Hyperactivity	.00	.00	.00	.33*	.00	.00
Well-being	.00	.00	.00	.00	.40*	.00
Tolerance	.00	.00	.00	.00	.00	.44*
Alcohol problems	.00	.00	.00	.00	.00	.00
Anxiety	.00	.00	.00	.00	.00	.00
Dominance	.00	.00	.00	.00	.00	.00
Control	.00	.00	.00	.00	.00	.00
Socialization	.00	.00	.00	.00	.00	.00
Communality	.00	.00	.00	.00	.00	.00
Unusual experiences	.00	.00	.00	.00	.00	.00
Flexibility	.00	.00	.00	.00	.00	.00
Suspicion	.00	.00	.00	.00	.00	.00
Shrewdness	.00	.00	.00	.00	.00	.00
Responsibility	.00	.00	.00	.00	.00	.00
Tension	.00	.00	.00	.00	.00	.00
Driving problems	.00	.00	.00	.00	.00	.00
Anger issues	.00	.00	.00	.00	.00	.00

Personality Assessment in Police Psychology

Table 3
SAMPLE META-ANALYSIS RESULTS FOR COGNITIVE ABILITY

Criterion	K	N	r	95% Confidence Interval		p	90% Credibility Interval		Var	Q_w
				Lower	Upper		Lower	Upper		
Academy Grades	61	14,437	.41	.33	.48	.62	.44	.81	78%	77.82
Supervisor Ratings	63	16,507	.16	.14	.18	.25	.24	.26	84%	74.63

K=number of studies, N=sample size, r = mean correlation, = mean correlation corrected for range restriction and criterion unreliability, VAR = percentage of variance explained by sampling error and study artifacts, Qw = the within group heterogeneity

Table 4
UNCORRECTED VALIDITY COEFFICIENTS FOR THE MMPI:
UPDATE OF AAMODT (2004A)

MMPI Scale	Supervisor Ratings	Discipline Problems	Commendations	Academy Grades
L	-.01	.01	-.01	-.02
F	-.08*	.02	.05	-.11*
K	.05	-.01	-.06	.08*
Hs	-.01	-.03	-.05	-.09*
D	-.04	-.01	.02	-.07*
Hy	.01	-.01	-.01	.02
Pd	-.07	.03	-.06	-.04
Mf	-.05	-.01	-.02	-.02
Pa	.00	.03	-.03	.04
Pt	-.05	-.01	-.08	-.03
Sc	-.07	.01	-.05	-.07*
Ma	-.10*	.03	-.01	-.11*
Si	-.01	.00	-.03	-.01

* Correlation is statistically significant

Table 5

META-ANALYSIS OF PSYCHOPATHOLOGY FACTORS IN PREDICTING SUPERVISOR RATINGS OF PERFORMANCE

Psychopathology Factor	K	N	r	95% Confidence Interval		ρ	90% Credibility Interval		Var	Q_w
				Lower	Upper		Lower	Upper		
Test Taking Style										
Defensiveness	59	8,404	-.02	-.10	.05	-.04	-.45	.37	36%	162.45*
Malingering	24	3,416	-.08	-.15	-.02	-.15	-.45	.15	49%	48.22*
Psychopathology Construct										
Hypochondriasis	36	7,376	-.04	-.09	.01	-.07	-.33	.19	47%	76.56*
Depression	31	5,731	-.04	-.10	-.01	-.07	-.30	.15	48%	64.69*
Hysteria	25	3,334	.02	-.04	.08	.04	-.19	.27	54%	45.82*
Antisocial/aggressive	31	4,247	-.09	-.17	-.02	-.18	-.55	.20	44%	70.33*
Paranoia	36	6,894	-.02	-.09	.05	-.03	-.43	.36	31%	113.40*
Psychasthenia	30	6,068	-.04	-.09	.01	-.08	-.30	.14	50%	60.41*
Schizophrenia	31	5,840	-.06	-.14	.02	-.11	-.54	.32	29%	107.75*
Mania	30	4,081	-.10	-.17	-.04	-.02	-.50	.10	55%	54.04*
Social introversion	30	3,872	-.04	-.11	.02	-.08	-.40	.24	51%	58.41*
Anxiety	5	811	-.09	-.16	-.02	-.15	-.15	-.15	100%	0.61
Substance abuse	9	1,645	-.07	-.15	.01	-.12	-.43	.19	33%	27.22*
Family problems	9	1,433	-.13	-.20	-.07	-.23	-.37	-.08	74%	12.13
Sexual concerns	4	668	-.13	-.21	-.06	-.22	-.22	-.22	100%	3.74

Table 6
META-ANALYSIS OF PSYCHOPATHOLOGY FACTORS IN PREDICTING DISCIPLINARY PROBLEMS

Psychopathology Factor	K	N	r	95% Confidence Interval		p	90% Credibility Interval		Var	Q_w
				Lower	Upper		Lower	Upper		
Test Taking Style										
Defensiveness	26	9,835	-.01	-.04	.02	-.02	-.15	.11	62%	41.77*
Malingering	15	5,025	.02	-.01	.06	.14	-.08	.17	71%	21.07*
Psychopathology Construct										
Hypochondriasis	17	4,486	-.03	-.06	.00	-.05	-.18	.09	73%	23.04*
Depression	19	7,505	-.02	-.05	.02	-.03	-.19	.13	56%	33.50*
Hysteria	19	7,769	-.03	-.06	.01	-.05	-.21	.11	57%	33.39*
Antisocial/aggressive	26	7,367	.04	.00	.08	.08	-.11	.27	56%	46.42*
Paranoia	19	7,390	.02	-.01	.05	.04	-.09	.17	67%	28.29*
Psychasthenia	22	7,447	-.02	-.05	.00	-.04	-.13	.04	84%	28.05*
Schizophrenia	22	7,905	-.01	-.04	.02	-.01	-.11	.09	77%	28.25*
Mania	20	5,573	.03	-.01	.07	.06	-.11	.23	61%	32.37*
Social introversion	21	5,677	.01	-.02	.04	.02	-.08	.11	78%	26.74*
Borderline	2	1,111	.00	-.06	.06	.00	-.15	.16	42%	4.79*
Anxiety	3	1,857	-.01	-.06	.04	-.01	-.11	.09	59%	5.09
Substance abuse	8	3,102	.05	.01	.08	.09	.09	.09	100%	4.61

Table 7
VALIDITY OF MMPI-2 SPECIAL SCALES:
UPDATE TO AAMODT (2004B) META-ANALYSIS

Criterion/Scale	K	N	R	95% Confidence Interval		Var%	Q
				Lower	Upper		
Performance Ratings							
GCBC (2 levels)	8	567	- .19	- .31	- .06	39.4	19.55*
GCBC (3 levels)	6	451	- .15	- .31	.02	35.9	18.35*
Huesmann Index	6	498	- .06	- .15	.02	100.0	1.43
Aamodt Index	6	498	- .06	- .14	.03	100.0	2.85
Goldberg Index	6	498	.02	- .07	.11	100.0	2.02
Gonder Index	5	412	- .01	- .11	.09	96.0	5.02
Factor I	5	412	- .04	- .14	.06	99.4	5.02
Factor II	5	412	.00	- .10	.09	88.6	5.64
Factor III	5	412	.13	.03	.22	100.0	1.55
Factor IV	5	412	.06	- .04	.15	100.0	1.14
Factor V	5	412	.01	- .09	.11	80.7	6.20
Discipline Problems							
GCBC (2 levels)	5	2,546	.10	.06	.14	100.0	3.53
GCBC (3 levels)	5	2,245	.11	.07	.15	100.0	4.37
Huesmann Index	6	2,653	.11	.07	.15	100.0	2.96
Aamodt Index	5	2,546	.18	.14	.22	100.0	3.10
Goldberg Index	6	2,707	.14	.11	.18	79.1	6.66
Gonder Index	5	2,546	.10	.04	.16	42.1	11.08*
Factor I	6	2,637	.10	.04	.16	39.0	14.49*
Factor II	6	2,637	- .06	- .10	- .02	71.0	8.26
Factor III	6	2,637	.02	- .03	.06	59.7	10.04
Factor IV	6	2,637	.01	- .03	.05	100.0	4.76
Factor V	7	2,837	.09	.05	.12	92.1	7.27

Note: K = number of studies, N = total number of subjects, r = mean correlation weighted by sample size, Var% = percentage of variance expected by sampling error, and Q = a chi-square statistical test of the homogeneity of the correlation coefficients (significance is indicated by an asterisk)

Table 8
UNCORRECTED VALIDITY COEFFICIENTS FOR THE CPI:
UPDATE OF AAMODT (2004A)

CPI Scale	Supervisor Ratings	Discipline Problems	Academy Performance
Dominance	.04	.06	.11*
Capacity for status	.05*	.03	.16*
Sociability	.02	.01	.13*
Social presence	.05*	.01	.12*
Self-acceptance	.01	.03	.08*
Well-being	.15*	-.13*	.13*
Responsibility	.11*	-.10*	.14*
Socialization	.09*	-.18*	.05
Self-control	.15*	-.15*	.06
Tolerance	.19*	-.15*	.22*
Good impression	.10*	-.07	.01
Communality	.10*	-.12*	.09*
Ach via conformity	.16*	-.03	.18*
Ach via independence	.11*	-.11*	.13
Intellectual efficiency	.13*	-.04	.17*
Psych mindedness	.11*	-.06	.12*
Flexibility	.05	-.09	.09
Femininity	.10*	-.05	-.09

Table 9
META-ANALYSIS OF BIG 5 PERSONALITY FACTORS (INVENTORIES OF NORMAL PERSONALITY)

Psychopathology Factor	K	N	r	95% Confidence Interval		p	90% Credibility Interval		Var	Q_w
				Lower	Upper		Lower	Upper		
Academy Grades										
Openness to Experience	26	5,555	.13	.08	.18	.19	-.08	.46	32%	80.99*
Conscientiousness	23	6,154	.10	.05	.15	.15	-.08	.38	33%	68.80*
Extraversion	41	8,753	.09	.06	.13	.14	-.05	.33	47%	87.26*
Agreeableness	22	7,382	.03	-.00	.06	.05	-.05	.14	67%	32.69*
Emotional stability	21	6,587	.08	.04	.12	.12	-.05	.28	44%	47.27*
Performance Ratings										
Openness to Experience	74	8,651	.05	.02	.08	.08	-.20	.35	42%	177.95*
Conscientiousness	66	9,494	.08	.05	.12	.12	-.12	.36	44%	151.68*
Extraversion	87	12,660	.04	.03	.07	.07	-.01	.14	89%	97.44*
Agreeableness	64	7,510	.06	.03	.09	.09	-.10	.27	60%	106.41*
Emotional stability	53	8,448	.06	.03	.09	.09	-.12	.30	47%	112.06*
Discipline Problems										
Openness to Experience	19	5,508	-.03	-.08	.01	-.05	-.23	.12	42%	45.76*
Conscientiousness	27	8,939	-.06	-.09	-.03	-.09	-.23	.04	53%	51.01*
Extraversion	34	13,167	.00	-.02	.03	.01	-.09	.11	60%	56.19*
Agreeableness	29	13,347	-.04	-.07	-.01	-.05	-.22	.11	33%	88.01*
Emotional stability	31	11,921	-.07	-.11	-.04	-.11	-.28	-.09	37%	82.04*

REFERENCES

Aamodt, M.G. (2004a). *Research in law enforcement selection.* Boca Raton, FL: BrownWalker.

Aamodt, M.G. (2004b). Special issue on using MMPI-2 special scale configurations in law enforcement selection: Introduction and meta-analysis. *Applied H.R.M. Research, 9*(2), 41–52.

*Abraham, J.D., & Morrison, J.D. (2003). Relationship between the Performance Perspectives Inventory's Conscientiousness scale and job performance of corporate security guards. *Applied H.R.M. Research, 8*(1), 45–48.

*Azen, S.P., Snibbe, H.M., & Montgomery, H.R. (1973). A longitudinal predictive study of success and performance of law enforcement officers. *Journal of Applied Psychology, 57*(2), 190–192.

*Azen, S.P., Snibbe, H.M., Montgomery, H.R., Fabricatore, J., & Earle, H. (1974). A longitudinal predictive study of success and performance of law enforcement officers. *American Journal of Community Psychology, 1*(2), 79–86.

Baczynska, G.A. (2006). "Validation of clinician judgments of MMPI-2 profiles in law enforcement selection." Unpublished master's thesis, Radford University, Radford, VA.

*Balch, D.E. (1977). "Personality trait differences between successful and non-successful police recruits at a typical police academy and veteran police officers." Unpublished doctoral dissertation, United States International University.

*Banks, D.E. (1988). "The relationship of personality styles to police job performance." Unpublished doctoral dissertation, California School of Professional Psychology.

*Bartol, C.R. (1991). Predictive validation of the MMPI for small-town police officers who fail. *Professional Psychology: Research and Practice, 22*(2), 127–132.

*Bartol, C.R. (1982). Psychological characteristics of small-town police officers. *Journal of Police Science and Administration, 10*(1), 58–63.

*Bartol, C.R., Bergen, G.T., Volckens, J.S., & Knoras, K.M. (1992). Women in small-town policing. *Criminal Justice and Behavior, 19*(3), 240–259.

*Bernstein, I.H., Schoenfeld, L.S., & Costello, R.M. (1982). Truncated component regression, multicollinearity and the MMPI's use in a police officer selection setting. *Multivariate Behavioral Research, 17*, 99–116.

*Beutler, L., Storm, A., Kirkish, P., Scogin, F., & Gaines, J.A. (1985). Parameters in the prediction of police officer performance. *Professional Psychology: Research and Practice, 16*(2), 324–335.

*Black, J. (2000). Personality testing and police selection: Utility of the "Big Five." *New Zealand Journal of Psychology, 29*(1), 2–9.

*Blau, T.H., Super, J.T., & Brady, L. (1993). The MMPI good cop/bad cop profile in identifying dysfunctional law enforcement personnel. *Journal of Police and Criminal Psychology, 9*(1), 2–4.

*Blunt, J.H. (1982). "The prediction of police officer performance utilizing the

---

* Study was used in the meta-analysis calculations.

MMPI." Unpublished master's thesis, University of Central Florida.

*Boes, J.O., Chandler, C.J., & Timm, H.W. (1997). *Police integrity: Use of personality measures to identify corruption-prone officers.* Monterey, CA: Defense Personnel Security Research Center.

*Boyce, T.N. (1988). "Psychological screening for high-risk police specialization." Unpublished doctoral dissertation, Georgia State University.

*Bozza, C.M. (1990). "Improving the prediction of police officer performance from screening information." Unpublished doctoral dissertation, United States International University.

*Bradford, A.C. (1991). "Psychological screening for narcotics officers and detectives." Unpublished doctoral dissertation, Miami University of Ohio.

*Brewster, J. (1996). Hypervigilance and cynicism in police officers. *Journal of Police and Criminal Psychology, 10*(4), 7–9.

*Brewster, J., & Stoloff, M.L. (2004). Using MMPI special scale configurations to predict supervisor ratings of police officer performance. *Applied HRM Research, 9*(2), 53–56.

*Brewster, J., & Stoloff, M.L. (1999). Using the good cop/bad cop profile with the MMPI-2. *Journal of Police and Criminal Psychology, 14*(2), 29–34.

*Brown, G.V. (1996). "Acceptable vs. marginal police officers' psychological ratings: A longitudinal comparison of job performance." Unpublished doctoral dissertation, Florida International University.

*Campion, T.R. (2005). "Predicting police aggression with the psychopathic deviate scale on the MMPI-2." Unpublished doctoral dissertation, Walden University.

*Castora, K., Brewster, J., & Stoloff, M. (2003). Predicting aggression in police officers using the MMPI-2. *Journal of Police and Criminal Psychology, 18*(1), 1–8.

Cave, S.B., & Westfried, E. (2001). "Do scores on pre-employment psychological evaluations correlate with final academy scores?" Paper presented at the annual meeting of the Society for Police and Criminal Psychology, Austin, Texas.

Cave, S.B., & Westfried, E. (2002). "Linkage between pre-employment evaluations, academy performance, and first year job performance ratings with a state police agency." Paper presented at the annual meeting of the Society for Police and Criminal Psychology, Orlando, FL.

*Clopton, W. (1971). "Comparison of ratings and field performance data in validating predictions of patrolman performance: A five-year follow-up study." Unpublished master's thesis, University of Cincinnati.

*Cope, J.R. (1981). "Personality characteristics of successful versus unsuccessful police officers." Unpublished doctoral dissertation, Florida Institute of Technology.

*Cortina, J.M., Doherty, M.L., Schmitt, N., Kaufman, G., & Smith, R.G. (1992). The "Big Five" personality factors in the IPI and MMPI: Predictors of police performance. *Personnel Psychology, 45,* 119–140.

*Cortina, J.M., Doherty, M.L., Schmitt, N., Kaufman, G., & Smith, R.G. (1991). "Validation of the IPI and MMPI as predictors of police performance." Paper presented at the annual meeting of the Society for Industrial-Organizational Psychology.

*Costello, R.M., & Schoenfeld, L.S. (1981). Time-related effects on MMPI profiles of police academy recruits. *Journal of Clinical Psychology, 37*(3), 518–522.

*Costello, R.M., Schneider, Schoenfeld, L.S., & Kobos, J. (1982). Police applicant screening: An analogue study. *Journal of Clinical Psychology, 38*(1), 216–221.

*Cuttler, M.J., & Muchinsky, P.M. (2006). Prediction of law enforcement training performance and dysfunctional job performance with general mental ability, personality, and life history variables. *Criminal Justice and Behavior, 33*(3), 3–25.

*Daley, R.E. (1978). "The relationship of personality variables to suitability for police work." Unpublished doctoral dissertation, Florida Institute of Technology.

*Davidson, N.B. (1975). "The predictive validity of a police officer selection program." Unpublished master's thesis, Portland State University.

*Davis, R.D., & Rostow, C.D. (2004). Using MMPI special scale configurations to predict law enforcement officers fired for cause. *Applied HRM Research, 9*(2), 53–56.

*Davis, R.D., Rostow, C.D., Pinkston, J.B., Combs, D.R., & Dixon, D.R. (2004). A reexamination of the MMPI-2 aggressiveness and immaturity indices in law enforcement screening. *Journal of Police and Criminal Psychology, 19*(1), 17–26.

*de Meijer, L.A.L., Born, M.P., Terlouw, G., & Van der Molen, H.T. (2008). Criterion-related validity of Dutch police-selection measures and differences between ethnic groups. *International Journal of Selection and Assessment, 16*(4), 321–332.

*Detrick, P., Chibnall, J.T., & Luebbert, M.C. (2004). The revised NEO personality inventory as predictor of police academy performance. *Criminal Justice and Behavior, 31*(6), 676–694.

*Dorner, K.R. (1991). "Personality characteristics and demographic variables as predictors of job performance in female traffic officers." Unpublished doctoral dissertation, United States International University.

*Enright, B.P. (2004). "Personality measurement in the prediction of positive and negative police officer performance." Unpublished doctoral dissertation, University of Missouri, St. Louis.

*Fabricatore, J., Azen, S., Schoentgen, S., & Snibbe, H. (1978). Predicting performance of police officers using the Sixteen Personality Factor Questionnaire. *American Journal of Community Psychology, 6*(1), 63–69.

*FitzGerald, P.R. (1986). "The prediction of police performance using the MMPI and CPI." Unpublished doctoral dissertation, Saint Louis University.

*Forero, C.G., Gallardo-Pujol, D., Maydeu-Olivares, A., & Andres-Pueyo, A. (2009). A longitudinal model for predicting performance of police officers using personality and behavioral data. *Criminal Justice and Behavior, 36*(6), 591–606.

*Funk, A.P. (1997). "Psychological assessment of military federal agents using the MMPI-2: A closer look at employment selection and performance prediction." Unpublished master's thesis, Florida State University.

*Gardner, J.F. (1994). "The predictive validity of psychological testing in law enforcement." Unpublished master's thesis, University of Alabama.

*Gelbart, M. (1978). "Psychological, personality, and biographical variables related to success as a hostage negotiator." Unpublished doctoral dissertation, University of Southern California.

*Geraghty, M.F. (1986). "The California Personality Inventory test as a predictor of law enforcement officer job performance." Unpublished doctoral dissertation, Florida Institute of Technology.

Gettys, V.S., & Elam, J.D. (1985). Validation demystified: Personnel selection techniques that work. *The Police Chief,* April, 41–43.

Goldberg, L.R. (1965). Diagnosticians vs. diagnostic signs: the diagnosis of psychosis vs. neurosis from the MMPI. *Psychological Monographs, 79,* 1–28.

*Gonder, M.L. (1998). "Personality profiles of police officers: Differences in those that complete and fail to complete a police training academy." Unpublished master's thesis, University of North Carolina-Charlotte.

*Gonder, M.L., & Gilmore, D.C. (2004). Personality profiles of police officers who successfully complete academy training. *Applied HRM Research, 9*(2), 59–62.

*Gottlieb, M.C., & Baker, C.F. (1974). Predicting police officer effectiveness. *The Journal of Forensic Psychology, 6,* 35–46.

*Grayson, L.J. (1986). "Narcissistic personality stules and their effects on job functioning in police officers." Unpublished doctoral dissertation, California School of Professional Psychology, Los Angeles.

*Greenberg, B.E., Riggs, M., Bryant, F.B., & Smith, B.D. (2003). Validation of a short aggression inventory for law enforcement. *Journal of Police and Criminal Psychology, 18*(2), 12–19.

*Griffith, T.L. (1991). "Correlates of police and correctional officer performance." Unpublished doctoral dissertation, Florida State University.

*Hankey, R.O. (1968). "Personality correlates in a role of authority: The Police." Unpublished doctoral dissertation, University of Southern California.

*Hargrave, G.E. (1985). Using the MMPI and CPI to screen law enforcement applicants: A study of reliability and validity of clinician's decisions. *Journal of Police Science and Administration, 13*(3), 221–224.

*Hargrave, G.E. (1987). Screening law enforcement cadets with the MMPI: An analysis of adverse impact. *Journal of Police and Criminal Psychology, 3*(1), 14–19.

*Hargrave, G.E., & Hiatt, D. (1989). Use of the California Psychological Inventory in law enforcement officer selection. *Journal of Personality Assessment (2),* 267–277.

*Hargrave, G.E., & Hiatt, D. (1987). Law enforcement selection with the interview, MMPI, and CPI: A study of reliability and validity. *Journal of Police Science and Administration, 15*(2), 110–117.

*Hargrave, G.E., Hiatt, D., & Gaffney, T.W. (1986). A comparison of MMPI and CPI test profiles for traffic officers and deputy sheriffs. *Journal of Police Science and Administration, 14*(3), 250–258.

*Hargrave, G.E., Hiatt, D., & Gaffney, T.W. (1988). F+4+9+Cn: An MMPI measure of aggression in law enforcement officers and applicants. *Journal of Police Science and Administration, 16*(3), 268–273.

*Hargrave, G.E., Norborg. J. M., & Oldenburg, L. (1986). Differences in entry level test and criterion data for male and female police officers. In Reese, J.T. & Goldstein, H.A. (Eds). *Psychological services for law enforcement,* pp 35–42. Washington, D.C.: U.S. Government Printing Office.

*Hart, R. (1981). "The use of the Clinical Analysis Questionnaire in the selection of police officers: A validation study." Unpublished doctoral dissertation, Florida State University.

*Henderson, N.D. (1979). Criterion-related validity of personality and aptitude scales: A comparison of validation results under voluntary and actual test conditions. In Charles D. Spielberger (Ed.). *Police selection and evaluation: Issues and techniques.* New York: Praeger Publishers.

*Hess, L.R. (1972). "Police entry tests and their predictability of score in police academy and subsequent job performance." Unpublished doctoral dissertation, Marquette University.

*Heyer, T. (1998). "A follow-up study of the prediction of police officer performance on psychological evaluation variables." Unpublished doctoral dissertation, Minnesota School of Professional Psychology.

*Hiatt, D., & Hargrave, G.E. (1988). MMPI profiles of problem police officers. *Journal of Personality Assessment, 52*(4), 722–731.

*Hiatt, D., & Hargrave, G.E. (1988). Predicting job performance with psychological screening. *Journal of Police Science and Administration, 16,* 122–125.

Hogan, J., & Holland, B. (2003). Using theory to evaluate personality and job performance relations. *Journal of Applied Psychology, 88,* 100–112.

Hogan, R. (2005). In defense of personality measurement: New wine for old whiners. *Human Performance, 18*(4), 331–341.

*Hogan, R. (1971). Personality characteristics of highly rated policemen. *Personnel Psychology, 24,* 679–686.

*Horstman, P.L. (1976). "Assessing the California Psychological Inventory for predicting police performance." Unpublished doctoral dissertation, University of Oklahoma.

Huesmann, L.R., Lefkowitz, M.M., & Eron, L.D. (1978). Sum of MMPI scales F, 4, and 9 as a measure of aggression. *Journal of Consulting and Clinical Psychology, 46*(5), 1071–1078.

Hunter, J.E., & Schmidt, F.L. (1990), *Methods of meta-analysis: Correcting error and bias in research findings.* Newbury Park, CA: Sage.

Hurtz, G.M., & Donovan, J.J. (2000). Personality and job performance: the Big Five revisited. *Journal of Applied Psychology, 85*(6), 869–879.

*Hwang, G.S. (1988). "Validity of the California Psychological Inventory for Police Selection." Unpublished master's thesis, North Texas State University.

*Inwald, R.E. (1988). Five-year follow-up of department terminations as predicted by 16 preemployment psychological indicators. *Journal of Applied Psychology, 73*(4), 703–710.

*Inwald, R.E., & Brockwell, A.L. (1991). Predicting the performance of government security personnel with the IPI and MMPI. *Journal of Personality Assessment, 56*(3), 522–535.

*Inwald, R.E., & Shusman, E.J. (1984). The IPI and MMPI as predictors of academy performance for police recruits. *Journal of Police Science and Administration, 12*(1), 1–11.

*Inwald, R.E., & Shusman, E.J. (1984). Personality and performance sex differences of law enforcement officer recruits. *Journal of Police Science and Administration, 12*(3), 339–347.

*Kauder, B.S. (1999). "Construct-related evidence of validity for the Inwald Personality Inventory and its usefulness for predicting police officer performance." Unpublished doctoral dissertation, Pacific University (Forest Grove, OR).

*Kleiman, L.S. (1978). "Ability and personality factors moderating the relationships of police academy training performance with measures of selection and job performance." Unpublished doctoral dissertation, University of Tennessee, Knoxville.

*Kleiman, L.S., & Gordon, M.E. (1986). An examination of the relationship between police training academy performance and job performance. *Journal of Police Science and Administration, 14*(4), 293–299.

*Knights, R.M. (1976). "The relationship between the selection process and on-the-job performance of Albuquerque police officers." Unpublished doctoral dissertation, University of New Mexico.

*Kwaske, I.H. (2006). "An exploratory, multi-level study to validate individual psychological assessments for entry-level police and firefighter positions." Unpublished doctoral dissertation, Illinois Institute of Technology.

*Macintyre, S., Ronken, C., & Prenzler, T. (2005). Relationship between MMPI-2 scores and police misconduct in Australia. *Applied HRM Research, 10*(1), 35–38.

*Mandel, K. (1970). "The predictive validity of on-the-job performance of policemen from recruitment selection information." Unpublished doctoral dissertation, University of Utah.

*Mass, G. (1980). "Using judgment and personality measures to predict effectiveness in policework: An exploratory validation study." Unpublished doctoral dissertation, Ohio State University.

*Matyas, G.S. (1980). "The relationship of MMPI and biographical data to police performance." Unpublished doctoral dissertation, University of Missouri-Columbia.

McCrae, R.R., & Costa, P.T. (2003). *Personality in adulthood: A five-factor theory perspective* (2nd ed). New York: Guilford Press.

*McEuen, O.L. (1981). "Assessment of some personality traits that show a relationship to academy grades, being dismissed from the department, and work evaluation ratings for police officers in Atlanta, Georgia." Unpublished doctoral dissertation, The Fielding Institute.

*Mills, C.J., & Bohannon, W.E. (1980). Personality characteristics of effective state police officers. *Journal of Applied Psychology, 65*(6), 680–684.

Mufson, D.W., & Mufson, M.A. (1998). Predicting police officer performance using the Inwald Personality Inventory: An Illustration from Appalachia. *Professional Psychology: Research and Practice, 29*(1), 59–62.

Murphy, K.R., Dzieweczynski, J.L., & Yang, Z. (in press). Positive manifold limits the relevance of content-matching strategies for validating selection test batteries. *Journal of Applied Psychology*, in press.

*Ofton, M.A. (1979). "The relationship between Minnesota Multiphasic Personality Inventory (MMPI) profiles of police recruits and performance ratings in their rookie year." Unpublished master's thesis, Abilene Christian University.

*Palmatier, J.J. (1996). "The big-five factors and hostility in the MMPI and IPI: Predictors of Michigan State Trooper job performance." Unpublished doctoral dissertation, Michigan State University.

*Plummer, K.O. (1979). "Pre-employment factors that determine success in the police academy." Unpublished doctoral dissertation, Claremont Graduate College.

*Powers, W.P. (1996). "An evaluation of the predictive validity of the MMPI s it relates to identifying police officers prone to engage in the use of excessive force." Unpublished doctoral dissertation, Adler School of Professional Psychology.

*Provines, J.L. (2006). "Investigation of police officer selection procedures." Unpublished doctoral dissertation, Wichita State University.

*Pugh, G. (1985). The California Psychological Inventory and police selection. *Journal of Police Science and Administration, 13*(2), 172–177.

*Raditz, B.S. (1985). "A study of the efficacy of the MMPI and clinical interview for screening correction officers." Unpublished doctoral dissertation, Memphis State University.

*Raynes, B.L. (2004). Using MMPI special scale configurations to predict supervisor ratings of police officer performance. *Applied HRM Research, 9*(2), 67–70.

*Raynes, B.L. (1997). "Predicting difficult employees: the relationship between vocational interest, self-esteem, and problem communication styles." Unpublished master's thesis, Radford University.

Richardson, D.W., Cave, S.B., & La Grange, L. (2007). Prediction of police officer performance among New Mexico state police as assessed by the Personality Assessment Inventory. *Journal of Police and Criminal Psychology, 22,* 84–90.

Roberts, M.D., Thompson J.A., Johnson M. (2004) *PAI Law Enforcement, Corrections, and Public Safety Selection Report: Software Program.* Odessa, FL: Psychological Assessment Resources.

Ronan, W.W., Talbert, T.L., & Mullet, G.M. (1977). Prediction of job performance dimensions: Police officers. *Public Personnel Management,* May-June, 173–180.

*Rostow, C.D., Davis, R.D., Pinkston, J.B., & Corwick, L.M. (1999). The MMPI-2 and satisfactory academy performance: Differences and correlations. *Journal of Police and Criminal Psychology, 14*(2), 35–39.

*Sarchione, C.D. (1995). "Personality constructs and California Psychological Inventory Subscales as a predictor of job difficulty n police officers." Unpublished master's thesis, University of North Carolina, Greensboro.

*Sarchione, C.D., Cuttler, M.J., Muchinsky, P.M., & Nelson-Gray, R.O. (1998). Prediction of dysfunctional job behaviors among law enforcement officers. *Journal of Applied Psychology, 83*(6), 904–912

*Saxe, S.J., & Reiser, M. (1976). A comparison of three police applicant groups using the MMPI. *Journal of Police Science and Administration, 4*(4), 419–425.

*Schneider, B.M. (2002). "Using the big-five personality factors in the Minnesota Multiphasic Personality Inventory, California Psychological Inventory, and Inwald Personality Inventory to predict police performance." Unpublished doctoral dissertation, Florida International University.

*Schuerger, J.M., Kochevar, K.F., & Reinwald, J.E. (1982). Male and female corrections officers: Personality and rated performance. *Psychological Reports, 51*(1), 223–228.

Scogin, F., Schumacher, J., Gardner, J., & Chaplin, W. (1995). Predictive validity of psychological testing in law enforcement settings. *Professional Psychology: Research and Practice, 26*(1), 68–71.

*Sellbom, M., Fischler, G.L., & Ben-Porath, Y.S. (2007). Identifying MMPI-2 predictors of police officer integrity and misconduct. *Criminal Justice and Behavior, 34*(8), 985–1004.

*Serko, B.A. (1981). "Police selection: A predictive study." Unpublished doctoral dissertation, Florida School of Professional Psychology.

*Shaver, D.P. (1980). "A descriptive study of police officers in selected towns of northwest Arkansas." Unpublished doctoral dissertation, University of Arkansas.

*Shaw, J.H. (1986). Effectiveness of the MMPI in differentiating ideal from undesirable police officer applicants. In Reese, J.T. & Goldstein, H.A. (Eds). *Psychological services for law enforcement*, pp. 91–95. Washington, D.C.: U.S. Government Printing Office.

*Shusman, E.J., Inwald, R.E., & Knatz, H.F. (1987). A cross-validation study of police recruit performance as predicted by the IPI and MMPI. *Journal of Police Science and Administration, 15*(2), 162–169.

*Shusman, E.J., Inwald, R.E., & Landa, B. (1984). Correction officer job performance as predicted by the IPI and MMPI: A validation and cross-validation study. *Criminal Justice and Behavior, 11*(3), 309–329.

*Spielberger, C.D., Spaulding, H.C., Jolley, M.T., & Ward, J.C. (1979). Selection of effective law enforcement officers: The Florida police standards research project. In Charles D. Spielberger (Ed.). *Police selection and evaluation: Issues and techniques.* New York: Praeger Publishers.

*Spielberger, C.D., Spaulding, H.C., Ward, J.C., & Vagg, P.R. (1981). *The Florida Police Standards Research Project: The Validation of a Psychological Test Battery for Selecting Law Enforcement Officers.* Tampa, Florida: University of South Florida.

*Sterrett, M.R. (1984). "The utility of the Bipolar Psychological Inventory for predicting tenure of law enforcement officers." Unpublished doctoral dissertation, Claremont Graduate College.

*Super, J.T. (1995). Psychological characteristics of successful SWAT/tactical response team personnel. *Journal of Police and Criminal Psychology, 11*(1), 60–63.

*Surrette, M.A., Aamodt, M.G., & Serafino, G. (2004). Using MMPI special scale configurations to predict performance ratings of police officers in New Mexico. *Applied HRM Research, 9*(2), 71–72.

*Surrette, M.A., Aamodt, M.G., & Serafino, G. (1990). "Validity of the New Mexico Police Selection Battery." Paper presented at the annual meeting of the Society for Police and Criminal Psychology, Albuquerque, NM.

*Sweda, M.G. (1988). "The Iowa law enforcement personnel study: Prediction of law enforcement job performance from biographical and personality variables." Unpublished doctoral dissertation, University of Iowa.

Swope, M.R. (1989). "Validating state police trooper career performance with the Sixteen Personality Factor questionnaire." Unpublished doctoral dissertation, Wayne State University.

*Talley, J.E., & Hinz, L.D. (1990). *Performance prediction of public safety and law enforcement personnel.* Springfield, IL: Charles C. Thomas.

*Tesauro, R.R. (1994). "The MMPI/MMPI-2 Immaturity Index as a predictor of police performance." Unpublished doctoral dissertation, Tennessee State University.

*Thomas, J.C., & Kauder, B. (2004). Using MMPI special scale configurations to predict field training officer ratings of probationary police officer performance. *Applied HRM Research, 9*(2), 73–74.

*Tomini, B.A. (1995). "The person-job fit: Implications of selecting police personnel on the basis of job dimensions, aptitudes and personality traits." Unpublished doctoral dissertation, University of Windsor.

*Topp, B.W., & Kardash, C.A. (1986). Personality, achievement, and attrition: Validation in a multiple-jurisdiction police academy. *Journal of Police Science and Administration, 14*(3), 234–241.

*Uno, E.A. (1979). "The prediction of job failure: A study of police officers using the MMPI." Unpublished doctoral dissertation, California School of Professional Psychology-Berkeley.

*Varela, J.G., Scogin, F.R., & Vipperman, R.K. (1999). Development and preliminary validation of a semi-structured interview for the screening of law enforcement candidates. *Behavioral Science and the Law, 17*(4), 467–481.

*Vosburgh, B.V. (1987). "Police personality and performance: A concurrent validity study." Unpublished doctoral dissertation, California School of Professional Psychology - Los Angeles.

*Ward, J.C. (1981). "The predictive validity of personality and demographic variables in the selection of law enforcement officers." Unpublished doctoral dissertation, University of South Florida.

*Weiss, W.U., Davis, R., Rostow, C., & Kinsman, S. (2003). The MMPI-2 L scale as a tool in police selection. *Journal of Police and Criminal Psychology, 18*(1), 57–60.

*Weiss, W.U., Rostow, C., Davis, R., & DeCoster-Martin, E. (2004). The Personality Assessment Inventory as a selection device for law enforcement personnel. *Journal of Police and Criminal Psychology, 19*(2), 23–29.

*Weiss, W.U., Serafino, G., Serafino, A., Wilson, W., & Knoll, S. (1998). Use of the MMPI-2 to predict the employment continuation and performance ratings of recently hired police officers. *Journal of Police and Criminal Psychology, 13*(1), 40–44.

*Weiss, W.U., Serafino, G., Serafino, A., Wilson, W., Sarsany, J., & Felton, J. (1999). Use of the MMPI-2 and the Inwald Personality Inventory to identify personality characteristics of dropouts from a state police academy. *Journal of Police and Criminal Psychology, 14*(1), 38–42.

*Wells, V.K. (1991). "The MMPI and CPI as predictors of police performance." Unpublished doctoral dissertation, Saint Louis University.

*West, S.D. (1988). "The validity of the MMPI in the selection of police officers." Unpublished master's thesis, University of North Texas.

Wilson, A. (1980). "Reported accidental injuries in a metropolitan police department." Unpublished doctoral dissertation, Boston University.

*Workowski, E.J., & Pallone, N.J. (1999). Previously unscored pre-service MMPI data in relation to police performance over a decade: A multivariate inquiry. *Journal of Offender Rehabilitation, 29*(3/4), 71–94.

*Wright, B.S. (1988). "Psychological evaluations as predictors of police recruit performance." Unpublished doctoral dissertation, Florida State University.

*Wright, B.S., Doerner, W.G., Speir, J.C. (1990). Pre-employment psychological testing as a predictor of police performance during an FTO program. *American Journal of Police, 9*(4), 65–83.

Chapter 10

EFFECT SIZES IN POLICE PSYCHOLOGY PERSONALITY ASSESSMENT RESEARCH: A PRIMER

JOHN H. HITCHCOCK, ROSEMARIE O'CONNER, and PETER A. WEISS

This chapter will not contribute new insights into the effect size (ES) literature; its purpose is instead to provide an overview of how the application of ES metrics (those of the correlation and standard mean difference varieties) can be applied to police selection and treatment work. A review of the literature in this area suggests a need for such a primer. Journals such as *Journal of Police and Criminal Psychology, Criminal Justice and Behavior*, and *Law Enforcement Executive Forum* make regular use of group comparison and regression techniques to measure treatment/intervention impacts and assess proposed police selection procedures. Many studies describe the statistical significance of observed relationships among variables, but fewer use ESs to supplement reporting. This is at odds with wider calls to report ESs given the limited utility of null hypothesis statistical significance testing (NHSTs) (cf. Cohen, 1994; Kline, 2004; Morgan, 2003; Thompson, 1993; Wilkinson & the Task Force for Statistical Inference, 1999), suggesting a need to describe and justify using these metrics.

The intended audience for this chapter is clinicians who contribute to and regularly consume research in the arena of police work, but not those with more advanced methodological training and/or experience with ESs. Whole books are available on the topic (e.g., Grissom & Kim, 2005; Kline, 2004; Rosenthal, Rosnow & Rubin, 2000) and related matters such as meta-analysis (e.g., Cooper, 1998; Hedges & Olkin, 1985; Hunter & Schmidt, 1990; Lipsey & Wilson, 2001), whereas this is only one chapter. Rather than offer an updated treatise on these issues, the goals of this work are to offer an introduction to ES applications and later demonstrate that they need to be considered more carefully within the subfield. The chapter is therefore divided into two sections. The first is an overview of the general merits of ESs and adding these to NHSTs. This section also includes a presentation of common approaches for standardizing mean differences (i.e., differences between a given treatment group and some counterfactual condition), correlational ESs, and indices that can be used with dichotomous outcomes. The second section illustrates a few common analytic scenarios the authors have encountered in the police-personality assessment literature that can benefit from the inclusion of ES metrics. Efforts are made to provide standard interpretive guidance while considering factors such as statistical power and magnitude of the observed effect. In the conclusion, we repeat wider calls in the social sciences to regularly apply ESs within this corner of research.

Why Bother with ESs?

NHSTs have been and continue to be a confusing approach toward understanding if effects appear to be a function of some relationship in datasets and/or the presence of some treatment (Cohen, 1994; Kline, 2004; Morgan, 2003; Thompson, 1998; Wilkinson & the Task Force for Statistical Inference, 1999). Indeed, there has even been a call for banning their use because of the confusion they purportedly cause (Kline, 2004), which served as part of the impetus for developing a task force convened by the American Psychological Association to investigate how psychologists apply NHSTs. Since the above citations offer far better treatments of the issue than what can be handled here, the debate is not discussed in detail. Suffice it to say that current practice has fallen on the side of continuing to use the application of NHSTs while supplementing their interpretation with ES estimates (and confidence intervals for ESs). Indeed, some journals are now requiring that quantitative studies report ES indices (Kline, 2004; Thompson, 2002a); we encourage the continuation of both approaches in future work in this subfield. This is because although NHSTs can help one investigate the probability that some observed relationship is in essence due to chance, they are not designed to yield insight on the magnitude of the relationship. Consider that if a treatment impact has been observed (i.e., a null hypothesis has been rejected) critical questions remain:

1. How large is the impact?
2. How does this finding compare to those from similar studies?
3. Procedure is heavily dependent on sample size. So does it seem reasonable that a Type II error (i.e., failure to reject the null hypothesis when it is false) may have occurred?

The answers to the first two questions depend on the literature. But, as discussed further below, ESs simplify comparisons across studies. In terms of the third question, the answer is "yes" (a Type II error may have occurred) if the sample is relatively small and an important ES was gleaned from the sample data. On the other side of the same coin, very well powered studies (i.e., those with really large samples) can find unimportant relationships to be statistically significant. Indeed, in a statistical power analysis (i.e., the probability a test will reject a false null hypothesis) ESs must be considered because power increases as the ES increases. If there is reason to believe the impact of whatever phenomena to be studied will be large, a smaller sample will be needed to detect the effect. At the same time, should a smaller effect be of interest, then a larger sample is required to detect it (this assumes all other design aspects being equal and the effect is indeed there). Put another way, concerns about Type II error can be mitigated if a researcher identifies the lower range of a clinically meaningful effect and powers the study accordingly. That is, it is ideal if a study has a sufficiently large sample so that failure to detect a given effect means it must have been so small it is not worth pursuing anyway. This discussion of power highlights the importance of thinking of a study as a link in a wider chain of research. This perspective, of course, comes naturally when describing previous literature in introductory and discussion sections of an article. But ESs can also help other researchers plan and make sense of their own results when describing results. They can help the researcher think through whether an observed effect was larger than what has been seen in previous work and focus on why, or vice versa. Such comparisons are not easy to make when working with NHSTs that apply dichotomous decisions (i.e., the null hypothesis was retained or not); hence, there is wider benefit to any field when ESs and their components are clearly reported (Thompson, 2002b).

An Overview of ESs

Much of the applied work in police psychology deals with police selection and often more distal applications in terms of supporting the psychological needs of officers. These are enormously important tasks. When one considers the potential social costs of hiring a candidate who is ill-suited for the job or when the psychological needs of current officers are not met, the merits of determining the capacity of some predictor variable (e.g., a psychological measure) to explain variance in a dependent variable (e.g., job performance), or for that matter estimating the impact of therapy becomes clear. Indeed, the literature suggests these are real concerns played out in precincts on a near daily basis. Furthermore, estimates of police turnover rates (Orrick, 2008) and high level stress (Brown & Campbell, 1994; Scott, 2004) buttress the need for ongoing work in this area.

ESs are germane to this discussion and indeed have already been introduced above when mentioning estimates of treatment impacts and explaining variance. Estimates of an effect can be calculated for most designs that compare groups, and statisticians know much about the distribution theory, conditional variance (i.e., variance of the different groups and variance pooled across groups), and how to translate from one index to another. Dealing with the first of the two analytic goals, in the context of a simple study with two groups an ES can be viewed as a mean difference between a treatment group and some counterfactual condition (i.e., what might have happened in absence of a treatment). In order to be confident that an observed difference is due to a treatment, and only the treatment, random assignment of study units to each condition is ideal (cf. Shadish, Cook, & Campbell, 2002). But the concept of mean differences clearly applies to observational studies where random assignment is not possible, which appears to be the status quo in this field. Getting back to simple mean differences, these are often easily interpretable in work where an outcome measure has concrete meaning. Consider for an example a weight loss study where a sample of chronically obese males in the United States is randomly assigned either to some promising weight-loss therapy or to some standard option focusing on diet and exercise. If at the end of the study the treatment group weighs, on average, 300 pounds and the control group weighs, on average, 315 pounds, we have an immediately interpretable ES, a 15-pound loss. One could *standardize* the ES, and for reasons to be discussed later should do so, but the outcome is straightforward. But even in this case, a 15-pound difference might be confusing to those who prefer the metric system. Of course, it would be a simple matter to convert the amount of observed weight loss, 15 pounds, to the corresponding weight in kilograms, about 6.8 kg. The point here is that the conversion does not change the observed difference in weight but re-expresses it into units that will be more readily understood by some.

This idea is especially important in assessment because we use measures that require specialized knowledge to interpret, such as subscales on the Minnesota Multiphasic Personality Inventory-2 (MMPI-2), Personality Assessment Inventory (PAI), IQ scores, and so on. Putting aside the need to understand underlying constructs of these measures, standardized score reports such as t-scores (with a mean of 50 and standard deviation of 10) are not readily understood by consumers of personality research (e.g., police administrators who make hiring decisions); even doctoral level psychologists should not necessarily be expected to know all of the forms of standardization that have been developed. Standardizing an effect will help communicate findings to a broader audience and this also goes a long way towards making cross-study comparisons (Cooper, 1998; Lipsey & Wilson, 1993).

The process of standardization is one where score differentiation within a sample (i.e., variance) is divided out to achieve a universal scale (essentially Z scores). Consider the process used whenever one converts different fractions to decimal points so as make comparisons; for example, we can readily see that 7/92 is smaller than 9/63 since 0.076 (7 divided by 92) is smaller than 0.14 (9 divided by 63). Here, decimals can be thought of as a universal scale to which fractions can be converted. This process is not unlike what is being used when converting mean differences to standardized mean differences. In the ES world, this is a ratio of the mean difference divided by an estimate of variance (i.e., the dispersion of scores in a sample). An implication of this ratio is that wider variance yields a larger denominator, and thus a smaller standardized effect. This can be understood visually. Suppose Figure 1 below represents two distributions of scores (assume these are normally distributed density curves), one for a treatment and a second for a control group. These scores represent performance on a measure of depression so that scores to the left, lower scores, are indicative of less depression. Imagine these scores were observed at post-test after some treatment, and at pre-test a single, normally distributed density curve well represented the entire sample (i.e., the amount and variance of depression was roughly the same for both groups, which is reasonable to expect if the groups were formed via random assignment).

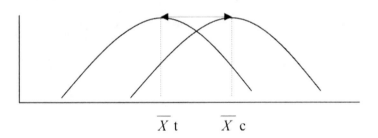

$\overline{X}$ t $\overline{X}$ c

Figure 1. Visual Representation of an ES Estimate.

These conditions allows one to think of mean difference as a function of distance (the mean for the treatment is represented by the vertical dashed line to the left, the mean for the control is higher on the scale, and is the vertical dashed line to the right). The double-headed, horizontal arrow represents the distance between the treatment and control means ($\overline{X}$ t and $\overline{X}$ c respectively). One can clearly see the two groups performed differently on the outcome measure, with the treatment group members obtaining, on average, lower depression scores than those in the control group. It is also apparent that there is considerable overlap of scores, meaning there are cases where control group members are less depressed than those in the treatment group. This leads to the issue of the probability that the observed difference was in essence due to chance, which gets into the application of NHSTs. Note that the unstandardized mean difference (i.e., the mean difference between the treatment and control group) does not account for score overlap. Indeed, the amount of information represented by simple mean differences is shown in Figure 2.

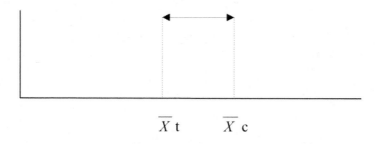

Figure 2. Simple Mean Difference That Does not Consider Sample Variance.

The point here is that the process of dividing the mean difference by an estimate of the variance is important not just to obtain a universal scale, but also because doing so accounts for the spread of scores between and within groups. Such accounting contextualizes the distance between means; the same distance in the context of wider score dispersion is less noteworthy and vice versa. The next figure, which shows the same mean difference as above, provides a sense of this, as the visual is formed by greater score variance.

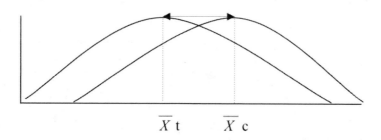

Figure 3. Mean Difference with Greater Sample Variance.

The mean distance remains unchanged from previous graphs. Hopefully this characterizes what is meant by understanding the relative distance between two means in context of wider overall score dispersion. Given the greater overlap of scores, it is much more likely a member of a treatment group is more depressed than a member of the control, suggesting a weaker effect in the context of the sample, even though the average difference is unchanged. The reverse of this is true as well, as demonstrated in Figure 4.

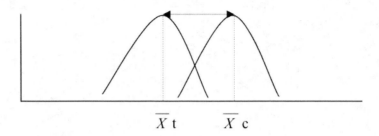

Figure 4. Mean Difference with Less Sample Variance.

Here the mean difference continues to be unchanged but the graph depicts far smaller variance and less overlap between groups. In this case, it is still possible for a control group member to be less depressed than someone in the treatment but this is less likely, suggesting a stronger treatment impact.

There is one more introductory idea to offer, and that is dealing with contexts where the variance of the treatment group is different from that of the control, a condition that can be assessed with most conventional software. Suppose the treatment of interest entailed some form of group therapy where happy people in a group tended to lift the mood of others (i.e., others are made happier) so that there was less variance in the treatment. At the same time, more depressed people tended to influence those around them in a way that also reduced score variance, but the untreated control maintained a normal spread of scores. See Figure 5.

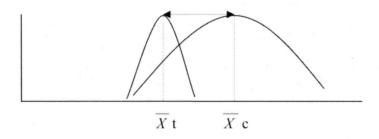

Figure 5. Mean Difference in the Context of Heterogeneous
Treatment Group Variances.

In this case the treatment group scores vary less than those in the control, so it would be advisable not to apply the treatment group variance in the overall estimate of the treatment impact. Put another way, the control group variance yields a better referent point as it represents a spread of scores that has not been altered by the treatment (Grissom & Kim, 2005). Judging from the figure, the control group standard deviation is larger, and this would thus yield a smaller ES. The metric one uses to derive such an effect is referred to as Glass' Delta, which is the mean of the treatment minus the mean of the control divided by the control group standard deviation. The formula is expressed as:

$\bar{X}$ t - $\bar{X}$ c/Control Group SD

Other options pool the standard deviations of the treatment and control groups, which has the relative advantage of estimating a standard deviation based on a larger group and thus should yield a less biased and variable estimate (Grissom & Kim, 2005; Lipsey & Wilson, 2001). The formula for pooling the two standard deviations is as follows:

$$S_{pooled} = \sqrt{\frac{(n_1 - 1)S_1^2 + (n_2 - 1)S_2^2}{(n_1 + n_2 - 2)}}$$

Hedges & Olkin (1985).

Dividing the result of $\bar{X}$ t - $\bar{X}$ c by this pooled standard deviation yields *Hedges g*. As a side note, pooling using *n* in lieu of n-1 yields *Cohen's d*, which is a sample and not a population estimate. In practice, however, the two options yield the same value within rounding (Grissom & Kim, 2005).

The fact that different denominators are available leads to a critical issue since inappropriate effect size estimation is a threat to making valid inferences (Shadish et al., 2002). Knowing there are options, broad guidance from applied statisticians would be to perform sensitivity analyses to see if conclusions seem to be dependent upon using a given procedure or assumption, or if findings appear to be robust and it matters little what approach is used. But an important caution would be that it is unacceptable to simply report the ES metric that is most supportive of a researcher's a priori assumptions, in those cases where it does matter which procedure is used. But this is the case for any given analysis. If there is reason to explore data properties and presentation options with more than one effect size metric, then it is important to report what was done, why it was done and discuss the most reasonable metric to apply. In this spirit, during times when one might want to calculate more than one version of an ES it becomes critical to think through how to best report substantive differences if they are found.

To get a sense of this issue, suppose again the mean of the control group is 315 pounds and the treatment mean is 300, for that difference of 15 pounds (i.e., 315 - 300 = 15). If the control group standard deviation is, say 30, then 15/30 - 0.50, meaning that 15-pound difference[1] is expressed as a Z score unit. The interpretation here is that a member of a treatment group can be expected to, on average, weigh about half a standard deviation less than a member of the control group. To provide a sense of score dispersion's impact on the estimate, suppose the control group standard deviation had been 60. Glass' Delta would then be 15/60 or 0.25, a smaller effect. Another way to interpret this figure is to think of there being a one-quarter standard deviation between the treatment and control means. A standardized mean difference of 0.25 versus 0.50 will generally be noteworthy, so should both figures be reported, an explanation should be offered along with figures used to derive the estimate (i.e., sample means, ns and standard deviations for the treatment and control groups). As noted above, one should probably stick with Glass' Delta in this case.

Some Options Dealing with Standardized Mean Differences

To this point, ESs were presented as the difference between two independent groups divided by a sample standard deviation (be it pooled across two groups or only by a control group standard deviation). It is also common to report ESs for the differences between two dependent groups (e.g., a pre and post design) where the denominator can be a pooled standard deviation based on variances from pre and post tests or just one of the measurement occasions.[2] The formulas are essentially the same as what has been reported above although the interpretation is quite different. In this case the result is a standardized mean difference between two measurement occasions of dependent groups, and note that Lipsey and Wilson (2001) have stated that meta-analysts should not mix ESs from these designs with ones that employ independent groups.

Another option to consider when dealing with widely available, normed tests such as the MMPI-2 or PAI is to divide mean differences by the standard deviation of the norming group (Grissom & Kim, 2005). This is an inter-

[1] In this case the difference is -15, but recall that absolute values are typically used in the numerator and a positive or negative sign should be used to express the direction of the impact.
[2] Most analysts would work with the pretest standard deviation. See Glass (1977).

esting idea because sample variances can in practice vary widely from study to study, yielding widely different estimates of an effect even if the mean differences are relatively similar. When doing programmatic research with a commonly used measure this might facilitate comparisons, although we encourage authors to still provide sample standard deviations to facilitate future efforts to synthesize research and allow readers to calculate their own effect sizes from reported findings.

The ES options considered so far deal with differences in the denominator; however, many designs will yield different choices for the numerator as well. Consider, for example, the use of adjusted means in the context of post-test adjusted means when a covariate is used in an analysis (e.g., ANCOVA). In some cases, the covariance adjustment may be done primarily to improve statistical power (Raudenbush, Martinez, & Spybrook, 2007)[3] whereas in other cases the adjustment is closely aligned with internal causal validity (in this case, the degree to which one is willing to believe a treatment effect is due to the actual treatment and not some competing explanation). For example, a quasi-experimental design that did not use random assignment may attempt to equate treatment and control groups on a baseline measure via ANCOVA in order to make the case that treatment groups were similar prior to treatment (for that matter, randomized controlled trials that observed baseline differences on measured characteristics might also do covariance adjustments). In this analysis post-test means are adjusted for pre-test differences so the researcher may wish to use adjusted mean differences in the ES numerator. The same denominator might still be used, however, as this would allow for comparisons of ESs across studies.

Simple Correlational ESs

Moving away from standardized mean differences, researchers often wish to present results in terms of how much variance in a dependent variable can be accounted for by an independent variable. Assuming both variables are continuous and working with Pearson's r, this is the oft used coefficient of determination, or r^2.[4] The value is simply derived from squaring a correlation coefficient so as to obtain a sense of how well one can predict a score on a dependent variable (i.e., degree of variance) from an independent (or predictor) variable. This can be understood by thinking about the range of

---

[3] If the varience in post-test data can be accounted for by an appreciable degree by knowledge of a pre-test then this information can be used within an analysis to increase staistical power. Functionally, this is like having a larger sample when running a NHST.

[4] There is also a sample coefficient of determination which is often used to estimate the relationship in a population.

potential values of this metric, which is zero to one. If $r^2 = 1.0$, this means a perfect association between two variables (since this is a squared value the correlation itself could be -1.0 or +1.0). In this rare if not unheard of set of circumstances, one can perfectly predict the value of one score by knowing the other score that informed the correlation. Should $r^2 = 0.0$ then knowledge of one variable tells you nothing about the other variable, assuming a bivariate, linear relationship.[5] Of course, the size of this metric will almost always be somewhere between the two values and most NHST work in this regard deals with whether an observed effect is statistically different from zero (although some NHSTs can be based on higher bars, such as whether a correlation is greater than 0.4 with $r^2 > .16$).

It is of course the case that most regression studies will use multiple predictor variables since behavior is typically multiply determined. Hence, one would rarely attempt to use a single sub-score from, say, the MMPI or PAI, to predict the outcome of an officer candidate and instead use a battery of tests. This will yield a multiple coefficient of determination (typically denoted as R2). This leads to additional issues such as making prudent choices around what predictor variables (Xs) to use, mulitcollinearity, and remaining cognizant of over-fitting meaning there may be too many Xs relative to the sample size (Huck, 2009).[6]

ESs for Dichotomous Outcomes

Dichotomous outcomes might be used in police work such as examining whether an officer remains employed after a given period of time, was suspended from the job for disciplinary reasons, and so on. In this sort of scheme, group differences are presented as proportions or, put another way, probabilities a given event occurred in one group versus another. One way to handle this in the ES world is to utilize odds ratios. The odds that an event will occur in a group are basically $p/1 - p$, where **p** is the probability of the event occurring. The odds ratio is the ratio between the odds for the two groups, or $p1(1 - p2)/p2(1 - p1)$. In this case, $p1$ is the probability of the event occurring in the treatment group, and $p2$ is the probability of the event

---

[5] There are cases where a relationship is curvilinear. Consider anxiety and performance where the two variables increase together up to a point, where ever-increasing anxiety is then associated with drops in performance. Put another way, it often helps to worry a little but excessive anxiety is oftern counterperductive. In such cases, statistical adjustments are needed to understand the relationship at hand since r^2 might equal 0 despite there being a strong association. Also note there are often complexities that can alter interpretation. For example, there are cases where Pearson's r cannot equal 1.0 and there certainly are other ways to derive correlation coefficients, so it is not always a matter of simply squaring the reported correlations (See Huck, 2009).

[6] A general recommendation is to have an N to X ratio of 20 to 1 (i.e., 20 cases for every X).

occurring in the control group. This is then transformed using a Logged Odds Ratio, which has a mean of zero and a standard deviation of 1.81. There are different ways of transforming this metric onto a scale that is comparable to standardized mean differences but it appears the Cox index is the least biased approach (Sanchez-Meca, Marin-Martinez, & Chacon-Moscoso, 2003). This is the Logged Odds Ratio divided by 1.65 (Cox, 1970).

A Word on Interpreting Magnitude

What can facilitate description of ESs is to take into account Cohen's (1988) heuristics of small (0.2), medium (0.5) and large (0.8) ESs, which were later validated somewhat by Lipsey and Wilson (1993). These values are, however, meant to serve as starting points and should be trumped by literature documenting prior effects within a field. It is also critical to consider the relative value of the outcome, which in the context of police selection work can be quite high (Weiss, Hitchcock, Weiss, Rostow, & Davis, 2008) since poor hiring decisions can bring enormous cost to society. Interpretation can be further facilitated by converting indices from one metric to another. For example:

$$r = \frac{d}{\sqrt{d^2 + 4}} \qquad\qquad d = \frac{2r}{\sqrt{1 - r^2}}$$

or

(Cooper, 1998; Lipsey & Wilson, 2001).

This allows for comparisons between d, r, and r^2, yielding another useful feature of ESs since researchers will often find interpretive value via such conversions.

Small values of r^2 have at times led to confusion about the importance of ESs (Rosenthal & Rubin, 1982). Consider that $r^2 = .138$, an apparently small value, equates to r = .371, which in turn converts to a standardized mean difference of 0.8 (which meets Cohen's threshold for a large effect). These values can also be converted to a statistic called U_3, which is the percentage of scores in the group with a lower mean that are exceeded by the average score in the group with the higher mean. Put another way, the statistic answers the question: "What percentage of the scores in the lower-meaned group was exceeded by the average score in the higher-meaned group?" (Cooper, 1998, p. 129). An ES of d = 0 would translate into a U_3 of 0.50, whereas d = 1.0 yields a U_3 of 84.1. Assuming the effect favors the treatment group, this means 84.1 percent of the scores in the treatment group exceed those in the comparison condition. Getting back to the value $r^2 = .138$, this yields a U_3 of 78.8, which suggests the effect may not be so small after all, depending on what has been found in previous work and the nature of the outcome measure.

The discussion offered by Rosenthal et al. (2000) offers a great example of why it is so important to contextualize ESs when interpreting their magnitude. They describe a randomized controlled trial investigating the effects of aspirin on mortality rates (Steering Committee of the Physician's Health Study Research Group, 1988). Briefly, the study was a five- year randomized trial with 22,071 physicians with a history of heart problems. These physicians were randomly assigned to receive either aspirin or a treatment/placebo condition. The study was ended early because an r^2 of .001 (from a correlation of .034) was detected and it was concluded that aspirin clearly worked. Readers not familiar with this story might be taken aback by the ES, which in most contexts is miniscule. The r^2 described here translated to a 3.4 percent decrease in the risk of a heart attack in an at-risk population of physicians if following the treatment regimen in a hypothetical case where half the sample was treated *and* half the sample experienced a heart attack. Put another way, this scenario was established via the Binomial Effect Size Display (BESD), which is essentially a 2 x 2 (heart attack vs. no heart attack and treated vs. not treated) contingency table (Rosenthal & Rubin, 1982; Rosenthal et al., 2000). Such a table essentially shows what the odds of the possible outcomes are, given a certain number of subjects in a hypothetical scenario. In the case of the 3.4 percent decrease in the likelihood the sample would experience a heart attack, it is important to emphasize the figure is not based on the actual sample but rather a case where one might assume a 50/50 chance of experiencing a heart attack when there is no treatment impact. The split becomes apparent when applying the the $r_{counternull}$, or:

$$r_{counternull} = 2r/\sqrt{1+3r^2}$$

(Rosenthal, Rosnow & Rubin, 2000, p. 20). The counternull in essence provides a weight (multiplier) that can be applied to determining the likelihood of an outcome. In cases of a simple treatment/control or yes/no design, the counternull figure becomes the percentage added to 50 in one cell and subtracted from 50 in the other, which then provides the percentage of participants who fall into each category. Examples of BESD applications in the context of police personality assessment are offered later in this chapter to better illustrate this concept.

In the aspirin study, the small effect was in fact viewed as sufficient reason to stop the study. The major take-home point then is that very small effect sizes can be quite important. Now consider the notion that small ESs in the business of identifying good vs. poor officer candidates should not be taken lightly given the importance of the outcome. In law enforcement settings, officers have the power to take life and liberty in certain instances (Rostow & Davis, 2006). Small effects may well be important and researchers and journal editors should remain cognizant that there are many options for how to report and interpret the magnitude of an effect (Kline, 2004; Morgan, 2003). A final step that is useful in interpreting ESs is to construct confidence intervals (CIs) around them. ESs will be increasingly less likely to reflect a population parameter as sample sizes decrease. Procedures for constructing CIs are available in Grissom and Kim (2005).

Some Applied Examples

As previously stated, it appears that many of the published studies in the field present statistically significant findings without the inclusion of ESs. However, the sample sizes in the studies are often large and, as noted above, it becomes easier to find statistically significant findings as the sample size increases. This emphasizes the importance of ESs and the need to distinguish between trivial and meaningful effects. Following the above overview of ES options and some interpretive guidance, it may be useful to provide some brief examples from the related literature where these indices have not been used but could have been. Rather than being critical of existing studies we have opted to identify scenarios that, in our judgment, appear to be common. The purpose of the following examples is to illustrate the importance of small, yet meaningful effects.

In 1996, the National Symposium on Police Integrity called for research into the relationship between psychological screening measures and deviant police behaviors (Sellbom, Fischler, & Ben-Porath, 2007). As a result, a popular statistical analysis used in the research literature is Pearson's r correlation. Researchers investigate the relationship between an assessment used for personnel screening (e.g., MMPI-2) and supervisory ratings including behavioral incidents (e.g., citizen complaints, unprofessional conduct) and departmental actions (e.g., suspensions, terminations). In some studies, the predictive validity of the assessment with respect to aggressive or abusive behaviors is explored using regression analyses. In the correlational or regression analyses, the ES (r^2 - the percent of variance accounted for) is usually not reported.

CORRELATIONAL ES EXAMPLE 1. Weiss, Rostow, Davis, and DeCoster-Martin (2004) investigated the use of the Personality Assessment Inventory (PAI) for police candidate selection. The PAI results for 800 police officers were correlated to a series of performance behavior variables. Several of the PAI scales had low but statistically significant correlations with behavior variables. In particular, the number of times a police officer discharged a weapon in the line of duty was significantly related to the Physical Aggression scale raw score ($r = .169$, $p < .01$). This correlation would have an r^2 of .029, meaning that 3 percent of the variance in the number of times an officer has discharged a weapon in the line of duty can be accounted for by the Physical Aggression score on the PAI. This explanation may not sufficiently inform readers and practitioners of the importance of the finding, as discharging a weapon is both rare and just about as serious an outcome one can measure. Yet at first blush one might focus on statistical significance being only a function of the large sample size. We believe that translating r to d (which is .343 allowing for rounding error) helps highlight the idea that this is not a miniscule effect. It certainly wouldn't be in the context of many group comparison studies, yet it seems reasonable that the r^2 value of .029 might cause one lose perspective that the PAI is helping to predict a very serious but rare outcome.

CORRELATIONAL ES EXAMPLE 2. Weiss and his colleagues (2003) investigated the L Scale (Lie) of the MMPI-2 in an analysis of 938 police officers who were conditionally hired. Higher scores on the L scale of the MMPI-2 were significantly related to several problematic behaviors, including being terminated for cause ($r = -.118$) and insubordination ($r = -.092$). Using the BESD (again assuming equal sample sizes), officers with higher L scale scores are almost 12 percent more likely to be terminated by their law enforcement agency, and 9 percent are likely to be insubordinate (see Tables 1 and 2 for insubordination and termination of cause data).

Table 1
BESD EXAMPLE USING L-SCALE OF MMPI-2
AS A PREDICTOR OF INSUBORDINATION

	Insubordination	
L-Scale Score	Yes	No
High	54.6%	45.4%
Low	45.4%	54.6%

Table 2
BESD TABLE DEALING WITH TERMINATION FOR CAUSE

	Termination for Cause	
L-Scale Score	Yes	No
High	55.9%	44.1%
Low	44.1%	55.9%

CORRELATIONAL ES EXAMPLE 3. In another study, Davis et al. (2004) and his colleagues investigated the relationship between the Aggressiveness and Immaturity Indices of the MMPI-2 and supervisory ratings for 1,020 law enforcement officers. Both indices were significantly related to several termination reasons and problematic police behaviors. The correlation coefficients were small, which would result in small effect sizes. Table 2 illustrates the relationship between the Aggressiveness Index and supervisory ratings.

Table 3
RELATIONSHIP BETWEEN AGGRESSIVENESS INDEX
AND SUPERVISORY RATINGS FOR THE MMPI-2

Rating	R	P	r^2	D
Number of Undesirable Off-Duty Conduct	.088	.007	.008	.1
Number of Suspensions/ Reprimands	.064	.05	.004	.1
Corruption/Criminal Conduct	.078	.01	.006	.1
Insubordination	.066	.03	.004	.1

When interpreted as the percent of variance accounted for, the relationship appears trivial, with only 1 percent of the variance in problematic police behaviors being accounted for by the Aggressiveness Index of the MMPI-2. However, when interpreted in terms of the BESD, the magnitude and importance of these relationships become more evident. Assuming the equal sample size conditions of the BESD are met, officers with high scores on the Aggressiveness Index are 6.6 percent more likely to be insubordinate, 6.4 percent more likely to be suspended/reprimanded, 7.8 percent more likely to be involved with criminal conduct and 8.8 percent more likely to engage in undesirable off-duty conduct compared to those with low scores on the index. The degree to which these effects may seem large is a matter of comparing them to those found in other studies, but it seems clear the nature of these outcomes is quite important.

Conclusion

The purpose of this chapter was two-fold. First, we wanted to present an overview of effect sizes. There are many different types of effect sizes and the choice of an ES depends on the outcomes, research designs, and analyses used. Secondly, we wanted to illustrate the importance of ESs. There is a difference between statistical significance and practical significance. Statistical significance is a function of both sample size and effect size, where studies with large samples are more likely to find statistically significant findings. As a result, researchers and journal editors view practical significance (ES) in a more favorable light than statistical significance. Yet imposing Cohen's guidelines as the determinant of a meaningful versus trivial effect is flawed. Sometimes what appears to be small is quite important (Rosenthal et al., 2000). It is imperative that researchers look at the potential outcome of their study and use this context to judge the magnitude of the effect. In the area of police officer screening, a small effect is very meaningful. This is partially because, as has been well documented, police applicant samples have narrow ranges on personality assessment instruments. Because of this issue, effect sizes may be small due to the lack of extreme scores. Therefore, these small effects may be highly important, and the outcome of personality assessments can prevent poor candidates from becoming police officers. Overlooking the "small effects" can have a considerable impact on society.

In sum, we hope this introductory overview of effect sizes and their application to the police psychology literature will serve as yet another voice calling for regular reporting of effect sizes. We also hope that our intended audience will be able to apply some of the formulas presented here when reviewing the existing literature and obtain their own sense of study impacts.

REFERENCES

Brown, J.M., & Campbell, E.A. (1994). *Stress and policing: Sources and strategies.* Chichester: Wiley.

Cohen, J. (1988). *Statistical power analysis for the behavioral sciences* (2nd ed.). New York: Academic Press.

Cohen, J. (1994). The earth is round (p < .05). *American Psychologist, 49,* 997–1003.

Cooper, H.M. (1998). *Synthesizing research: A guide for literature reviews* (3rd ed.). Thousand Oaks, CA: Sage.

Cox, D.R. (1970). *Analysis of binary data.* New York: Chapman & Hall/CRC.

Davis, R.D., Rostow, C.D., Pinkston, J.B., Combs, D.R. & Dixon, D.R. (2004). A reexamination of the MMPI-2 aggressiveness and immaturity indices in law enforcement screening. *Journal of Police and Criminal Psychology, 19*(1) 17–26.

Glass, G.V. (1977). Integrating findings: The meta-analysis of research. *Review of Research in Education, 5,* 351–379.

Grissom, R.J., & Kim, J.J. (2005). *Effect sizes for research: A broad practical approach.* Mahwah, NJ: Lawrence Erlbaum Associates.

Hedges, L.V., & Olkin, I. (1985). *Statistical methods for meta-analysis.* New York: Academic Press.

Huck, S.W. (2009). *Statistical misconceptions.* New York: Routledge.

Hunter, J.E., & Schmidt, F.L. (1990). *Methods of meta-analysis: Correcting error and bias in research findings.* Newbury Park, CA: Sage.

Kline, R.B. (2004). *Beyond significance testing: Reforming data analysis methods in behavioral research.* Washington, DC: American Psychological Association.

Lipsey, M.W., & Wilson, D.B. (1993). The efficacy of psychological, educational, and behavioral treatment: Confirmation from meta-analysis. *American Psychologist, 48*(12), 1181–1209.

Lipsey, M.W., & Wilson, D.B. (2001). *Practical meta-analysis.* Thousand Oaks, CA: Sage Publications.

Morgan, P.L. (2003). Null hypothesis significance testing: Philosophical & practical considerations of a statistical controversy. *Exceptionality, 11*(4), 209–221.

Orrick, W.D. (2008). *Recruitment, retention and turnover of police personnel: Reliable, practical and effective solutions.* Charles C Thomas Publishing.

Raudenbush, S.W., Martinez, A., & Spybrook, J. (2007). Strategies for improving precision in group-randomized experiments. *Educational Evaluation and Policy Analysis, 29*(1), 5–29.

Rosenthal, R., Rosnow, R.L., & Rubin, D.B. (2000). *Contrasts and effect sizes in behavioral research: A correlational approach.* Cambridge University Press.

Rosenthal, R, & Rubin, D.B. (1982). A simple general purpose display of magnitude of experimental effect. *Journal of Educational Psychology, 74,* 166–169.

Rostow, C.D., & Davis, R.D. (2006). Psychological police officer selection part I: History and forensic implications, *Law Enforcement Executive Forum, 6*(1), 27–31.

Sanchez-Meca, J., Marin-Martinez, F., & Chacon-Moscoso, S. (2003). Effect-size indices for dichotomous outcomes in meta-analysis. *Psychological Methods, 8*(4), 448–467.

Scott, Y.M. (2004). Stress among rural and small town police officers: A survey of Pennsylvania municipal agencies. *Police Quarterly, 7*(2), 237–261.

Sellbom, M., Fischler, G.L., & Ben-Porath, Y.S. (2007). Identifying MMPI-2 predictors of police officer integrity and misconduct. *Criminal Justice and Behavior, 34*(8), 985–1004.

Shadish, W., Cook, T., & Campbell, D. (2002). *Experimental and quasi-experimental designs for generalized causal inference.* Boston: Houghton Mifflin.

Steering Committee of the Physician's Health Study Research Group. (1988). Preliminary report: Findings from the aspirin component of the ongoing physician's health study. *New England Journal of Medicine, 318*, 262–264.

Thompson, B. (1998). Statistical significance testing and effect size reporting: Portrait of a possible future. *Research in the Schools, 5*(2), 33–38.

Thompson, B. (2002a). "Statistical," "practical," and "clinical": How many kinds of significance do counselors need to consider? *Journal of Counseling and Development, 80*, 64–71.

Thompson, B. (2002b). What future quantitative social science research could look like: Confidence intervals for effect sizes. *Educational Researcher, 31*(3), 24–31.

Weiss, W.U., Davis, R., Rostow, C., & Kinsman, S. (2003). The MMPI-2 L scale as a tool in police selection. *Journal of Police and Criminal Psychology, 18*(1), 57–60.

Weiss, P., Hitchcock, J.H., Weiss, W.U, Rostow, C., & Davis, R. (2008). The Personality Assessment Inventory borderline drug and alcohol scales as predictors of overall performance in police officers: A series of exploratory analyses. *Policing and Society, 18*(3), 301–310.

Weiss, W., Rostow, C.D. Davis, R.D., & DeCoster-Martin, E. (2004) The Personality Assessment Inventory as a selection device for law enforcement personnel. *Journal of Police and Criminal Psychology, 19*(2), 23–29.

Wilkinson, L., & the Task Force for Statistical Inference. (1999). Statistical methods in psychology journals: Guidelines and explanations. *American Psychologist, 54*, 594–604.

Chapter 11

THE FUTURE OF PERSONALITY ASSESSMENT RESEARCH IN POLICE PSYCHOLOGY: WHAT'S NEXT AND WHAT DO WE NEED?

JOHN H. HITCHCOCK, PETER A. WEISS, WILLIAM U. WEISS, CARY D. ROSTOW and ROBERT D. DAVIS

INTRODUCTION

There has been a rise in the promotion of evidence-based practice in multiple areas of the social sciences including, for example, psychology (e.g., Braden & Shernoff, 2008; Kratochwill & Shernoff, 2003, Shernoff & Kratochwill, 2005; Stout & Hayes, 2004), education (Cook, 1999, 2002; Odom, Bratlinger, Gersten, Horner, Thompson, & Harris, 2005; Raudenbush, 2005; Schneider, Carnoy, Kilpatrick, Schmidt, & Shavelson, 2007; Slavin, 2002; U.S. Department of Education, 2005), and subfields such as personality assessment (American Educational Research Association [AERA], American Psychological Association [APA], and National Council on Measurement in Education [NCME], 1999). Indeed, this push has had considerable impacts on federal and state legislation, such as the No Child Left Behind Act. Although it is clear that there is a new push for establishing practice supported by evidence, the authors do not wish to suggest that social scientists practicing prior to this movement were somehow bereft of a desire to apply a sense of empiricism to their work. Our point is only that we are now operating in a world where clinicians must frequently defend their practices on the basis that there is evidence that they work, but at the same time there is considerable debate over how to define evidence. Indeed, the general literature on this matter is rife with long-standing paradigm wars between quantitative and qualitative camps (Maxwell, 2004; Onwuegbuzie,

2002; Tashakkori & Teddlie, 1998, 2003). Furthermore, there are arguments within these camps, such as the relative importance of external and internal-causal validity (Campbell, 1986; Shadish, Cook & Campbell, 2002). Despite lack of consensus, the importance of evidence and how it should inform practice is now a central matter in the social science landscape.

This all serves as a backdrop for the purpose of this chapter, which is to list a series of research issues within personality assessment research in police psychology that might be tackled in future work. Our focus is on contemporary assessment practices, particularly in pre-employment screening, and working through psychometric and experimental designs that might yield better overall evidence for defending a practice, or for that matter, altering the status quo. Part of this discussion examines the practice of using measures of pathology within police work. The chapter also comments on related matters such as screening candidates for special unit selection (e.g., roles in special weapons and tactics [SWAT], detectives, etc.), Fitness-for-Duty Evaluations (FFDEs) and promoting overall mental health among officers. The chapter does not provide data of any kind, or fully worked out designs, but instead provides fodder for a research agenda.

Pre-employment Screening

The purpose of pre-employment psychological testing is, of course, to avoid the hiring of candidates who will perform poorly as officers. This practice has considerable weight in terms of social validity (Messick, 1995) due to the potential costs that poor hiring decisions entail. Police must necessarily exercise individual judgment in stressful situations and their legal authority demands a sense of trust. Clinicians therefore need to be well informed about testing characteristics relative to the assessment context. At first blush this may seem like an obvious point but consider the multiple issues involved with general assessment. At a minimum, there is (1) the varying perspectives of the test's purpose,[1] (2) professional standards in test administration, scoring, and reporting, (3) specific technical details of a measure relative to the exact reason for the assessment, and (4) guidance on score interpretation relative to the hiring decision (AERA, APA, NCME, 1999). In the context of personality assessment, all of these matters can become especially complex because interpretation of scores requires expert understanding of theoretical constructs and their interrelationships.

---

[1] Anastasi and Urbina (1997) make mention of cultural bias in testing as well as understanding of why the measurement is being conducted. Nastasi and Schensul (2005) draw from ethnographic work that can elucidate cultural differences by acknowledging the etic and emic perspectives (i.e., view points of test administrators [etic] will often differ from viewpoints of responders [emic]).

A good start for describing evidence-based practice in assessment might then be to review issues of construct validity, since this topic serves as a cornerstone for understanding and applying evidence in any social science discipline be it in the form of test development, experimental design, or both (cf. Anastasi & Urbina, 1997; Crocker & Algina, 1986; Messick, 1995; Pedhazur & Schmelkin, 1991; Shadish et al., 2002). Such validity is central to psychological assessment, because all other forms of validity are threatened when the veracity of a construct cannot be defended. Simply put, one could not be sure how to interpret or apply assessment results without having a clear grasp of that which is being assessed. This can be enormously complex in personality assessment since constructs of interest (e.g., anti-social personality disorder, depression, anxiety) cannot for the most part be directly observed (i.e., they are latent constructs to be measured via item responses) and assessment strategies tend to be heavily intertwined with detailed theoretical structures (cf. Exner, 2003; Butcher, Graham, Ben-Porath, Tellegen, Dahlstrom, & Kaemmer, 2001; Morey, 2007).

Three broad strategies are used to establish construct validity: logical, internal-structure and cross-structure analyses (Pedhazur & Schmelkin, 1991). Logical analysis deals with whether a construct is sufficiently concrete for measurement purposes and is akin to operationally defining whatever is being measured. Internal structure analyses often entail approaches such as factor analyses to determine if test items appear to assess some underlying trait (Kline, 1994), which of course should be consistent with theory and logical analysis. Cross-structure analyses apply convergent and discriminant validation procedures (Pedhazur & Schmelkin, 1991). Convergent validity refers to agreement between different methods designed to measure a given construct (usually done via validity coefficients). Discriminant and convergent validity are often assessed together to develop supportive evidence for a construct, and this is typically done using the multitrait multimethod matrix, in which a variety of related measures are correlated with one another to assess their convergent/divergent relationships (Campbell & Fiske, 1959).

We describe all of this because the field might benefit from a renewed interest in a holistic view of construct validity. Consider that many of the oft-used tests for assessing the personality of police candidates tend mainly to deal with pathology issues (Minnesota Multiphasic Personality Inventory 2 [MMPI-2], Personality Assessment Inventory [PAI], etc.). This represents a methodological concern because most candidates will not be struggling with pathology per se. In essence, overreliance on such measures generates a construct mismatch that manifests itself in several ways. One related limitation is that if a measure of pathology is used as a "screen out" instrument, not all of the information gained from these tests is necessarily job relevant. This issue is also discussed in other chapters in this book (see Weiss, Chapter 12, this volume). Another concern is that tests of psychopathology cannot be used in the pre-offer phase of the evaluation process because of the Americans with Disabilities Act. Furthermore, datasets that might inform a connection between measures of pathology and police performance will typically be truncated because those who score within clinical ranges should be rare, making subsequent statistical analyses (e.g., regression procedures) harder to carry out. Even if smaller samples were not a primary concern, statistical models perform better when data have an opportunity to vary along the dimensions of interest. Therefore if one is hoping to regress scores of a measure on some later indicator of job performance, then the pre-screening score should have items that tap both good and bad performance (more on this later).

This discussion is not meant to suggest that practicing psychologists should discard measures of psychopathology when consulting on candidate selection decisions. At present, research in police psychology has validated some of these measures for use in law enforcement applications (Graham, 2006; Weiss, Weiss, & Gacono, 2008). In particular, there is now an extensive literature on both the MMPI-2 and PAI in conducting these evaluations. However, the difficulty with both of these measures is that the correlations associated with them are often significant but low (see, for example, Aamodt, 2004; Weiss, Davis, Rostow, & Kinsman, 2003; Weiss, Hitchcock, Weiss, Rostow, & Davis, 2008). Some work has suggested that overreliance on such measures does occur. Then, there seems at times to be a gap between common assessment practices and what can be supported by research (Aamodt, 2004).

Another avenue to consider would be to focus more on tests and variables that have more to do with personality or behaviors (liability) than pathology. Examples are that occur to use are the Rorschach, Matrix-Predictive Uniform Law Enforcement Selection Evaluation Inventory (M-PULSE), and the California Psychological Inventory (CPI). To provide some sense of this, compare the relative advantages and disadvantages of the MMPI-2 and Rorschach. The former measure will present items that any intelligent candidate will think of as wrong answers in most employment screening contexts; one should therefore assume the standard social desirability phenomenon that endangers any self-report measure may be at work (Graham, 2006). Of course the MMPI-2 offers some scales (for example, L, F, and K) that can help detect such response behavior. In fact, many of the decisions that can be made about employment on the basis of these measures of psychopathology are made using these validity scales (Weiss et al., 2003; Weiss, Rostow, Davis, & Decoster-Martin, 2004). After all, the purpose of these scales is generally to assess response bias and the degree to which it threatens the validity of overall measurement results.

By comparison, the Rorschach, particularly in the context of the Exner Comprehensive System (Exner, 2003) may offer more subtle measurement where it is not as easy for candidates to present socially desirable traits. In addition to the fact that it would be highly unusual for candidates to know anything at all about the Comprehensive System (CS), they would be working with a psychologist conducting direct observations while paying attention to traits that lend themselves to police work (or not). Keeping in mind that the CS requires specialized training, it might offer a useful measurement approach in some cases. Some literature (Weiss, 2002; Weiss, Weiss, & Gacono, 2008; Brewster, Wickline, & Stoloff, Chapter 8, this volume) suggests that this may be helpful in the future to police psychologists who are engaged in selection, fitness-for-duty evaluations, and treatment planning. Assessment researchers in police psychology are therefore encouraged to continue validation research on the Rorschach for these purposes. In addition, the CPI (Gough & Bradley, 1996) represents a test of normal personality and can be added to a test battery in addition to a test of psychopathology in order to provide more information. Overall, further work is needed to help clinicians optimally apply traditional measures of pathology in pre-employment screening by examining ways in which they can be included within a battery of assessment and carefully parsing out how their results can inform measurement goals.

Creating Direct Measures of Potential Performance and Measurement Systems

Having established the point that personality measures exist that can help with hiring decisions, they often speak to distally-related constructs. Job-specific measures need to be created that are not easily swayed by social desirability or at least have ways of assessing response bias. Options may include knowledge and skill assessments that assess how candidates think about scenarios an officer might encounter, as well as items that measure personality traits that are not readily perceived as having right and wrong answers. Developing new items would of course have to rely on advanced psychometric techniques such as item response and generalizability theory (respectively, IRT and G-Theory). These perspectives can be contrasted with classical test theory, which assumes a single trait is responsible for response behaviors and a singular/undifferentiated score error is at work. Modern techniques, by contrast, can better handle assumption that multiple latent traits of examinees (i.e., officer candidates) can account for item responses (IRT), and that error variance can differ by context (e.g., assessment from one police department to another). These matters are complex and cannot be adequately covered here, so suffice it to say that item development and scoring procedures will generally entail these techniques and clinicians should be aware of their basic features so as to better understand manuals.

Developing a widely available measure would entail some logistical and technical challenges, the first of which is developing measures designed to directly assess constructs of interest (i.e., predicting on-the-job performance). Measures would have to be informed by a normative sample that is representative of legally agreed upon characteristics and skill sets. Furthermore, the wording and content of some screening items might take into account cultural and regional variation. From there, measures would have to meet satisfactory evidence of psychometric reliability and validity (see AERA, APA, & NCME, 1999).

A logistical concern is that current practice in assessment for selection purposes focuses on psychological evaluations performed after a conditional offer of employment has been made, mainly due to Americans with Disabilities Act mandates. However, recent research and practice (see for example Jones et al., Chapter 8, this volume) suggests that a bifurcated model involving "nonmedical" evaluation pre-offer and then a more traditional psychological evaluation post-offer will probably improve screening procedures. Therefore, the present authors believe that research focusing on the process of selection, particularly involving a multistage system of assessment, that considers personality as one of several hiring factors, would be worthwhile.

A multistage assessment system might follow approaches used in prevention science, where a short screener is given to all candidates. These would have to be psychometrically sound measures that are easy to administer, score, and provide a quick sense of whether a candidate has the requisite skills needed to warrant more intense evaluation (e.g., interviews, background checks, physical tests, and personality assessments). Of course, any such screener should provide evidence for its incremental validity (i.e., it must add new and useful information to the selection process). Therefore the screener must be very well aligned with the construct of interest, and be compatible with existing assessment techniques.

A multistage screening system might be able to yield several estimates of concurrent validity, which would be a simple correlation between scores on the measure and some other measure collected at the same time. For example, scores on a screener might correlate well with quantified scores on structured interviews, academic indicators such as a grade point average of recent graduates, knowledge tests and so on. This could serve as the basis for continued checks on convergent and divergent validity (which are similar but need not rely on data points collected at roughly the same time of the screener) and developing a system for ongoing item calibration.

Criterion Related Validity

To address predictive and concurrent validity (combined, these two forms of validity establish criterion-related validity), standard statistical practice is to regress scores of the measure on measures of on-the-job performance. The aforementioned standards put forth by AERA, APA and NCME (1999) point out that the key question in criterion relationships is: How accurately do test scores predict criterion performance (p. 14)? This yields another question, which is: How should criterion data be selected? Combined, these questions are compelling matters for officer selection. Direct performance criteria would seem to best handle social and legal consequences of testing. For example, the authors of this chapter have done some initial work looking into how well scores on the PAI predict later officer misconduct (Weiss, Hitchcock et al., 2008). The criterion variable was a 32-item survey of the number of times officers were disciplined for actions such as procedural mistakes, undesirable off duty conduct, reprimands from supervisors, substance abuse and so on. The results of the exploratory analyses yielded small but significant correlations. One regression model was statistically significant (keeping in mind the particular procedure must be replicated before being confident of the predictive capacity of the PAI in this context). This is a start but more robust findings might be derived from predicting good performance as well. From a purely technical point of view, this would have allowed us to determine if lower PAI scores are associated with indicators of good performance (not just focusing on performance problems). If this relationship held, then more compelling models would be generated. Taking it a step further, looking at quantified estimates of a range of job performance would be an excellent option, indeed, even a gold standard for this type of work. This is by no means an advanced observation; many researchers would like to obtain access to such criteria but such information seems to be hard to come by. Hence, future research might focus on the social and policy barriers to collecting job performance data for the long-term goal of conducting more criterion validity studies.

Special Unit Selection

Related to overall police selection is the issue of using personality assessment for selection of candidates for particular jobs within law enforcement and many of the above points apply here. For example, traffic management is a very different job than other aspects of law enforcement. That is, some traits are probably better suited to traffic matters than, say, homicide investigation or serving as a SWAT officer. If so, personality assessment should be useful for selection of particular individuals for special assignments within the police force after the officers have actually worked for a time on other assignments. As an example, Cunningham, Jones, and Behrens (2009) have performed an interesting study of how to select a police chief which incorporated psychological assessment data. They used a specialized assessment battery called the LH-STEP to evaluate leadership potential in candidates. Perhaps future studies can address these issues to further enhance the effectiveness of police officers. For example, if personality assessment instruments can be used to identify successful SWAT officers, traffic officers, or detectives, this could help police departments operate more efficiently. Conversely, finding out if certain personality assessment instruments identify individuals who have problems at a particular job would be useful also.

Effect Sizes and Research Syntheses

The aforementioned issue of effect sizes needs more attention in this field. Hitchcock, Weiss, and O'Conner (Chapter 10, this volume) demonstrated that after even a cursory review of the literature it was noted that several pieces limit discussion of estimates of the magnitude of a treatment impact or how much variance in a dependent variable can be accounted for by some independent variable (i.e., r^2 if dealing with a single predictor or R^2 if multiple predictors are involved). In some of the larger studies, there must be careful accounting for the fact that small effects may be found to be statistically significant by virtue of a large sample size and not necessarily some relationship of substantive interest. At the same time, because prediction is often based on somewhat distally related measures, small effects should often be expected and sometimes these are quite meaningful. For example, research on police selection (Weiss, Davis, Rostow, & Kinsman, 2003) has shown with some degree of consistency that high scorers on the MMPI-2 L (Lie) scale often exhibit performance problems as law enforcement officers when hired. However, the correlations and effect sizes are relatively small, largely because the hiring situation pulls for modest elevations on the L scale (Weiss, Weiss, Cain, & Manley, in press). This is not surprising given the aforementioned construct matching issue. The L scale was not explicitly designed to predict performance and instead gives a sense of response bias, which are two different things. This is not to suggest such work is in any way ill-advised since clinicians should want to be able to think through L scale results within a larger pattern of screening data. But at the same time, it is hard to imagine a scenario where the L scale would yield a large r square value.

A tricky point here is that large studies might easily yield statistically significant observations, yet in practice such relationships might be of little value to clinicians. This of course is due to the fact that statements of statistical significance are very much sample dependent. This means unimportant effects could be overemphasized in the context of a large sample. At the same time, clinically (not statistically) significant findings might be underemphasized in a small study (Kline, 1994). Hence, some attention needs to be paid to separating out statistical noise from important findings. Theory is the fulcrum where the difference between the two types of observations (i.e., statistical noise versus findings of substantive importance) and elucidating a priori versus exploratory work continues to be a critical way for identifying important effects. Rather than relying too much on Cohen's (1988) indicators of small, medium, and large effect sizes,[2] studies in personality assessment need to focus on the types of effects found in prior work when presenting literature reviews, and contrasting current and prior findings when interpreting data (Grissom & Kim, 2005; Rosenthal, Rosnow, & Rubin, 2000). Meta-analytic work of course can provide this very sort of service and can help convey the true meaning of observed effects to those running studies and clinicians who stay on top of the literature.

We are aware of one series of meta-analytic work that investigates strength of association between predictor and criterion variables (Aamodt, 2004). In general the results found that personality inventories are useful in law enforcement selection, but that some work better than others. The advantage of the Aamodt (2004) study is that it incorporates studies that utilized a variety of assessment instruments. But it seems that more work is needed in the area of summarizing findings across studies so as to advise practitioners what to look for during assessment. Indeed, syntheses are in need of updates because Bronfenbrenner's (1995) work reminds us that findings change over time and once predictors are established, one has to wonder how long they will be valid in a world of changing criteria. Furthermore, syntheses of the research can look at time from yet another angle, such as whether the ages of candidates factor into studies of criterion validity.

In the spirit of methodological plurality, there are also strong theoretical and practical reasons to maintain a reporting mechanism for case study findings (see Yin, 2009), which can supplement larger quantitative investigations and meta-analytic work. Indeed, some mixed methods researchers have even suggested that research syntheses combine evidence from quantitative and qualitative work (e.g., Hart, Smith, Swars, & Smith, 2009). If the police assessment field is to advance it will help to have careful descriptions of these decisions and honest reporting of how they turned out. That is, what was the competing evidence that compelled the psychologist to override other assessment results and how did the decision work? An overview of these cases can

---

[2] Cohen did not intend for these markers to become some sort of convention; they are, however, still useful particularly when there is minimal literature available for comparison purposes.

potentially go a long way in helping quantitative researchers make a priori decisions about analyses and later interpretation. In sum, we would like to see a stronger connection between research syntheses and study design in the world of personality assessment research along with clearer delimitation of exploratory and confirmatory findings. This is not to say that exploratory work has no place but it is critical to understand the difference between these two research goals and how they can inform practice.[3] The clinical versus statistical prediction controversy is still with us after a half century (Meehl, 1954). Statistical prediction is the most rigorous and in the long run preferred. But the process of clinical prediction continues to provide important insights into the relevant factors that guide successful police candidate selection. The question in clinical prediction is: What information was most significant for the psychologist for making the decision? Exploratory studies provide hypotheses. Confirmatory studies provide answers.

Advancing the Evidence via Experimental and Quasi-Experimental Trials

Regression analyses appear to be the standard approach for investigating the validity of personality assessment. But different types of studies could be developed that look at the impact of using different types of assessment systems in police selection work. Consider a study by Gould et al. (2005), where they used a randomized controlled trial (RCT) to investigate the impacts of a screening system for adolescent suicide risk. The treatment entailed a universal screening system while working with 2,342 students across six high schools. Classrooms were the level of random assignment and the outcome measure was an assessment of stress, suicidal ideation, depression symptoms, and substance abuse problems. The study's primary concern was determining if such screening might actually yield iatrogenic effects on psychological health (some expressed concerns that suicide screening could yield such negative outcomes by bringing up the topic) and found that it did not. The results of the study suggest suicide screening might therefore be a safe component of prevention programming.

Can this work provide some guidance for future research in personality assessment when selecting officers? The short answer is yes. The general design would test the impact of assessment where a researcher might assign departments to use a novel approach to measurement or business as usual screening practices. Any number of outcome measures that are typically already collected could be used for post-testing purposes. These might

---

[3] In short, the former can help establish research agendas whereas the latter is better used to inform practice and policy.

include turnover rates (i.e., do departments that use the new system experience lower average turnover rates relative to the counterfactual condition?), number of discipline referrals or, even better, overall job evaluation metrics. Such a study might also yield insight on use of actuarial decision making models for predicting liabilities. That is, the effort might help establish cutoff scores to guide decisions.

Given that outcomes would be at an officer level, the impact model (i.e., the analyses that would ascertain if treatment units outperformed control units) would have two levels, where officers were nested by department, the unit of assignment. This would necessitate use of hierarchical linear models in the analysis so as to properly account for the data structure (Raudenbush & Bryk, 2002). It would probably be necessary to constrain recruiting to within a state or some other organizing body so as to standardize procedures for rating performance as well as candidate training approaches. In the end, such a design could be used so as to test the incremental validity of the new approach and a RCT would be the only design, with the possible exception of a regression discontinuity design, that can yield an unbiased estimate of the program effect (Shadish et al., 2002). Of course, given that such a design would in essence be comparing two competing options for candidate screening, one should anticipate a small difference (i.e., effect size) between groups if one is to be found at all. The implication here is the study would have to be fairly large and well funded.

Some might argue the design would be infeasible because of legal concerns and/or unwillingness on the part of administrators to allow random assignment. These concerns would override the desire of administrators to use novel assessments in the recruitment process. Similar concerns have been noted in other fields and overcome (Boruch, 1997; Cook, 1999, 2002; Gueron, 2002). On ethical grounds, the hope here would be to identify better assessment systems. We do not know whether a new approach would be better. On legal grounds, the competing assessment systems would have to be equally justifiable at the outset of the trial. If candidates would take umbrage with an employment decision that is informed in part by personality assessment, then the two competing options would have to be equally defensible. There may well be some departments who would outright refuse to join the study but this is always a concern. Most trials therefore deal with a convenience sample of participants who agreed to the parameters of the study. While this limits the study this is not sufficient reason to desist. Finally, RCTs are used in other high stakes contexts all the time such as medicine, psychological and educational settings. There are no doubt barriers that have yet to be identified here but other fields have contended with strong barriers as well, in the name of obtaining strong causal evidence of program effects.

Assuming for a moment that a RCT is indeed unrealistic, then nonrandom assignment mechanisms (i.e., a quasi-experiment) remain an option. For example, one might compare departments that apply personality assessments in their recruiting process to ones that do not. Or for that matter, one could compare departments that use different types of measures to see if one appears to yield better outcomes than another. Except for the important fact that random assignment is not used the study could be just like the one described above. Taking this approach would introduce threats to internal-causal validity (see Boruch, 1997; Shadish et al., 2002) but would simplify recruiting and potential legal concerns. If this less desirable design were to be used it might be strengthened by using propensity score matching techniques where treatment and control departments could be matched on several, indeed dozens of variables so as to approximate the RCT design. Briefly, such a design might show departments are similar in terms of multiple variables such as their size, types of neighborhood served, experience levels of current staff, average discipline rates among officers, community complaints and accolades, and so on. If departments were matched on so many variables their similarity would approximate what can be achieved via random assignment (see Hong & Raudenbush, 2005, 2006, for an excellent demonstration of the procedure). The overall idea of the design would be to argue that if the only important difference between departments is the type of assessment system used, then any differences in outcome measures could be attributed to the assessment system. Failure to observe differences might yield to the equally helpful conclusion that there is no difference and thus no reason to change practice until test developers can come up with something different to be tested in a future study. Having said all of this, keep in mind that evidence suggests that even the best quasi-experiments should not be expected to remove bias in the way that an RCT can (Bloom, 2005; Boruch, 1997; Shadish et al., 2002).

Whether random assignment is used or not, such a study designed to compare the effects of one assessment system against another could be supplemented via qualitative inquiry. Stakeholders such as candidates, personnel responsible for officer training, administrators and even those who were filtered out by the process might all be interviewed. Psychologists could also conduct individual case studies by carefully describing the battery of scores of randomly sampled recruits while putting this information into the context of departmental needs and decisions. Representative cases within the study could be identified via random sampling procedures. Indeed, some stratification could be implemented within the sampling process so as to make sure the case studies were done at all levels of the screening process (i.e., recruits who sail past the process, close calls and seemingly obvious candidates for screening out). Qualitative work itself could be subjected to standard techniques for promoting validity of inferences, such as member checks, performing external audits, data triangulation, thick description and so on

(Brantlinger, Jiminez, Klingner, Pugach, & Richardson, 2005; Maxwell, 2004; Nastasi & Schensul, 2005; see also Yin, 2009, for other options). The sum result of such a study would be a rigorous test of the benefits, if any, of changing selection approaches that make systematic use of personality assessment data. This would be supplemented with excellent descriptive information documenting whether the system was implemented as planned, perceptions the various stakeholders had of the process and documentation of the overall assessment process.

Research in Police Treatment

Psychological evaluations using personality assessment instruments have for many years been used for treatment planning purposes, and their usefulness for this application has been well documented with a variety of instruments (Exner, 2003; Graham, 2006; Weiss, Weiss, & Gacono, 2008). However, law enforcement officers present unique problems related to the psychological assessment process and its relationship to treatment. Treating law enforcement officers with psychologically based therapy is problematic because of the stigma associated with mental health treatment, especially in police circles (Rostow & Davis, 2004; Weiss, Weiss, & Gacono, 2008). Many law enforcement officers, even though they face considerable job-related stress and are susceptible to job-related psychological difficulties, do not wish to present to treatment because it is perceived as being a sign of weakness.

Also, there are often ethical issues in the application of evaluation information to the treatment of police officers. There is an inherent conflict of interest between protecting the public interest and confidentially treating a rejected or impaired police candidate or officer (Rostow & Davis, 2004). This does not mean that personality assessment instruments cannot be applied to impaired or rejected police officers or candidates. It does mean that the psychologist must fully understand his or her role in the evaluation and treatment process. The present authors know of no systematic studies of assessment for treatment planning of law enforcement officers. Further research might attempt to deal with stigma against psychologically based treatment for law enforcement, and finding out if evaluations can help determine appropriate interventions for law enforcement officers having psychological difficulties. For example, can personality inventories such as the MMPI-2 be useful in planning treatment interventions? Or are test batteries effective in indicating such issues as number of sessions or length of treatment for psychologically troubled officers? Or could testing be useful in breaking through the treatment resistance typically found with police officers? Unfortunately, this has been an often overlooked, yet potentially useful application of personality assessment in police settings.

One option that might help would be a quick screening system for both newly hired and veteran officers who report distress. Fairly common measures of distress such as The Beck Depression Inventory (Beck, Steer, & Brown, 1996) might be administered to all officers who are willing to self-report distress. This is complete conjecture but it might be the case that more universal screening will normalize assessment, although officers would be able to refuse to participate. The overall point, however, is that officers do experience disproportionate levels of distress (Scrivner, 2006) and there is reason to believe treatment systems can be improved. Identifying how exactly goes beyond the scope of this chapter. But we do wish to note that new systems may yield more fodder for a RCT or quasi-experiment, particularly ones with qualitative components that might entail interviews with stakeholders involved with the treatment process.

Fitness-for-Duty Evaluations

While police psychologists frequently perform Fitness-for-Duty Evaluations (FFDE) there is, in fact, very little peer-reviewed research on FFDEs. While there are some excellent sources available for conducting FFDEs based on current legal and practice guidelines (Gormally, 2008; Rostow & Davis, 2004) there are relatively few peer-reviewed studies of the use of psychological testing in FFDEs, although a few do exist (Caillouet, Rostow, & Davis, 2004; Grossman, Haywood, Ostrov, Wasyliw, & Cavanaugh, 1990; Schmit & Stanard, 1996). Admittedly, much of the psychological practice of FFDEs is justified by research in other areas of psychology, but studies specific to the personality assessment and law enforcement FFDEs would be helpful in promoting evidence based practice.

Research on several topics here may be helpful in further refining FFDE procedures. One would be on which tests are most helpful in assisting police psychologists with making recommendations. Another type of research study would be to use regression or discriminant models to show which tests and personality assessment scales are helpful for making accurate recommendations. For example, do clinically elevated MMPI-2 or PAI scores, or unusual Rorschach scores, accurately predict whether or not an officer is fit for duty? Although difficult to obtain, performance records of officers subsequent to FFDE's involving personality assessment data could be used for such studies. Of course, only a few suggestions are presented here and readers may be able to think of others. Regardless, police psychologists are encouraged to attempt to further explore the role of personality assessment instruments in conducting FFDE's.

CONCLUSION

The emerging field of positive psychology (see Seligman & Csikszentmihalyi, 2000) points out that too much in the psychological sciences focuses on that which is maladaptive and not on strengths. There is good reason to keep these tools within a practitioner's repertoire but it is important not to lose sight of the fact that the measures are used in a context where the primary goal might be to evaluate candidate strengths as well as weaknesses. To this end, we propose not only continuing to research measures of psychopathology and other measures used to "screen out" applicants or evaluate fitness for duty, but also more positive applications. For example, understanding through assessment what instruments will help plan treatments or find the best job for a particular officer has positive connotations.

While this chapter has been able only to scratch the surface of possibilities in doing research in police assessment in law enforcement, the authors hope it has been informative. We also hope that future researchers in the field will find it useful in designing the next generation of assessment studies.

REFERENCES

Aamodt, M.G. (2004). *Research in law enforcement selection.* Boca Raton, FL: Brown Walker Press.

American Educational Research Association, American Psychological Association, & National Council on Measurement in Education. (1999). *Standards for educational and psychological testing.* Washington, DC: American Educational Research Association.

Anastasi, A. & Urbina, S. (1997). *Psychological testing* (7th Ed). Upper Saddle River, NJ: Prentice Hall.

Beck, A.T., Steer, R.A., & Brown, G.K. (1996). *BDI-II Manual.* San Antonio, TX: Psychological Corporation.

Bloom, H.S. (2005). *Learning more from social experiments: Evolving analytic approaches.* New York: Russell Sage Foundation.

Boruch, R. F. (1997). *Randomized field experiments for planning and evaluation: A practical guide.* Thousand Oaks, CA: Sage Publications.

Braden, J.P., & Shernoff, E.S. (2008). Why the need for evidence-based interventions? In R.J. Morris & N. Mather (Eds.), *Evidence-based interventions for students with learning and behavioral challenges* (pp. 9–30). Mahwah, NJ: Lawrence Erlbaum Associates.

Brantlinger, E., Jiminez, R., Klingner, J., Pugach, M., & Richardson, V. (2005). Qualitative studies in special education. *Exceptional Children, 71*(2), 195–207.

Bronfenbrenner, U. (1995). Developmental ecology through space and time: A future perspective. In Moen, P. & Elder, G.H. (Eds.). *Examining lives in context:*

Perspectives on the ecology of human development (pp. 619–647). Washington, DC: American Psychological Association.

Butcher, J.N., Graham, J.R., Ben-Porath,Y.S., Tellegen, A., Dahlstrom, W.G., Kaemmer, B. (2001). *MMPI-2 (Minnesota Multiphasic Personality Inventory-2): Manual for administration, scoring, and interpretation, revised edition.* Minneapolis, University of Minnesota Press.

Caillouet, B.A., Rostow, C.D., & Davis, C.D. (2004). Law enforcement officer seniority and PAI variables in psychological fitness-for-duty examinations. *Journal of Police and Criminal Psychology, 19*(2), 49–52.

Campbell, D.T. (1986). Relabeling internal and external validity for applied social scientists. In W. M. K. Trochim (Ed.), *Advances in quasi-experimental design and analysis: New Directions for Program Evaluation.* San Francisco: Josey-Bass.

Campbell, D.T., & Fiske, D.W. (1959). Convergent and discriminant validation by the multitrait-multimethod matrix. *Psychological Bulletin, 56,* 81–105.

Cohen, J. (1988). *Statistical power analysis for the behavioral sciences* (2nd ed.). Mahwah, NJ: Lawrence Erlbaum.

Cook, T.D. (1999). "Considering the major arguments against random assignment: An analysis of the educational culture surrounding evaluation in American schools of education." Paper presented at the Harvard Faculty Seminar on Experiments in Education, Cambridge, MA.

Cook, T.D. (2002). Randomized experiments in educational policy research: A critical examination of the reasons the educational evaluation community has offered for not doing them. *Educational Evaluation and Policy Analysis, 24* (3), 175–199.

Crocker, L., & Algina, J. (1986). *Introduction to classical and modern test theory.* Belmont, CA: Wadsworth Group.

Cunningham, M.R., Jones, J.W., & Behrens, G. (2009, October). "Psychological assessment of chief of police candidates: Scientific and practice issues." Paper presented at the Annual Meeting of the Society for Police and Criminal Psychology, Hartford, CT.

Exner, J.E., Jr. (2003). *The Rorschach: A comprehensive system:* (4th Ed.). New York: Wiley.

Gormally, J.F., (2008). The Rorschach in fitness-for-duty evaluations. In C.B. Gacono & F.B. Evans (Eds.), *The handbook of forensic Rorschach psychology,* (pp. 301–322). New York: Routledge.

Gough, H.G., & Bradley, P. (1996). *CPI manual.* (3rd Ed.). Palo Alto, CA: Consulting Psychologists Press.

Gould, M.S., Marrocco, F.A. Kleinman, M., Thomas, J.G., Mostkoff, K., Cote, J., & Davies, M. (2005). Evaluating Iatrogenic risk of youth suicide screening programs: A randomized controlled trial. *Journal of the American Medical Association, 293*(13), 1635–1643.

Graham, J.R. (2006). *MMPI-2: Assessing personality and psychopathology.* (4th Ed.). New York: Oxford University Press.

Grissom, R.J. & Kim, J.J. (2005). *Effect sizes for research.* Mahwah, NJ: Lawrence Earlbaum.

Grossman, L.S., Haywood, T.W., Ostrov, E., Wasyliw, O., & Cavanaugh, J.L. (1990). Sensitivity of MMPI validity scales to motivational factors in psychological evaluations of police officers. *Journal of Personality Assessment, 55,* 549–561.

Gueron, J.M. (2002). The politics of random assignment: Implementing studies and affecting policy. In F. Mosteller & R. Boruch (Eds.), *Evidence matters: Randomized trials in education research* (pp. 15–49). Washington, D.C.: Brookings Institution.

Hart, L.C, Smith, S.Z., Swars, S.L., & Smith, M.W. (2009). An examination of research in mathematics education (1995–2005). *Journal of Mixed Methods Research, 3*(1), 26–41.

Hong, G. & Raudenbush, S.W. (2005). Effects of Kindergarten retention policy on children's cognitive growth in reading and mathematics. *Educational Evaluation and Policy Analysis, 27*(3), 205–224.

Hong, G. & Raudenbush, S.W. (2006). Evaluating kindergarten retention policy: A case study of causal inference for multilevel observational data. *Journal of the American Statistical Association, 101*(475), 901–910.

Kline, P. (1994). *An easy guide to factor analysis.* London: Routledge.

Kratochwill, T.R., & Shernoff, E.S. (2003). Evidence-based practice: Promoting evidence-based interventions in school psychology. *School Psychology Quarterly, 18*, 389–408.

Maxwell, J.A. (2004). Using qualitative methods for causal explanation. *Field Methods, 16*(3), 243–264.

Meehl, P. (1954). *Clinical versus statistical prediction: A theoretical analysis and a review of the evidence.* Minneapolis: University of Minnesota Press.

Messick, S. (1995). Validity of psychological assessment: Validation of inferences from persons' responses and performances as scientific inquiry into score meaning. *American Psychologist, 50*, 741–749.

Morey, L.C. (2007). *Personality Assessment Inventory: Professional manual.* (2nd Ed.). Odessa, FL: Psychological Assessment Resources.

Nastasi, B.K., & Schensul, S.L. (2005). Contributions of qualitative research to the validity of intervention research. Special issue of *Journal of School Psychology, 43* (3), 177–195.

No Child Left Behind. (n.d.). Retrieved October 24, 2004 from http://www.ed.gov/nclb/accountability/ayp/testing-faq.html#4

Odom, S.L., Brantlinger, E., Gersten, R., Horner, R.H., Thompson, B., & Harris, K. R. (2005). Research in special education: Scientific methods and evidence-based practices. *Exceptional Children, 71*, 137–148.

Onwuegbuzie, A.J. (2002). Why can't we all get along? Towards a framework for unifying research paradigms. *Education, 122* (3), 518–530.

Pedhazur, E.J. & Schmelkin, L.P. (1991). Measurement, design and analysis: An integrated approach. Hillsdale, NJ: Prentice Hall.

Raudenbush, S.W. (2005). Learning from attempts to improve schooling: The contribution of methodological diversity. *Educational Researcher, 34*(5), 25–31.

Raudenbush, S.W., & Bryk, A.S. (2002). *Hierarchical linear models: Applications and data analysis methods* (2nd ed.). Thousand Oaks, CA: Sage Publications, Inc.

Rosenthal, R., Rosnow, R.L., & Rubin, D.B., (2000). *Contrasts and effect sizes in behavioral research: A correlational approach.* Cambridge University Press.

Rostow, C.D. & Davis, R.D. (2004). *A handbook for psychological fitness-for-duty evaluations in law enforcement.* Binghamton, NY: Haworth.

Schmit, M.J., & Stanard, S.J. (1996). The utility of personality inventories in the employee assistance process: A study of EAP referred police officers. *Employee Assistance Quarterly, 11*(4), 21–42.

Schneider, B., Carnoy, M., Kilpatrick, J., Schmidt, W.H., & Shavelson, R.J. (2007). *Estimating casual effects using experimental and nonexperimental designs.* Washington, D.C.: American Education Research Association.

Scrivner, E. (2006). Psychology and law enforcement. In I.B. Weiner & A.K. Hess (Eds.), *The handbook of forensic psychology* (3rd ed.) (pp. 534–551). New York: Wiley.

Seligman, M.E.P., & Csikszentmihalyi, M. (2000). Positive psychology: An introduction. *American Psychologist, 55*, 5–14.

Shadish, W.R., Cook, T., & Campbell, D. (2002). *Experimental and quasi-experimental designs for generalized causal inference.* Boston: Houghton Mifflin Company.

Shernoff, E.S. & Kratochwill, T.R. (2005). Evidence-based practice. In M. Hersen, G. Sugai, & R. Horner (Eds.), *Encyclopedia of behavior modification and cognitive behavior therapy* (pp. 1306–1311). Thousand Oaks, CA: Sage.

Slavin, R.E. (2002). Evidence-based education policies: Transforming educational practice and research. *Educational Research, 31* (7), 15–21.

Stout, C.E. & Hayes, R.A. (2004). *The evidence-based practice: Methods, models, and tools for mental health professionals.* John Wiley and Sons.

Tashakkori, A., & Teddlie, C. (1998). *Mixed methodology: Combining qualitative and quantitative approaches.* Thousand Oaks, CA: Sage.

Tashakkori, A., & Teddlie, C. (2003). *Handbook of mixed methods in social and behavioral research.* Thousand Oaks, CA: Sage.

U.S. Department of Education. (2005). *Scientifically based evaluation methods.* Retrieved May 24, 2005 from the American Evaluation Association Web site http://www.eval.org/doepage.htm

Weiss, P.A. (2002). Potential uses of the Rorschach in the selection of police officers. *Journal of Police and Criminal Psychology, 17* (2), 63–70.

Weiss, P.A., Hitchcock, J.H., Weiss, W.U., Rostow, C., & Davis, R. (2008). The Personality Assessment Inventory Borderline, Drug, and Alcohol Scales as predictors of overall performance in police officers: A series of exploratory analysis. *Policing and Society, 18*(3), 301–310.

Weiss, P.A., Weiss, W.U., & Gacono, C.B., (2008). The use of the Rorschach in police psychology: Some preliminary thoughts. In: C.B. Gacono and F.B. Evans, eds. *The handbook of forensic Rorschach assessment.* New York: Routledge, 527–542.

Weiss, W.U., Davis, R., Rostow, C., & Kinsman, S. (2003). The MMPI-2 L scale as a tool in police selection. *Journal of Police and Criminal Psychology, 18*(1), 57–60.

Weiss, W.U., Rostow, C., Davis, R., & Decoster-Martin, E. (2004). The Personality Assessment Inventory as a selection device for law enforcement personnel. *Journal of Police and Criminal Psychology, 19*(2), 23–29.

Weiss, W.U., Weiss, P.A., Cain, S., & Manley, B. (in press). Impression management in police officer candidacy on the MMPI-2. *Journal of Police and Criminal Psychology.*

Yin, R.K. (2009). *Case study research: Design and methods* (4th Ed.). Thousand Oaks, CA: Sage.

Part IV

APPLICATIONS OF PERSONALITY ASSESSMENT IN POLICE PSYCHOLOGY

Chapter 12

PROCEDURAL CONSIDERATIONS IN SECURITY PERSONNEL SELECTION

WILLIAM U. WEISS

PURPOSE AND IMPORTANCE OF PERSONALITY ASSESSMENT IN POLICE SELECTION

In their article about the use of the MMPI-2 to predict the employment continuation of recently hired police officers, Weiss, Serafino, Serafino, Willson, and Knoll (1998) note that police officers are often the interface between the local government and the public. They note that no other official of the municipality or state engages the average citizen as directly as does the police officer. Also, the police officer deals with the citizen at times when he or she is most vulnerable. Domestic violence is an example. Couples are at their most vulnerable during episodes of domestic violence. Children who are neglected are also vulnerable. Citizens who are the victims of crime require the assistance of police officers for protection. Police officers are exposed to many opportunities to display excessive force or corruption (Stone, 1995). Impulsivity, antisocial tendencies, paranoia, cynicism and contempt on the part of the officer can lead to destructive behavior which is not only legally and criminally inappropriate but also ethically so (Rostow & Davis, 2004). Inappropriate behavior of officers can lead minimally to contempt for officers and the local government on the part of the local populace but also at worst to expensive lawsuits. In addition, officers also carry weapons for the defense of the ordinary citizen and themselves. The potential for the misuse of these weapons exists and, concomitantly, the potential for the use of excessive force exists (Stone, 1995). Any number of examples of excessive force have been publicized, including the Rodney King beating and the Abner Louima abuse case where a nightstick was shoved into the rectum of an arrested individual. Police beatings and the use of excessive force come to the attention of the news media and the public frequently, more so because of the increasingly ubiquitous presence of surveillance cameras. Officers have even been photographed employing excessive force by cameras attached to their own police vehicles. In the interests of public safety, personality screening of police officer candidates is a necessary procedure. Police officers have a greater potential to do harm to members of the public than do other governmental representatives. Corrupt and/or violent police officers create public outrage and thwart the administration of justice in our society. They also increase the human and financial costs of doing governmental business.

There is no doubt that a professional police force is a necessity for the existence of civilized society. Weiss (2008) noted that, in England, before the organization of the Westminster Constables by Sir Robert Peel in 1829, policing was in the hands of the citizenry themselves and therefore law enforcement was erratic and unpredictable. The professional police officer changed that. The populace could rely upon the behavior and professionalism of the trained officer. This made personality assessment of police officers all the more important. Corrupt, violent and unethical officers poisoned the trust of the ordinary citizen both in fair and impartial law enforcement and in government.

With the growth and increasing expertise of the professional discipline of psychology, particularly after World War II, a vehicle was created to assess the personality of officer candidates so that officers with negative characteristics and potential could be screened out. Indeed, psychologists were assisting police departments actively during the 1960s, according to Archibald (1995). Although it is beyond the scope of this chapter to trace further the historical development of such work, the interested reader may wish to refer to several short discussions in the recent literature. A concise personal "behind-the-scenes" account by Inwald (2008) of her work in 1978 as a consultant to a large urban public safety agency acknowledges that evaluation requirements at that time were elusive and ill defined. Davis and Rostow also discuss the history of police testing in their technical manual (2008).

Following this summary of the purpose and importance of personality screening for police candidates, it is appropriate to review the process by which this is accomplished. This chapter discusses the method by which an appropriate personality screening program can be developed so that inappropriate candidates can be eliminated from the applicant pool. It also discusses how a fair and impartial personality assessment process can be developed so that not only the police agency but the candidates as well can have confidence in it.

The Referral Process

Police departments do seek the assistance of psychologists in making personnel decisions about police officers. In many jurisdictions psychological evaluations of police officers are required by law. In some jurisdictions even a part of the method is specified by law. There are states and municipalities requiring that one of the tests administered be the MMPI-2 (Weiss, Serafino, Serafino, Willson, Sarsany, & Felton, 1999). Most jurisdictions are more general in their specifications, however, requiring only that a psychological evaluation be administered to the candidate. In many jurisdictions either a psychiatrist or a psychologist is allowed to perform the evaluation. However, psychologists are uniquely trained to administer and interpret tests and therefore their expertise is more relevant to the selection process. It is important to note that personality assessment of the police officer candidate now takes place at the very end of the hiring process, as a result of the passage of the Americans with Disabilities Act. The Act was passed to protect Americans who have a disability from discrimination. A mental disability or physical disability that may not be relevant to performance on the job as a police officer should not prevent a candidate from being hired. For example, depression compensated by medication may not be a deterrent to being a successful police officer. Certain personality characteristics such as passiveness may not be as well. These can influence a rating or a ranking by a physician or a psychologist. In past years all candidates were evaluated and rank ordered as to suitability. Following the passage of the Americans with Disabilities Act, candidates are seen one at a time after the decision to hire has been made. This means that the psychological evaluation is usually the last hurdle for the candidate along with the polygraph test and the medical evaluation.

Sometimes the city or police department seeks the assistance of an organization such as the local mental health center or the occupational medicine department of a local hospital. However, it is more appropriate that the department seek the assistance of a psychologist who specializes in police selection. A specialist can be defined as one holding the Diplomate in Police Psychology of the Society for Police and Criminal Psychology or having publications in the area of police selection suggesting a strong professional interest in the area. Usually there are specialists in the local jurisdiction but often the police department has difficulty identifying them without some initiative on the part of the police psychologist. This is why it is important for the police psychologist to make himself or herself known to the local and state police departments. The police selection specialist can put together a brochure outlining the services provided and the costs of such services, as well as providing a curriculum vita. In this way, the department can be encouraged to hire a specialist in the area of police selection to perform the evaluations.

Once there is a desire on the part of the department to hire the psychologist there should be a letter of intent or a contract delineating the type and nature of the services to be provided and the fee for such services. Fees are important. Sometimes the department will have very little money for the evaluation process and it may be insufficient to provide for a comprehensive evaluation that the psychologist can defend. If there is a meeting of the minds the contract or letter of intent can be signed. If there is a reluctance or an inability on the part of the agency to sign a letter or contract, it behooves the psychologist to send a letter delineating the type of services to be provided, the methods to be used and the cost of such services so that there can be no misunderstandings about the nature of the services in the future. In this letter should be a discussion of the requirements of the Americans with Disabilities Act, particularly if there is a lack of clarity about it on the part of the agency.

The experience of most psychologists who do police selection is that it is a "hurry-up" scenario. Usually the permission to hire comes without much advance notice to the police chief or city manager. All of a sudden money is available for hiring the officer. There may be an academy deadline. Having the process in place before the first evaluation is very helpful to the psychologist and can prevent misunderstandings on the part of the agency from the beginning. Often the department needs the results by the next day. Therefore, immediate scoring of tests is required. Delays in a machine scoring process will lead to dropping of some test materials or will delay the submission of the report. Hand scoring may be necessary. The psychologist should be prepared to have the report ready in 24 hours. The police agency will be appreciative because there is often a narrow window of opportunity for hiring candidates. If the agency does not act quickly, the position will be eliminated or the hiring of the individual cannot be completed because the candidate will be delayed in attending the academy.

Preliminary Data

One question that is frequently posited relates to the type of information that the psychologist should obtain from the municipality and/or the police department prior to interviewing the candidate. Certain types of tests, those related to so-called normal personality characteristics, can be available prior to interviewing the individual. However, one must be careful that these instruments are not used to screen out a candidate prior to the psychological evaluation, to satisfy the requirements of the Americans with Disabilities Act. There are basic skills, however, which can be assessed prior to the evaluation. Literacy skills are one of these. Reading and writing assessment should be performed. It is necessary that a police officer be literate so that he/she can read and write reports and testify in court. Also, the ability to handle basic arithmetic should be assessed. Intelligence tests and achievement tests are inappropriate, but tests such as the Wide Range Achievement Test, which assesses reading, spelling, and arithmetic, or the Wonderlic Personnel Test (Wonderlic, Inc., 2007) are appropriate screens that can be administered prior to the psychological evaluation. However, it is only necessary that the candidate meet the minimum standard for passing. A candidate should not be judged on the academic skills since these are not relevant to the actual work as a police officer.

The psychologist should receive a copy of the background investigation if this is available. Lautenschlager (1994) refers to this type of information more succinctly as biodata. Basically, it is biographical information. During the interview, candidates are not always truthful. They may omit problematic behavior which has been detected on the background analysis, seeing it as an omission rather than a prevarication. Arrest records, domestic violence and drug use are often reported or identified by the background check. These can be valuable information for the assessment of the officer. If the information on the background check is available, the psychologist should obtain it and review it prior to interviewing the candidate. Biodata are routinely obtained prior to hiring. It would not violate ADA regulations if the psychologist were to obtain this information prior to the interview, particularly because the candidate has been offered the position before the psychologist becomes involved. Arrest and jail records are germane to the hiring process and can be obtained prior to the psychological evaluation. In some jurisdictions, for example, it is illegal to hire someone who has been convicted of a felony to be a police officer.

It is also valuable for the psychologist to have a copy of the polygraph report if available. It is recognized that the validity of polygraph information is controversial (Terris, 1985). If given by the department it is usually provided at the same time as the psychological evaluation–that is, after the candidate has been offered the position and is usually not available to the psychologist. However, polygraph information, within the context of a psychological evaluation and used judiciously, may have some value. Primarily, then, the background information report is the most important piece of prior information that the psychologist should attempt to obtain.

Informed Consent

The most important issue in the area of informed consent is the fact that the privilege lies not with the client in this particular set of circumstances but with the city or police organization (Archibald, 1995; American Psychological Association, 2002; Rostow & Davis, 2004). The police officer candidate is not entitled to a copy of the evaluation at any time. This is unlike other medical or psychological information that can be shared with the candidate and in some cases is shared by law with the candidate. The candidate has a right to see his or her medical or psychological records. The only information that the candidate is entitled to receive from the psychological screening evaluation is the conclusion: acceptable for work as a police officer or unacceptable. Of course, the candidate has the right to confidentiality. Release of information to any other party must be approved by the candidate. Although it is understood as a function of the evaluation that a report will be released to the agency, it is important that the psychologist understand the nature of the privilege and the limits of confidentiality. Basically, the issue is whether the candidate is considered psychologically fit for the job or not. If deemed psychologically unfit, then the employment offer is rescinded and the candidate is not hired. If deemed fit by the psychologist, the candidate is hired and if the candidate has not already completed police academy training he or she starts working as an apprentice officer until he or she is sent to the academy. There are times when the candidate may be deemed fit but with reservations. Psychologists should avoid this conclusion if possible because it does present a decision problem to the city or police department. Under these circumstances the city or police department may on the basis of the reservations reject the candidate or put conditions upon the candidate such as expecting a good performance at the academy. Depending upon the contract between the psychologist and the department, the psychologist may see the candidate later, explaining the reason for non-selection or for the reservations but this is not necessary. The psychologist and the department do not have to provide reasons for the decisions made. Again, the privilege is with the department or the city, not with the candidate. Other issues in the informed consent procedure are permission for the evaluation given by the candidate. It is also helpful to provide some explanation of the rationale for the tests, and to specify that the report is sent directly to the city or police department. It is also important to explain that the report is confidential and will not be shared with any other organization or person other than the department or the city. The city or department is the only party to whom the report and the results will be presented.

The Evaluation

The evaluation usually begins with a mental status interview, although in some cases psychologists move directly to testing (Mullins & McMains, 1995). During the interview informed consent is explained. With some modifications the standard mental status evaluation can be used. There is no chief complaint as there is with the clinical mental status. The psychologist should not forget that the individual with whom he or she is interacting is likely to be healthier than the average person in the American population. The following outline for the mental status is a good model to follow:

Mental Status Examination

1. Informed consent
2. History, including education, job history, and current job
3. Motivation for police work–Why does the candidate want to be an officer?
4. Previous experience as a police officer, either going to the academy or actual work as an officer
5. Marital history. Histories of conflict with the spouse or former spouse. Any history of domestic violence or Domestic Violence Orders. Any separations. Divorces, how many, and whether there are any children and who has custody of them. Are there any child support issues and is the individual up to date with the child support payments?
6. If single, what kinds of personal relationships does the individual have? For example, does the candidate live with parents or with a significant other. If the latter, what are the plans for the future?
7. Personal hobbies and recreational activities
8. Mental health history. Has the person ever had counseling and why... Has the candidate ever been in a psychiatric hospital? Does the person have a tendency toward depression or anxiety? Has the person ever been paranoid or hallucinatory?
9. Administration of the standard mental status exam, beginning with Proverb Interpretation
10. Drug and alcohol history. Does the person drink alcohol? When did he or she last have a drink? Has the candidate ever been a heavy drinker? Ever had treatment for alcohol? Ever smoked marijuana? When was it and how often? Has the individual ever been addicted to marijuana? Ever used cocaine or crack? Used it more than once and, if so, how often? Ever used intravenous drugs? If so, how frequently? Ever been in a drug or alcohol treatment program?
11. Legal history. Has the candidate ever been convicted of a DUI? When and where? What was the alcohol level? Involved in an accident? Ever been convicted of a misdemeanor or a felony? When and for what? Ever been in jail? Which one and for how long? How many traffic violations has the individual had? What is their nature and when did they occur? Has the driver's license ever been suspended?

One can see that this is a mental status examination, but it is combined with elements of an employment interview. The mental status interview is the basis for the decision- making process with regard to acceptability. The psychologist combines the information from the mental status with the test and background information to come to an informed decision about acceptability.

Test Selection

Test selection is an important issue for the psychologist. Actually, it has been narrowed by the Americans with Disabilities Act. In the past, Hibler and Kurke (1995) noted, there were two approaches to test selection. One traditional approach was "screening out" (hereafter SO). This one emphasizes potential problems. In other words, the emphasis is upon eliminating candidates who will become problem police officers. In general the Americans with Disabilities Act has led to a de-emphasis on "screening in." or SI. Care must be used not to overinterpret instruments used prior to a job offer and proffer psychological disability statements based upon them. In the past candidates were often "rank-ordered" based upon pre-offer testing information. However, there are still some pre-offer measures that are legal and appropriate. The Wonderlic Personnel Test (Wonderlic, 2007) as a measure of educational skills is one of these. The National Police Officer Selection Test (POST) developed by Stanard and Associates (1991) is another one of these in that it assesses the cognitive skills associated with being a police officer such as Arithmetic, Reading Comprehension, Grammar and Incident Report Writing. There are also some biodata measures that are appropriate. Two examples of SI instruments that have been used are the Kuder and Strong Vocational Interest Inventories (Weiss, Yates, & Buehler, 1995). These instruments can predict life satisfaction with work as a police officer but they do not predict problematic performance. They do not predict that the candidate's performance as an officer will be inadequate. Life satisfaction is important but it cannot be a criterion for withholding a position from a police officer candidate.

For further reference, Aumiller and Corey (2007) discuss the bifurcated model which does involve pre-offer and post-offer measures. However, the emphasis in selection is upon SO. The psychological evaluation can only conclude that the candidate can or cannot do the job effectively. Selection on the basis of longevity in the job or happiness in the job cannot be used as a criterion for selection, though these do represent valuable information. However, one can be unhappy in a position and still do it well.

The psychologist evaluator must focus upon screening out potential problematic officers. The question then arises as to what type of measures are appropriate. A mental status as described above is a necessary part of the process. Super (2006) recommends one test of psychopathology and one test of normal personality at a minimum. However, in the employment (SO) process, an instrument specifically designed for security employees is extremely important. As Super (2006) states, more recently there has been greater emphasis upon instruments specifically designed for high security candidates. Therefore a combination of the MMPI-2 or PAI, measures of general psychopathology, along with a test specific to security personnel such as the Inwald Personality Inventory or the Matrix-Predictive Uniform Law Enforcement Selection Evaluation Inventory (M-PULSE) would be an appropriate test battery when accompanied by a mental status examination. Such instruments are "screening out" measures, and one instrument emphasizing general psychopathology and one more specifically emphasizing the identification of potential problem behavior in security employees would appear to be more appropriate than a measure of psychopathology and a measure of the normal personality. The CPI, a measure of normal personality, because of the validity information associated with it, could replace either the measure of general psychopathology or the more specific measure. However, almost all other measures of normal personality would not be appropriate for candidate selection. The two most appropriate measures of general psychopathology that have been validated with police officer candidates are the MMPI and the PAI. Descriptions of these measures are provided below.

The Minnesota Multiphasic Personality Inventory-2

The MMPI-2 (Butcher, Graham, Ben-Porath, Tellegen, Dahlstrom, & Kaemmer, 2001) is an empirically constructed measure of psychopathology using a dichotomous response format which includes a number of scales specifically measuring psychopathology. Also included are validity scales which measure response sets. Scale construction has been based upon statistical decision theory in that a T score of 65, one and one-half standard deviations above the mean is the criterion for identifying psychopathology. Therefore, elevations on the scales of 65 or greater are cause for concern. Elevated scores of the L scale of the MMPI-2 have been shown in multiple studies to be related to potential disciplinary actions and corruption (Boes, Chandler, & Timm, 1997; Herndon, 1998; Weiss, Davis, Rostow, & Kinsman, 2003). The MMPI-2 is one of the instruments that can be used for SO. More than that, the MMPI-2 is mandated by law in many states and must be used in the evaluation. The new RC scales have not as yet been fully investigated (Tellegen et al., 2003). Further research with them is needed to demonstrate their utility in the police selection process but they do have potential in this area.

The Personality Assessment Inventory

The Personality Assessment Inventory, or PAI (Morey, 2007), has scales similar to those of the MMPI-2 and has been used as a part of the test battery for police candidate selection (Weiss, Zehner, Davis, Rostow, & DeCoster-Martin, 2005; Weiss, Rostow, Davis, & DeCoster-Martin, 2004; Weiss, Serafino, & Serafino, 2000; DeCoster-Martin, Weiss, Davis, & Rostow, 2004; Weiss, Hitchcock, Weiss, Rostow, & Davis, 2008). However, rather than using a True-False dichotomy, the PAI uses a 4-point scale of agreement, which is more realistic when answering personality questions. It is also an SO instrument. In addition, its scales are general measures of maladaptive tendencies.

Two other tests that deal with security personnel more specifically are the Inwald Personality Inventory, or IPI (Inwald, 1982) and the Matrix-Predictive Uniform Law Enforcement Selection Evaluation Inventory (M-PULSE) (Davis & Rostow, 2008).

The Inwald Personality Inventory

The scales of the Inwald Personality Inventory were mainly validated with potential problematic behaviors related to police and security work. The Inwald Personality Inventory (Inwald, 1982) is a 310-item "True-False" inventory designed to identify a variety of personality and behavioral characteristics in public safety/law enforcement applicants. The Inwald contains several scales designed to measure behaviors, attitudes, and characteristics of individual applicants. Inwald presented validity studies in the test manual (1982). One of these involved a discriminant function equation used to correctly predict successes and failures in selection. Scales measuring "acting out" behaviors, suspiciousness and rigidity predicted the retention and termination status of police officer applicants. (See also the more recent discussion in Inwald, 2008.) Twenty-five clinical scales and one validity scale, Guardedness, are used in the assessment. In addition to the scales mentioned above other important scales are Alcohol, Drugs, Substance Abuse, Job Difficulties, and Antisocial Attitudes. The scales have a strong clinical emphasis, but they have been validated with security personnel.

The Matrix-Predictive Uniform Law Enforcement Selection Evaluation (M-PULSE) Inventory

The Matrix-Predictive Uniform Law Enforcement Selection Evaluation Inventory, or M-PULSE (Davis & Rostow, 2008), is a recently published selection inventory specifically developed for hiring law enforcement officers. It consists of several sets of scales. First of all, there are the liability scales, associated with officer misconduct areas. Secondly, there are the empirical scales which gauge attitudes, values and beliefs that have direct relevance to law enforcement work. Included here are groups of subscales called Negative Self Issues, Negative Perceptions Related to Law Enforcement, Unethical Behavior, and Unpredictability. Thirdly, there are validity scales which assess impression management and test attitudes. The validity of the M-PULSE is based upon data collected from 2,000 prior police candidacy decisions and follow-ups. Scales were developed using these validity data. Validity studies have shown that 86 percent of the liability events could have been predicted correctly using the M-PULSE. Scales have high reliability. Matrix continues to collect validity data related to the M-PULSE, and investigation of the validity of the M-PULSE is an ongoing process.

A battery of tests using a mental status exam, the MMPI-2 or the PAI, and the IPI or the M-PULSE would certainly be appropriate in a police selection procedure attempting to screen out those individuals who would present problem behavior as police officers. There is one additional test, however, of normal personality variables which could be used for screening out because of the validity data associated with it. This is the California Psychological Inventory (CPI).

The California Psychological Inventory

An instrument that is both SO and SI is the California Psychological Inventory, or CPI (Gough & Bradley, 1996; Super, 2006; Hargrave & Hiatt, 1989). The CPI was constructed to measure normal personality variables. For example, it assesses such constructs as Dominance, Well-being, Socialization, and Intellectual Efficiency. A meta-analytic researcher, Aamodt, has emphasized the value of the Tolerance scale of the CPI (2004). Super (1995) reported that the best predictors of SWAT team performance were scales V2, a measure of conscientiousness and self-discipline, and the Socialization and Self-Discipline scales. These personality variables may have value in screening out problematic candidates and, indeed, there are useful data on this test which suggest that it can be used in this way.

Scoring

Computer scoring for psychological tests is readily available. The advantage is that it provides a large number of variables that can be used for the analysis. Also, it tends to be more accurate than hand scoring (Evans, 2009).

However, one must remember that if a test is given, one is obligated ethically to use the information obtained from the instrument. Ethical obligations also exist for the publisher, who must provide a rapid and reliable system of scoring to test users. Fortunately, most publishers now do. However, one disadvantage to the use of computer scoring–it provides many more variables than are actually needed to make the decision. While lots of data can be helpful, there is no need for the collection of voluminous data that goes unused. Computers being what they are the computer program may be nonfunctional for a time due to technical difficulties. Hand scoring, in this author's view, remains an alternative emergent way to do scoring for police selection purposes. Unfortunately, it is not available for every test. It is available for the MMPI-2, which is one of the many reasons the MMPI-2 has such great value in police officer candidacy. One should attempt to select the most available and reliable computer scoring system for any test that provides only computer scoring and not hand scoring.

Interpretation

Of course, clinical acumen and clinical prediction remain important in the use of tests and should remain so. The psychologist's clinical judgment can be a great assist in making appropriate decisions. Paul Meehl introduced and discussed the clinical versus statistical prediction controversy (1954). Usually decisions about acceptability as a police officer are made with a combination of these two methods. The MMPI-2, for example, is an instrument that compiles test data statistically but often the entire profile is interpreted clinically. Both clinical and statistical methods have their strengths and weaknesses (Meehl, 1954). It sometimes appears as if clinical compilation is an intuitive method and not scientifically based. The cognitive processes of the clinician are often obscure. From the statistical perspective it is noted that very few variables account for statistical significance and increasing the number of variables beyond five gives so little additional predictability that it is not worth the effort to compile additional variables. The important issue in interpretation of tests is not whether the clinical or statistical method is superior but what the research tells us. "Evidence-based practice" is important. We must be familiar with what the psychological literature tells us is effective. For example, the L scale appears to be one of the most effective testing variables in the area of police selection. The validity scales of both the MMPI-2 and the PAI have shown major promise for police selection. So have the clinical scales of the MMPI-2. The psychologist who does police selection should be aware of the research literature and incorporate it into his or her practice. In so doing, there can be better and more reliable prediction for the evaluation of police officer candidates. Evidence-based practice can be based upon reading journals such as the *Journal of Police and Criminal Psychology* and continuing education experiences.

The Report

The report should address the following issues:

A. Referral Information

The report should describe the source of the referral and the purpose of the referral. Since the referral is from a police organization, the name should be given and who the contact person is. The purpose is a psychological evaluation is to determine suitability for work as a police officer.

B. History

A psychological, social, medical, and family history is obtained and described. The decision is based partially upon this information.

C. Review of Records

Any records such as a background investigation are reviewed and summarized.

D. Mental Status Examination

A standard mental status exam is administered and reported.

E. Test Results

The results of the tests administered and scored are interpreted and the interpretation is presented in the body of the report under this heading.

F. Conclusion and Recommendations

Under this heading the psychologist rates the candidate as acceptable or unacceptable. The psychologist, if he or she wishes, may use the category "Excellent" for a candidate that is deemed to be outstanding. The category "Acceptable with reservations" may also be used, but it is not recommended since it places the police agency in a dilemma. The agency is unable to turn down an acceptable candidate. Yet it is urged to use caution in selecting this individual. Of course, the agency has to accept the individual but may feel anxiety in so doing because of the nature of the "reservations." Using this category is problematic for the department and the individual officer who is hired. It implies that this individual needs to be observed more closely than are other hires. This may not be possible. Also, it may create morale problems among the newly hired police officers.

Communication of Results

In the case of an unacceptable decision for a candidate, the psychologist may want to communicate personally with the police chief or the city manager, if possible. If a candidate is deemed unacceptable the reasons for the rating should be communicated personally in addition to completing a report. The call should be made before the completion of the report. Sometimes the police chief is very positive about the candidate and may request additional evaluation measures of the psychologist to ensure that the individual does have personality problems that will interfere with police work. Sometimes the candidate, because of an unusual test-taking set, may have answered questions in a unique way. This can be examined with additional exploration. The psychologist, however, in re-interviewing, retesting or further testing the client, must be cognizant of ethical guidelines and adhere to them. The psychologist should not be pushed into activities which are unethical because of the ideas or needs of the security agency. Of course, any additional evaluation that is done should be fully presented in the final report to the agency.

Communication of Results to the Candidate

Communication of the results to the candidate should not be performed except with the expressed permission of the security agency. It must be remembered that the agency owns the report. The privilege lies with the agency and not with the candidate. Provided that there is an understanding between the psychologist and the agency, communication to the candidate may occur. In such communication the psychologist may tell the candidate about the reasons for the conclusion.

Appeals Process

Some agencies allow an appeals process, and some do not. Some states or jurisdictions allow an appeals process and some do not. The psychologist should be familiar with the law in the particular state or jurisdiction where the evaluation takes place. The psychologist can then advise the candidate and/or the agency appropriately. In general, it is appropriate for the jurisdiction or agency to allow an appeals process. It often circumvents expensive lawsuits. The reader should see the chapter by Khadivi (2009) in this volume for more information.

Follow-Up

Validation and cross-validation are key concepts in the area of police selection. Hibler and Kurke (1995) discuss various types of validity, but the only real validation procedures involve criterion validity. Face or content validity is insufficient. Simply because a question or test looks appropriate does not mean it is valid for police selection. Criterion validity procedures are appropriate for validation (Kaplan & Saccuzzo, 2005). They identify particular criteria and assess the capacity of the procedure to predict the criteria. Predictive validity procedures are impractical, since it is not possible to place all individuals who seek a position in the position. However, concurrent validity procedures are practical and useful in validating security personnel selection procedures and instruments. Cross-validating any selection procedure is also highly desirable. Data collection following hiring can often prove to be very useful in evaluating the effectiveness of selection. However, data need to be organized appropriately. For this reason it is recommended that the psychologist, if not personally a researcher, attach himself or herself to someone who is, so that meaningful analysis of the data can be performed.

One model for follow-up is provided by the developers of the M-PULSE (Davis & Rostow, 2008) directly related to the scales of the test and their construction. They continue to follow up on hiring decisions made with the M-PULSE on 18 liability misconduct areas and other criteria. Their continuing data collection will allow them to further refine their scales and improve the validity of their hiring decisions. They will be able to develop statistically-based validity coefficients and allow their test to continue to improve with such development.

REFERENCES

Aamodt, M.G. (2004). *Research in law enforcement selection.* p. 100. Boca Raton, FL: BrownWalker, Press. p. 100.

Americans with Disabilities Act, 42 U.S.C. §12112© (3) and (4) (1990)

American Psychological Association. (2002). Ethical principles of psychologists and code of conduct. *American Psychologist, 57* (12): 76–89.

Archibald, E.M. (1995). Managing professional concerns in the delivery of psychological services to the police, pp 45–54. In M.I. Kurke & E.M. Scrivner (Eds.), *Police psychology into the 21st century.* New York: Lawrence Erlbaum Associates.

Aumiller, G.S., & Corey, D. (2007). Defining the field of police psychology: Core domains & proficiencies. *Journal of Police and Criminal Psychology, 22* (2), 65–76.

Boes, J.O., Chandler, C.J., & Timm, H.W. (1997). *Police integrity: Use of personality measures to identify corruption-prone officers.* Monterey, CA: Defense Personnel Security Research Center.

Butcher, J.N., Graham, J.R., Ben-Porath, Y.S., Tellegen, A., Dahlstrom, W.G., & Kaemmer, B. (2001). *MMPI-2 (Minnesota Multiphasic Personality Inventory-2) manual for administration, scoring, and interpretation.* Revised Edition. Minneapolis: University of Minnesota Press.

Davis, R.D., & Rostow, C.D. (2008). *Matrix-Predictive Uniform Law Enforcement Selection Evaluation (M-PULSE) Inventory - technical manual.* Toronto: MHS, Inc.

DeCoster-Martin, E., Weiss, W.U., Davis, R.D., & Rostow, C.D. (2004). Compulsive traits and police officer performance. *Journal of Police and Criminal Psychology, 19* (2), 64–71.

Evans, F.B. (2009, May). "Therapeutic assessment in clinical and forensic practice." Paper presented at the Society for Personality Assessment Continuing Education Workshop, New York, NY.

Gough, H.G., & Bradley, P. (1996). *CPI manual.* (3rd Ed.) Palo Alto, CA: Consulting Psychologists Press.

Hargrave, G.E., & Hiatt, D. (1989). Use of the California Psychological Inventory in law enforcement officer selection. *Journal of Personality Assessment (2)*, 267–277.

Herndon, J. (1998, Oct.). "Correlates of MMPI-2 L scale: Elevations in an LEO selection test battery." Paper presented at the 27th annual meeting of the Society for Police and Criminal Psychology, Portland, OR.

Hibler, N.S., & Kurke, M.I. (1995). Ensuring personal reliability through selection and training. In M.I. Kurke & E.M. Scrivner (Eds.), *Police psychology into the 21st century.* pp. 57–91. New York: Lawrence Erlbaum.

Inwald, R.E. (1982). *Inwald Personality Inventory (IPI) technical manual.* New York: Hilson Research, Inc.

Inwald, R. (2008). The Inwald Personality Inventory (IPI) and Hilson Research inventories: Development and rationale. *Aggression and Violent Behavior, 13,* 298–327.

Kaplan, R.M., & Saccuzzo, D.P. (2005). *Psychological testing: Principles, applications, and issues.* (6th Ed.). Belmont, CA: Wadsworth/Thomson.

Lautenschlager, G.J. (1994). Accuracy and faking of background data. In G.S. Stokes, M.D. Mumford, & W.A. Owens (Eds.), *Biodata handbook: Theory, research and use of biographical information in selection and performance prediction* (391–419). Palo Alto, CA: CPP Books.

Meehl, P. (1954). *Clinical versus statistical prediction: A theoretical analysis and a review of the evidence.* Minneapolis: University of Minnesota Press.

Morey, L.C. (2007). *Personality Assessment Inventory: Professional manual* (2nd ed). Lutz, FL: Psychological Assessment Resources.

Mullins, W.C., & McMains, M. (1995). Predicting patrol officer performance from a psychological assessment battery: A predictive validity study. *Journal of Police and Criminal Psychology, 10* (4), 15–25.

Rostow, C.D., & Davis, R.D. (2004). *A handbook for psychological fitness-for-duty evaluations in law enforcement.* New York: Haworth Press.

Stanard & Associates, Inc. (1991). *The National Police Officer Selection Test (POST).* Chicago, IL: Author.

Stone, A.V. (1995). Law enforcement psychological fitness for duty: Clinical issues. In M.I. Kurke & E.M. Scrivner (Eds.), *Police psychology into the 21st century,* pp. 109–131. New York: Lawrence Erlbaum.

Super, J.T. (1995). Psychological characteristics of successful SWAT/tactical response team personnel. *Journal of Police and Criminal Psychology, 19* (3), 60–63.

Super, J.T. (2006). A survey of pre-employment psychological evaluation tests and procedures. *Journal of Police and Criminal Psychology, 21* (2), 83–87.

Tellegen, A., Ben-Porath, Y.S., McNulty, J.L., Arbisi, P.A., Graham, J.R., & Kaemmer, B. (2003). *MMPI-2 Restructured Clinical (RC) Scales: Development, validation, and interpretation.* Minneapolis, University of Minnesota Press.

Terris, W. (1985). Altitudinal correlates of employee integrity. *Journal of Police and Criminal Psychology, 1* (1), 60–68.

Weiss, P.A., Hitchcock, J.H., Weiss, W.U., Rostow, C., & Davis, R. (2008). The Personality Assessment Inventory Borderline, Drug, and Alcohol scales as predictors of overall performance in police officers: A series of exploratory analyses. *Policing & Society, 18,* 301–310.

Weiss, W.U. (2008). "Gun violence in the U.K." Paper presented at the 34th annual conference of the Society for Police and Criminal Psychology, October 2008, Walnut Creek, CA.

Weiss, W.U., Davis, R., Rostow, C., & Kinsman, S. (2003). The MMPI-2 L scale as a tool in police selection. *Journal of Police and Criminal Psychology, 18* (1), 57–60.

Weiss, W.U., Rostow, C., Davis, R., & DeCoster-Martin, E. (2004). The Personality Assessment Inventory as a selection device for law enforcement personnel. *Journal of Police and Criminal Psychology, 20* (1), 16–20.

Weiss, W.U., Serafino, G., & Serafino, A. (2000). A study of the interrelationships of several validity scales used in police selection. *Journal of Police and Criminal Psychology, 15* (1), 41–44.

Weiss, W.U., Serafino, G., Serafino, A., Willson, W., & Knoll, S. (1998). Use of the MMPI-2 to predict the employment continuation and performance ratings of recently hired police officers. *Journal of Police and Criminal Psychology, 13,* No. 1, 40–44.

Weiss, W.U., Serafino, G., Serafino, A., Willson, W., Sarsany, J., & Felton, J. (1999). Use of the MMPI-2 and the Inwald Personality Inventory to identify the personality characteristics of dropouts from a state police academy. *Journal of Police and Criminal Psychology, 14,* (2), 38–42.

Weiss, W.U., Yates, D., & Buehler, K., (1995). Occupational satisfaction and competence of police officers as predicted by the Kuder Interest Inventory. *Journal of Police and Criminal Psychology, 10* (4), 53–56.

Weiss, W.U., Zehner, S. N., Davis, R.D., Rostow, C., & DeCoster-Martin, E. (2005). Problematic police performance and the Personality Assessment Inventory. *Journal of Police and Criminal Psychology, 20* (1), 16–21.

Wonderlic, Inc., (2007). *Wonderlic Personnel Test*. Libertyville, IL.

Chapter 13

ISSUES IN THE LAW ENFORCEMENT FITNESS-FOR-DUTY EVALUATION*

CARY D. ROSTOW and ROBERT D. DAVIS

INTRODUCTION

The professional and scientific application of psychological methods and findings to the behavioral problems of law enforcement and public safety occupations may be called police psychology (Rostow & Davis, 2002). As with any explicit application of applied psychology, the basic foundation of the profession must be adapted to new uses by detailed examination of the specific issues inherent in any application. In general terms, the Fitness-for-Duty Evaluation (FFDE) involves an assessment of the psychological ability of incumbent police officers to safely and effectively execute their job functions. It is a subdivision of police psychology which deals with all elements of the interrelationship between law enforcement organizations and psychology.

FFDEs in law enforcement are of particular importance as compared to general psychological fitness assessments because only law enforcement officers have the authority in civil occupations, under certain circumstances, to take life and liberty in the normal course of their duties (Rostow, Davis, Levy, & Brecknock, 2001). The purpose of the following chapter is to expand the researchers' and the practitioners' understanding of the current FFDE as a unique element of police psychology practice and to clarify the issues that distinguish this methodology from other forms of psychometric or professional service. The chapter will also reflect on the more recent forensic forces that have impacted the FFDE methodology.

---

*Author Note: Special thanks to Dr. Amy L. Copeland of LSU for her assistance with this chapter.

Clinical, Forensic and Fitness-for-Duty Evaluations

All professions ultimately are compelled to develop methods or procedures that are standardized for specific purposes with specific populations to answer specific questions. For example, medical blood panels generally include standard collection and testing methods for specific purposes and such procedures result in an established analysis that yields well-understood biochemical values with which almost all physicians are familiar (Starr, 2002). In a like manner, the form (if not content) of a psychology evaluation in the twenty-first century should demonstrate some degree of uniformity in goals and referents to other psychological evaluations when the purposes of the assessments are equivalent. The differential tools and methods among evaluation subtypes within recognized specialties (e.g., neuropsychology, legal competency assessments, etc.) are usually informed by a number of factors, such as the development of distinctive instrumentation, as well as the legal issues, contexts and intended purposes to which the evaluation may be applied (Reisman, 1991). Unfortunately, it is common for research and practicing psychologists to inadequately appraise the statistical, psychometric and forensic nature of evaluations which they undertake, resulting in the inappropriate application of psychological methods and instrument for the question at hand (Grove & Meehl, 1996).

Three Types of Psychological Evaluations

Rostow & Davis (2004) have proposed that the confusion and misapplications of psychological evaluations may be effectively reduced if there were clear definitions of the nature and purpose of various types of evaluations as they apply to specific settings (see Table 1 at end of chapter). The authors recommended that the **Clinical Psychology Evaluation** be considered a psychometric and interview-based psychological procedure conducted with a person who has voluntarily submitted for (or whose legal guardian has requested) examination, often at direct or indirect cost, because of some suspected mental, emotional or medical difficulty. A confidential, patient-doctor relationship is usually established as part of this process and it is generally understood that the client controls the use and disposition of the evaluation (as per HIPAA, P.L. 104-191). The evaluation provider cannot release any part of a report or transmit identifying information without the explicit permission of the client under ordinary circumstances. The basic goal of the evaluation is usually to diagnose a pathology or conditions with respect to some pre-established system (such as the *DSM-IV*), and offer possible therapy recommendations for treatable conditions. The patient may self-refer for the evaluation, or be referred by a physician (e.g., neurologist) or by a significant other (e.g., family member). Treatment may begin simultaneously with or successively to the evaluation and the evaluator may be the treatment provider. Clinical evaluation reports often extensive and contain personal, hypothetical and heuristic information for use by a therapist in reflection upon the patient's life issues, in addition to the central diagnostic issue of the referral.

Rostow & Davis (2004) have also proposed that the **Forensic Psychological Evaluation** (sometimes called Independent Medical Evaluation or IME) may be considered a psychometric and interview-based psychological procedure conducted with a person who may or may not have voluntarily submitted for examination. The examinee is usually referred for evaluation as part of the process of making some claim of injury (as in a tort case) or disability in an administrative case (Worker Compensation) or may be part of a criminal, civil or family court procedure regarding a claim of diminished capacity or the well-being of some party (e.g., child protection, insanity defense or interdiction due to mental incapacity). A confidential, patient-doctor relationship is usually absent and the referring party (e.g., attorney, court, trustee, compensation or administrator) pays for and controls the disposition of the report. The forensic evaluation examiner can, under the auspices of a legal authority, release the report or transmit information to specified parties without explicit permission from the examinee in most cases. The goal of the evaluation, in addition to diagnosing problems or conditions, may also include the establishment of causation of the reported impairment, determine the degree of impairment and consideration possible therapy modalities for treatable conditions. Treatment does not usually begin simultaneously with the evaluation, and the evaluator frequently does not provide treatment services to the patient. Reports of a forensic nature are often extensive and contain personal, hypothetical and heuristic information for reflection upon issues that may not be the central issue of the claimed injury or disability, such as pre-existing conditions, employment restrictions and secondary gain.

Finally, Rostow & Davis (2004) described the **Fitness-for-Duty Evaluation (FFDE)** as a psychometric and interview-based psychological procedure conducted with a person who usually does not request examination. The referring party is usually the employer who has sound reason to believe the employee suffers a mental or emotional difficulty that represents a safety risk or that the employee is unable to perform essential duties of the job because of mental illness or defect. FFDEs should be conducted at no cost to the employee as part of the arrangement by which there is no Duty to Treat or Duty to Care. A confidential, patient-doctor relationship should be absent and it is generally understood that the referring source controls the use and disposition of the report, although specific employee rights may be retained in law or by agreement (e.g., in union contract or civil service regulations). The provider must be able to release the report or transmit information to the employer once proper prior consent is obtained within the context of the use and purpose of the evaluation. The primary goal of the evaluation is neither to diagnose problems, nor to convey medical or technical findings to the employer (e.g., proposed personality dynamics, psychological jargon, etc.), but it is to determine the degree to which the employee presents a danger in the workplace or the likelihood that he/she unable to perform essential job duties because of mental or emotional factors. FFDE reports are typically focused on the job-related issue that motivated the referral and contain minimal unneeded personal information so as to maintain the privacy and dignity of the employee. In that regard, FFDEs should avoid speculative or tangential reports, such as unconfirmed stories of infantile sexual abuse, since the role such information may play is disconnected with or remote from the reason for referral.

Definition of the Law Enforcement Psychological Fitness-for-Duty Evaluation

As regards law enforcement work, a Fitness-for-Duty Evaluation (FFDE) has been defined as by Rostow & Davis (2004) as: "A specialized inquiry conducted under the authority of a police or security agency by a specifically qualified mental health professional in response to complaints of an officer's reported inability to perform official duties in a safe and effective manner because of impaired or deviant behavior" (p. 56). More recently, Rostow (2007) had proposed the following definition:

> A FFDE is a specialized inquiry conducted by a specifically qualified mental health professional that is informed by applicable civil rights and employment law in response to credible reports of an employee's inability to perform job related duties in a safe and/or necessary and sufficient manner because of what may reasonably be thought to be the burden of a medical or mental illness or defect by an Law Enforcement Executive or official of comparable authority and experience.

It is worth noting that the term Fitness-for-Duty Evaluation may also be used in nonlaw enforcement contexts, such as for the civilian assessments of violence or danger potential, such as a workplace threat (Turner & Gelles, 2003). The term is also used regarding the medical (non-psychological) ability of a employees to perform physical work, such as the ability of a person to lift heavy loads following back surgery (Cox, Edwards & Palmer, 2000).

Research in Police Psychology

In the past, few psychological guidelines existed for hiring or examining police officers (Blau, 1994). Psychologists made the first attempts at involvement in police matters when Lewis Terman published a study regarding measures of general intelligence (and something called "moral integrity") in successful police officers (Terman, 1917). For many reasons, including poorly developed and occasionally inappropriate psychometric and examination methods, little usefulness was seen by some authors for most early police psychology testing procedures (Kurke & Scrivner, 1995).

However, in recent years an extensive research literature has developed regarding the use of assessment instruments in police psychology. Numerous studies have demonstrated the efficacy of a variety of different psychological tests for applications in police psychology. A large number of these studies are referenced in the appropriate chapters in the present volume which deal with specific tests. While an understanding of this research literature and test use is important in conducting law enforcement FFDEs using personality assessment instruments, other factors (primarily legal ones) also come into play. The remainder of this chapter discusses many of those issues, and how they affect relevant psychological testing in these evaluations.

The ADA and Employment Law

The entire field of employment evaluations underwent a revolution with the passage of the Americans with Disabilities Act of 1990 (ADA). This federal law offered civil rights protections to individuals with disabilities and prohibited discrimination against people with disabilities in employment (Title I), which EEOC is responsible for enforcing. The ADA prohibited inequity in all employment practices, including job application procedures, hiring, firing, advancement, compensation, training, and conditions and privileges of employment for those persons with qualified disabilities. It applied to all employment-related activities. Amendments to the Americans with Disabilities Act (ADA) signed into law on September 25, 2008 (P.L. 110-325), extending the definitions of who is covered by the law's civil rights protections and revising the definition of "disability" to more broadly encompass impairments that substantially limit a major life activity. The changes also expanded coverage of impairments that are episodic or in remission that substantially limit a major life activity when active, such as epilepsy or post traumatic stress disorder. The amendments took effect January 1, 2009.

The ADA prohibited employment discrimination against applicants and employees who are "qualified individuals with disabilities." An individual is considered to have a disability "if s/he has a physical or mental impairment that substantially limits one or more major life activities or has a record of such impairment." The ADA applies to persons who have impairments that substantially limit major life activities such as seeing, hearing, speaking, walking, breathing, performing manual tasks, learning, caring for oneself and working (Americans with Disabilities Act of 1990) .

An ADA qualified individual with a proven disability is one who meets legitimate skill, experience, education, or other requirements of an employment position that s/he holds or seeks, and who can perform the "essential functions" of the position with or without reasonable accommodation. Requiring the ability to perform essential functions assures that an individual with a disability will not be considered unqualified simply because of inability to perform marginal or incidental job functions, such as expecting a police dispatcher to lift heavy weights.

ADA and Examinations

If an individual is unfit because a psychological examination revealed a disability, a change in employment status (a determination of unfitness and subsequent actions) must be job-related and consistent with either *direct threat* or *business necessity*, meaning that the impairment or disability makes the practical performance of the job unattainable. With an incumbent employee, a medical (or psychological) examination or inquiry must be job-related and the employers may conduct employee medical examinations only where there is evidence of job performance or safety problems that is reasonable thought to be of abnormal or pathological origin. For example, evidence that a police officer had suffered a panic attack in his patrol car and was unable to respond to a radio call is a reason to conduct a Fitness-for-Duty Examination, but the simple fact that an officer accepted a bribe without evidence of illness is not a reason for a FFDE.

The Americans with Disabilities Act (ADA) allows employers to refuse to hire or retain a disabled person only where that person poses a direct threat to the health or safety of others in the workplace. *Direct threat* means a significant risk to the health or safety of the employee or others that cannot be eliminated by reasonable accommodation (42 U.S.C. §12113). Therefore, an employee who poses a direct threat is not a qualified individual with a disability (*Daugherty v. City of El Paso*, 1995). The determination that an individual poses a direct threat must be based on an *individualized assessment* of the individual's present ability to safely perform the essential functions of the job.

Business Necessity means that the employee must be able to perform the essential tasks that comprise a job or employment position. For example, an employer can refuse to hire a disabled person who suffers from uncontrol-lable seizures for a position that requires flying aircraft. In law enforcement work, the ability to operate vehicles, devices (such as weapons) and to engage in physical confrontations may be critical business necessities, where the officer's duties involve such work. The inability to perform such func-tions may be described as failing to meet the business necessity of the job in the workplace.

Personality Disorders under ADA

Personality or social interaction problems are not usually covered under ADA (in contrast with "illness"), implying that simply being a difficult or unpleasant person alone is not a qualified disability. Indeed, in *Duncan v. Wis. of Dept. Health* (1999) a three judge Federal appellate panel ruled that "per-sonality disorder" is not covered by the ADA, while mental illness is cov-ered. Understanding the complexities of ADA regarding behavioral prob-lems is an important dual function of the attorney and the FFDE provider.

In *Watson v. Miami Beach* (1999) a police commander reported that an offi-cer was unusually offensive and antagonistic toward coworkers and supervi-sors. In a three-year period, there were eleven grievances by or against this officer. When he was relieved of duty pending a Fitness-for-Duty Evaluation, he brought suit under the ADA. The appeals court rejected the claim of being psychologically disabled because the department had shown he had "serious personality conflicts," a problem not covered by ADA. The panel ruled that these characterizations "merely show he had serious personality conflicts" with coworkers and "such conflicts do not rise to the level of a mental impairment under the ADA." Further, the rules of the department had demonstrated a business necessity to remove him and not to wait until "perceived threat became real or questionable behavior resulted in injuries."

In *Garner v. Gwinnet Co.* (1999), a police officer was reportedly "tired, angry, (and) hated work," had suicidal thoughts and a "vivid fantasy . . . of killing his supervisor." Three independent FFD examiners found that he was unfit for law enforcement work. He was demoted to the position of animal control officer. When he demanded reinstatement, he was fired. He sued the chief and agency claiming he was terminated in violation of the ADA, both because his superiors perceived him ("regarded as" standard) as suffering from a mental illness, and in retaliation for taking FMLA leave. He also claimed that the horror of seeing animals euthanized caused him to suffer psychological injury. The court ruled:

> Plaintiff denies that he actually suffered from an impairment at the time of the
> adverse employment decision. However, he contends that defendants regard-

ed him as having an impairment–namely, emotional or stress-induced problems preventing him from safely handling a gun and engaging in confrontations with citizens.

The Court found that plaintiff's perceived impairment did not substantially
limit any major life activity and that the impairment does not constitute a
"disability" within the meaning of the ADA. The department had competent
medical evidence that Garner posed a threat to himself and to others. The
ADA does not require departments to ignore this information, rely on the
conflicting medical opinions of officer's therapists, and take the risk that officer would injure his coworkers or a member of the public once reinstated.

    A youth counselor in *Duncan v. Wis. Dept. of Health* (1999) was referred for
a FFDE following a period of disagreeable and explosive incidents involving
his loss of personal temper control. An examining psychiatrist opined that
the employee suffered episodic temper outbursts that imposed "serious limitation" on his ability to serve in this occupation. The counselor claimed that
the complaints about his behavior to be "profoundly offensive" and he,
therefore, resisted by refusing rehabilitation and avoiding therapy sessions
that the examiner had recommended. After his termination, he sued under
the ADA, but a three-judge appellate panel noted that a personality disorder
does not affect a major life activity, especially if the "disability" is relevant
only to a specific job.

Replacing Pathology with Liability Risk

    The Matrix-Predictive Uniform Law Enforcement Selection Evaluation
Inventory (M-PULSE), a law enforcement liability-based selection instrument (Davis & Rostow, 2002; Rostow & Davis, 2006b, Githua, Leark, &
Skidmore, 2007; Leark, Catanese, Topchyan, & Githua, 2008), has been
investigated as a means to more fully understand the role of nonpathology
factors in police FFDEs. Rostow, Davis and Hill (2009, in press) administered the M-PULSE, MMPI-2 and the PAI, to 71 serving law enforcement
officers who had been referred by their departments because of some form
of misconduct that was believed to originate with mental impairment.
Officers were then found to be fit (mentally impaired in connect with police
misconduct) or unfit (not mentally impaired) based on the MMPI-2, PAI and
interview/historical information. The most common reasons for referral
were excessive force, racial or sexual misconduct, substance abuse and
apparent depression. Reasons for referral were categorized as being either
emotional in nature (such as depressive disorder) or concerning misconduct
on the part of the officer (such as the use of excessive force). One-way

ANOVAs performed on the M-PULSE™ data yielded significant group differences be- tween the FFDE groups determined to be either fit (n=43) or unfit (n=27) for duty on the following scales: test attitude, negative self-perception, negative emotions, negative actions, negative attitudes, alienated attitudes, risk-taking, competiveness, motor vehicle accidents, unprofessional conduct, social incompetence, lack of team work, reckless impulsivity, lack of integrity/ ethics, and emotional instability/stress intolerance. For officers who were referred for misconduct, the following M-PULSE™ scales and subscales yielded significant Mann-Whitney U test group differences between officers who were found to be fit (n=17) or unfit for duty (n=9): negative self-perceptions negative emotions negative actions inappropriate attitudes about use of force risk taking social incompetence reckless impulsivity emotional instability/stress intolerance), and poor decision making and judgment. For officers who were referred for reasons of an emotional nature, the following M-PULSE™ scales and subscales yielded significant group differences between officers who were found to be fit (n=28) or unfit for duty (n=18): test attitude, negative self-perception, negative emotions, alienated attitudes, competitiveness, motor vehicle accidents, unprofessional conduct, lack of team work and emotional instability/stress intolerance.

The use of tests specifically developed of nonpathological vocational law enforcement instruments, especially pertaining to relevant liability outcomes, may address both scientific and forensic problems in future professional assessments. The focus of research over the last half century has continued to push the frontiers of psychometric variables as an indication of better vs. worse officer conduct using clinical indicators (Rostow & Davis, 2006a). The need to develop valid and reliable indicators of officer behavior (as compared to general population indicators) remains a problem and recent research has indicated that attempts to forecast officer conduct which are limited exclusively to standard, pathological-oriented psychometric findings may create difficulties and may sometime not signify anything in police populations.

Some authors have attempted to renorm standard clinical instruments for vocational use with law enforcement populations. That is, a psychometric instrument with original test items meant to measure pathology is administered to a sub-population of interest, such as police officers, and the new distribution of responses may be used to create an altered raw score to standard score relationship that be me differ from the original clinical instrument norms. The underlying rationale appears to be that item response distributions may be systematically different for a vocational sub-population than it had been for the original population and the meaning of a given raw score would, therefore, be interpreted differently. Thus, a raw score elevation on the MMPI-2 Pd scale, for example, may be a pathological indicator in the general population, but that same raw score may be within the average range for a cohort of police officers (who may be suspicious for professional reasons), and, therefore, not indicative of dysfunction or impaired conduct. Renormed instruments are meaningful only if validity studies can confirm that clinical elevations of officers' examination outcomes are or are not predictive of later misconduct that is dangerous or that results in the officer becoming dysfunctional in his or her occupations role. For this reason, the use of renormed testing (such as The Minnesota Report™: Revised Personnel System, 3rd Edition, and the PAI® Law Enforcement, Corrections, and Public Safety Selection Report™ Module for the PAI-SP™), while a step in the correct direction, is of limited use without subsequent concurrent, construct and/or predictive validity studies regarding the meaningfulness of the new variable outcomes.

The meaningfulness issue is well presented in *Standards for Educational and Psychological Testing* (1999):

> Tests are commonly administered in the expectation that some benefit will be realized from the intended use of the scores. A few of the many possible benefits are selection of efficacious treatments for therapy, placement of workers in suitable jobs, prevention of unqualified individuals from entering a profession, or improvement of classroom instructional practices. A fundamental purpose of validation is to indicate whether these specific benefits are likely to be realized. Thus, in the case of a test used in placement decision, the validation would be informed by evidence that alternative placements, in fact, are differentially beneficial to the persons and the institution. In the case of employment testing, if a test publisher claims that use of the test will result in reduced employee training costs, improved workforce efficiency, or some other benefit, then the validation would be informed by evidence in support of that claim (pp. 16–17).

A great deal of work needs to be performed before test variables alone can be considered reliable and valid indicators of fitness for duty in employment settings. Testing that focuses on pathology must play a part in FFDEs of the future, but the specific manner in which they are applied to the fitness question will require study and verification.

CONCLUSION

It is clear that FFDEs are shaped and constrained by factors that are very different from the other major forms of psychological assessment, the clinical and the forensic evaluations, especially since the passage of the ADA.

FFDE professional considerations that flow from civil rights, labor and administrative legal factors guide FFDEs to a far greater degree than is the case for other forms of evaluation or such factors may be applied in a different manner for FFDEs than other evaluations. Research and practice methods that depend upon "clinical analysis" (predictions and generalizations from interview and psychometric findings in non-occupational settings) and extrapolations from the personality constructs and theory are unlikely to produce strong predictive validity based findings. In any case, even if such traditional methods were shown to be valid for general psychometric application, the passage and strengthening of the ADA has made the use of conclusions which are not based upon clear and evident relationships to job-related findings impermissible as a matter of law. The authors recommend that future research and practice refocus FFDEs efforts away from considerations of traits that "good" or "bad" officers are thought to possess, and toward liability and risk management variables that are defendable in the current atmosphere of civil right and employment law. Indifference to forensic changes by the psychological community may render FFDE research and practice inapplicable when challenged and may expose the FFDE provider and his/her client (the law enforcement employer) to legal sanctions and unanticipated expense.

Such a shift is appropriate when consideration is given to the powerful issues of both certifying an unfit officer to remain in a position of power as well as the damage to individual officers and departments that may occur if an officer is compelled to suffer the dislocation and economic harm of an improperly conducted FFDE. Superimposed upon scientific and professional standards of evidence, the specialized forensic environment has created a need for a distinctive approach to FFDEs that should inform future applications of the psychological method of assessment.

The following are recommendations in the refocusing of FFDE research and practice in the coming era:

1. Since the fundamental goal of a FFDE is not to diagnose or treat illness, but to identify liability risk, the use of tools for the identification of pathology should be used only when the outcome of the instrument or method is clearly connected to Direct Threat and Business Necessity as those concepts evolve within the ADA. This connection should not be based on theoretical speculation or extrapolation from clinical observations, but should derive from relevant and replicable research. In a related manner, diagnostic instruments that are uninformed by the ADA should be avoided as the basis for decision when engaging in vocational assessments because of the substantial risk of violating the officer's rights when the officer suffers an illness that is not connected

with Direct Threat and Business Necessity. It is especially important that there be significant evidence to support the validity of any medical or psychological test or method that was originally designed for diagnostic or clinical uses, even if they are renormed for vocational purposes because of the danger of adverse impact upon persons with mental pathologies who are otherwise entitled to protection under the ADA (*Krarraker v. Rent-a-Center, Inc.* 7th Circuit, June 14, 2005, No. 04-2881).

2. Once an instrument or method is shown to be of potential value in a law enforcement FFDE evaluation, a program of construct and predictive validation should be undertaken to verify its utility in actual law enforcement application. Research findings that are presented in isolation (small *N*, no cross validation, small subsumed variance in the yielded relationships, etc.) can be misleading and before such findings are employed in actual practice, the findings must be based upon a significant body of evidence, as noted in the *Standards for Educational and Psychological Testing* (1999).

3. It is self-evident that there are a broad range of impairments to which officers may be vulnerable. Research efforts should be extended into the area of the categorization and identification of such impairments as relates to job performance so that a more precise determination of FFD can be achieved in fairness to the officer and to his department. It is likely that there is no unitary concept of unfitness, as there is no such concept for mental illness that is distinct for the specifications of the pathological condition or state in question.

4. An officer may be unsuited for police work due to cultural, personality, cognitive and other reasons, without that officer being different from others in terms of pathology. Most available data appears to indicate that pathology is far from the only cause of improper and impermissible office conduct. In the NIJ grant study (Tolson, Davis & Rostow, 2005), excessive force findings for officers who were previously psychologically examined were unrelated to Bizarre Mental States, suggesting that classical illness parameters were not good indicators of later misconduct. A great deal of work lies ahead of the police psychology profession in making distinctions between those who are unsuitable, and presumable not entitled the ADA protection, and those who are ill and are so entitled.

In all science, static assumptions tend to lead to moribund and cryptic procedural methods that reduce the utility and defensibility of the eventual work product. Police psychology, especially regarding FFDE methodologies, is of vital importance because of the real harm to society, the law enforcement agency, and the impaired officer that can result from the behavior of individuals whose mental conditions that are incompatible with the demands of police work. An effective and fair science underpinning FFDEs is unlikely to emerge in a mature state from typical clinical or forensic practices. Personality or psychopathological variables may or may not prove useful as the field moves forward. Only focused police psychology research is likely to provide meaningful answers in the future.

Table 1
SIMPLIFIED COMPARISON OF CLINICAL, FORENSIC AND
PSYCHOLOGICAL FITNESS-FOR-DUTY EVALUATIONS (MATRIX, INC.)

	Clinical Eval	*Forensic Eval*	*FFD Evaluation*
Reason	Treatment	Forensic Service	Safety/Work 1
Confidential	Yes	Limited	Limited
Cost to Patient 2	Yes	Not Usually	No
Requests service	Patient	Attorney/Court/WC	Employer
Control of Evaluation	Patient	Attorney/Court/WC	Employer 3
Diagnosis	Yes	Yes	No 4
Rx Plan	Yes	Possibly	No 5
Evaluator Therapy	Yes	Possibly 6	No 7
Self-Referral	Yes	Yes	No 8
Purpose	Diagnose	Guidance	Occupation
Examinee Feedback	Yes	Possibly	Not Usually 9
Duty to Care 10	Yes	Unlikely	No
Detail Report	Yes	Yes	No

1. FFDE evaluations only are meaningful within the context of employment law. The employer has reason to believe that the employee is a Direct Threat to others or is unable to do the fundamental tasks of his/ her job position (Business Necessity).
2. Although clinical evaluations may be produced at government expense, more typically they are paid for by the patient or their insurance coverage or family members' resources.
3. The employer requests the evaluation based on a reasonable, documented suspicion of impairment and the report is delivered to the employer.
4. Diagnosis is defined as the process of determining the nature and cause of a disease or injury through evaluation of patient history, examination, and review of laboratory data. The employer (as compared with a treatment provider) is not entitled to such information under the ADA because it may be misunderstood and may create a bias against the impaired employee.
5. While it is advisable to indicate that an unfit employee may benefit from some generic forms of treatment (medication management, cognitive therapy, substance abuse treatment, etc.), it is strongly recommended that the evaluator avoid specifying a particular provider or program in exclusion of others.
6. In Worker Compensation systems, the evaluator may be able to offer clinical services.

7. Treatment services offered by the evaluator may seem to be a conflict of interest in which the examiner/treater may benefit financially by finding an employee to be unfit.
8. There are conflict of interest in accepting commissions to perform FFDEs directly from an officer.
9. Any implication of a doctor-patient relationship should be avoided to protect the integrity of the FFDE process.
10. Duty to Care involves a legal obligation imposed requiring that they adhere to a reasonable standard of care while performing professional services and a breach is part of a claim of negligence.

REFERENCES

American Educational Research Association, American Psychological Association, & National Council on Measurement in Education. (1999). *Standards for educational and psychological testing.* Washington, D.C.: American Educational Research Association.

Americans with Disabilities Act of 1990 (1991). Pub. L. No. 101-336, § 2, 104 Stat. 328.

Blau, T.H. (1994). *Psychological services for law enforcement.* New York: John Wiley and Sons, Inc.

Cox, R., Edwards, F., & Palmer, K. (2000). *Fitness for Work,* 3rd Edition. USA: The Medical Aspects, Oxford University Press.

Daugherty v. City of El Paso, 56 F.3d 695, 4 A.D. Cases 993, 11 A.D.D. 229 (5th Cir.(Tex.) Jul 03, 1995) (NO. 94-50212), Rehearing Denied (Aug 08, 1995), Certiorari Denied, 516 U.S. 1172, 116 S.Ct. 1263, 134 L.Ed.2d 211, (U.S. Mar 18, 1996) (NO. 95-1083)

Davis, R.D., Rostow, C.D., Pinkston, J.B. and Cowick, L.H. (1999). An investigation into the usefulness of the MMPI and MMPI-2 in municipal and state police candidate selection, *Journal of Police and Criminal Psychology, 14,* 100–106.

Davis, R.D. and Rostow, C.D. (2002). M-PULSE©: The Uniform Law Enforcement Selection Evaluation. *The Forensic Examiner, 11,* 19–24.

Decoster-Martin, E., Weiss, W.U., Davis, R.D., & Rostow, C.D. (2004). Compulsive traits and police officer performance. *Journal of Police and Criminal Psychology, 19,* 64–71.

Duncan v. Wis. Dept. of Health #97-2198, 166 F.3d 930 (7th Cir., 1999), 1999 U.S. App. Lexis 1444

Garner v. Gwinnet Co., 1999 U.S. Dist. Lexis 6370 (N.D. Ga.).

Gough, H.G. (1996). *California Psychological Inventory Manual.* Palo Alto, CA: Consulting Psychologists Press.

Graham, J.R. (2000). *MMPI-2 Assessing Personality and Psychopathology,* 3rd Edition. New York, NY: Oxford University Press, Inc.

Githua, O., Leark, R.A. & Skidmore, S. (2007). "Predictive Ability of the M-PULSE to Detect Fitness-for-Duty Decisions." Paper presented at the 3rd International Congress of Psychology and Law, Adelaide, Australia.

Grove, W.M., & Meehl, P.E. (1996). Comparative efficiency of informal (subjective, impressionistic) and formal (mechanical, algorithmic) prediction procedures: The clinical-statistical controversy. *Psychology, Public Policy, and Law, 2*, 293–323.

Herndon, J. (1998). "Correlates of MMPI-2 L scale: Elevations in an LEO selection test battery." Paper presented at the 27th annual meeting of the Society for Police and Criminal Psychology, Portland, OR.

Krarraker v. Rent-a-Center, Inc. 7th Circuit, June 14, 2005, No. 04-2881).

Kurke, M.I. & Scrivner, E.M. (1995). *Police psychology into the 21st century.* Hillsdale, NJ: Lawrence Erlbaum.

Leark, R.A., Catanese, S., Topchyan, A., & Githua, O. (2008). "Research on the M-PULSE Inventory." Paper presented at the Society for Police and Criminal Psychology Annual Conference. Walnut Grove, CA.

Reisman, J.M. (1991). *A history of clinical psychology (Series in Death Education, Aging, and Health Care,* 2nd Edition). New York, NY: Taylor & Francis.

Rostow, C.D. & Davis, R.D. (2002). Psychological screening. *Law and Order, 50,* 100–106.

Rostow, C.D. & Davis, R.D. (2004). *A handbook for psychological fitness-for-duty evaluations in law enforcement.* Binghamton, NY: Haworth Press, Inc.

Rostow, C.D., Davis, R.D., Levy, J.P., & Brecknock, S. (2001). Civil liability and psychological services in law enforcement administration. *The Police Chief, 68,* 36–43.

Rostow, C.D. & Davis, R.D. (2002). Psychological fitness-for-duty evaluations in law enforcement. *The Police Chief, 69,* 58–66.

Rostow, C.D. & Davis, R.D. (2006a). Psychological Police Officer Selection Part I: History and Forensic Implications. *Law Enforcement Executive Forum, 6,* 27–31.

Rostow, C.D. & Davis, R.D. (2006b). Psychological Police Officer Selection Part II: The M-PULSE© Methodology and Inventory. *Law Enforcement Executive Forum 6,* 32–38.

Rostow, C.D. (2007). "The Matrix-Psychological Uniform Law Enforcement Selection and Fitness-for-Duty Evaluation." Paper presented at Alliant International University, Forensic Seminar, Fresno, CA.

Rostow, C.D., Davis, R.D., & Hill, B. (in press). Reasons for referral and outcomes for law enforcement officers in fitness-for-duty evaluations. *Journal of Police and Criminal Psychology.*

Starr, D. (2002). *Blood: An epic history of medicine and commerce.* New York, NY: Alfred Knopf, Inc.

Terman, L. & Otis, A. (1917). A trial of mental and pedagogical tests in a civil service examination for policemen and firemen. *Journal of Applied Psychology, 1,* 17–29.

The President's Commission on Law Enforcement and Administration of Justice. (1973). *Task force report: The police.* Washington, D.C: U.S. Government Printing Office.

Tolson, I.A., Davis, R.D. & Rostow, C.D. (2005). Grant No. 02-523702, National Institute of Justice, Office of Justice Programs, U.S. Department of Justice.

Turner, J. & Gelles, M. (2003). *Threat assessment: A risk management approach,* Routledge, 1st Edition, Binghamton, NY: Haworth Press, Inc.

Watson v. City of Miami Beach, 177 F.3d 932(11th Cir., 1999) (98-4163), 1999 U.S. App.

Lexis

Weiss, W.U., Rostow, C.D., Davis, R.D., & Decoster-Martin, E. (2004). The Personality Assessment Inventory as a selection device for law enforcement personnel. *Journal of Police and Criminal Psychology, 19*, 23–29.

Weiss, W.U., Buehler, K., & Yates, D. (1995). The Psychopathic Deviate scale of the MMPI in police selection. *Journal of Police and Criminal Psychology, 10*, 57–60.

Weiss, W.U., Davis, R.D., Rostow, C.D., Serafino, G., Serafino, A., Willson, W., & Knoll, S. (1998). Use of the MMPI-2 to predict the employment continuation and performance ratings of recently hired police officers. *Journal of Police and Criminal Psychology, 13*, 40–44.

Weiss, W.U., Davis, R.D., Rostow, C., & Kinsman, S. (2003). The MMPI-2 L scale as a tool in police selection. *Journal of Police and Criminal Psychology, 18*, 57–60.

Chapter 14

CONDITIONAL SECOND OPINION PSYCHOLOGICAL EVALUATION OF LAW ENFORCEMENT CANDIDATES

ALI KHADIVI

Prospective law enforcement candidates undergo a psychological assessment that includes a face-to-face clinical examination and the administration of various self-report psychological tests. The majority of law enforcement agencies in the United States use the psychological assessment as part of their pre-employment evaluation (Delprino & Bahn, 1988; Weiss, Davis, Rostow & Kinsman, 2003). The candidates who are deemed psychologically unsuitable for law enforcement employment are given a chance to appeal the outcome of their evaluation. As part of this appeal process, a law enforcement candidate (LEC) must undergo a *conditional second opinion psychological evaluation.* Law enforcement agencies handle this appeal processes differently. Some law enforcement agencies conduct the second opinion evaluation internally, using their own consultants. More often than not, however, the LEC is given the responsibility of finding an outside psychologist to conduct the evaluation. The objective of this chapter is to critically discuss the conditional second opinion psychological evaluation of LECs by outside clinicians. Most of the literature on the use of psychological assessment in law enforcement agencies focuses either on the pre-employment screening of prospective candidates, or on the fitness-for-duty examination of already employed law enforcement agents (Blau, 1994; Borum, Super & Rand, 2003; Johnson, 1984; Ostrov, 1995; Stone, 2000). Although there are many similarities between the assessment methods used for pre-employment screening fitness-for-duty examinations, and second opinion evaluations, there are also significant differences. The conditional second opinion psychological evaluation presents a unique set of challenges to the evaluation processes. This chapter discusses the nature of these examinations, the assessment process-

333

es, and the unique psychological and ethical issues to be considered in the conditional second opinion evaluation of LECs.

Processes of Pre-employment Psychological Screening of LECs

The use of psychological assessment by law enforcement agencies has increased from 52 percent in 1988 to 91 percent in 2003 (Cochrane, Tett & Vandecreek, 2003). Despite this increase, the application of psychological assessment is variable, with some law enforcement agencies using more sophisticated methodology than others (Cochrane et al., 2003). A LEC can be deemed psychologically unfit through the process of a pre-employment screening evaluation on the basis of psychological symptoms or personality characteristics that are incompatible with law enforcement work. To make this decision, psychologists often seek out converging clinical evaluation data to form their opinion. Among the challenges involved in the pre-employment psychological evaluation is the fact that there are no clear criteria for disqualification. Aside from obvious disqualifiers such as the presence of a major AXIS I psychiatric disorder, recent or current substance use, and a history of aggressive behavior, no specific criteria are outlined. As a result, competent examining psychologists may disagree with each others' findings and conclusions.

Evaluating psychologists are expected to understand the characteristics that are required for effective functioning as a law enforcement agent, and then to apply their assessment skills to identify any psychological deficits, symptoms, or personality features that interfere with the LEC functioning (Borum et al., 2003; Super, 1997). Trompetter (1998) has described eighteen psychological characteristics that are necessary for effective functioning as a law enforcement officer. They include anger management, stress tolerance, acceptance of criticism, impulse control, positive attitude, assertiveness, persuasiveness, integrity, reliability, achievement motivation, conformance to rules/regulations, adaptivity, vigilance, interpersonal sensitivity, social concern, teamwork, practical intelligence/decisions making ability, and objectivity/tolerance.

Psychologists are capable of determining the negative impact of psychological symptoms and maladaptive personality traits on LEC's ability to function effectively. They may, however, have a different threshold for disqualifying LECs. For example, one psychologist might view a history of two speeding tickets as reflection of poor judgment and impulsivity, whereas another might argue that the traffic violation occurred few years ago, not giving as much weight to it as an indicator of impaired judgment.

Processes of Referral for Conditional Second Opinion Evaluation of LEC

As part of the appeal process, a LEC who is deemed not psychologically qualified makes a formal request to appeal the law enforcement department decision. The LEC is then asked to obtain a second psychological evaluation by a qualified psychologist. Most law enforcement agencies have specific criteria for the psychologist who will be conducting the second opinion examination. For example, they may require several years of clinical experience or other qualifications to conduct the examination. The LEC will then inform the law enforcement department, in writing, of the name and address of the chosen examiner. The LEC will sign the consent to release his or her psychological evaluation results to the second opinion-examining psychologist. After accepting the qualifications of the second opinion-examining psychologist, the law enforcement agency directly forwards all the relevant material to him/her. This usually includes the specific reasons for the LEC's disqualification, a copy of the psychological report, and all the tests profiles. Law enforcement agencies require that the second opinion-examining psychologist keep all the material confidential, and not share the report or profiles with the LEC. Upon completion of the second opinion evaluation, the examining psychologist must send a copy of the psychological report and the results of any tests administered. The law enforcement departments expect a plainly written recommendation regarding suitability. Unlike fitness-for-duty examination assessments, in which examining psychologists can offer different levels of suitability (Borum et al., 2003), in the conditional second opinion psychological evaluation the final opinion must indicate whether the LEC is psychologically suitable or not. The law enforcement agencies are under no obligation to accept the second opinion psychologist's recommendation. Some departments may even ask the LEC to see a third consultant for yet another opinion.

The importance of defining the examiner's role, clarifying confidentiality issues and obtaining informed consent has been emphasized in forensic psychological assessment (Greenberg & Shuman, 1997; Heilbrun, Grisso & Goldstein, 2009) and in pre-employment and fitness-for-duty examination of law enforcement (Borum et al., 2003; Flanagan, 1995; Ostrov, 1995). However, there are special considerations and unique challenges involved in this type of evaluation that require further discussion.

Understand the Impact of Psychological Unsuitability on the Law Enforcement Candidate

Since the psychological screening processes of law enforcement almost always takes place after the successful completion of a background check and other requirements, a LEC who is deemed psychologically unsuitable can have strong emotional reactions to this news. Some of the LECs who decide to appeal the law enforcement agency's decision may openly express surprise, disappointment, shock or anger. Others may question the validity of pre-employment psychological screening or of the psychologist's decision-making process. As a result, the examining psychologist who is planning to conduct a second opinion evaluation needs to be sensitive and empathic to the LEC's emotional reactions. It is advisable for the examiner to be extremely transparent regarding the evaluation process. Providing a very detailed, clear, and understandable written informed consent that includes the risks and benefits of participating in the conditional second opinion psychological assessment may help the LEC to make the best decision for him/herself. This can also potentially protect the psychologist from any future ethical complaints or legal action (for an excellent general discussion of these issues see Heilbrun et al., 2009).

Obtain Informed Consent

According to the American Psychological Association's ethical guidelines (2002), all psychologists have an ethical obligation to explain the purpose of any psychological evaluation and to obtain informed consent. The informed consent should be presented to the LEC both verbally and in writing. The written consent must be signed by the LEC. It is advisable to break down the informed consent processes into four, clearly explained components.

Explain the Nature of the Examination

The LEC must be informed that the examining psychologist will review the results of the previous examination, conduct a face-to-face interview, administer psychological tests, and gather collateral information. The examining psychologist must clearly indicate to the LEC that the result of this second opinion evaluation might support the previous evaluator's findings. Furthermore, a LEC should be informed of the possibility that the examination may identify psychological characteristics other than those identified by the first evaluation that could indicate that the LEC not suitable for a law enforcement position.

Clarify Your Role

Since the LEC directly contracts the examining psychologist and pays for the evaluation, he or she may have an expectation that the examining psychologist will advocate for him or her. As a result, the need for role clarification is especially important for psychologists conducting conditional second opinion evaluations. The examining psychologist should clearly explain that even though the LEC is paying for the evaluation, the LEC is not the client. It is best to inform the LEC that the examiner will conduct an objective and independent psychological evaluation, and that neither the LEC nor the law enforcement agency will be advocated for in the evaluation. In short, the examiner will advocate only for his or her evaluation.

Clarify the Limits of Confidentiality

The LEC should be informed that the findings of the evaluation are not confidential. Super (1997) argues that the second opinion psychologist should only offer information that is directly relevant to the LEC's employment suitability. The LEC should also be informed that he has a right to refuse the evaluation and to seek the services of another psychologist any time during the process. However, it should be made clear that the impact of changing the examiner and selecting another psychologist after the examining psychologist becomes the designee evaluator by the law enforcement agency is not known. Furthermore, it is possible that the law enforcement agencies will not look positively on changing the examining psychologist during the course of evaluation. The LEC can choose to change clinicians for the evaluation after the initial session and before signing the informed consent. If the switch is made during this phase, the law enforcement agency is not informed, since the LEC has not yet chosen the examining psychologist.

Obtain Payment Prior to the Start of the Examination

LECs who request a conditional second opinion evaluation are responsible for its payment. Since the purpose of this evaluation is not treatment, the LEC should also be informed that health insurance will not pay for the evaluation. It should be clearly explained to LEC that it is unethical for a psychologist to receive payment contingent on the results of the evaluations (see the Specialty Guidelines for Forensic Psychologists, 1991). To this end, the full payment of the evaluation should be received before the start of the evaluation.

Relevant Legal Issues

Since a law enforcement employment evaluation is a type of forensic assessment, understanding relevant legal issues is essential. What follows are selected legal cases that may be relevant to conducting conditional second opinion evaluations. While a detailed discussion of the issues involved in each of these cases is beyond the scope of this chapter, readers who are involved in conducting second opinion evaluations may wish to become familiar with these cases if they are not already.

McKenna v. Fargo (1978)

Several fire department applicants complained to the Court that the pre-employment screening psychological tests that assess stress tolerance are a violation of their civil rights. The Court denied their claims and made a ruling that screening candidates including who might not be able to handle job-related stress is in the interest of the city. As a result, some violation of candidate privacy is justified.

Bonsignore v. City of New York (1981)

A plaintiff won a settlement arguing that the police department was negligent in not conducting psychological evaluations of police officers.

Nilsson v. City of Mesa (2007)

A police officer candidate who passed all the other requirements failed the psychological evaluation. She filed a lawsuit under Americans with Disabilities Act (1990) and argued that she did not understand the waiver that she signed, waiving her legal rights regarding to background evaluation. The Court ruled in favor of the police department, arguing that with a college education and past work experience with the police department, she was in a position to understand the waiver.

Murray v. County of Nassau (2007)

A LEC who failed to meet the psychological requirement of the police department underwent a second evaluation. After failing the second evaluation, he sued the police department, complaining that they acted arbitrarily. He then underwent a third psychological evaluation by an examiner of his choosing. This examiner found him psychologically suitable for the position. The department then conducted another psychological examination, and again found the LEC to be psychologically unfit. After reviewing all the evidence the Court ruled that the police department did not act arbitrarily and that the decision was factually supported. The case was dismissed.

Assessment

The conditional second opinion psychological evaluations of LEC are more comprehensive than the pre-employment screenings. The evaluation methodology is similar to that used for the fitness-for-duty assessments. While there are no published guidelines for conditional second opinion evaluations of LEC, there are published guidelines for pre-screening and fitness-for-duty examinations. Many aspects of those guidelines are indeed relevant for second opinion evaluations and can be incorporated in these assessment processes. These guidelines were developed by the Police Psychological Services Section of The International Association of Chiefs of Police (IACP, 1998a). The following is the summary of clinically relevant points: validated instruments that measure job-related constructs should be used, test results should be available to the evaluator before screening interviews, only validated written tests are used, psychologist should interpret any computer test that are used, and finally in accordance with the Americans with Disabilities Act guidelines (ADA, 1990) the evaluation must be conducted after a conditional has been offered.

The IACP guidelines for fitness-for-duty evaluation (IACP, 1998b) advocate a multi-method assessment. It includes the following: review the requested background information, conduct a face-to-face clinical interview, conduct a mental status examination, use validated objective psychological tests, obtain a biopsychosocial history, and obtain collateral information. A face-to-face clinical interview should be conducted before a final report is written. A semi-structured, job-related interview format should be always be employed. The interviewer should allow sufficient time to review background and test result verification.

Conduct a Multi-method Comprehensive Assessment

After obtaining written informed consent and receiving all materials from the law enforcement agencies, the assessment can begin. Consistent with the IACP guidelines (1998a), it is essential to conduct a multi-method assessment including record review, clinical interview and mental status exam, collateral information and psychological testing.

Review of Previous Records Including the Test Data

The first task is to conduct a careful review of the psychological report of the law enforcement examiner. The focus should be on the rationale and supporting data for the disqualification of the LEC. The second opinion psychologist should re-interpret all the test profiles. The examining psychologist should identify all the data supporting the LEC disqualification. Then, for each point, the psychologist should attempt to offer an alternative or counter explanation. Like any forensic psychological examination, the examiner does not want to be overly influenced by the previous psychological evaluation of the LEC, nor wants to dismiss it (Heilbrun, Warren & Picarello, 2003).

Conduct a Thorough Clinical Interview and Mental Status over Two or More Sessions

Psychologists cannot solely depend on the history that was obtained as part of the LEC's pre-employment psychological screening. Using a semi-structured format, the examiner's interview should focus initially on obtaining personal, educational, social, vocational, military and medical history. In addition, any history of substance use and any mental health history should be explored. Subsequent areas of inquiry should focus on history of traffic violations, or any past contact with police. History of aggressive behavior as an adult is another area of focus. It is best to conduct several separate interviews of the LEC to observe the behavior and mental status on different occasions. This also affords the examiner time for further inquiry following the administration and scoring of tests, and the communication with collateral contacts. The second part of the interview should focus on detailed inquiry regarding the reasons for disqualification.

Obtain Third Party Collateral Information

In contrast to pre-employment psychological evaluations, the conditional second opinion evaluation should contain collateral information. The psychologist can ask the LEC to provide names of current and former employers, past supervisors, coaches, and/or teachers. After obtaining informed consent, collateral contact can be made by telephone. There is evidence to suggest that telephone collateral contacts are as effective as face-to-face contact (Rohde, Lewinsohn & Seeley, 1997). One major challenge in obtaining third party information is that the collaterals might be reluctant to provide negative information or may not provide accurate information (Heilbrun et al., 2003). One approach to dealing with this is to begin by inquiring about specific factual information. For example, psychologists can ask LEC's past or current employers about promotions, absentee rate, and any probationary or disciplinary action. This information should then be compared with what the LEC provides during the interview.

Administer Another Multiscale Personality Inventory

The type of psychological tests used in the conditional second opinion depends on the reasons for the LEC's disqualification. However, providing a second opinion without using any psychological testing is not advisable. First, the second opinion evaluator must decide whether to readminister the test that was given at the pre-employment screening. In general, it is advisable to readminister if the previous test was invalid or was highly inconsistent with other findings of the examination. Sometimes the LEC reports that during the pre-employment psychological testing his or her level of alertness was compromised due to fatigue. In that case, readministering the test is recommended.

It is advisable to administer either the Minnesota Multiphasic Personality Inventory-2 (MMPI-2; Butcher et al., 2001) or the Personality Assessment Inventory (PAI; Morey, 2007). Both instruments have shown to have potential utilities including predicative validity in evaluating law enforcement evaluations (Brewster & Stoloff, 1999; Weiss, Hitchcock, Weiss, Rostow & Davis, 2008; Weiss, Rostow, Davis, & Decoster-Martin, 2004; Weiss, Serafino, Serafino, Willson, & Knoll, 1998; Weiss, Zehner, Davis, Rostow, & Decoster-Martin, 2005). Both instruments also have law enforcement norms that are essential for this type of evaluation. As a recommended rule, if the LEC was examined using the MMPI-2, administrating the PAI will be helpful, and vice versa.

The second consideration is whether to use instruments that measure normal personality dimensions. Both the California Personality Inventory (CPI, Gough, 1987) and the NEO-Personality Inventory Revised (NEO-PI-R, Costa & McRae, 1992) have been used with LECs.

The third consideration is whether to use the Inwald Personality Inventory (IPI; Inwald, 1992). This instrument measures behaviors that are directly relevant to law enforcement and other high-risk professions. Studies have shown that the IPI is useful in pre-employment screening (Mufson & Mufson, 1998) and has demonstrated predictive validity with regard to job related outcomes (Inwald, 1988; Inwald & Shuman, 1984; Shuman, Inwald & Knatz, 1987). The decision to use these should be made case-by-case, and depends on the reason for the LEC's psychological disqualification.

Communicating the Findings to the Law Enforcement Agency

In communicating the final opinion to the law enforcement agencies it is essential for the examiner to clearly address the specific concerns held by the agency's psychologist regarding the LEC's qualification. If the findings do not support the previous evaluation result, that fact should be clearly communicated, point by point. This is also the case when the second opinion evaluation results are consistent with the pre-employment psychological screening. The following is an illustrative case showing how multiple sources of data were used in the second opinion to address specific disqualification findings of an LEC.

Case Discussion

Mr. B is a 26-year-old, Caucasian, college-educated, single man who lives with his girlfriend. He works full time as an armed guard in a major security company. Mr. B applied to be a law enforcement agent and he passed the entire requirement except for the pre-employment psychological evaluation of the police department (PD). The evaluation found Mr. B to have personality traits that were incompatible with the unique demands and stress of employment as a law enforcement agent. He appealed the department's decision and was asked to obtain another psychological evaluation at his own expense.

The PD's psychologist raised concerns about Mr. B's judgment and anger management. The PD examiner offered three findings from the evaluation as the basis for Mr. B's disqualification: 1) During the background interview Mr. B. indicated that he has had friends that used illegal drugs, at times in his presence. The PD examiner argued that such behavior reflected poor judgment. 2) Mr. B produced an unusual MMPI-2 protocol, charactized by a high elevation on the F p (raw score = 4, T-score of 70), which is a scale that was developed to assess symptom exaggeration and malingering (Arbisi & Ben-Porath, 1998). The PD evaluator correctly stated that the elevation on F p suggested a trend in overreporting, unusual given the context of the evaluation. The PD examiner argued that this represented another example of Mr. B's poor judgment. The pattern of Mr. B's other MMPI-2 validity scales showed no evidence of any inconsistent response style (VRIN scale=T54), no evidence of maximization (F scale=T51, FB scale=T42), or minimization, or defensiveness (L scale=T48, K scale =T49 and S scale=T52). 3) Mr. B also showed elevation on the Overcontrolled hostility scale (O-H scale=T68). The PD examiner argued that such an elevation suggests underlying hostility and proclivity toward explosiveness that are incompatible with functioning as a police officer. There is some support that O-H scale is associated with poor job performance in police officers (Weiss, Johnson, Serafino & Serafino, 2001). However, the study has a small sample and has not been replicated.

During the conditional second opinion evaluation, Mr. B was pressed by the examiner to clarify what he meant by saying he knew people who used drugs. He stated that he understood the question as whether he had known people who used drugs. He stated that when he was a teenager he knew other teenagers who used drugs but he did not associate with them and they were not his friends. He further indicated that he only once saw people using drugs in front of him. He stated that when he was 16 years old he walked into a party where he saw people using drugs and he reportedly walked out of the party.

Regarding his MMPI-2 findings, a possible reason for Mr. B's elevation on the Fp could be due to the items on this scale that are from the L-scale. These items assess self-favorable descriptions. It could also be due to four other items on the scale that tap family relationships. Individuals who endorse L-scale or family problem items may produce elevations on the Fp scale (Greene, 2008). Examination of the specific items indeed indicated that he had endorsed the L-scale and family problem items. This endorsement was consistent with Mr. B's report during the clinical interview that he was experiencing some family tension as a result of his career choice.

With regard to his elevation on the O-H scale, it was argued that O-H scale is considered a "post-diction" scale and is interpretatively meaningful only if an individual has a history of violence. Based on all available data, including collateral information, there is no evidence that Mr. B had any history of violent behavior. In the absence of a history of aggression, the elevation on O-H is interpreted as a capacity to control one's aggression. Furthermore, the O-H elevation is not uncommon in other professions, with no history of violence, who are seeking employment and may suggest a well controlled and highly socialized person (Butcher & Williams, 1992).

Since Mr. B had taken the MMPI-2 for his pre-employment screening, the PAI was administered. Mr. B produced a valid profile. He showed no evidence of inconsistent reporting (INC=T34), nor or idiosyncratic responses (INF=T40). There was also no evidence of minimization (PIM= T53 and DEI=3) or maximization (NIM=T44 and MAI=0) response styles. His profile does not suggest any psychopathology. His profile was similar to individuals who are likely to be positive, sociable, and may adapt easily to different social work environments.

Collateral information was obtained with the focus on identifying any potential indication of poor judgment or anger management difficulties. Mr. B's former soccer coach stated that he found Mr. B to be a "highly dedicated, hard working" man who "never missed practice" and always "pushed himself to excel." He indicated that Mr. B "always showed good judgment," and he never acted inappropriately or got into altercations. She indicated that Mr. B demonstrated commitment to the game and team and displayed "leadership with his peers."

Mr. B's supervisor at his current job described him as one his best employees. He indicated that since the start of his job four years ago, Mr. B has always been punctual, dedicated, and he exhibited excellent judgment. The supervisor reported that Mr. B interacted with many different people on a daily basis, never with any incidents or complaints that might call his judgment into question.

Mr. B's coworker describes him as "a professional" and stated, "I never had any problems with him." He reported that Mr. B had "good judgment" and that he is "careful," "responsible," and "thoughtful." He also reported being very happy working with Mr. B.

Mr. B's collaterals stated never having seen him intoxicated or engaging in behaviors that might suggest drug or alcohol abuse.

The examiner argued that Mr. B is psychologically suitable for the position of police officer. There was no evidence suggestive of poor judgment, and there were no indications of anger management problems. The evidence from the interview, psychological testing and collateral showed no convincing evidence of any maladaptive personality traits or psychological symptoms that could impair his ability to function as a police officer. Based on the systematic refutation of the disqualification findings, the Police Department accepted Mr. B. to the police force.

REFERENCES

Americans with Disabilities Act. (1990). 42 U.S.C.A. 12101 et seq.

American Psychological Association. (2002). Ethical principles of psychologists and code of conduct. *American Psychologist, 57,* 76–89.

Arbisi, P.A., & Ben-Porath, Y.S. (1998). The ability of MMPI-2 validity scales to detect "fake bad" responses in psychiatric inpatients. *Psychological Assessment, 10,* 221–228.

Blau, T.H. (1994). *Psychological services for law enforcement.* New York: Wiley.

Bonsignore v. City of New York, 683 F.2d 635 (1982).

Borum, R., Super, J., & Rand, M. (2003). Forensic assessment for high-risk occupations. In A. M. Goldstein (Ed.), *Forensic psychology: Vol 11 of Handbook of psychology* (pp.133–147). Hoboken, N.J.: John Wiley & Sons.

Brewster, J., & Stoloff, M.L. (1999). Using the good cop/bad cop profile with the MMPI-2. *Journal of Police and Criminal Psychology, 14*(2), 29–34.

Butcher, J.N., Graham, J.R., Ben-Porath, Y.S., Tellegen, A., Dahlstrom, W.G., & Kaemmer, B. (2001). *Minnesota Multiphasic Personality Inventory-2 (MMPI-2): Manual for administration and scoring* (revised ed.). Minneapolis: University of Minnesota Press.

Butcher, J.N., & Williams, C.L. (1992). *Essentials of MMPI-2 and MMPIA Interpretation.* Minneapolis: University of Minnesota Press.

Cochrane, R.E., Tett, R.P., & Vandecreek, L. (2003). Psychological testing and the selection of police officers. *Criminal Justice and Behavior, 30* (5), 511–537.

Committee on Ethical Guidelines for Forensic Psychologists. (1991). Specialty guidelines for forensic psychologists. *Law and Human Behavior, 15*, 655–665.

Costa, P.T., & McRae, R.R. (1992). *Revised NEO Personality Inventory (NEO-PI-R) and NEO Five Factor Inventory (NEO-FFI): Professional manual.* Odessa, Fl: Psychological Assessment Resources.

Delprino, R. & Bahn, C. (1988). National survey of the extent and nature of psychological services in police departments. *Professional Psychology: Research and Practice, 19*, 421–425.

Flanagan, C.L. (1995). Legal issues regarding police psychology. In M.I. Kurke & E. M. Scrivner (Eds.), *Police psychology into the 21st century* (pp. 93–107). Hillsdale, NJ: Lawrence Erlbaum Associates.

Gough, H.G. (1987). *California Psychological Inventory Administrator's Guide.* Palo Alto, CA: Consulting Psychologists Press, Inc.

Greene, R.L. (2008). The Minnesota Multiphasic Personality Inventory. In I.B. Weiner & R.L. Greene (Eds.), *Handbook of personality assessment,* (pp. 135–204). Hoboken, N.J.: John Wiley & Sons.

Greenberg, S.A., & Shuman, D.W. (1997). Irreconcilable conflict between therapeutic and forensic roles. *Professional Psychology: Research and Practice, 28*, 50–57.

Heilbrun, K., Grisso, T., & Goldstein, A.M. (2009). *Foundations of forensic mental health assessment.* Oxford University Press: New York.

Heilbrun, K., Warren, J., & Picarello, K. (2003). Third party information in forensic assessment. In A.M. Goldstein (Ed.), *Forensic psychology: Vol 11 of Handbook of psychology,* (pp. 69–86). Hoboken, NJ: John Wiley & Sons.

IACP Police Psychological Services Section. (1998a). *Pre-employment psychological evaluation guidelines.* Alexandria, VA: Author.

IACP Police Psychological Services Section. (1998b). *Fitness-for-duty evaluation guidelines.* Alexandria, VA: Author.

Inwald, R. (1988). Five-year follow-up study of departmental termination as predicted by 16 pre-employment psychological indicators. *Journal of Applied Psychology 73*, 703–710.

Inwald, R. (1992). *IS5 Technical manual.* Kew Gardens, NY: Hilton Research, Inc.

Inwald, R., & Shusman, E. (1984). The IPI and MMPI as predictors of academy performance for police recruits. *Journal of Police Science and Administration, 12*, 1–11.

Johnson, E. (1984). Problems in assessing police and firefighter candidates. *Journal of Police Science and Administration, 12*, 404–406.

Matter of Murry v. Co. of Nassau Civ. Serv. Cmsn, N.Y. Misc. (2007).

McKenna v. Fargo, 451 F. Supp 1355 (1977).

Morey, L. (2007). *The Personality Assessment Inventory (PAI) professional manual* (2nd Ed). Lutz, FL: Psychological Assessment Resources.

Mufson, D., & Mufson, M.A. (1998). Predicting police officer performance using the Inwald Personality Inventory: An illustration. *Professional Psychology: Research and Practice, 29*(1), 59–62.

Nilsson v. City of Mesa, 9th Cir (2007).

Ostrov, E. (1995). Legal, psychological, and ethical issues in police-related forensic psychology evaluations. In M. Kurke & E. Scrivner (Eds.), *Police psychology into the 21st century,* (pp. 133–145). Hillsdale, NJ: Erlbaum.

Rohde, P., Lewinsohn, P., & Seeley, J. (1997). Comparability of telephone and face-to-face interviews in assessing Axis I and II disorders. *American Journal of Psychiatry, 154,* 1593–1598.

Shusman, E., Inwald, R., & Knatz, H. (1987). A cross-validation study of police recruit performance as predicted by the IPI and MMPI. *Journal of Police Science and Administration, 15,* 162–169.

Soroka v. Dayton Hudson Corporation, Cal. Rptr. 2d 77 (cal. App. 1 Dist, 1991).

Specialty guidelines for forensic psychologists. (1991). *Law and Human Behavior, 15,* 655–665.

Stone, A. (2000). *Fitness for duty: Principles, methods, and legal issues.* Boca Raton, FL: CRC Press.

Super, J. (1997). Legal and ethical aspects of pre-employment psychological evaluations. *Journal of Police and Criminal Psychology, 12,* 1–6.

Trompetter, P. (1998, October). Fitness-for-duty evaluations: What agencies can expect. *Police Chief, 60,* 97–105.

Weiss, P.A., Hitchcock, J.H., Weiss, W.U., Rostow, C., & Davis, R. (2008). The Personality Assessment Inventory borderline, drug, and alcohol scales as predictors of overall performance in police officers: A series of exploratory analyses. *Policing and Society, 18,* 301–310.

Weiss, W. U., Davis, R., Rostow, C., & Kinsman, S. (2003). The MMPI-2 L scale as a tool in police selection. *Journal of Police and Criminal Psychology, 18*(1), 57–60.

Weiss, W.U., Johnson, J., Serafino, G., & Serafino, A. (2001). A three-year follow-up of the performance of a class of state police academy graduates using the MMPI-2. *Journal of Police and Criminal Psychology, 16*(1), 51–55.

Weiss, W. U., Rostow, C., Davis, R., & DeCoster-Martin, E. (2004). Use of The MMPI-2 to predict the employment continuation and performance rating of recently hired police officers. *Journal of Police and Criminal Psychology, 13,* 40–44.

Weiss, W.U., Serafino, G., & Serafino, A., Wilson, W., Knoll, S. (2001). A three-year follow-up of the performance of a class of state police academy graduates using the MMPI-2. *Journal of Police and Criminal Psychology, 16*(1), 51–55.

Weiss, W. U., Zehner, S. N., Davis, R. D., Rostow, C., Decoster-Martin, E. (2005). problematic police performance and the Personality Assessment Inventory. *Journal of Police and Criminal Psychology, 20*(1), 16–21.

Chapter 15

USING MULTIPLE SOURCES OF INFORMATION WHEN CONDUCTING MANDATORY OR REQUIRED POLICE PSYCHOLOGICAL EVALUATIONS

Eric Ostrov

INTRODUCTION

The purpose of this chapter is to comment upon the unique problems posed in performing mandatory or required psychological evaluations of police officers. It will be contended that overlapping evaluative procedures are necessary to reach correct and defensible conclusions when conducting these kinds of evaluations. While the emphasis in this chapter will be on mandatory fitness-for-duty evaluations, the methodology discussed is equally applicable to other kinds of mandatory or required evaluations such as disability, promotional, special squad or police officer candidate evaluations.

Typically, in medical settings, it is assumed that patients are motivated to reveal the facts regarding their physical or psychological condition so as to enhance the doctor's ability to evaluate them and help alleviate whatever condition they might have. In the legal system, this expectation is reflected in the hearsay rule exception for statements made to treating physicians in the course of providing treatment to the person making those statements.

In the case of mandatory evaluations, the opposite motivation often pertains. The officer may have a strong motive whether consciously or nonconsciously not to reveal or to distort pertinent facts. This motive, as is well known, can take one of two forms: either the officer may be motivated to exaggerate his symptoms in order to realize a desired sick role or disability status (malingering) or, in practice more often, the officer may be motivated to conceal a psychological disability so as to not jeopardize his position or career with the police force (dissimulation through minimization or denial).

An officer evaluee's possible motivation to conceal or distort requires careful use of multiple data sources Reliance on a single source of information is almost never sufficient. In the end, these data sources must be integrated and tested against one another in order to effectively address whether the officer can meet the essential job requirements of his or her position, which should always be spelled out in detail in a job description provided by the requesting police department.

Fitness evaluations in particular can concern officers still on active duty, officers on sick leave or on disability who want to return to active duty, or officers who have resigned from or have been terminated from the police force and want to be rehired. In all of these cases, the same basic paradigm pertains: multiple data sources must be used and taken into account to perform a competent and useful assessment.

Police departments usually request such evaluations when questions have been raised about an officer's emotional functioning relevant to his ability to perform essential job requirements. Questions usually are raised based on specific observations or other information about that officer's present or past life circumstances, behavior, demeanor or mood. For example, questions may have been raised on the basis of on-duty incidents or reports that the officer has recently been hospitalized psychiatrically.

In all cases, from the referring department's point of view, what is needed is a legally and ethically defensible evaluation that presents a clear recommendation regarding the officer's capacity on a psychological basis to remain on (or return to) full active duty. Temporizing by emphasizing diagnostic issues and not drawing implications for capacity to be on duty, or by saying the officer may or may not be fit for duty, will rarely meet the administrative needs of the referring department. What should be performed and what should be presented is an evidence-based, logically sound opinion as to whether the officer is or is not able to meet essential job requirements along with any ancillary recommendations.

Optimally, the report should spell out in detail, based on multiple sources of information, the basis for the opinions rendered and recommendations made. There are instances, however, when departments want only the "bottom line," that is a determination of whether the officer is fit or not with no supporting data presented in the final report. The examiner, nevertheless, should be prepared to defend in a hearing or in court the bases for his or her determination again citing multiple sources of evidence integrated and addressed specifically to essential job requirements.

Problems in Doing Mandatory Psychological Evaluations

Clinical evaluations often just present problems in making inferences from accepted facts. For example, it may not be disputed that the patient has had hallucinations and is delusional. Questions center on what condition may have caused these symptoms and how best to remediate it.

In fitness-for-duty evaluations in particular, the facts themselves often are highly disputed. Often allegations are far removed temporally and spatially from the evaluation itself. Rarely is the examiner able to decide what is going on clinically just by observing and listening in the course of the evaluation itself.

With police officers this problem is compounded by the fact that experienced officers are themselves usually experienced investigators. It seems likely that a person who is an expert in detecting the truth can adopt the reverse role and become proficient at concealing it. Some officers or law enforcement personnel have served in undercover capacities, a duty that requires ability to think quickly and dissimulate effectively in trying circumstances. In any event, the evaluator may find him or herself in the clinically unusual role of having to decide between rival versions of what occurred or transpired. These rival versions may be the subject of litigation or potential litigation increasing the level of contentiousness.

To illustrate, the officer may intimate he or she is being set up or picked on for political reasons and that the examiner is just being used as a pawn for this purpose. A variation on this theme is that the officer being evaluated contends that his supervisors have a problem, not him or her. The referring department itself may be divided with some supervisors believing the officer is highly disturbed while others believe he or she is faking illness to get a pension or a light duty position.

Problems also pertain to the use of standard psychological tests. These tests typically were not developed for the specific purpose of evaluating candidates or evaluating police officers for fitness, for duty, or promotions. Standard norms as a result are generally not applicable. This is true whether norms were developed on clinical populations or on persons volunteering or being paid in some way to take the test as part of a "normal" reference group. In the case of the clinical group, it often is the case that their motivation is to highlight or fully reveal their disturbance by endorsing symptoms since usually they are present in the testing facility precisely because they are seeking help for those problems. Normal subjects may not have a motive to conceal or reveal but that absence of motive itself differentiates them from the typical police officer undergoing a fitness for duty or other kind of required evaluation.

The Problem of Standards

This problem goes beyond establishing facts or inferences with respect to an individual officer. This problem concerns the interests and needs of the individual police department requesting the evaluation. After doing a great deal of psychological investigatory work, the evaluator may feel he or she has reached a good understanding of the individual officer or candidate being assessed. Nevertheless, the evaluator may feel he or she does not know what recommendation to make because the department's tolerance for or capacity to deal with certain risks or performance deficits is unknown. For example, the examiner may believe that an officer has been depressed and irritable due to domestic problems he or she has been suffering. The officer and his or her spouse may be willing to engage in counseling. But it may not be clear whether the department is willing to accept the level of functioning the officer is now showing pending possible remediation through therapy.

Similarly, the department may have alternative positions an officer could fill in the interim, which are less demanding psychologically. This issue often is critical especially when time off represents a significant loss of income to the officer who may not have enough sick time to cover the period of potential recovery or may suffer due to a loss of overtime pay. Ideally, the department would address this issue with the examiner before the final report is issued. This would require the examiner's educating the department as to what the situation is and what the risks of continuing on full or light duty might be and the department's providing feedback to the examiner as to what solutions are feasible or desirable from their point of view.

It should be noted in this context that in the case of fitness-for-duty evaluations it is not always clear in a sense what side the department is on. To illustrate, from the department's point of view, a great deal of time and expense has gone into training an experienced officer and the loss of that officer either permanently or for a significant amount of time, could be very costly to that department and to the public. This is particularly true since in many departments an officer removed from duty continues to collect half- to full-pay for protracted periods of time. An officer's being off-duty unnecessarily would be unfair and demoralizing to other officers.

On the other hand, the potential cost to the individual is very great. An experienced officer often has invested his entire career efforts into being a police officer. Were he to lose his job, he might not only lose the benefits he accrued during his years with the department but also, based on the associated stigma, might not be able pursue his career as a police officer at all.

The public interest is a powerful factor as well with the average citizen almost certainly being on the side of not having a disturbed officer on active duty. At the same time, the average citizen almost certainly would not want an officer whose career has entailed protecting the public to be the object of unfair or unjust administrative actions. Being hired as a police officer may be a candidate's primary career goal. But again the public would not want an unsuitable person carrying a weapon and exercising arrest powers.

These considerations show that the best stance for the examiner in all types of police-related evaluations is one of neutrality. No matter who is paying for the evaluation the examiner must render a fair and maximally substantiated opinion while at the same time knowing the opinion may displease some party and might be challenged in court or in the course of a formal hearing.

Proposed Solutions to Fitness Evaluation Challenges

In the rare cases where facts are not in dispute, the challenge is reduced to making relevant inferences from those facts. The general solution is that in making inferences, relevant scientific research should be applied to observations as often as possible. In doing mandatory or required psychological evaluations for police departments, certain research results seem particularly pertinent.

An example is the often recurring problem of alcohol addiction. The facts may not be in dispute and it may be fully conceded by the officer and all other parties that the officer has had a severe drinking problem. What is at issue may be how likely it is that the officer will remain sober and whether given his or her extensive history of alcohol abuse, he or she is cognitively able to perform essential job requirements. In this case, neuropsychological testing would be particularly relevant. Research indicating probability of relapse as a function of number of years of sobriety and commitment to programs such as AA also would be relevant. Brain damage itself might enhance the likelihood of relapse (*Filskov* and *Boll, 1981*; *Prigatano, 1977*). Since brain damage often can be objectively assessed, especially when the officer is motivated to return to duty, and since participation in programs such as AA often can be substantiated at least to a degree through records and collateral contacts such as an AA sponsor or spouse, reasonably accurate prognostications regarding the risks associated with allowing such an individual to return to active duty can be made.

Another case in point would be the officer who has had a bipolar psychotic episode and has been stabilized on medication. In such a case, the facts, such as his or her having been hospitalized for a psychotic episode, may not be in dispute. What is at issue is whether, now that the officer has been stabilized on medication, he or she is capable on a long-term basis of fulfilling the duties of being a police officer. In this case, research results pertaining to the likelihood of relapse and treatment records concerning the officer's commitment to treatment would be relevant as would the attestations of collateral informants such as treating physicians and psychotherapists. These data would be essential in assessing the risk of returning such a person to duties as demanding and potentially dangerous as those involved in police work.

In the more usual case, when facts are in dispute, the examiner must to some extent (him or herself) become an investigator. In this case, the sole use of traditional evaluative procedures, such as the psychiatric interview or psychological testing alone, is particularly inadequate. To do adequate mandatory psychological evaluations of police officers, the following data sources usually must all, when possible, be used: (1) use of a structured psychiatric interview that systematically covers all pertinent areas of psychiatric functioning; (2) careful observation during the interview, preferably accompanied by verbatim notes when appropriate, describing such matters as the evaluee's mood, level of cooperation and affect as well as the logic and coherence of his statements; (3) use of specialized interview methodology such as a modified version of Scientific Content Analysis (SCAN) to enhance testing of the evaluee's credibility; (4) use of psychological tests such as the SIRS (Rogers et al., 2005) and the M-FAST (Miller, 2005) to test, when appropriate, for possible malingering; (5) use of psychological tests such as the Shipley Institute of Living Scale (SILS) to test for cognitive functioning and the Personality Assessment Inventory (PAI) (Morey, 2007) to test for both dissimulation and a wide spectrum of psychological symptoms or syndromes; (6) all relevant police departments including medical records, performance ratings, and history of complaints made against him (particularly important are administrative findings such as findings of rule-breaking behavior–these findings are important because they present a third-party determination regarding the facts of a particular event); (7) records stemming from any previous hospitalizations or treatment, whether for physical or psychiatric reasons and any other relevant records; and (8) interviews with collateral informants such as the officer's supervisors and with his or her permission the officer's psychotherapist, psychiatrist, or spouse.

Use of multiple sources of information helps the evaluator to avoid the problem posed by an officer's possible self-interested distortion of relevant facts. The goal of multiple assessments is convergence–when data from several sources begin to converge, the evaluator gains increasing confidence that he or she possesses the facts necessary to make informed inferences. Some problems noted earlier under this category also can be alleviated through this methodology. Clarification as to whether a problem is primarily individual or systemic in nature can be obtained through interviews with supervisors and careful reading of police department records concerning this individual. Comments on some of these procedures follow:

I use a memorized version of SCID (Steinberg, 1994) as the structured psychiatric interview. Asking the same comprehensive set of questions in the same order in each evaluation has the advantage of assuring that all relevant areas of functioning will be covered. Over time, moreover, the examiner gains a wealth of experience in regard to answers to these questions forming an informal data base for comparison purposes.

The observations during the interview follow standard psychiatric mental status formats. One of course must be aware of the anxiety-provoking circumstances under which these examinations often are done and not mistake idiosyncratic ways of handling tension as reflecting psychopathology. Nervous laughter or bantering, to cite one example, isn't necessarily reflective of psychopathology.

SCAN was originated by former polygrapher Avinoam Sapir as a verbal lie detector test. I use it as an interview technique that calls for a narrative regarding a critical incident and then focus on what is not said in that narrative rather than what is said. It is very useful for revealing narrative discrepancies when the evaluee is being less than forthcoming about what happened with respect to an alleged event. An example pertains to an officer who was accused of sexual improprieties. He adamantly denied the veracity of the charge, but SCAN interviewing revealed telling discrepancies in his narrative about what did occur.

Regarding use of psychological tests, norms appropriate for use with this population have been developed specifically. The literature contains, for example, characteristic PAI and CPI (Gough,1987) scores for various groups of officers. It must be cautioned, however, that psychological tests in general are not equivalent to more objective medical tests. Common use of language is revealing in this regard. One might say, "I went for an x-ray or I had a colonoscopy done." One wouldn't say, "I took an x-ray" or "I took a colonoscopy." But one does say, "I took an MMPI" or "I took an IQ test." The difference is that evaluees generally are passive recipients of medical tests. Their role in getting an x-ray for instance is primarily to keep still. When taking psychological tests, however, evaluees are almost always active participants. The results are products of the interaction between the evaluee and the test and the evaluee almost always plays a significant role in what the test supposedly reveals. For that reason, as much as psychologists might want to think their tests are "objective," they in fact are just samples of behavior even if they are elicited by standard stimuli and referenced to common norms. The meaning of those samples of behavior must always be supplemented by other information relevant to why this evaluee produced these results at this time.

Illustrative Cases

Use of Behavior During the Interview

This illustration concerns an officer who was on the disability pension roll and then leave-of-absence for six years after having served with the police department for four years. He was being evaluated because he wished to return to active duty. The record was not clear as to why this officer had been put on the disability pension roll in the first place. When put on disability pension, this officer was described as "suspicious and paranoid." It was also said that his thought processes displayed "looseness of association and tangential thinking." The record provided no specific illustrations of his alleged paranoia or thought disorder, however.

In the interview, this officer was well-groomed and calm; generally he related well to the examiner. He denied having any psychiatric symptomatology. He explained previous statements about him as emanating from resentment due to his union activities while he was on active duty.

It was not necessary to judge the validity of this officer's contentions about resentment though. This officer indicated in many ways during the interview that he had serious psychiatric problems. Thus, about the statements that were made about him, this officer evidenced paranoia when he said, "The object of the game was to break my finances." He intimated that the person who made the statement had been "gotten to." An even more clear indication of paranoid and illogical thinking on the part of this officer was his saying that a psychologist who he had once seen must have been fired because the psychologist said this officer did not need medication and that the psychologist would go to court for the officer if necessary. The evidence put forward by this officer for this conclusion was that when he went back to see this psychologist about seven months later, the psychologist was no longer employed. The officer concluded that since the psychologist was no longer employed, he must have been fired. He did not seek to verify this conclusion or his inferences about the reasons the psychologist was supposedly fired. This officer also showed narcissistic traits and grandiosity when, for instance, he boasted that he had put an invention he patented up for sale through a local newspaper for 2.5 million dollars.

It should be noted that in contrast to observations during the interview, former supervisors were ambiguous in their assessment of this officer, and MMPI results showed, when interpreted against the usual norms, only that he functioned in the mildly neurotic range. Generally, former supervisors' reports or current supervisors' reports can suffer from supervisors' reluctance to make consistently negative statements about supervisees, particularly when they know those supervisees might read their statements in a report and be able to infer who made them. Structured psychological testing can suffer from officers' awareness that the choices they make while responding to items will be scrutinized–particularly because on a test like the MMPI the officers have as much time as they want to reflect before choosing a particular answer. In this case, observations during the interview based on verbatim notes about verbalizations during the interview were better sources of information than interviews with former supervisors and psychological testing.

Use of Prior Records

This case concerned an officer who had been contending with his superiors for at least three years. Stacked back-to-back, the memos between this officer and his supervisors over a three-year period stood about half a foot high. The officer maintained during the interview that he was reasonable at each step during this period. It was the department, he said, and in particular his supervisor, who were picking on him.

To illustrate, this officer protested not being given an earned day on a specific date. The reason given to him for not being allowed to take his day on a specific date, he said, was manpower shortage problems. The officer protested that the commander who turned him down himself took an earned day when the manpower situation was similar to that prevailing on the day for which this officer was turned down. Later, this officer said, he felt that his performance evaluations were being decreased in retaliation for his protesting not being given the specific earned day he had requested.

Based on this perception, the officer began filing grievances with respect to the manner in which his evaluations were given. Thus, he protested on one occasion not being given a five-day notice as required by the rules prior to receiving his evaluation. At one point, this officer even filed charges against supervisors for allegedly breaking rules for giving evaluations. In a separate incident, one supervisor had claimed that this officer cursed at and threatened him. During the interview, this officer denied the charge and said that, on the contrary, it was the supervisor who threatened the officer.

While there were specific clues during the interview that this officer was paranoid, police department records were most informative in leading to a correct diagnosis. For one thing, careful reading of departmental records showed that the officer had disputes with many supervisors, not just one. He had disputes with supervisors who initially were favorable to him. Several supervisors, the records showed, including the Chief of Police, had gone out of their way to accommodate this man's grievances when problems with him first began. It was of special interest that this officer, years before, had protested not being allowed to transfer to a different district within his department. Several years later, when asked to make the same transfer, he protested being "forced" to make that transfer and did so in the strongest terms, alleging harassment.

Surprisingly, after the officer read the examiner's report, based on the record and the interview—that this officer was antagonistic and resentful of authority and needed treatment—he did not protest and consented to pursue treatment through psychotherapy.

Use of Collateral Informants

This case concerned a tall, distinguished-looking, well-built police officer who had been on the force for 24 years. For approximately 15 years, he had accumulated many excessive force complaints and most recently had been the subject of a great deal of media publicity based on allegations that he had used excessive force with respect to various citizens.

The records showed that very few of the allegations made against him had been sustained. None of the contemporary allegations made against him had been sustained. Another charge that had been leveled against him recently was that he had attacked a youngster in a high school where he worked off-duty as a security guard. Contract rules prohibited use of prior incidents in adjudging a current incident. Thus, administratively, the fact that this officer had many complaints against him presented by diverse persons unknown to each other could not be used administratively to judge his case. The same rule, however, did not pertain to psychological evaluations.

In the interview, this officer related well to the examiner. He denied all the charges made against him. He said that he had received many excessive force complaints only because he is a very active officer who will not back down when confronted by an unruly citizen.

For this evaluation, five informants were interviewed. This officer's immediate supervisor stated that he had known this officer for four and a half years and that this officer was "a perfect gentleman." This supervisor denied that this officer had ever been abusive. "It's just that he won't back down for anything," this supervisor said. "He doesn't start it." A high school teacher at the school where this officer allegedly attacked a youth said that the youth picked up a chair, though he could not say whether the youth picked up a chair first or the officer began to hit him first. That the youth picked up a chair was a confirmation of a statement the officer had made during the interview. Another teacher at the same high school said he had known this officer 20 years and that the officer was not unduly aggressive during that entire time period. The principal of the high school stated that were it not for the adverse publicity accompanying the incident between the officer and the student, he would have retained the officer as a security guard in the high school. Prior to that incident, this principal said, the officer had presented no problems while working as a security guard.

The father of the student the officer allegedly used excessive force against stated when interviewed that witnesses claim the officer "jumped on" his son for no reason. This informant, though, conceded that his son was emotionally disturbed and was not a student at the school where the incident had taken place, and had engaged in provocative behavior before the incident in question. The mother of a person alleged to be a victim of the officer's actions while on duty stated that she thought the officer's judgment was very poor. She also said she knew another person alleged to be a victim of the officer's actions and that alleged victim was a very cooperative and nonaggressive individual.

Despite the different pictures of this officer painted by various informants, certain common elements seemed to emerge through the interviews, psychological testing, and police department records. Each time the officer was accused of using excessive force, the officer was confronting an individual in his capacity as an enforcer of laws or rules. In each case, the officer delivered a limited number of blows that led to visible injuries but in no case led to injuries severe enough to warrant hospitalization or to lead to permanent injury. The most favorable informant described the officer as not willing to back down in a confrontation and as merely acting in self-defense. The officer described himself as using only enough force to effect an arrest and contrasted using his fists to drawing and using a gun. An adverse witness described the officer as having poor judgment. One informant told the examiner that the officer was a former boxer with "very quick hands."

It seemed likely in the light of all this evidence that in each instance of alleged excessive use of force, the officer had felt justified in his responses. The problem seemed to be his quickness to perceive an arrest situation as getting out of control and as requiring physical intervention. When the officer began to fight, it seemed likely that some of his hostile feelings broke through and he hit someone harder than he needed to. Being an ex-boxer in excellent physical condition, it also seemed likely that when this officer hit, he did more damage than most people would do under the same circumstances showing the same response.

This case illustrates not only the use of informants, but also the need for standards. Clearly, the most certain way to prevent this officer from using excessive force would have been to take him off active duty. But then his long years of experience and apparently effective police work would have been lost; he would have been at home drawing pay, not performing his duties. Clear standards, however, were not available. Instead, it was adjudged that labeling this officer psychiatrically ill was not appropriate.

Rather than remove him from active duty, it was recommended that he be counseled directly about being so quick to use physical force when he perceived that an arrest was being resisted. It also was recommended that he should be encouraged to try to call for backup assistance whenever possible and if he were found to use excessive force, then appropriate administrative sanctions would be applied to him as soon as possible to make it clear particular in that case his behavior was not acceptable. To the present author's knowledge, no further complaints about this officer's conduct were received after the suggested interventions were made.

Use of SCAN

This officer was arrested after allegedly shoplifting from a store in a mall. He maintained that he drove to a mall and went to the store to buy a present for his wife and the next thing he knew he was being placed under arrest. In effect, he was claiming amnesia for the event and was claiming that he had taken the item (a wrench) he had concealed up the sleeve of his jacket while in a type of fugue state.

As I use it, SCAN involves simply asking the officer to write or relate all that he or she recalls before, during and after the event starting at the beginning of the day in question. If the narrative is spoken it should be written down verbatim. The analysis of the narrative, as mentioned earlier, focuses on what is not said rather than what is said. In this case, for example, the officer did not mention in his narrative how he felt or what happened during or after his arrest. He did not mention at what point exactly his memory allegedly faltered. Logical questions included (given what he did not mention) do you remember parking your car, thinking about what you wanted to buy, deciding what store to go to, and so on. He concluded by saying he recalled all events up to his entering the store but nothing thereafter until the moment of his arrest.

Logically, following the thread of his narrative, he seems likely that he would have been confused, shocked and bewildered-first, about finding himself outside the store when he only recalled entering it, second, about being arrested when he recalled having done nothing wrong, and third, about having a wrench up his sleeve when he did not recall taking it.

But when asked about his thoughts and feelings at the moment of his arrest, the officer mentioned none of these things. He didn't mention having been surprised that he stole anything at all or bewildered that anyone said he did. He only mentioned being scared about the possible ramifications for his career that he, an enforcer of the law, broke the law in such an egregious way.

In fact, store security camera videos showed that the officer looked around several times before he took the wrench in what appeared to be an apprehensive manner. Moreover, arrest records reflected that his first approach to the arresting officers was to show his credentials and badge and ask for special consideration. At that point, at not time did he communicate to security officers being bewildered about what had occurred or mention not recalling what he evidently had done.

My judgment (as might be expected) was that his claim of amnesia and fugue was not credible.

CONCLUSIONS

In this chapter, an attempt was made to point out some of the difficulties in doing mandatory or required psychological evaluations with police officers. As is often the case in forensic psychology or psychiatry, complicating the task of making correct inferences from observations is the fact that the individuals being evaluated are usually motivated to one degree or another to conceal or distort the truth. Making evaluations even more difficult is the possible law enforcement experience of the persons being assessed. This problem is similar to investigating an investigator. Perhaps no one is more skilled in covering up the truth than someone who is trained to uncover it or, in certain roles, conceal it.

Suggested in this chapter is that there is no simple or magical way to validly assess another human being who is motivated to and/or is skilled at presenting a certain view of him or herself. Occasionally, one source of information about a person is sufficient. For example, if an officer is trying to return to work just before his benefits run out and shows clear signs of thought disorder during the interview, it would seem to be clear that officer is not fit to be on duty.

Under ordinary circumstances, however, no one source of information is sufficient. Unless an evaluee is grossly psychotic, psychological test responses can be manipulated and appropriate behavior can be shown for the length of time a psychiatric interview takes. Conversely, there is evidence that psychiatrists and psychologists relying on only one source of information can be fooled fairly easily by persons trying to look psychiatrically ill (e.g., Rosenhan, 1973; Anthony, 1971).

Before an evaluator can feel comfortable in reaching a conclusion regarding the psychiatric status of an evaluee, converging information should be obtained from many different sources of data. Psychological testing results are much more convincing when they agree with observations during a psychiatric interview or an interview using SCAN methodology. Evidence contained in an officer's prior records is much more cogent when reinforced by attestations from contemporary informants who know the officer well.

When results conflict or, after all sources of information are used, and results are still ambiguous, the problem described earlier as one of standards comes into play. Persons who are able to become police officers and remain police officers for years and even decades usually are not flagrantly psychiatrically ill unless they have become very ill suddenly and recently. Most often, when officers manifest psychological problems those problems have been escalating for many years with no clear delineation as to when a threshold of intolerability from the point of view of not being able to meet essential job requirements is crossed.

Ideally, the individual department would set up presumptions that could guide the examiner. The department could decide, for instance, that unless shown clearly to be severely psychiatrically ill, an experienced officer will be presumed to be able to remain on active duty. Conversely, a department could presume that an officer who shows appreciable signs of mental illness or psychiatric disturbance is not suitable for full active duty.

It is my experience, however, that police departments are reluctant to specify such criteria. The reason is probably that the stakes seem too high. If it is presumed than an officer is fit for duty, even if that officer is showing appreciable, if ambiguous signs of mental illness, then the concern is that officer might hurt someone, or, through an act of omission, allow someone to get hurt. In retrospect, it will then be asked how someone who showed even ambiguous signs of being mentally ill was allowed to be on full active duty. If, on the other hand, an officer is presumed not to be fit even though signs of disturbance are ambiguous, the officer, perhaps justifiably, might complain that he was unfairly stigmatized and deprived of his livelihood, though no unambiguous evidence was presented. Moreover, other persons might maintain that the officer was being given the opportunity not to work and, at the same time, collect disability benefits even though there were no unambiguous signs that he is mentally ill. In this no-win situation, the easy solution may be to let the psychologist decide. But psychologists may or may not be the best persons to set what really should be departmental policy.

In short, mandatory or required evaluations of police officers can be thought of as a three-step process. The first step, which is uniquely difficult in this situation, is to establish accurate data about what led to the referral in the first place. Because many of the salient facts may not be directly observable, or if directly observable may be distorted by witnesses or the officer himself, either in a favorable or unfavorable direction, multiple sources of information should be used. The second stage is the traditional clinical one, one of inference based on the most accurate picture that can be obtained across data sources. As is true in all good clinical practice, these inferences must be based on scientific research results as much as possible. The third stage of this process is providing a recommendation consistent with the referral question as to, for example, whether or not the evaluee should be promoted or remain on active duty. As appropriate, ancillary recommendations such as psychotherapy or referral for possible prescription of psychotropic medication should be made.

REFERENCES

Barefoot vs. Estelle, 103 S Ct 3383 (1983).

Filskov, S.B. & Boll, T.J. (1981). *Handbook of clinical neuropsychology.* New York: John Wiley & Sons.

Gough, H.G. (1987). *California Psychological Inventory (CPI) Administrator's Guide.* Palo Alto, CA: Consulting Psychologists Press, Inc.

Judd, L.L. (1979). Effect of lithium on mood, cognition, and personality function in normal subjects. *Archives of General Psychiatry, 36,* 860–865.

Miller, H.A. (2005). *Miller Forensic Assessment of Symptoms Test.* Lutz FL: PAR.

Morey, L.C. (2007). *Personality assessment inventory professional manual* (2nd Ed.). Lutz FL: PAR.

Nair, N.P.V., Muller, H.F., Gitbrodi, E., Buffet, L, & Schwartz, G. (1979). Neurotropic activity of Lithium: Relationship to Lithium levels in plasma and red blood cells. *Res. Commum. Psychol. Psychiatr. Behavior, 4,* 169–180.

Prigatano, G.P. (1977). Neuropsychological functioning in recidivist alcoholics treated with Disulfiram. *Alcoholism, 1,* 81–86.

Rogers, R., Bagby, R.M. & S.E. Dickens, (2005). *Structured Interview of Reported Symptoms (SIRS).* Lutz FL: PAR.

Rosenhan, D.L. (1973). On being sane in insane places. *Science, 179,* 250–258.

Saxe, S.J. & Reiser, M. (1976). A comparison of three police applicant groups using the MMPI. *Journal of Police Science and Administration, 4,* 419–425.

Shipley, W.C. (1991). *Shipley Institute Of Living Scale (SILS),* Los Angeles, CA: Western Psychological Services.

Steinberg, M. (1994). *Interviewers guide to the structured clinical interview for DSM- IV.* Washington, DC: American Psychiatric Press.

Chapter 16

THE POLITICS OF PERSONALITY ASSESSMENT IN POLICE AGENCIES

JAMES S. HERNDON

INTRODUCTION

The use of psychological assessment in the law enforcement personnel selection process is fraught with issues of concern. It is not an exaggeration to say that, in general, cops do not like psychologists. Each profession attracts and shapes different types of people. To expect them to share similar world views is asking a lot. Police officers tend to see the world in black or white terms; good or bad; us vs. them. Psychologists tend to see the world in shades of gray; on the one hand . . . , and on the other hand. . . . Thus, law enforcement managers expect certainty when it comes to predictions of human behavior; psychologists tend to couch their predictions in terms of probabilities. No wonder, then, that the use of psychological tests in pre-employment situations leaves a bad taste in some mouths (metaphorically speaking).

People make up organizations, and organizations have cultures. The culture of law enforcement organizations can have a tremendous influence on the success or failure of a psychological testing program. The purpose of this chapter is to present and discuss some of the issues that can emerge to undermine the effectiveness of psychological testing. These issues will be collectively referred to as the "politics" of psychological testing in a law enforcement agency. In no particular order, several personally encountered issues are presented and discussed. The list is not all-inclusive, and there are, no doubt, examples that have not been encountered, but which exist nevertheless. Future authors may wish to address those areas.

362

Issues

In-House vs. Contract

Probably one of the first issues of psychological testing as utilized by law enforcement agencies is the question of in-house vs. contract. This is taken to address the options available to police officials; whether to provide psychological services by means of an in-house staff, or to rely upon external contractors. On the surface, this may appear to be essentially a dollars and cents (or money sense) issue. But, it is more than that.

In the United States, there are approximately 166,000 psychologists (BLS, 2006). Within the specialization of police psychology, there are probably less than 200 full-time practitioners (Bartol, 1996). Thus, a large number of psychologists in general does not translate into plenty of available police psychologists. With approximately 18,000 police agencies employing an estimated 800,000 officers (DOJ, 2004), the need for psychological services would seem great. And, while some surveys of utilization indicate most departments rely upon psychological services to some degree (Delprino & Bahn, 1988), it is only the larger agencies that can afford to hire full-time in-house staff.

STAFF VS. HIRED CONSULTANT. Large law enforcement agencies, such as the LAPD and the NYPD are noted for their in-house staff of psychologists. Whether located in a psychological services section or a behavioral science unit, these psychologists perform a range of services dedicated to law enforcement needs. As many as 8–12 psychologists are available in some agencies for assessment services, as well as counseling, crisis intervention, and operational support. There is a tendency, however, to contract out assessment services and retain clinical (therapeutic) services as an in-house function. This is not always the case, especially in smaller agencies where the few (sometimes sole) psychologists are expected to provide all services irrespective of role conflict. In the vast majority of cases, smaller agencies find it more convenient and practical to contract out psychological services.

COST VS. EFFECTIVENESS. When it comes to the in-house vs. contract out decision, the paramount factor is cost. Maintaining an in-house staff is expensive. Salaries and benefits are recurring budget items, as are office rental fees, take-home cars, pagers, cell phone, etc. The advantage of an in-house staff is that psychologists are available 24/7/365; they are employees who work for the agency and are, thus, optimally responsive to the needs of law enforcement But, the big disadvantage is, of course, cost. In tight budget times, and in agencies with small budgets, it may be difficult, if not impossible, to maintain an in-house staff. Since September 11, 2001, many agencies have felt the need to realign their budgets to enhance homeland security efforts. Civilian functions (such as psychological services) are prime targets for contracting out in order to free the funds for sworn functions.

There is a downside to contracting out psychological services after they have been historically performed by an in-house staff. In a word, that downside is responsiveness. Some agencies have found, after contracting out psychological services, that it is challenging to obtain the same quick turnaround for pre-employment testing and/or specialty assignment assessment. Furthermore, delays have been encountered when requesting on-site assistance during crisis calls. Contractors are not employees and feel less pressure to respond to the demands of a chief or a sheriff. Besides, contractors often serve multiple agencies and, thus, have competing and potentially conflicting demands. While it may be cheaper in the short run to obtain psychological services a la carte from a contractor/vendor, in the long run the agency may find itself being penny wise and pound foolish.

There is another drawback from the contract approach as compared to the in-house approach. Historical records of psychological services maintained by in-house staff are agency property and can be treasure troves for future research, such as validation studies and program effectiveness evaluations. But, once contracted out, these records are no longer accessible to the agency. There is one sad case that comes to mind where the agency contracted out the psychological services function that existed in house for 25 years, and then systematically destroyed more than 20 four-drawer file cabinet's worth of psychological records. This is tremendously unfortunate.

Assuming that the function of psychological services remains in-house and is found to be cost efficient and effective, there are some other concerns that should be addressed. Those concerns include who decides which tests to use; how much weight is given to science versus issues of practicality and expediency; and, who does the work, gets the credit or shares the blame for assessment outcomes.

Dictating Tests

Oftentimes, the psychologist and/or the section/unit in a law enforcement agency is assigned to an administrative bureau or a human resources division. As Blau (1994) has pointed out, this is not the level at which the psychologist should be located; he maintains that the staff psychologist should report to the highest level of the organization, viz., chief/deputy chief or sheriff/undersheriff. When psychological services get subordinated in the organization, bad things can happen.

It is one thing to hire a psychologist to conduct psychological tests (such as pre-employment screening) for police agencies; it is altogether another thing to dictate which tests shall be used in that process. When a human resource director tells the psychologist to use a particular test (e.g., the MBTI) for a particular purpose, and the psychologist knows better based on the state of the practice of police psychology, that can be a serious issue that confronts a subordinate professional against a higher level manager who most likely lacks any professional training in psychology. The dilemma becomes, do what you are told or stand firm to your beliefs. The reality is, however, not doing what you are told and/or bucking the system means your days, in all likelihood, will be numbered. This situation is not fictional; accounts are known.

Some state laws requiring pre-employment suitability and fitness-for-duty evaluations actually go so far as to specify that the MMPI shall be used (e.g., Iowa, 1999). This is clearly a case where politics overrides science. Sure, the MMPI can be used; but, there are many other suitable tests that can be used with equal or superior reliability and validity. The choice should remain with the competent police psychologist and not state legislature.

When cost is a factor, as it often is in tight budgets, the decision to use a cheaper test may not be in the best interest of psychological assessment. In an effort to reduce the budget for psychological services, some agencies have tried to limit the type of tests used to a select few, taking the decision away from the psychologist. Other agencies have disapproved budget requests for such costly items as optical scanners and testing software, forcing (believe it or not) staff to resort to archaic hand scoring. Without access to modern technology, psychological assessment can be reduced to faulty clinical judgment instead of actuarial, data-driven science.

Ignoring Science

GOING WITH THE FAD OR STUCK IN A RUT. As the foregoing discussion reveals, there may be some bureaucratic/organizational/political reasons why psychologists are forced to use certain tests, or may not be permitted to upgrade their technology. External forces can be strong, and clearly this is a consideration for those seeking to work in-house. But, those forces not withstanding, it is incumbent upon police psychologists to be aware of and current in the state of the practice. Knowledge of recent relevant research regarding the validity of assessment devices should drive decisions to continue or discontinue the use of particular tests. Popularity of tests or friendship with a test publisher should not be a deciding factor in building an assessment battery. Psychology as a science demands that techniques be empirically validated. Research and data must outweigh personal preferences and old habits. The responsible police psychologist stays current with science and does not become rigid and fixed in the ways of the past.

SELECTION TESTING VS. CLINICAL ASSESSMENT. For many years, police psychology was viewed as the domain of the clinically trained psychologist. The traditional model of assessment was based on the desire to screen out pathology. In that sense, a thorough understanding of clinical theory and contemporary diagnostic criteria seems appropriate. But, behavior in organizations (especially police organizations) requires a broader skill to understand than just the clinical approach. Selection testing and organizational consultation require training in and proficiency with the industrial model that seeks to "select in" for best fit, rather than "screen out" due to pathology. Sufficient evidence, empirical and anecdotal, exists to demonstrate that freedom from pathology is no guarantee that an applicant will become a good law enforcement officer. The science of modern day police psychology needs to utilize a balanced approach to assessment and other service areas that encompasses lessons learned from clinical, industrial, organizational, and operational psychology. Not to do so opens many doors for ridicule and blame when things go wrong.

The Assessor as Scapegoat

Assessing personality or behavioral traits for predictive purposes, such as in selection testing, specialty assignment evaluation, or fitness-for-duty determination, carries with it a tremendous burden and a great risk. When things go according to expectations (from a management perspective), meaning the employee performs well or within acceptable standards, not much fallout occurs. But, when an employee messes up, meaning predictions go wrong, a scapegoat is needed. That scapegoat is often the assessor (psychologist). Never mind that the assessment may have been done months or even years before an incident occurred that questioned the psychological suitability of the employee; somehow, psychological assessment gets the blame. The power of the environment and the passage of time get minimized. Critics are quick to fault the unreliability of psychological assessment.

Truth be told, there is plenty room for blame to be spread around. What about the pressure not to test periodically, which would make more sense? There is an erroneous belief in the law enforcement culture that one test at the beginning of a career is sufficient to predict success or failure over the next twenty years. Requirements to the contrary that were at one time part of law enforcement agency accreditation standards are slowly being rescinded (CALEA, 2009). And, what about the effect of organizational socialization on behavior? Good police officers can become bad police officers when surrounded and shaped by negative influences. Should not the organization share the blame with the psychologist? We've all heard the old aphorism "one bad apple can spoil the bunch." But, it is no less true that a bad bunch can potentially spoil the good apple.

Dual Roles

EVALUATOR AND COUNSELOR. Working in-house as a staff psychologist, especially where there is a small staff, presents opportunities that put the psychologist in a potential bind (Herndon, 2000a). There are many functions to be performed–from assessment, to counseling, to training, to consultation. No one person can be skilled to perform all functions equally well. But, more than that, there are situations where one should not perform functions that present role conflict. APA ethical principles clearly prohibit dual relationships (APA, 2002). A psychologist who is an assessor/evaluator should not be the treating psychologist when problems of behavior emerge. Nevertheless, cases of organizational pressure are known where the psychologist was ordered to do both assessment functions and supportive counseling functions for the same employee. With the admonition, "what are we paying you for?" the staff psychologist felt that he was being coerced into behavior that violated ethical principles. Standing firm for professional principles was seen as insubordination.

ON THE TEAM AND AGAINST THE TEAM. While being a member of the Crisis (Hostage) Negotiation Team (CNT), one staff psychologist found that he was required to work with the same people he had not recommended for the team when he wore the assessor hat. Resentment was evident and was openly displayed during team calls-out. Even worse, credibility was questioned when the team knew that the psychologist's judgment was completely ignored about team member suitability. How, then, could the psychologist serve as an effective member of the team? Perhaps, another psychologist could be found to do the testing and a different one could serve on the CNT?

Opinion Shopping

YES MAN. So, in the case where the opinions of an in-house psychologist are ignored for convenience, it becomes organizationally necessary (as in CYA) to have a document on file that recommends an applicant or candidate who was initially not recommended by the staff psychologist. This calls for finding another psychologist (in the *Yellow Pages*) who is willing to provide a report that the agency can live with (and present to the media or the court when and if necessary). Lest you think this is fictional, be assured that it can and does happen. Rather than take a clear and firm stand on suitability, or even design a prediction of future success on the job, some reports examined by the author were worded in such a fashion as to leave the reader unconvinced of anything good or bad. Such despicable behavior on the part of an unethical psychologist and a corrupt administration is a reality.

HIDING NEGATIVE REPORTS. A difficulty that ensues from buying convenient reports is what to do with the official report prepared by the staff psychologist. One solution is to make the report conveniently disappear from the official records maintained by human resources. Trouble is, there's always a copy somewhere. The danger is great that a challenge to the bought opinion might bring out the fact that it was provided by someone other than the psychologist who was routinely used for selection testing. Very odd. Very risky.

In one moderately large southern law enforcement agency, 19 cases were examined where individuals were hired against the advice of the psychologist (HAAP). Other, second opinion reports were inserted into the files. Discovering this led to some observational tracking of job success (a fortuitous validation study). Within one year of hiring, 10 of the 19 HAAP employees had been fired or quit. Five remaining were showing signs of performance difficulty and two of them were currently under investigation by Internal Affairs. The other four were seemingly doing okay. A recent follow-up found that after five years, only one of the 19 still remains employed by the agency. These findings have never been published for obvious reasons. Yet, they serve to highlight the dangers of opinion shopping and not trusting the in-house psychologist.

The Issue of Competence

YELLOW PAGE SHRINKS. Speaking of the Yellow Page psychologist above, it is disturbing to find that no knowledge of police testing is required to provide services to law enforcement agencies. All psychologists are not created (trained and experienced) equally. "A psychologist is not a psychologist is not a psychologist." Some are clinical, some are industrial. Some are therapists, some are career counselors and life coaches. Some specialize in marital issues; some specialize in child and adolescent issues. Some are trained in substance abuse and addiction. Some are academics and researchers. But, as was pointed out in the beginning of this chapter, less than 200 psychologists nationwide are actually police psychologists. It would seem reasonable that a police administrator would seek out a police psychologist when services are needed. But, unfortunately, most police officials (and certainly the public) make no distinctions among and between psychologists. A shrink is a shrink. If they are in the *Yellow Pages*, they are called upon when needed.

ASSURING COMPETENCE. It is up to the practicing psychologist to maintain professional integrity and work only within the bounds of his/her competence. Police psychology is now a recognized specialty within the field of psychology (Corey, 2008). Training and experience can lead to board certification (Diplomate in Police Psychology) through the Society for Police and Criminal Psychology (SPCP). SPCP has also begun a program of certification in police psychology in conjunction with several universities, the aim being to raise the standards within the profession by providing an avenue for continuing education and credentialing.

There are divisions representing police psychology within the American Psychological Association (APA Division 18 - Psychologist in Public Service, Police and Public Safety Section) and the International Association of Chiefs of Police (IACP - Police Psychological Services Section). A psychologist not affiliated with these organizations, and not trained and experienced in police psychology should refrain from engaging in work with law enforcement agencies. And, police administrators should insist on demonstrated competence in police psychology from service providers.

The IACP has issued a series of guidelines to improve the practice of police psychology and ensure the competency of practitioners (e.g., IACP, 2004). Police psychologists (actual or wannabe) and police administrators and managers would do well to become thoroughly familiar with these documents. Guidelines include pre-employment psychological evaluation, fitness-for-duty evaluation, and consulting police psychologists, among others. These guidelines are available in PDF format from the IACP web site (www.theiacp.org).

Navigating the Waters (Playing Politics)

If you are a police psychologist, or aspire to be one, there are some thoughts to consider about working in or for a law enforcement agency. You need to give serious consideration as to your own suitability to work, survive, and thrive in the environment as it actually is, rather than what the entertainment media portrays it to be. Police psychology is not like the movies (Herndon, 2000b).

THE POSITION VS. THE PROFESSION. The first, and perhaps most important, issue is the question of where you place your loyalty. Are you a psychologist (loyal to the profession), or are you an employee (loyal to the organization)? A quick, but not so easy, answer would be both. But, the reality is you must choose which one overrides the other. Working in-house for a law enforcement agency will challenge your loyalties. You will be reminded regularly as to who signs your paycheck. You will be asked/told/ordered to do things that test your ethics. You must decide just how to play it to survive. It comes down to a delicate balancing act; how to be ethical and professional in an environment that demands and challenges issues of boundaries and competencies.

SINK OR SWIM. In order to survive in bureaucratic organizations, one must sanctify the hierarchy (Merton, 1968). To expect to rise in an organization, one must pay tribute in the form of obedience and respect to those higher up the pyramid. Doing otherwise, (bucking the system, bad-mouthing the boss, challenging authority) is a sure way to get expelled from the organization. Thus, organizational reality for a police psychologist is to swim with the tide or risk being overtaken by the current, drowning, and sinking to the bottom.

MY WAY OR THE HIGHWAY. Authoritarian management styles tell rather than ask. Police managers give orders and expect compliance. Police psychologists, no matter how highly placed within the organization, still ultimately work for the chief or the sheriff. As an employee, you have someone to which you must answer. And even as a contractor/vendor, if you displease the chief/sheriff, you won't be around long. You, no doubt, will be occasionally (if not often) reminded that it's "my way or the highway." Of course you are free to leave. But, if you want to make a difference, you want to stay. So, the struggle is to be a good employee while being a good police psychologist.

CONCLUSION

Personality assessment is never done in a vacuum. There are always contexts. Within police agencies, the contexts are palpable. Law enforcement organizations are bureaucratic hierarchies staffed by individuals with strong values about right and wrong, good and bad, legal and illegal, ethical and unethical. Even so, the environment can put pressure on individuals to make choices and compromises. Police psychologists are not exempt. The politics of conducting assessments (or performing any type of psychological services) within police agencies require that employees or contractors open their eyes to the dynamics and conform accordingly, or leave with head held high.

REFERENCES

APA. (2002). *Ethical principles of psychologists and code of conduct.* Washington, DC: American Psychological Association.

Bartol, C. (1996). Police psychology: Then, now and beyond. *Criminal Justice and Behavior, 23* (1), 70–89.

Blau, T.H. (1994). *Psychological services for law enforcement.* New York: John Wiley & Sons.

BLS. (2006). *Occupational outlook handbook.* Washington, DC: Bureau of Labor Statistics.

CALEA. (2009). *Standards for law enforcement accreditation.* Fairfax, VA: Commission on Accreditation for Law Enforcement Agencies, Inc.

Corey, D. (2008). APA recognizes police psychology. IACP *Police Psychological Services Section Newsletter, 8* (2), 1.

Delprino, R.P. & Bahn, C. (1988). National survey of the extent and nature of psychological services in police agencies. *Professional Psychology: Research and Practice, 19* (4), 421–425.

DOJ. (2004). *Summary findings.* http://www.ojp.usdoj.gov/bjs/lawenf.htm.

Herndon, J. (2000a) Readdressing role conflicts in police psychology: Inside, outside, upside, downside. Presentation at the Annual Conference of the American Psychological Association, Washington, DC, August.

Herndon, J. (2000b). The police psychologist on the silver screen: Reviewing the roles on the reels. *Journal of Police and Criminal Psychology, 15* (2), 30–40.

IACP. (2004). Pre-employment psychological evaluation services guidelines. Ratified by the IACP Police Psychological Services Section, Los Angeles, California.

Iowa. (1999). Minimum standards for Iowa law enforcement officers. Iowa Administrative Code , Section 80B, Chapter 2 Law Enforcement Academy.

Merton, R.K. (1968). *Social theory and social structure.* New York: The Free Press.

INDEX

A

A Futurist View of Psychology's Emerging Role in Police Agencies, 11
AA, 351
Aamodt Index, 235, 248
Aberrant Experiences (RC8) scale, MMPI-2 RF, 67
Absence Abuse (AA) scale, IPI, 121
Academic Interest (AI) scale, IPS, 100
Academic Interest/New Skills Development (AI) scale, IPS, 126
Ach via conformity scale, CPI, 249
Ach via independence scale, CPI, 249
Achievement History (AH) scale, HPP/SQ, 121
Adaptability Quotient (AQ) Total Score, IPS, 127
Adaptability/Flexibility competency, 168
Addiction Admission (AAS) scale, MMPI-2, 66, 68
Admission of Faults (AF) scale, IPS, 100, 126
Admission of Shortcomings (AD) scale, HMI, 99
Admission of Shortcomings (AD) scale, HMS, 121
adolescents, 95
Affection/Physical Compatibility (AF) scale, ICCP, 123
Aggression (AGG) scale, PAI, 73, 81, 84, 87
Aggression/Hostility (AG) scale, HCSI, 122
aggressiveness index, MMPI-2, 275
agreeableness dimension, FFM, 166, 231, 250
agreeableness global factor, 168, 169
Alcohol Problems (ALC) scale, PAI, 73, 78, 79

Alcohol problems scale, Test of Personality, 243
Alcohol Use (AL) scale, IPI, 94, 121, 308
Alcohol Use Patterns (AU) scale, IPPI, 125
alcohol/drug, 16, 80
Alienated Attitudes scale, M-PULSE, 325
Allen, Scott, 12
Alliant International University, 136
American Board of Forensic Psychology (ABFP), 14
American Board of Professional Psychology (ABPP), 14, 38
American Educational Research Association (AERA) Guidelines, 37
American Psychological Association (APA), 11, 12, 15, 16, 21, 37, 48, 261, 369
American Psychological Association Ethics Code, 33-35, 39, 69, 367
American Psychological Association Insurance Trust (APAIT), 31
Americans with Disabilities Act (ADA), 16, 17, 37, 46, 60, 73, 86, 133, 134, 136, 161, 162, 167, 182, 183, 231, 282, 284, 301-303, 306, 321-323, 326-328, 338
Americans with Disabilities Amendment Act, 183, 321
Amorality scale, M-PULSE, 150, 153
Anger (ANG) scale, MMPI-2, 66
Anger issues scale, Test of Personality, 243
Anger Patterns (AP) scale, HCSI, 97
Anger/Hostility Patterns (AP) scale, HCSI, 122
Anger/Hostility subscale, NEO-PI R, 167
Antisocial Attitudes (AS) scale, IPI, 94, 121, 171, 308
anti-social attitudes/behaviors, 92
Antisocial Behavior (RC4) scale, MMPI-2 RF, 67

anti-social behavior patterns, 91, 94
antisocial conduct, 159
Antisocial Features (ANT) scale, PAI, 73, 79, 80, 83
antisocial History, RPSR, 170
antisocial/aggressive construct, 246, 247
Anxiety (AI) scale, HLAP, 122
Anxiety (AN) scale, IPI, 94, 121
Anxiety (ANX) scale, PAI, 73
Anxiety about Organization (AX) scale, HPP/SQ, 95, 121
anxiety construct, 246, 247
Anxiety scale, Test of Personality, 243
Anxiety subscale, NEO-PI R, 167
anxiety, 132
Anxiety-Related Disorders (ARD) scale, PAI, 73, 78, 83
APA Division 18
  Psychologists in Public Service, 11, 38
APA Guidelines, 37, 49
appeals process, 312
appeals, 47, 333, 335, 342
Army Alpha Intelligence test, 6
Assertive Management Style (AM) scale, HMS, 121
assertiveness competency, 168
Attitudes: Antisocial Behaviors (A1) scale, IS2, 122
Attitudes: Antisocial Behaviors (AB) scale, IS5-R, 122
Aumiller, Gary, 20, 21
Avoidance of Criticism (AV) scale, IPPI, 125

B

Background Compatibility (BC) scale, ICCP, 100, 123
Beck Depression Inventory, 292
Beck method, Rorschach scoring, 189
Behavior Patterns: Integrity Concerns (B1) scale, IS2, 122
Behavior Patterns: Integrity Concerns (BP) scale, IS5-R, 122
bifurcated assessment model, 183, 284, 306
Binomial Effect Size Display (BESD), 272, 274, 275
bipolar psychological inventory, 239
Bonsignore v The City of N.Y., 11
Borderline Features (BOR) scale, PAI, 73, 80, 81, 83

Bottom Line (BL) scale, ICCP, 100
Bottom Line Summary (BL) scale, ICCP, 125
Broadfoot, Phil, 214
Brown, Diane, 17
business ethics & practices competency, 165, 168

C

California Peace Officer Standards and Training (POST), 20, 35, 42, 45
California POST Psychological Screening Dimensions, 137, 144, 146, 151
California Psychological Inventory (CPI), 10, 11, 13, 16, 18, 35, 45, 188, 229, 231, 240, 241, 282, 283, 307, 309, 341, 353
Caliper Profile, 231
Candor (CA) scale, HPP/SQ, 95, 96, 99, 121
Capacity for status scale, CPI, 249
Cashel Discriminant Function (CDF), PAI, 77, 78
Chandler, James, 12
chaos management competency, 168
Chemical Abuse/Dependency scale, M-PULSE, 137, 139, 149, 152
Chicago Police Department, 169
Civil Rights Act of 1871, 133
Civil Rights Act of 1991, 17
Clinical Assessment Questionnaire (CAQ), 231, 239
Coaching/Counseling Orientation (CC) scale, HMS, 121
Cohen's d, 267, 276
communality scale, CPI, 249
communality scale, Test of Personality, 243
Compatibility Quotient (CQ) scale, ICCP, 125
Competitive Spirit (CO) scale, HPP/SQ, 95, 121
Competitiveness scale, M-PULSE, 325
Composure Under Stress Difficulties (CS) scale, IAS, 128
computer test scoring, 310
Concerns about Health (CH) scale, HLAP, 97, 122
conditional offer of employment (COE), 35, 37, 41
conditional second opinion psychological evaluation, 333-342

Conscientiousness Big-5 factor, 168, 169, 175
Conscientiousness dimension, FFM, 165, 166, 181, 183, 231, 250
Conscientiousness scale, Personal Perspectives Inventory, 230
conscientiousness, construct, 230
Consortium of Police Psychologists (COPPS), 12
Content scales, MMPI-2, 60, 65, 66
Control scale, Test of Personality, 243
Controlling Behavior (CB) scale, ICCP, 100
Copeland, Amy L., 317
Coping Deficit Index (CDI), RCS, 200, 201, 204, 210, 211, 213
Corey, Dave, 21
coworker relations supervisor evaluations, 172
Cox index, 271
Criminal Conduct scale, M-PULSE, 138, 141, 149, 152
criminal Justice and Behavior, 260
Criminal Justice Orientation scale, LEAI, 173
Crisis Negotiation Team (CNT), 367
Critical Events (CE) scale, HLAP, 122
Critical Items (CI) scale, IPPI, 126
Critical Items, ICCP, 119
Critical Items, IPI, 94, 98, 111
criticality index (CI), 164
cross-cultural adaptability competency, 168
curiosity competency, 168
Curran, Stephen, 17
customer relations supervisor evaluation, 172
Cuttler, Michael, 21
Cynicism (RC3) scale, MMPI-2 RF, 67

D

D scale, MMPI-2, 63,195, 215, 245
Daubert v Merrill Dow Pharmaceuticals, 134, 190
Davis, Doug, 214
Defensive Responses: Validity Style (DF) scale, HSRI, 122
Defensiveness (DN) scale, HCSI, 96,122
Defensiveness Index (DEF), PAI, 77
defensiveness style, 246, 247
defensiveness, 132
Delegation Skills (DK) scale, HMS, 121
Denial of Shortcomings (DL) scale, IS2, 122
Depression (DE) scale, IPI, 94, 98, 121

Depression (DEP) scale, PAI, 73, 85
depression construct, 246, 247
Depression Index (DEPI), RCS, 201
Depression scale, MMPI, 171
Depression subscale, NEO-PI R, 167
Detroit Police Department, 6
Diagnostic and Statistical Manual-IV (DSM-IV), 50, 63, 161, 318
diplomate in police psychology, 20, 38, 301, 369
directiveness competency, 168
Discharge of Weapon scale, M-PULSE, 137, 140, 149, 152
Disciplinary History (DH) scale, HCSI, 122
Dissatisfaction with Career (DC) scale, HCSI, 122
Dissatisfaction with Job (DJ) scale, HCSI, 122
Dissatisfaction with Supervisor (DS) scale, HCSI, 122
Distrust of Others (DI) scale, IS5-R, 122
diversity tolerance competency, 168
Domestic Concerns (DC) scale, IS5-R, 96,122
Domestic Violence by Police Officers, conference, 19, 20
domestic violence issues, 96, 305
domestic violence, 299
Dominance (DOM) scale, PAI, 73, 82, 87
Dominance scale, CPI, 249, 309
Dominance scale, Test of Personality, 243
Drive (DR) scale, HPP/SQ, 121
driving ability competency, 168
Driving Behaviors (DB) scale, HSRI, 122
Driving problems scale, Test of Personality, 243
Driving Violations (DV) scale, IPI, 94, 95, 98, 121
Drug and alcohol history, 305
drug avoidance competency, 165, 168
drug Avoidance scale, LEAI, 173
Drug Problems (DRG) scale, PAI, 73, 78, 79, 84
Drug Use (DG) scale, IPI, 94, 308
Drug Use (DO) scale, IPI, 121
Drug Use Patterns (DU) scale, IPPI, 125
Drug/Alcohol Abuse (DA) scale, HCSI, 122
due diligence, 132
Dysfunctional Negative Emotions (RC7) scale, MMPI-2 RF, 67

E

Edwards Personal Preference Schedule (EPPS), 10, 231
effect size (ES), 260-264, 267-276, 286
Effort towards Responsibilities (EF) scale, IPS, 100,127
Egocentricism scale, M-PULSE, 150, 153
Eisenberg, Terry, 8, 9
Emotional instability dimension, FFM, 166, 167, 182
Emotional Instability/Stress Intolerance scale, M-PULSE, 325
Emotional Instability-Stress Intolerance dimension, CA POST, 144, 151, 153
emotional intelligence, 92
Emotional stability dimension, FFM, 231, 250
emotional stability global factor, 168, 169, 183
Empathy/Helping Others (EM) scale, IPS, 100,126
Empirical scales, M-PULSE, 137, 150
Employee assistance program (EAP), 92, 93, 99
Employment Problems (EP) scale, IPPI, 100, 125
energy competency, 168
Equal Employment Opportunity Commission (EEOC), 9, 133, 134, 162, 321
evidence-based practice, 279, 282, 310
Excessive Force scale, M-PULSE, 137, 141, 149, 152
excessive force, 299, 300, 324, 356-358
Excusing Attitudes (EA) scale, HCSI, 96,122
Exner Comprehensive System, Rorschach, 283
Extraversion dimension, FFM, 165, 166, 168, 169, 231, 250
Extraversion scale, Test of Personality, 243
Extroversion (EX) scale, HPP/SQ, 97, 121
extroversion, 132

F

F scale, MMPI-2, 60, 63, 64, 215, 235, 245, 282, 342-343
Fabricatore, Joseph, 8, 9, 11
Factor 1: Emotional Adjustment Difficulties/ Psychopathology (EM) scale, HLAP, 122
Factor 1: Lack of Conscientiousness/Reli- ability-F1 scale, IS5-R, 122

Factor 1: Leadership Potential-F1 scale, HMS, 121
Factor 2: Employee Performance Mgmt Skills-F2 scale, HMS, 121
Factor 2: Lack of Work Ethic-F2 scale, IS5-R, 122
Factor 2: Recent Activity Level/General Functioning (RA) scale, HLAP, 122
Factor 3: Lack of Social Initiative-F3 scale, IS5-R, 122
Factor 3: Team-Oriented Style-F3 scale, HMS, 121
Family Achievement History (FE) scale, HPP/SQ, 121
Family Compatibility (FA) scale, ICCP, 124
Family Conflicts (FC) scale, IPI, 94, 121
family problems construct, 246, 247
FBI Academy, 9, 12
FBI World Conference on Police Psycho- logy, 14
FBI, 8, 9, 14, 18, 19, 93
Federal Rules of Evidence, 134, 145, 190
feedback, 47
Femininity scale, CPI, 249
Financial Compatibility (FC) scale, ICCP, 100
Financial/Functional Compatibility (FD) scale, ICCP, 123
Firearms Interest (FI) scale, IS2, 97, 122
Fitness-for-duty evaluation (FFDE), 5, 8, 13, 17, 18, 22, 30, 32, 48, 50, 60, 61, 68, 92, 93, 96, 145, 214, 280, 283, 292, 293, 317- 330, 333, 335, 339, 347, 349-351
Five-Factor Model of general personality (FFM), 165-167, 174, 183, 230, 240
Flanagan, Catherine, 17
Flexibility (FL) scale, HMS, 121
Flexibility scale, CPI, 249
Flexibility scale, Test of Personality, 243
FMLA, 323
Forensic psychological evaluation, 319
Frustration/Anger Patterns (FR) scale, IS5-R, 122
Frye Standard, 134, 190
Furcon, John, 9

G

G.E. v Joiner, 134, 190
Galbo, Charles J., 9
Generalizability theory (G-Theory), 283
Gentz, Douglas, 12

Glass' Delta, 267, 268
Global Assessment of Functioning (GAF), 50
Goal Orientation (GO) scale, HPP/SQ, 121
Goldberg Index, 234, 248
Goldstein, Harvey, 11, 12
Gonder Index, 235, 248
Good Cop/Bad Cop (GCBC) Profile, 234, 239
Good Cop/Bad Cop, 64, 65, 239
Good impression scale, CPI, 249
Guardedness (GD) scale, IPI, 76, 95, 121, 308
Guardedness scale, Test of Personality, 243
Gupton, Herb, 21

H

Habits/Issues Compatibility (HA) scale, ICCP, 124
Harris-Lingoes subscales, MMPI-2, 60, 65
Health Insurance Portability and Accountability Act (HIPAA), 37, 318
Hedges, G., 267
Hickey, Tom, 12
Hilson Background Investigation Inventory-Revised (HBI-R), 92, 98, 99, 112, 113, 122, 130
Hilson Career Satisfaction Inventory (HCSI), 13, 92, 96, 108, 122, 130
Hilson Job Analysis Questionnaire (HJAQ), 19
Hilson Life Adjustment Profile (HLAP), 19, 92, 96, 98, 109, 112, 122
Hilson Management Inventory (HMI), 98, 99, 113, 114, 121, 130
Hilson Management Survey (HMS), 18, 92, 99, 114
Hilson Personnel Profile/Success Quotient (HPP/SQ), 14, 15, 92, 95, 96, 99, 104, 105- 107, 110, 111, 113, 114, 121, 130
Hilson Research, Inc., 10, 17
Hilson Safety/Security Risk Inventory (HSRI), 18, 92, 122, 130
Hilson Spouse/Mate Inventory, 18
Hilson Test Battery for Fitness-for-Duty Evaluations, 96
Hilson Test Battery for Public Safety Officer Screening, 98
Hilson Trauma Recovery Inventory (HTRI), 20

Hispanics, 36
HLAP Total Score (TO) scale, HLAP, 122
Hogan Personality Inventory, 231
Honesty scale, LEAI, 173
honesty supervisor evaluation, 172
Hostility (HO) scale, MMPI-2, 66, 68
hostility, Rorschach variables as predictors of, 211
Hs scale, MMPI-2, 195, 215, 234, 235, 245
Huesmann Index, 235, 248
Hy scale, MMPI-2, 195, 215, 234, 235, 245
Hyperactivity (HP) scale, IPI, 94, 121
Hyperactivity scale, Test of Personality, 243
Hypervigilance Index (HVI), RCS, 197
Hypochondriasis (Hs) scale, MMPI-2, 63, 65, 215
Hypochondriasis construct, 246, 247
Hypomania (Ma) scale, MMPI-2, 64, 65
Hypomanic Activation (RC9) scale, MMPI-2 RF, 67
Hysteria (Hy) scale, MMPI-2, 63, 64, 65
hysteria construct, 246, 247

I

IACP Guidelines, 37, 49, 146
Ideas of Persecution (RC6) scale, MMPI-2 RF, 67
Illicit Substance Abuse, 172
Illness Concerns (IC) scale, IPI, 121
Immaturity index, MMPI-2, 275
impression management competency, 168
Impression Management scales, M-PULSE, 137, 148, 152
impression management, 76, 77
Inadequate Views of Police Work scale, M-PULSE, 150, 153
Inappropriate Attitudes About the Use of Force scale, M-PULSE, 150, 153
Inappropriate Use of Weapon scale, M-PULSE, 137, 140, 149, 152
Inconsistency (ICN) scale, PAI, 73-75
Independent Medical Evaluation (IME), 319
informed consent, 40, 41, 43, 47, 48, 87, 303, 335
Infrequency (INF) scale, PAI, 73-75
Initiative (IN) scale, HPP/SQ, 95, 96, 121
Institute for Personality and Ability Testing, Inc. (IPAT), 130
Integrity Issues (II) scale, IAS, 128

integrity issues, 92, 182, 183
integrity tests, 166, 168, 174, 182
integrity/honesty competency, 165, 168
Intellectual efficiency scale, CPI, 249, 309
Interests Compatibility (CI) scale, ICCP, 123
International Association of Chiefs of Police (IACP), 8, 12, 17, 38, 48, 50, 51, 160, 369
International Association of Chiefs of Police Guidelines, 34, 46, 163, 339, 369
Interpersonal Assertiveness (IA) scale, ICCP, 124
Interpersonal Difficulties (ID) scale, IPI, 121, 171
Interpersonal Difficulties scale, M-PULSE, 137, 139, 149, 152
Introverted Personality Style (IP) scale, IS5-R, 122
Inwald Attitude Survey (IAS), 21, 92, 99, 100, 118, 119, 127
Inwald Couples Compatibility Questionnaire (ICCQ), 21, 92, 99, 100, 115, 116, 119, 123
Inwald Partners Personality Inventory (IPPI), 21, 92, 99, 100, 116, 117, 125
Inwald Personality Inventory (IPI), 10, 11, 13, 15-17, 19, 21, 35, 50, 73, 86, 91, 93-96, 98, 102, 103, 111, 121, 130, 171, 188, 191, 214, 231, 239, 307-309, 341
Inwald Personality Survey (IPS), 21, 92, 99, 100, 117, 118, 126
Inwald Research Relationship Surveys, 92, 99, 100
Inwald Research, Inc., 131
Inwald Survey 2 (IS2), 18, 92, 96, 110, 113, 122, 130
Inwald Survey 5, 17, 19, 92, 96, 109, 112, 130
Inwald Survey 5-Revised, 19, 122
Inwald Survey 8 (IS8), 18
Inwald Trauma Recovery Inventory (ITRI), 92
Inwald, Robin, 9-14, 17
IQ scores, 263
IQ test, 353
IS2 Overall Score (OS), IS2, 122
Isolation Index, RCS, 206
Item response theory (IRT), 283

J

James Madison University, 214
Janik, James, 17

job analysis, 42, 47, 50
job description, 42, 50
Job Difficulties (JD) scale, IPI, 121, 308
Job/Career Adjustment Difficulties (JA) scale, IAS, 128
Johnson, Roberts Personal History Questionnaire (PHQ), 15
Journal of Police and Criminal Psychology, 260, 311

K

K scale, MMPI-2, 60, 62, 67, 76, 195, 215, 245, 282, 342
King County Sheriff's Department, 7
Koepfler, James, 214
Krakosky, Lauren, 214
Kuder, 306
Kumho Tire v Carmichael, 134, 190

L

L scale, MMPI-2, 43, 60-63, 65, 67, 68, 76, 77, 82, 195, 215, 245, 274, 282, 286, 307, 310, 342-343
Lack of Assertiveness (LA) scale, IPI, 121
Lack of Candor (LC) scale, HLAP, 122
Lack of Competitive Motivation (LM) scale, IS5-R, 122
Lack of Family Support (LF) scale, HLAP, 122
Lack of Hostility Control (HC) scale, HSRI, 122
Lack of Insight/Candor (LC) scale, IS5, 97
Lack of Insight/Candor (LC) scale, IS5-R, 122
Lack of Integrity Concerns (IY) scale, HSRI, 122
Lack of Integrity/Ethics dimension, CA POST, 144, 151, 153
Lack of Integrity/Ethics scale, M-PULSE, 325
Lack of Interpersonal Support (IS) scale, HCSI, 122
Lack of Jealous Behavior (JE) scale, ICCP, 100
Lack of Jealousy (JE) scale, ICCP, 124
Lack of Leadership Interest (LL), IS2, 122
Lack of Over-Controlling Behavior (CB) scale, ICCP, 124

Lack of Personal Integrity scale, M-PULSE, 150, 153

Lack of Satisfaction with Life (SL) scale, HLAP, 98, 122

Lack of Self Awareness (AW) scale, IAS, 127

Lack of Sensitivity (LS) scale, IS5, 97

Lack of Sensitivity (LS) scale, IS5-R, 122

Lack of Social Judgment (SJ) scale, HSRI, 122

Lack of Social Network (LN) scale, HLAP, 122

Lack of Social Sensitivity (SS) scale, IS2, 122

Lack of Team Work scale, M-PULSE, 325

Lack of Teamwork dimension, CA POST, 144, 151, 153

Lack of Temper Control (TC) scale, IS2, 122

Lack of Trusting Nature (TN) scale, IAS, 128

Lack of Work Ethic Concerns (WC) scale, HSRI, 122

Latinos, 36

Law Enforcement Academy, 36

Law Enforcement Assessment and Development Report (LEADR), 11

Law Enforcement Assistance Administration (LEAA), Dept. of Justice, 8, 9, 11

Law Enforcement Executive Forum, 260

Law Enforcement Families: Issues & Answers, conference, 18

Law enforcement officer (LEO) selection , 132, 136

Law Enforcement Personal History Questionnaire (PHQ), 11

Lawsuit Potential scale, M-PULSE, 137, 143, 149, 152

Leadership (LD) scale, HMS, 121

Leadership Avoidance (LE) scale, IS5-R, 122

Leark, Robert, 136

Legal Problems (LP) scale, IPPI, 100, 125

LH-STEP, 286

Liability scales, M-PULSE, 137, 149

Limited Tolerance of Frustration (TF) scale, IAS, 128

Logged Odds Ratio, 271

Loner Type (LO) scale, IPI, 95, 121

Los Angeles Police Department, 6, 8, 363

Low Activity Level (LV) scale, HLAP, 98, 122

Low Positive Emotions (RC2) scale, MMPI-2 RF, 67

M

Ma scale, MMPI-2, 195, 215, 235, 245

Maki, Bill, 214

Malingering Index (MAL), PAI, 77

malingering style, 246, 247, 347

Mania (MAN) scale, PAI, 73, 85

mania construct, 246, 247

Mania scale, MMPI, 171, 234

Manifest Hostility (HOS) scale, MMPI-2, 66

Mardi Gras, 12

Masculinity-Femininity (Mf) scale, MMPI-2, 63-65

Matrix-Predictive Uniform Law Enforcement Selection Evaluation (M-PULSE) Inventory, 21, 73, 86, 132, 135-56, 191, 282, 307-309, 313, 324, 325

MBTI, 365

McAndrew Alcoholism scale (MAC-R), MMPI-2, 65, 66, 68

Mental Status Examination, 61, 85, 86, 304, 305, 311

Meritorious Research Award, NY State Psychological Association, 13

Meta-analysis, 229, 235-238, 240, 241, 260, 287, 309

Mf scale, MMPI-2, 195, 214, 215, 235, 245

M-FAST, 352

MHS, Inc., 132, 136, 137

Millon Clinical Multiaxial Inventory (MCMI-III), 135, 231

Minnesota Multiphasic Personality Inventory (MMPI), 6, 10, 13, 15-17, 19, 35, 59, 60, 63-65, 68, 72, 161, 171, 181, 190, 192, 193, 231, 234, 235, 239, 241, 245, 270, 307, 353-355, 365

Minnesota Report: Revised Personnel System, 3rd Edition, 326

Misuse of Vehicle scale, M-PULSE, 137, 141, 149, 152

MMPI-2 RC scales, 21, 35, 59, 60, 66-69, 307

MMPI-2, 15, 21, 45, 59-69, 72, 73, 76, 77, 82, 85, 86, 88, 89, 135, 146, 188, 190-196, 212, 214, 215, 231, 234, 238, 241, 263, 268, 274, 275, 281, 282, 286, 291, 292, 299, 301, 307, 309, 310, 324, 341, 342-343

Motor Vehicle Accidents scale, M-PULSE, 137, 139, 149, 152, 325

M-PULSE Methodology, 135
Myers-Briggs Type Indicator, 231

N

National Advisory Commission on Annual
  Justice Standards and Goals, 7
National Computer Systems, (NCS), 13
National Police Officer Selection Test
  (POST), 306
National Symposium on Police Integrity, 273
National Symposium on Police Psychological
  Services, 12
National Working Conference on the
  Selection of Law Enforcement Officers, 9
Negative Actions scale, M-PULSE, 325
Negative Attitudes scale, M-PULSE, 325
Negative Emotions scale, M-PULSE, 150,
  153, 325
Negative Impression (NIM) scale, PAI, 73,
  75, 83
Negative Perceptions of Law Enforcement
  scale, M-PULSE, 143, 150, 153, 309
Negative Self-Issues scale, M-PULSE, 143,
  150, 153, 309, 325
Negative Views of Department/Leadership
  scale, M-PULSE, 150, 153
NEO-Personality Inventory Revised (NEO-
  PI R), 167, 231, 341
Neuroticism dimension, FFM, 165
Neuroticism dimension, NEO-PI R, 167
New Mexico Law Enforcement Academy, 44
New York City patrolmen, 188
New York City police, 6, 363
Niziurski, Julie, 214
No Child Left Behind Act, 279
Nonsupport (NON) scale, PAI, 73, 82
Non-Violence competency, 165, 168
Non-Violence scale, LEAI, 173
Novelty Seeking scale, M-PULSE, 150, 153
Null hypothesis statistical significance testing
  (NHST), 260-262, 265, 269, 270

O

Obsessive Personality (OB) scale, IPI, 121
Obsessive Style Index (OBS), RCS, 197
Obsessive-Compulsive Personality (OC)
  scale, HLAP, 97, 122

Off-Duty Misconduct scale, M-PULSE, 137,
  139, 149, 152
Office of Strategic Services, 7
Office of Technology Assessment (OTA), 15,
  16
O-H scale, MMPI-2, 342-343
Onion Fields kidnap-murder, 7
Openness global factor, 168, 169
Openness to experience dimension, FFM,
  165, 166, 231, 250
Organizational Issues in Law Enforcement
  conference, 18
Orientation (SO) scale, IS5-R, 122
Out-going Personality (OG) scale, IPS, 126
Overall Performance supervisor evaluation,
  172
Overall Score (OS) scale, HMS, 121
Overall Score (OV) scale, IPPI, 126
Overall Total Risk Score (OT), IAS, 128
Overall Total Score (OT) scale, IS5-R, 122
Overcontrolled Hostility (O-H) scale,
  MMPI-2, 65, 66, 68
Overly Traditional Officer Traits scale, M-
  PULSE, 150, 153

P

Pa scale, MMPI-2, 195, 215, 245
PAI Law Enforcement, Corrections, and
  Public Safety Selection Report, 87, 326
Paranoia (Pa) scale, MMPI-2, 64
Paranoia (PAR) scale, PAI, 73, 85
Paranoia construct, 246, 247
Paranoia scale, MMPI, 171
Paranoid Ideation (PI) scale, HLAP, 122
Passivity-Submissiveness dimension, CA
  POST, 144, 151, 153
Past Criminal Behavior, 172
Patience competency, 168
Pd scale, MMPI-2, 195, 215, 234, 235, 245,
  325
Pearson's r, 269, 273
Perceptual Thinking Index (PTI), RCS, 199
Performance Appraisal Ability (PA) scale,
  HMS, 121
Personality assessment instruments, 5, 7, 21,
  76
Personality Assessment Inventory (PAI), 19,
  45, 72-89, 231, 238, 263, 268, 270, 273,

274, 281, 282, 285, 292, 307-310, 324, 341, 343, 352, 353

Personality assessment techniques, 11

Personality Employment Test, 231

Phobic Personality (PH) scale, IPI, 121

Physical Aggression scale, PAI, 274

Police and Public Safety Section of APA, 11

Police culture, 31

Police Foundation, 8

Police Psychological Services, 2nd National Symposium on, 14

Police psychology, 5, 29, 68, 132, 133, 146, 262, 279, 282, 283, 293, 301, 321, 363, 369

Policy Compliance competency, 168

Polygraph Act of 1988, 15, 16

Polygraph, 303

Poor Decision-Making and Judgment dimension, CA POST, 144, 151, 153

Poor Decision-Making and Judgment scale, M-PULSE, 325

Poor Emotional Controls scale, M-PULSE, 150, 153

Popularity (PO) scale, HPP/SQ, 95-97

Popularity with Peers (PP) scale, IPS, 126

Popularity/"Charisma" (PO) scale, HPP/SQ, 121

Positive Impression (PIM) scale, PAI, 73, 76, 77, 83

Positive Work Attitudes (PW) scale, HMS, 121

Post-conditional offer, 18, 22, 41, 61, 145, 160-163, 183, 284, 306

Potential for Resignation scale, M-PULSE, 138, 142, 149, 152

Potential for Termination scale, M-PULSE, 138, 143, 149, 152

Pre-conditional offer, 17, 18, 22, 145, 160, 161, 163, 176, 177, 179, 180, 183, 231, 282, 306

Prediction of Termination, IPI, 94

Pre-employment assessment/screening, 5-8, 10, 11, 13, 18, 30, 32, 63, 68, 159, 160, 162, 163, 168, 169, 171, 174, 182, 188, 189, 193, 280, 333-336, 338-343, 362, 364

Preparation Concerns (PC) scale, HSRI, 122

Preparation Style (PS) scale, HPP/SQ, 121

Presidential Commission on Law Enforcement and the Administration of Justice, 7

Price, Caitlin, 214

Procedural and Conduct Mistakes scale, M-PULSE, 137, 140, 149, 152

Property Damage scale, M-PULSE, 137, 140, 149, 152

Psych mindedness scale, CPI, 249

Psychasthenia (Pt) scale, MMPI-2, 64

psychasthenia construct, 246, 247

Psychological Evaluations for Police Specialty Assignments (PEPSA), 52

Psychopathic Deviate (Pd) scale, MMPI-2, 43, 63-65

Pt scale, MMPI-2, 195, 215, 235, 245

Public Safety Attitude Scale, RPSR, 172

Public Safety Attitudes and Admissions, RPSR, 170

public safety officer selection, 10, 93

Q

Questioning competency, 168

R

Racially Offensive Conduct scale, M-PULSE, 137, 142, 149, 152

Randomized control trial (RCT), 288-290, 292

Realistic Expectations of Others (RE) scale, HMS, 121

Reckless Driving/Safety Patterns (RD) scale, IS2, 97, 122

Reckless Impulsivity scale, M-PULSE, 325

Reckless-Impulsivity dimension, CA POST, 144, 151, 153

Reese, James, 12, 14

Reid Integrity Attitude Scale (RIAS), 169-172, 175, 177, 181

Reid Public Safety Report (RPSR), 169-173, 177, 178, 181

Reid, John, 169

Reiser, Martin, 8, 11

Reisfeld, Ed, 130

Relationship with Co-workers (RC) scale, HCSI, 122

Reliability (RL) scale, IPPI, 126

Reprimands/Suspensions scale, M-PULSE, 138, 142, 149, 152

Respectful Treatment (RE) scale, ICCP, 124

responsibility competency, 168
Responsibility scale, CPI, 249
Responsibility scale, Test of Personality, 243
Return on Investment (ROI), 162
Revised Personality Inventory, 242
Rigid Type (RT) scale, IPI, 121, 171
Rigidity dimension, CA POST, 144, 151, 153
Risk Avoidance Scale, RPSR, 170
Risk Taking scale, M-PULSE, 150, 153, 325
Risk-Avoidance scale, LEAI, 173
Risk-Taking Patterns (RP) scale, HSRI, 122
Risk-Taking/Reckless Behavior (RI) scale, IS2, 122
Roberts, Michael, 8, 9
Rodriguez, Gabriel, 12
Rogers Discriminant Function (RDF), PAI, 77
Rorschach Comprehensive System (RCS), 188, 189, 193, 196, 283
Rorschach Inkblot Method, 6, 21, 86, 188-194, 196, 197, 206-208, 211-214, 216-222, 282, 292

S

S scale, MMPI-2, 342
Sackett, Paul, 17
Safety Attitudes (AT) scale, HSRI, 122
Safety Behaviors (SB) scale, HSRI, 122
Safety Orientation competency, 168
Safety Promotion competency, 168
Safety Risk (SR) scale, HSRI, 122
Safety scale, LEAI, 173
Sales Interest (SI) scale, HPP/SQ, 121,
San Jose, California, police department, 6, 8
Saxe-Clifford, Susan, 12
Sc scale, MMPI-2, 195, 215, 245
SCAN, 352, 353, 358, 360
Schizophrenia (Sc) scale, MMPI-2, 64
Schizophrenia (SCZ) scale, PAI, 73, 85
Schizophrenia construct, 246, 247
Schizophrenia Index (SCZI), RCS, 199
SCID, 352
screen in, 309
screen out, 231, 232, 281, 293, 306-309
Scrivner, Ellen, 11
Selecting in, 231
Selective Service Boards, 7
Self Worth (SW) scale, HPP/SQ, 99, 121

Self-acceptance scale, CPI, 249
Self-Belief (SB) scale, IPS, 127
Self-Confidence (SB) scale, IPS, 100
Self-Confidence competency, 168
Self-Consciousness subscale, NEO-PI R, 167
Self-control scale, CPI, 249
Self-Discipline scale, CPI, 309
Sensitivity (SE) scale, HPP/SQ, 95-97, 99, 121
Sensitivity about Responsibilities (SR) scale, IPS, 127
Sensitivity scale, Test of Personality, 243
Service Relations Scale, RPSR, 170, 177, 178
Sexual Concerns (SC) scale, IPI, 121
sexual concerns construct, 246, 247
Sexually Offensive Conduct scale, M-PULSE, 137, 142, 149, 152
Shaw, James, 7, 8, 9, 12
Shea, Leo, 12
Shealy, Allen, 9
Shipley Institute of Living Scale (SILS), 352
Shrewdness scale, Test of Personality, 243
Si scale, MMPI-2, 195, 215, 245
SIRS, 352
16 Personality Factor (16PF), 10, 11, 135, 231
Sociability scale, CPI, 249
Social Ability (SA) scale, HPP/SQ, 95, 121
Social Approval Concerns (SC) scale, IPS, 100, 127
Social Behavior, RPSR, 178, 180
Social Compatibility (SN) scale, ICCP, 100
Social Incompetence dimension, CA POST, 144, 151, 153
Social Incompetence scale, M-PULSE, 325
Social Introversion (Si) scale, MMPI-2, 64
social introversion, 246, 247
Social Network Compatibility (SN) scale, ICCP, 124
Social presence scale, CPI, 44, 249
Socialization scale, CPI, 249, 309
Socialization scale, Test of Personality, 243
Society for Police and Criminal Psychology (SPCP), 9, 20, 38, 43, 48, 301, 369
Somatic Complaints (RC1) scale, MMPI-2 RF, 67
Somatic Complaints (SOM) scale, PAI, 73, 85
Somodevilla, Al, 11
special assignments, 51

Special Weapons and Tactics (SWAT), 52, 280, 285, 286, 309

Spielberger, Charles, 9

Spilberg, Shelley, 144

Spouse/Mate Concerns (SP) scale, IPI, 121

Standards for Educational and Psychological Testing, 134

Stanford-Binet intelligence test, 6

Statement of Understanding (SOU), 41, 44, 49

Stress (STR) scale, PAI, 73, 82

Stress Patterns (ST) scale, HCSI, 122

Stress Symptoms (SY) scale, HCSI, 122

stress tolerance competency, 165, 168

Strong Vocational Interest Inventory, 306

Subject matter experts (SMEs), 163, 168, 175

Substance Abuse (SA) scale, IPI, 94, 121, 171, 308

substance abuse construct, 246, 247

Substance Abuse dimension, CA POST, 144, 151, 153

Substance Abuse, RPSR, 170, 178

Success Quotient (SQ) scale, HPP/SQ, 121

success quotient theory, 14

Suicidal Ideation (SUI) scale, PAI, 73, 82

Suicidal/Depressive Thoughts (SU) scale, HLAP, 122

supervisory relations competency, 168

Supplementary scales, MMPI-2, 60, 65, 66

Surrette Inventory, 230, 242

Suspicion scale, Test of Personality, 243

Suspiciousness scale, M-PULSE, 150, 153

T

teamwork competency, 168

Teamwork Orientation (TM) scale, HMS, 121

Temper Control (TE) scale, ICCP, 100, 124

Tension scale, Test of Personality, 243

Test Attitude scales, M-PULSE, 137, 148, 152, 325

test of personality, 230, 232, 233, 242, 243

theft, fraud, & dishonesty, 180

Thematic Apperception Test (TAT), 86

Timeliness about Responsibilities (TR) scale, IPS, 127

Tolerance scale, CPI, 229, 249, 309

Tolerance scale, Test of Personality, 243

Total Score HCSI (TS) scale, HCSI, 122

Total Score: Lack of Employee Reliability (ER) scale, IS5-R, 122

Total Score: Lack of Service scale, IS5-R, 122

treatment planning, 69, 214, 283, 291

Treatment Programs (TP) scale, IPI, 121

Treatment Rejection (RXR) scale, PAI, 73, 82

tree drawing, 6

Trompetter, Phil, 21

Trouble with Law & Society (TL) scale, IPI, 94, 98, 121, 171

U

Undue Suspiciousness (US) scale, IPI, 121

Undue Worry (UW) scale, HSRI, 122

Unethical Behavior scale, M-PULSE, 143, 150, 153, 309

Unpredictability scale, M-PULSE, 143, 150, 153, 309

Unprofessional Conduct scale, M-PULSE, 137, 141, 149, 152, 325

Unreliability dimension, CA POST, 144, 151, 153

Unusual experiences scale, Test of Personality, 243

Unusual Experiences/Thoughts (UE) scale, IPI, 95, 121

V

V2 scale, CPI, 309

Validity scales, M-PULSE, 137, 148

Vangent Competency Modeling System, 168

Vangent Reid Report Integrity Test, 169, 176

Vangent's Law Enforcement Applicant Inventory (LEAI), 173

violent behavior, 92, 94, 95, 102

W

WAIS, 190

Warmth (WRM) scale, PAI, 73, 82, 87

Watson, Nelson, 8

Watts riots, 7

Well-being scale, CPI, 249, 309

Well-being scale, Test of Personality, 243

Wells, Butch, 214

Wide Range Achievement Test, 303
Williams, Jim, 214
Winners Image (WI) scale, HPP/SQ, 121
Wonderlic Personnel Test, 302, 306
Work Adjustment Difficulties (WA) scale,
    IS5-R, 122
Work Background, RPSR, 178, 180
Work Difficulties (WD) scale, IS2, 122
Work Effort Concerns (WE) scale, IS5-R, 122
Work Efforts Concerns (WE) scale, IS5, 97
Work History and Personal Achievements,
    RPSR, 170
World War II, 7, 300

Y

Yerkes-Dodson Law, 82
Yuille, John, 14

Z

Zelig, Mark, 9